Ghosts of a Family

Dr Edward Burke is a historian at University College Dublin, specialising in the study of political violence, insurgencies and paramilitarism. His previous books are *An Army of Tribes: British Army Cohesion, Deviancy and Murder in Northern Ireland* (Liverpool, 2018) and *Ulster's Lost Counties: Loyalism and Paramilitarism since 1920* (Cambridge, 2024).

GHOSTS OF A FAMILY

*Ireland's Most Infamous Unsolved Murder,
the Outbreak of the Civil War and the
Origins of the Modern Troubles*

Edward Burke

MERRION
PRESS

First published in 2024 by
Merrion Press
10 George's Street
Newbridge
Co. Kildare
Ireland
www.merrionpress.ie

© Edward Burke, 2024

9781785375224 (Paper)
9781785375330 (Ebook)

A CIP catalogue record for this book
is available from the British Library.

All rights reserved. No part of this publication may be reproduced, stored in
a retrieval system, or transmitted, in any form or by any means (electronic,
mechanical, photocopying, recording or otherwise), without the prior written
permission of both the copyright owner and the publisher of this book.

Typeset in Minion Pro 11.5/17 pt

Cover design by Fiachra McCarthy

Merrion Press is a member of Publishing Ireland

For my aunt, Anna Burke

TABLE OF CONTENTS

	Acknowledgements	ix
	Abbreviations	xi
	Introduction	xiii

PART 1

1.	Killing the McMahons	3
2.	Belfast's Descent	27

PART 2

3.	Aftermath	79
4.	A Terrible Victory	98
5.	The Brown's Square Gang	125
6.	Taking a Delight in Killing	152

PART 3

7.	The Notorious David Duncan	167
8.	The Patient by the Window	216

	Epilogue	227
	Bibliography	237
	Endnotes	248
	Index	276

ACKNOWLEDGEMENTS

THERE IS ONE UNCONTESTED RULE in the discipline of history – historians can never thank archivists enough. I am especially indebted to Kate Thaxton, curator and archivist at the Royal Norfolk Regimental Museum in Norwich and Roberto Lima and his colleagues at the Archives of Ontario in Toronto who were determined to facilitate my research, even during the depths of COVID-19. Archivists at the Burns Library at Boston College, the Cardinal Ó Fiaich Library, the Churchill Archive at Cambridge University, the Imperial War Museum, the McClay Library at Queen's University Belfast, the Military Archives of Ireland, the National Archives of Ireland, the National Army Museum, National Museums of Northern Ireland, Orange Heritage Museum, the Police Museum of Northern Ireland, Princeton University Library Special Collections, Public Record Office of Northern Ireland, Royal Fusiliers Museum, the Royal Irish Fusiliers Museum, the Royal Ulster Rifles Museum, Staffordshire Regiment Museum and University College Dublin Archives also showed reserves of patience and kindness in responding to my requests. Not all the material cited in this book was publicly available at the outset of my research – I am especially grateful to those archivists who made the case for transparency, a century after the events described.

At a time when (my own) research funds for this project were exhausted, Douglas Delaney invited me to lecture at the Royal Military

ACKNOWLEDGEMENTS

College of Canada, which allowed me to consult archives in Toronto and discuss veterans' experiences with a range of outstanding historians. Doug has set a benchmark for collegiality. Family, friends and colleagues who offered essential advice included Huw Bennett, Angela Burke, Judy Burke, Lynsey Burke, Daniel Burke, Rory Cormac, Nadia Dobrianksa, John Dorney, Richard English, Hugh Forrester, Robert Gerwarth, Kieran Glennon, Peter Gray, Peter Hart, Francis Higgins, Jonathan Mattison, Ian McBride, Jim McDermott, Ronnie Meharg, Marc Mulholland, Patrick Mulroe, Conor Mulvagh, Caoimhe Nic Dháibhéid, Martin O'Donoghue, Connal Parr, Nicholas Perry, Colin Reid, Fionnuala Walsh, Gordon White, John Wilson and Tim Wilson. My agent at Northbank, Matthew Cole, provided eagle-eyed criticism and encouragement. I am also very grateful to Conor Graham, Síne Quinn, Wendy Logue, Ciara Kinsella, Conor Holbrook, Peter O'Connell and Heidi Houlihan at Merrion Press, who backed the book and made it much better.

A number of descendants of individuals and families that feature in the book generously spoke with me about inherited memories and legacies of violence, including Norah Glynn (Owen McMahon's grand-niece) and her husband Joe, as well as the granddaughter of District Inspector John Nixon, the son of District Inspector William Lynn and Reverend Brian Black, a relative of military veteran, Alick Kennedy. What follows is my account and analysis of political violence in Belfast in the 1920s. It does not pretend to be definitive; nor does it claim to represent the views of any of the families affected by the events described within.

ABBREVIATIONS

AOH	Ancient Order of Hibernians
AOO	Archives of Ontario
CHAR	Churchill Archives
CGM	County Grand Master
CO	Commanding Officer
Comd	Commander
GROI	General Registry Office of Ireland
GRONI	General Registry Office of Northern Ireland
HO	Home Office
IRA	Irish Republican Army
LAC	Library and Archives of Canada
LOL	Loyal Orange Lodge
LRI	Land Registry of Ireland
LRNI	Land Registry of Northern Ireland
MAI	Military Archives of Ireland
MFLF	Museum of the Foreign Legion of France
MSPC	Military Service Pensions Collection
NAI	National Archives of Ireland
NAM	National Army Museum of the United Kingdom
NCO	Non-Commissioned Officer

ABBREVIATIONS

NWHRM	The Royal Norfolk Regimental Museum
OBLDA	Orange and Black Loyalist Defence Association
OC	Officer Commanding
OHM	Orange Heritage Museum
PMNI	Police Museum of Northern Ireland
PRONI	Public Record Office of Northern Ireland
PULSC	Princeton University Library Special Collections
RFM	Royal Fusiliers Museum
RIC	Royal Irish Constabulary
R.Innis.F.	Royal Inniskilling Fusiliers
RIF	Royal Irish Fusiliers
RIR	Royal Irish Rifles
RUC	Royal Ulster Constabulary
TNA	The National Archives of the United Kingdom
TPA	The Parliamentary Archives of the United Kingdom
UCDA	University College Dublin Archives
UDA	Ulster Defence Association
UDR	Ulster Defence Regiment
UFTM	Ulster Folk and Transport Museum
UVF	Ulster Volunteer Force
USC	Ulster Special Constabulary
UULA	Ulster Unionist Labour Association
UVF	Ulster Volunteer Force
WM	Worshipful Master
WO	War Office

INTRODUCTION

SHORTLY AFTER 1.20 A.M. ON 24 March 1922, at the height of what became known as the 'Belfast pogrom', five men smashed their way into 3 Kinnaird Terrace, the family home of a well-known and prosperous fifty-five-year-old Catholic publican, Owen McMahon, and his wife, Eliza, who lived with their seven sons and a daughter. Four of the men wore police uniforms and carried revolvers. They went straight upstairs to the bedrooms where they ordered the members of the household downstairs to the ground floor. Eliza (49), her daughter Lily (13) and eighteen-year-old niece Mary Catherine were separated from the rest of the family. Eliza was brought downstairs to the drawing room, while Mary and Lily remained in their bedroom.

Owen, six of his sons – Bernard (26), Frank (24), Patrick (22), John (19), Thomas Gerald (15), Michael (11) and an employee of the family, Edward McKinney (26) – were brought to the dining room. (Another son, fourteen-year-old Leo, was in hospital recovering from an operation.) There they were lined up by the fireplace and addressed by a man with 'a round soft looking face and very black eyes' wearing a light brown trench coat, and who appeared to be the leader of the group. He told his captives to say their prayers. Seconds later, he raised his revolver and shot Owen in the head. Owen's sons – with the exception of Michael – were then shot in turn. (John survived his wounds; the rest perished.) Hearing the shot, his wife Eliza pulled up

INTRODUCTION

a window at the back of the house and screamed 'Murder!' into the night sky.[1]

Seventy-nine years after the McMahon and McKinney murders, David Trimble, then First Minister of Northern Ireland and a Nobel Peace Prize laureate, wrote a blistering letter to the chairman of the BBC's board of governors in London.[2] The BBC had commissioned a historical drama, *Rebel Hearts,* based on the Irish independence movement, the British counter-insurgency campaign and the formation of Northern Ireland from 1916–23. In a scene that closely resembles accounts of the shocking murders at Kinnaird Terrace, a character called 'Inspector Nelson' leads a police murder gang in Belfast that enters a home at night and shoots the men of the family in the dining room. ('Nelson' also finishes off some of the family with a knife.) Trimble condemned the series for its inaccurate portrayal of the city during 1920–22. This, Trimble complained, was more republican propaganda than historical reality.[3]

The shadow of 3 Kinnaird Terrace, the original sin of Northern Ireland's foundation, has loomed over Belfast – for years rumours about who killed the McMahons and Eddie McKinney were whispered in the city. During the centenary year of the McMahon murders the Royal Irish Academy published a history pointing the finger of blame for the murders at one District Inspector John William Nixon of the Royal Irish Constabulary (RIC), stating, 'It is generally accepted that it was this unit [Nixon's] that planned and executed the McMahon attack.'[4] A recent BBC documentary, *The District Inspector,* also suggested that Nixon led the attack on the McMahons, firing many of the fatal shots.[5] Those who objected to the Irish government's plans to hold a service 'to commemorate the place of the Royal Irish Constabulary and Dublin Metropolitan Police in Irish history' a hundred years after the disbandment of both forces pointed to John Nixon and the McMahon murders as exemplifying why such an event could not be held. (The government backtracked; the event was cancelled.)[6]

The main sources drawn upon to implicate Nixon are reports produced by the Irish Republican Army (IRA) in Belfast that were collected and summarised by the Irish government.[7] But John Nixon had successfully won two libel cases, one in 1925 and another ten years later, when his accusers dared to put their allegations in print. And so for nearly a century historians – and politicians – have typically lined up on two sides, one quick to damn, the other eager to cast doubt on allegations of police murder. (One historian dismissed the allegation that police had taken part in the McMahon murders as 'Sinn Féin propaganda'.)[8] Archives or documents written by one side to the conflict or the other have repeatedly been held up as proof of guilt or innocence.

Was Nixon really the monstrous figure who singled out the McMahons for death? It is now possible to identify the most compelling motive for the massacre of the McMahons and the family's most deadly enemy and likely killer. To understand the case against this man, it is first necessary to understand the politics, poverty and violence that stained Belfast's streets and to know the gangs that ruled them. The leaders of these gangs were some of the most violent men in Belfast's history, among them a man who has been hidden in plain sight for more than a century.

✱✱✱

In the autumn of 2019, while scrolling through the military archives section of the Norfolk Museums Collections online catalogue for a research project on paramilitary violence in Ulster, I came across a vaguely titled 'intelligence report' that had been produced by the 1st Battalion of the Norfolk Regiment. Clicking on the link brought me to a description which read, 'Record of riots, disturbances, shootings and investigations in Belfast, Northern Ireland 1921–1922 including descriptions of violent incidents amongst individuals and groups; index

INTRODUCTION

contains names of civilians mentioned either as victims or aggressors.' The intelligence reports were from September 1921 to June 1922, the height of the 'Belfast pogrom' and the most violent ten months in Northern Ireland's bloodied century.

I immediately sent an enquiry to the Royal Norfolk Regimental Museum, who informed me that, following discussions with the National Archives, the Ministry of Defence and the Royal Anglian Regiment (successors to the Norfolks), the file was closed to the public and I would not be granted access to it under any conditions. Frustrated, I appealed the decision. Finally, four months later I boarded a train from my home in Derby in the English Midlands to Norwich. As the train rattled slowly across the flat fens of eastern England, I wondered whether my months of pestering the museum would be worth the effort. I had often visited regimental archives where a closely guarded item turned out to be full of anodyne material such as receipts for the officers' mess.

The Royal Norfolk Regimental Museum archive is located beneath the magnificent Norman limestone keep of Norwich Castle. Once inside, the curator Kate Thaxton showed me a hefty grey ledger with a crown symbol and 'George V' written on the front. This was not a short intelligence summary or perfunctory series of notes. Here was a volume of contemporaneous, extensively detailed daily reports of successive military intelligence officers on street violence and murder in Belfast. It contained information on the identity of suspected IRA leaders. (These later proved to be generally accurate when compared with IRA files held in the Military Archives in Ireland.) The reports also detailed loyalist attacks and offered an unprecedented insight into the British Army's conflict with the elements of the police in late 1921–22, including intelligence on the work of police 'murder gangs'.[9]

After a century here was a contemporary source, one not produced by the IRA, that threw light on the loyalist paramilitary organisations whose members committed Northern Ireland's most infamous massacre

xvi

of the early twentieth century, the brutal murder of five members of the Catholic McMahon family and Edward McKinney on 24 March 1922.

Who were the intelligence officers who wrote the reports? Kate Thaxton showed me a detailed officers' digest of services, offering a short but precise biography of individual Norfolk officers. There were three officers whose principal job it was to gather intelligence and report to the commanding officer of 1 Norfolks as well as the British Army's headquarters in Belfast. The first was Captain Harry Papworth. Born in 1882 and the son of a coachman, Papworth enlisted in the Norfolks as an ordinary soldier in 1902. He distinguished himself in the first months of fighting in France in 1914 and was commissioned as an officer.

First Lieutenant Eric Hayes was fourteen years younger than Papworth. He was a brilliant young officer who had been employed by the War Office to raise a militia in Northern Persia in 1918 to carry out attacks against Ottoman forces in the Caucasus. He later served in Siberia where he was taken prisoner by the Red Army. (Hayes was decorated for his service in Russia, including receiving the Medal of Saint Vladimir from the 'White' government – one of the very last recipients.) The final intelligence officer was 2nd Lieutenant Harold Watling. Born in 1900, Watling joined the Norfolks at the end of the First World War. Belfast was his first operational tour of duty. None of these men had any obvious connection to Ireland. All three men showed little liking for any side, although they did sympathise with the victims of Belfast's sectarian inferno and persistently tried to hunt down and kill the perpetrators.

A second item relating to Belfast is also kept in the Norfolks' museum. Kate Thaxton brought out a large red box; inside was a .303 rifle that had been modified by an officer called Lieutenant Robert Scott for street-fighting in Belfast. Its barrel was cut down and its stock shortened so that it could easily be fired at close range. It resembled a pistol of sorts.

Born in London in 1898, Bob Scott was commissioned as a second lieutenant into the Norfolk Regiment aged eighteen. He was over six feet tall – by his own account 'the biggest bloody man in the British Army'. He was also exceptionally courageous; he had been wounded three times in the First World War, losing his sight in one eye at the Battle of Arras on the Western Front in 1917.

As part of his convalescence, Scott was posted to the Officers' Cadet Battalion at the University of Oxford. He also enlisted as a student in Balliol College where he was constantly chased for unpaid bills. By the time he re-joined 1 Norfolks in 1920 he was being sued by the fellows of Balliol and had incurred several other large debts in England. Scott tried to claim a further disability allowance from the War Office when he re-joined his regiment in Ireland, stating that he was twice 'wounded' in the testicles, while playing rugby for the North of Ireland club and when his horse reared up on a beach. (The claims were, unsurprisingly, rejected.) Carrying his cut-down rifle and wearing an eyepatch, Bob Scott acquired a near mythical reputation among Belfast's republicans and loyalists.[10]

Other than the military, few better understood the British government's loyalist dilemma in Belfast – whether to muster the forces to take on loyalist paramilitarism or avoid confrontation and accept the consequences of nationalist anger – than the Royal Ulster Constabulary's first commander or 'inspector general' in 1922, Lieutenant Colonel Charles Wickham. In 2019 I wrote a letter to his grandson John Ramsden, a long-serving British diplomat who served as Britain's ambassador to Croatia after the Balkan Wars in the 1990s. Did he have any surviving papers belonging to his grandfather? Months later – the address was an old one – he replied. By coincidence he had recently sifted through Wickham's letters and had just published a selection of them. His grandfather may have carefully avoided conflict with his political masters but he had some sharp views on his subordinates, which he divulged to his close family.

A son of minor Yorkshire gentry, Wickham was commissioned into the Norfolk Regiment in 1899. His career was anything but orthodox.

INTRODUCTION

After serving as a staff intelligence officer in the Second Boer War he was then attached to a mounted unit of former Boer rebels turned militia – the Western Transvaal Reserve. Wickham returned to his regiment at the outbreak of the First World War and saw action in France.[11]

In early 1918, now holding the rank of major, Wickham volunteered for the British military mission to aid the Russian 'Whites' during the Civil War against the Bolshevik 'Reds'. He spent over a year as a staff officer in Vladivostok under the command of Major General Sir Alfred Knox, an Ulsterman, Royal Irish Rifles officer and Russophile who preferred the furs and *ushanka* [hat] of the White Army to his British Army uniform. Wickham's experience working with militia in South Africa, Knox's favour and his regiment's lead responsibility for security in Belfast were all important factors in explaining why he was selected to command the police in Ulster. In 1922 he formally left the army and served as inspector general of the newly established Royal Ulster Constabulary (RUC) for twenty-three years.[12]

At the end of the Second World War Wickham became the commander of the British Police Mission to Greece, a position he held until 1952. Years later Wickham's grandson discovered a suitcase full of letters and photographs. Pictures of Wickham in the Mediterranean show a trim, elderly man looking quite uncomfortable in a tight (and unsuitably warm) RUC police uniform. In his letters to his family Wickham offered a forthright analysis of the various political factions involved in the Greek Civil War.

Wickham believed that the situation in Greece so resembled Northern Ireland that he started calling the communists 'RCs' [Roman Catholics] and those on the right 'Prots'. While in Athens Wickham was compelled to work with the Greek Minister for Public Order, Napoleon Zervas, a notorious right-wing paramilitary leader. Zervas reminded Wickham of 'a crooked bandit of the [Ulster] ultra-Protestant league

xix

INTRODUCTION

variety [who] wants to have his own gendarmerie ... The result of his regime so far has been an orgy of murders and reprisals by the right.'

For Wickham, the co-option of right-wing paramilitaries in Greece in an attempt to turn them into the police auxiliaries was a disastrous mistake – 'Our main difficulty is that the gendarmerie in the RC areas are frightened and in the Prot areas are in with the Prot murder gangs up to the eyeballs, because they hate and fear the communists and because the Prots don't shoot them up ... We are following the N. Ireland precedent to the letter.'[13] From reading these letters it became clear that the RUC's own most senior officer believed that at least some members of the police in Northern Ireland, like those in Greece, collaborated with murder gangs.

✷ ✷ ✷

Here were new sources and an opportunity to dig further into the identities and motives of those who were responsible for atrocities such as the murders of the McMahons and Edward McKinney. During my research, it did not take long to establish the identity of the most dangerous loyalist killer in north Belfast, a decorated former soldier and policeman. Just over two months before the Kinnaird Terrace murders, he had been charged with shooting at a publican called Patrick McMahon who ran a prosperous spirit grocery – a type of pub with an ancillary shop – on York Road, a main thoroughfare in the north of the city. I searched for publicans in Belfast by the name of Patrick McMahon. Only one name stood out – Owen McMahon's brother.[14]

Tracing the lives of the lower ranks of the British Army or the police – in this case the alleged would-be murderer of Patrick McMahon – is not straightforward. Unlike aristocratic or middle-class officers, such men – the working-class non-commissioned officers (sergeants, corporals, etc.)

INTRODUCTION

of the British Army – did not leave 'papers' for consultation by historians a century later. However, I discovered that he had emigrated to Canada in the years after the McMahon murders. Glancing at his death certificate I noticed an unusual address for the place of death: 999 Queen Street West, Toronto. An internet search revealed that he had been a patient at what had been known as the Toronto Lunatic Asylum. I submitted a Freedom of Information Request.

A few months later, at the height of the COVID-19 pandemic, I received an email from the Archives of Ontario with an in-patient file on the man who was believed to have attacked Patrick McMahon. In it were extensive details of war trauma, paranoid schizophrenia, domestic violence and murder. This man had not only served in the First World War, he had also fought in a specially-raised British Army unit, drawn from the Royal Fusiliers regiment, that was sent to aid the anti-Bolshevik 'Whites' during the Russian Civil War (1918–20). From 1925 to 1926 he soldiered in North Africa with the French Foreign Legion (*La Légion Étrangère*).

And so, in the summer of 2022 I travelled to another Norman castle, the Tower of London, to sift through the unpublished accounts of Royal Fusiliers' soldiers who had been sent to the Archangel front during the Russian Civil War. This was a conflict in which British soldiers not only faced the superior numbers of the Red Army but also increasingly feared betrayal or murder at the hands of mutinying 'Whites'. Meanwhile, Dónal Hassett, a historian at Maynooth University, generously volunteered to search the Legion's museum in Aubagne, near Marseille. There he found more evidence of violent and erratic behaviour by the same man. After more than a century, had the McMahons' killer finally been identified?

* * *

PART 1

CHAPTER ONE

Killing the McMahons

ON THE NIGHT OF THE massacre at 3 Kinnaird Terrace, 24 March 1922, the McMahons' immediate neighbours were Rosabell Purdy at 1 Kinnaird Terrace, who owned a boarding house, and a nursing home run by Matron Mabel McMurtry at no. 5. Shortly after 1.20 a.m. residents of the nursing home recalled being awakened by the sound of the McMahons' door being smashed in, followed by the crash of breaking glass. They listened to screams for help from the house and shots being fired. Nobody moved. Matron McMurtry heard Eliza McMahon shouting to her to call the police, followed by the sound of more screams. Then Eliza again called to her again, telling her to 'ring up the hospitals and get ambulances'.

Matron McMurtry phoned Glenravel police barracks, the headquarters of the Royal Irish Constabulary's 'D' District, which was situated a few hundred yards from Kinnaird Terrace. A nurse at the home saw a group of men running away from the McMahon house but she couldn't make out their faces. It was a drizzly night – the men were concealed by an absence of street lighting at Kinnaird Terrace and little or no moonlight.

The manager of Purdy's boarding house, a man called Arthur Hamill, recalled that he was awakened by Beatrice Purdy, Rosabell's daughter,

3

who told him that shots were being fired and to get up. He looked out of a window and saw a bright light streaming out from the McMahons' house onto the street. As he pulled on his trousers he heard 'bang after bang, as if the shooting was in the very house with him, and long and terrible screams of agony'.[1] A few minutes later there was a knock on the Purdys' door. Hamill shouted to the men to identify themselves. 'Police on duty' came the response. Hamill opened the door. It was the police from Glenravel Street. He agreed to accompany them to the McMahon house next door.

Once outside on the street, Hamill saw that the door to the McMahon house was still ajar and there was smashed glass on the ground.[2] He entered what he described as 'a house of horrors'. He first saw John McMahon sitting on a chair near the hallway entrance to the dining room. Blood was seeping from his nightshirt and he was struggling to breathe. Hamill moved towards him to help but cut his feet on the smashed glass. He returned next door to get his shoes. When he came back, he saw Eliza McMahon in the hallway. He gave her his dressing gown to cover her son John.

Hamill then looked further into the dining room. Owen McMahon was 'writhing in agony on the floor' near the fireplace. Four of his sons and Eddie McKinney were dead or dying close by. Eliza ran to her son Michael who was hiding, wordless and in shock, under a large mahogany dining-room table. He had escaped the shooting. Two ambulances arrived at approximately 2 a.m. Frank, Patrick and Gerald McMahon and Eddie McKinney were already dead by the time they were brought to the Mater Hospital. Owen died shortly afterwards. Bernard lingered on, dying on 4 April, eleven days later. A doctor gave the shaken ambulance party and police a shot of brandy when their job of removing the bodies and wounded to the hospital was completed.[3]

A journalist who visited the McMahon home on the same day as the murders described it as 'a scene from a slaughterhouse … On either side of the fireplace lay large pools of blood – thick, heavy, coagulated stuff, that turned one sick with horror. In places it was rubbed and disturbed as if someone had rolled in it; in others it was clotted in lumps as if someone had macerated a fresh bullock's liver and strewn it about.' The dining room table was scarred by two bullet marks. On the table lay the remains of the victims' last meal – milk, butter, teacups, bread and oatcakes. On the sideboard stood an empty naggin of whiskey. An empty casing from a Webley revolver was also reported to have been found at the scene.[4]

Kinnaird Terrace was a Victorian terrace of eight large houses in north Belfast, built to accommodate the city's expanding managerial and professional classes. Spacious garages had been built beside the houses for large cars. No. 3 Kinnaird Terrace had five bedrooms and three reception rooms, including a dining room and a drawing room, spread out over three floors. It overlooked a small estate and mansion owned by the Bruce family, one of the city's oldest dynasties. Before it was acquired by the Purdys, no. 1 had been the home of a Jewish family, the Berwitzes. From impoverished beginnings in Russia, Louis Berwitz had built up a substantial furniture business empire in Belfast; his son Charles served as an officer in the British Army. This was a middle-class enclave into which Belfast's sectarian street wars normally did not intrude.[5]

The McMahon murders stunned Belfast – a city that had already witnessed two years of violence by republicans (overwhelmingly Catholics, supporters of the Sinn Féin party and the Irish Republican Army) to secure Irish independence, and those who identified as unionists or loyalists (mostly Protestants) who wished to preserve the connection to Britain. They also sent a shiver across the Irish Sea to a normally war-jaded British public. Winston Churchill told the House of Commons that 'one would have to search all over Europe to find instances of equal atrocity, barbarity, cold-blooded, inhuman, cannibal vengeance – cannibal in all except the act of devouring the flesh of the victim – which will equal this particular event'.[6]

Captain Harry Papworth, a British Army intelligence officer, reported an eerie silence on the streets of Belfast in the hours after the murders: '[Protestants] believe there will be an awful reprisal for this deed.' Friday 24 March was payday for many but almost nobody ventured out to spend their wages in the city's bars. Papworth also passed on intelligence 'from a most reliable source' that the dreaded Irish Republican Army (IRA) commander Seán Mac Eoin, the 'Blacksmith of Ballinalee', was travelling to Belfast to take revenge.[7]

Owen McMahon and his three sons were buried in Milltown cemetery in west Belfast on Sunday 26 March. Huge crowds assembled along Belfast's streets to watch the carriage-borne hearses pass by. The funeral was preceded by an armoured car, but there was no trouble. Nonetheless, some Protestant residents took precautions against possible reprisals – groups of men were stationed at potential flashpoints in the west and north of the city. Bishop Joseph MacRory, assisted by a dozen other Catholic clergy, conducted the service. Owen's brothers John, Patrick, Daniel, Thomas and Bernard attended. 'Wee' Joe Devlin, the leading Irish nationalist MP in Belfast and a friend of Owen McMahon, was also among the mourning party.

But all eyes were on Eliza McMahon and her two children, Lily and Michael. (Bernard would later die from his wounds; John was too critically injured to attend.) Michael had to be carried into the graveyard, and fainted when the coffins were lowered into the graves.[8] Eddie McKinney's body was brought across the border to his native Buncrana in County Donegal for burial. There the local IRA attempted to set fire to the Masonic Hall and posted notices ordering 'all Orangemen to clear out'.[9]

Three months before the McMahon murders the Anglo-Irish Treaty – signed by the British government and Sinn Féin leaders – had created what was to become a twenty-six-county Irish Free State. Michael Collins, the erstwhile IRA spymaster and organiser, was appointed as the chairman of a provisional government in Dublin. South of the border, IRA 'volunteers' were now part of a new National Army; the violence of the preceding two years had largely ceased. In the six counties of what was now Northern Ireland a hellish cycle of sectarian atrocity had taken hold. Loyalists feared invasion and lashed out at a 'disloyal' population, while republicans – covertly supported by the provisional government and National Army – sought to make Northern Ireland ungovernable through burnings and assassinations.

In mid-February 1922 Michael Collins had sent Cork Sinn Féin activist Patrick O'Driscoll – his brother-in law and friend – to Belfast to act as a conduit between the Belfast IRA and the government in Dublin. O'Driscoll, a former editor of the *West Cork People*, compiled much of the reporting for Collins' publicity bureau bulletins on atrocities in Belfast. With local Sinn Féin and IRA support he also carried out investigations into specific murders in the city; he then presented his conclusions to the provisional government. Well-placed collectors of intelligence in Belfast included IRA medical officer Dr Russell McNabb, Seán Cusack, an intelligence officer who reported directly to Collins, and Desmond Crean, an IRA volunteer who kept in contact with a number of serving Catholic RIC constables. The Belfast IRA now moved quickly to make enquiries into the McMahon murders.[10]

Collins' investigators took a statement from John McMahon in hospital in the hours after the attack. He explicitly blamed the police for the killings: 'Four of the five men were dressed in the uniform of the RIC but from their appearance I know they are "Specials" not regular RIC. One was in plain clothes.' The subsequent report described John McMahon's extensive injuries, including 'a haemorrhage in the cavity of the left chest'.

The report also noted that John McMahon had given a 'similar statement' to the nationalist *Irish News*. But John's description of the killers 'was altered in the office of that paper by the editors who live in daily dread of the "Specials" who are threatening to burn down the premises'.[11] John McMahon's reference to police uniforms was changed to 'blue-coloured burberry coats which concealed the nature of their inner attire'.[12]

Based on the witness descriptions, Collins' investigators concluded that members of the Special Constabulary, not the regular RIC, were responsible for the McMahon murders. Terence O'Keeffe, the long-serving editor of the nationalist *Irish News*, also carried out his own enquiries into the McMahon murders. He recalled that, although there were many theories about who the perpetrators were, it was 'generally accepted' that they were members of the part-time, wholly Protestant 'B' Class of the Special Constabulary.[13]

Some republicans later claimed that Donegal native Eddie McKinney was an IRA volunteer, but that this was deliberately concealed at the time of his death. Such an admission could have also diverted some attention away from the horror of the murders. The McMahon family were apparently unaware of their barman's republicanism. Seán Montgomery, IRA officer, referred to Eddie McKinney in his memoirs as 'Volunteer McKinney'.[14]

Eddie McKinney never played a prominent role in republican activities in Belfast, however. Neither the police nor the British Army had any intelligence about his IRA membership. His cousin was a police constable serving in Leopold Street Barracks in north Belfast. Constable Michael McKinney served in the Irish Guards regiment of the British Army during the First World War. Some constables in Leopold Street were (correctly) suspected by their superiors of passing on intelligence to the IRA. But Michael McKinney did not fall within this category; he had an exemplary record as a policeman.[15] Eddie McKinney's murder was collateral. The attack was directed against the McMahons.

Owen McMahon was a respected publican and businessman, one of the emerging Catholic middle class who occasionally transcended

Belfast's sectarian lines of division. Although friends with Joe Devlin, who was vocally opposed to IRA violence, he was not politically active.

The day after the murders, the *Evening Echo* reported that 'the Specials are giving out that they had known that Mr Owen McMahon was a subscriber to *Sinn Féin* funds.' The *Echo*'s correspondent in Belfast immediately made inquiries among republicans who denied that this was the case.[16] Some years later, Belfast IRA officer Seán Montgomery recalled that Owen McMahon made a donation to Sinn Féin and that this had been recorded in a receipt book captured by the police a few days earlier. The RIC seized an IRA collection book, including a list of 'subscribers' to republican funds, during a raid on Sinn Féin headquarters in Belfast city centre six days before the McMahon murders.[17]

Belfast's police leaders assured the public that the murderers of the McMahons and Eddie McKinney would be found. The RIC published a notice in the city's main newspapers offering a £1,000 reward for evidence that would lead to a conviction. William Lynn, the DI in command of 'D' District, led the investigation. He wrote an initial report in which he summarised the witness accounts of the surviving members of the McMahon family and those of their neighbours.

Lynn concluded that the Bruce demesne was used as a staging point for the attack and as a point of exit afterwards. One of the men used a sledgehammer to break down the door. Lynn questioned the police on duty nearby but none had seen or heard anything of relevance before or after the murders. He also ordered searches of some houses in the Antrim Road and New Lodge Road areas of north Belfast. He does not appear to have taken a statements from the McMahons' immediate neighbours.[18]

Mabel McMurtry was a skilled nurse. She had served in the Queen Alexandra's Imperial Military Nursing Service. Her husband, James, was also a veteran; the son of a well-known doctor on the nearby Crumlin Road, he had joined the Guards Machine Gun Regiment during the First

World War and later worked as a clerk at the Ministry of Home Affairs. The McMurtrys had moved into 5 Kinnaird Terrace less than a year before the attack on the McMahons. In October 1921 a nurse who worked at the home complained that a sum of money had been stolen from her room. DI Lynn led the investigation – nobody was charged, and this event does not appear to be connected to the murders. There was nothing extraordinary about the McMurtrys. They did not have pronounced political views, and professionally had little in common with their neighbours.[19]

Among the eight houses of Kinnaird Terrace, the Purdys stand out as being committed loyalists. The Purdys moved into 1 Kinnaird Terrace eighteen months or so before the murders. Rosabell's husband was a publican who owned and ran a pub off North Street in the city centre (sold after his death in 1915). Their son William joined the militant loyalist youth group the Young Citizen Volunteers; he later served in the Royal Irish Fusiliers and was wounded during the First World War. In early 1922 he lived at 18 Corporation Square, just off York Street, Rosabell Purdy's former home before she moved to Kinnaird Terrace. This was the territory of a notorious loyalist paramilitary leader called David Duncan.[20]

As for a motive, DI Lynn wrote that he could find none. Owen McMahon was popular and well-known; neither he nor his family had offended anyone. Lynn reported that he had 'no clue' as to the identity of the perpetrators.

Eliza McMahon's niece Mary Downey was a guest in the house at the time of the murders. Mary and her cousin John gave the most detailed police statements. Eliza was treated for shock – her statement and those of her thirteen-year-old daughter, Lily, and eleven-year-old son, Michael, are only a few sentences long.

Eliza recalled that she was awoken in the bedroom she shared with her husband on the third floor by what she thought was the sound of a bomb exploding at their front door. Hurrying downstairs, she was met by a man in police uniform, carrying a revolver in his hand, who ordered her to go back to her bedroom. She saw another four or five uniformed policemen. One man wore a trench coat; he ordered members of the household downstairs, hurrying them as they went – 'Come on, come on.' Eliza repeatedly asked what they wanted with the men of the family. Her husband tried to reassure her that it was just a raid. Michael recalled his mother being told 'go you back to your bed' by the man wearing a trench coat. His mother refused, saying, 'I am going to go on down too.' She followed the men downstairs, entering the drawing room, a few yards away from where her husband and sons were being held.

Mary Downey was asleep in a bedroom she shared with her cousin Lily on the second floor of the house when she was awakened by a light being pointed towards her face. Looking up she saw a man wearing a light-coloured trench coat and a light-coloured cap. He had 'a round soft looking face and very black eyes, he was about 5 ft 9 in in height'. The man was clean-shaven but not 'very young'. She was sure she would recognise him again. He did not speak and left the room once Mary got out of bed. Moving to the door, Mary noticed that the gas had been lit on the landing. She observed the same man speaking to her aunt on the landing in 'a gruff voice'.

Mary then saw three men dressed in black waterproof police coats going up the stairs to the next floor. She went back into the bedroom but could hear her uncle asking, 'What are you going to do?' And the reply: 'Get on down.' After the murderers left, she ran downstairs to the dining room where she found Eddie McKinney dying near the door. Her uncle lay badly wounded on the rug in front of the fireplace. Frank and Patrick were slumped in the far-right-hand corner of the room; Mary believed they were already dead. At this point John – badly wounded but conscious – was lying on the ground between Pat and their father. Michael was cowering near a couch close to the fireplace, physically unhurt but trembling with fear.

Lily McMahon also recalled a man entering her room on the second floor and shining a light in her face. He did not speak, and left the room. She heard her father say, 'That is right, it is only searching for arms.' She then heard shots, twelve or thirteen, and the sound of her father moaning downstairs. She went onto the landing where she saw two men run out of the house; one dressed in a trench coat. He was the last to leave. She could also hear her mother shouting in the drawing room.

John McMahon shared a bedroom with his brothers Gerald and Michael on the second floor. He was awoken by the sound of smashing glass. He got up, went to the landing and looked down the stairs. He could see a faint light coming from the dining room on the bottom floor. His mother and father came downstairs to the second floor. Then he saw a man – dressed in a trench coat with a belt – who asked him if there was anybody else upstairs. The same man then went up to the third floor where he ordered his brother Bernard and Eddie McKinney out of their room.

On his way downstairs, John saw a man in police uniform standing at the door of the drawing room. Sensing that something was dangerously wrong, John pleaded with this man, telling him that he had a sick brother in hospital. The man reassured him, 'It is allright [*sic*] this is only a raid.' John was led into the dining room, where he was joined by his father, Bernard, Frank, Pat, Gerald, Michael and Eddie McKinney. The group, all wearing their nightclothes, were lined up beside the fireplace. They were then spoken to by the man in the trench coat: 'Do you boys say prayers?'

A few seconds later the same man 'shot straight before him at my father. Another man who was in uniform shot in my direction. I ducked my head and was shot in the neck. I fell on the floor under the table and lay there. There were two or three shots more fired and then they went out. I thought one filled his revolver, but I am not sure.'

Looking up, John saw his father lying on the rug beside the hearth; Eddie McKinney and Gerald were nearby. Bernard had fallen close to

John, beside the dining-room table. John waited until the men left. As well as being shot in the neck, a bullet was lodged half an inch from John's heart. Clearly in shock, John got up, took a swig of brandy from the drinks cabinet and left the room. He told the police that five men carried out the attack and that the man in the trench coat appeared to be the leader. This clean-shaven, smartly-dressed man was about thirty to thirty-five years old.

John saw only two men open fire – the man in the trench coat and a 'much taller man in uniform'. This man had a dark complexion and was about six feet tall. One of the five men appeared to have an English accent. Michael corroborated John's account of the man in the trench coat speaking to them in the dining room and then opening fire, although he recalled him saying, 'Did you never say your prayers?' When he saw the man lift his revolver to start shooting Michael ducked down and crawled under the dining-room table.

The men who murdered the McMahons and Eddie McKinney were in a hurry. Eliza saw two of the gang running off into Bruce's demesne across the street. The men who did the firing did not complete their task of murder; John survived. They did not shoot Michael, either because he successfully concealed himself or because one of the murderers decided not to kill an eleven-year-old boy.[21]

The men's haste should not obscure their evident coolness when it came to killing. The man in the trench coat was able to look his victim in the eye, speak to him and then shoot him in the head (and abdomen) a few second later. Frank and Gerald were both shot in the head and chest. Pat was shot in the chest and abdomen. Bernard was shot in the chest and spinal cord. Eddie McKinney was shot in the chest and abdomen.[22]

By John McMahon's account, after expending the bullets in his revolver, one of the murderers may have put his hand in his pocket and placed more rounds in the chamber. To do that in the midst of a mass-murder took a calmness that either betrayed past experience of violence or, at the very least, an unusual level of callousness. The shooting went on for some minutes, not seconds. Lily McMahon's figure of hearing twelve to thirteen shots come close to the estimated shots fired that inflicted fifteen separate wounds on seven men. This was a careful massacre. Shots were aimed; there was no wild firing. The only account of a misdirected shot was that aimed at John, who ducked just in time and was wounded in the neck. Even so, the next shot, fired a moment later, nearly hit him directly in the heart.

Notes made in the murder file indicate that the police suspected – or at least professed to believe – that the IRA may have carried out the murders. It was apparently irrational for members of the Special Constabulary to carry out murders while in uniform. The IRA could have stolen uniforms to falsely implicate the police. And Sinn Féin were known to terrorise 'respectable' Catholics such as the McMahons. The most senior official at the Ministry of Home Affairs in Belfast pointed out to his minister that the murderers told the McMahons 'to say their prayers'. The apparent importance – or hidden sectarian subtext – of this statement is not clear. No mention in the police file was made of any support given by Owen McMahon to Sinn Féin.[23]

What is missing from the otherwise very thin police murder file is any trace of an investigation into loyalists who were suspected of having carried out most of the murders in the area over the previous months. The five men who broke into 3 Kinnaird Terrace made no effort to cover their faces. In the days after the murders the *Sunday Express* newspaper published a 'scoop'; a number of people had come forward to identify the McMahon murderers. They had signed witness affidavits, and these had been given directly to the prime minister, Sir James Craig. The matter was especially serious since the men identified were members of the Special Constabulary who were based in a Belfast barracks.[24] If such evidence was made available to the Northern Irish government it has since disappeared.

In August DI Lynn also took charge of the inquests into the McMahon and McKinney murders. He initially could not discover the whereabouts of Eliza McMahon, her niece and her surviving children. They had left the city in the days after the killings; their relatives, including Owen's brothers, refused to divulge their location.

Lynn contacted the McMahons' family solicitor, Bernard Donnelly, to discuss making witnesses available for the proceedings. Donnelly replied that the family 'did not want to make any fuss'. Eliza McMahon was most likely terrified that she and the rest of her surviving family would also be killed if they gave evidence. Eventually, three members of the family were interviewed – Eliza McMahon and her two sons, John and Michael. Remarkably, the two other survivors, Mary Downey and her cousin Lily, played no part in proceedings. Lynn took the view that 'their evidence was nothing but what the other witnesses deposed'. This was obviously wrong – Mary had given by far the most detailed physical description of the leader of the group in her initial police statement.

Despite his glaring failure to making any progress in identifying the murderers, Lynn's conclusions were unambiguous: 'There was no suggestion on the part of the McMahons that the police were implicated in the murder and no attempt was made by them or their solicitor to go further than the statements which were taken by DI Williams and I the morning after the murder.' The statements of the survivors only *suggested* that the men wore police clothing – waterproof coats and caps. According to Lynn, that proved nothing.

There is no mention in the investigation file of the attack on the house of another leading publican in north Belfast a month after the McMahon murders.[25] John O'Keeney had purchased his landmark pub (and adjacent) house on the Oldpark Road in north Belfast from a Protestant publican who moved his business to the Shankill Road.[26] At 9 a.m. on Sunday, 23 April 1922 three men pushed their way past the maid into the O'Keeney house. The leader of the gang – a man of

GHOSTS OF A FAMILY

medium build wearing a blue coat – ordered the maid and the O'Keeney children to remain in the kitchen where they were guarded by one of the raiders. The other two men then went upstairs to the bedrooms.

John O'Keeney was in bed with his wife. When the men entered the room, Rose O'Keeney screamed 'murder!' and threw a blanket over her husband. She then grabbed a whistle, which she kept on a bedside table, blowing it repeatedly. (Many Catholics in north Belfast had taken to keeping whistles nearby so that they could summon help if targeted by a 'murder gang'.)

Instead of firing at her husband, the men ran downstairs and out of the house. Rose O'Keeney followed the men out of the bedroom and down the stairs. She then went into the drawing room at the front of the house, pulled open a window that faced the street and repeatedly shouted 'murder!' The raiders left just in time. A nearby police patrol, hearing the noise, ran towards the house, arriving seconds after the three men made their escape down nearby Byron Street.

Journalists who covered the raid and the police response reported that there was no doubt that the intention was to murder John O'Keeney. This time the attempted murder was in daytime, not during curfew hours – between 11 p.m. and 5 a.m. – and none of the men wore police uniforms. Oldpark Road was a busy thoroughfare. The raiders, rightly thinking that they had little time to escape, panicked when they encountered Rose O'Keeney's resistance.

Despite these differences there were some obvious resemblances to the attack on the McMahons. The profile of the victim was similar – O'Keeney was two years older than Owen McMahon; he also owned a number of valuable public houses in the city as well as trading in furniture, clothing and jewellery. (In July 1920 his pub on the Oldpark Road and his stock of goods were destroyed by loyalist arsonists.)[27]

A few weeks later, on the evening of 20 May 1922, another Catholic publican's home in north Belfast was attacked. This time the target was

Vincent Shields who, like the McMahons and O'Keeneys, lived in a large, spacious house – on Alexandra Park Avenue, between the Antrim and York roads. Shortly before 10 p.m. four men approached the house – two went to the rear of the house while two others knocked on the front door, which was opened by Kathleen Shields, Vincent's mother. Kathleen was alone in the house with her two grandchildren.

Kathleen Shields told the men that her son was not in. They drew revolvers, forced their way inside the hallway and ran upstairs to the bedrooms. There they found the two children sleeping in separate rooms. As the men returned downstairs they encountered Winifred Anderson, Kathleen's daughter, who had returned from mass to her mother's house. The men pushed both women into the kitchen, telling them that they had to search the house 'as it was part of their duty' and that, 'We could blow the head off you if we wanted but we won't.'

As Winifred Anderson begged the men for mercy, not to leave her children without a mother, two men came into the kitchen from the back of the house and opened fire, injuring both women. The four men then ran out of the house. Winifred collapsed, wounded in the thigh. Her mother, although shot in the chest, was able to stumble to a neighbours' house. An ambulance was called; both women survived.[28]

Vincent Shields had previously come under suspicion: British Army intelligence suggested that he kept arms and ammunition in his bar on North Derby Street off the York Road. His father, William, had been a prominent support of the National Volunteers in Belfast before his death in 1915. The RIC sergeant at York Street Barracks was more sceptical, informing military intelligence that Shields was 'a most inoffensive man, has sympathies, but is a man who in their opinion would not be trusted with either arms or ammunition'.[29] But rumours in Belfast could be fatal. Shields' pub was repeatedly attacked and looted. He moved with his family across the border to the town of Sligo.[30]

The attacks on the O'Keeney and Shields homes occurred weeks after the raid on 3 Kinnaird Terrace. Both were less than a mile from the McMahons' home. No. 60 Oldpark Road was close to the western edge of the Bruce demesne. Alexandra Park Avenue was an area favoured by middle-class unionists such as MP William Twaddell. This was a shocking intrusion into this suburban idyll.

The initial part of the raids also chimed with the experience of the McMahons – in the case of the O'Keeneys, securing the children and maids in a room before seeking out the man the leader of the gang called 'the boss' – John O'Keeney. Several members of the O'Keeney household had seen the would-be-murderers in daylight. An RIC constable witnessed the men make their escape. Kathleen Shields and Winifred Anderson spoke to two of the four men for some minutes and also had a clear view of the two men who shot them. Yet DI Lynn and other RIC officers never considered linking these other attacks on the homes of wealthy Catholic publicans in north Belfast to the McMahon murders.[31]

Forty-three-year-old DI William Lynn was an experienced police officer. A surviving picture taken around 1920 shows a strong, somewhat angular figure. He looks directly, confidently at the camera, gripping his dress sword. His slightly hooded eyes masked a restless brain. Lynn was one of the most intelligent officers of his generation. Ranked first in his examination to gain promotion to district-inspector, he was known for his exceptional ability to solve crimes. Fourteen years before the McMahon murders, as a young sergeant, Lynn had been lauded by superiors for successfully investigating a complex case of murder and attempted murder in County Meath. Lynn worked for many years in Belfast before his elevation to district inspector. He told his son that he saved the life of Éamon de Valera when the Sinn Féin president was addressing a meeting in the city and came under attack from a spanner-wielding supporter of Joe Devlin MP.

The reasons for the sudden incompetence of DI Lynn are not clear. Lynn was a Catholic from a rural Antrim background; his north Belfast family home on Cliftonville Avenue was not far from Kinnaird Terrace.[32] Lynn's Catholic predecessor in 'D' District had been shot by loyalists. The gaping silence in north Belfast over the identity of the McMahons' murderers suggested that their leader was a man whose power and violence were greatly feared.

Lynn finished his report on the McMahon murders by observing that, 'I do not see how there can be any future reflection on the Govt. or the police action in this case.' Everything had been done properly. Evidence could not be gathered; the police could not be incriminated. The report was sent up the chain of command and eventually landed on Northern Ireland Prime Minister Sir James Craig's desk, who offered no comments.[33] And so the case was effectively closed, never to be reopened.

Craig had often been unwell or absent from Belfast as the violence in the city intensified in early 1922. His friend and the secretary to the Northern Irish cabinet, Wilfred Spender, covered for him as much as he could, sending frequent letters to Craig while he recuperated in England in February and March of that year.[34]

Craig was not alone in vacillating over what to do about loyalist murder. The British cabinet wrestled with the possibility that Collins and others would rip up the Anglo-Irish Treaty and go to war over the 'pogrom' in Northern Ireland. For Prime Minister David Lloyd George, the year 1922 was supposed to mark an end or at least a pause to the 'Irish question' that had consumed so much British government attention during the preceding decades. Successive British cabinets had grappled with waves of political unrest and intermittent bouts of insurgency and terrorism. Home rule, limited self-government or autonomy for Ireland, had been voted into law in 1914 but then postponed due to political opposition and the exigencies of the First World War.

Protestants, largely committed to the union with Great Britain, made up a slim majority in Ireland's northern province of Ulster. They were mostly descendants of settlers 'planted' by the British crown in the seventeenth century to pacify this most rebellious part of the island. Between 1912 and 1914 northern unionists formed the well-armed, 90,000-strong paramilitary organisation the Ulster Volunteer Force (UVF), to resist all-island self-government by a parliament that would sit in Dublin – home rule. Intimidated by this show of force, the British government began drawing up plans for the partitioning of Ireland under any future home rule settlement. It was envisaged that both parts of Ireland would continue to return members of parliament to Westminster. Dublin would not raise its own military. Foreign policy and matters of external trade would be decided in London.

The First World War and the 1916 Easter Rising in Dublin changed everything. Irish nationalist leaders supported the Allied war effort; parallels were drawn between the rights of a small (Catholic) country like Belgium to determine its own future and that of Ireland. Members of the National Volunteers – set up to counter any potential loyalist UVF resistance to home rule – joined the British Army's 10th and 16th Divisions. A minority of more extreme nationalists, represented by Sinn Féin stayed at home and planned a rebellion. Their hard logic was that of previous generations of rebels: 'England's difficulty is Ireland's opportunity.'

The Easter Rising in April 1916 was a military failure. Orders were issued and countermanded. The rebellion was largely confined to the city centre in Dublin and most of the casualties were civilians. But the execution of the Rising's leaders, dragged out over successive days, fuelled a wave of political sympathy. The annihilation of much of the 10th Irish Division in 1915 during the failed Gallipoli campaign in the eastern Mediterranean and a bungled government proposal to extend wartime conscription into Ireland added kindling to the republican fire.

By 1918 a new generation of revolutionaries was coming of age. The executed leader of the Easter Rising, Patrick Pearse, was a teacher who fully appreciated the potential of directing the minds of children towards an extreme end.[35] So too did Countess Constance Markievicz – a west of Ireland aristocrat turned revolutionary – who had travelled to Belfast to help organise the boys' Fianna movement in the years before the First World War. One of her recruits was Roger McCorley, who joined the Fianna at the age of twelve. McCorley would become one of what Belfast IRA officer Thomas McNally called 'the super gunmen of the city'. In the hills above Belfast Lough, a Protestant ex-soldier and Ulster volunteer turned republican instructed the boys in military drill and the Japanese martial art of ju-jitsu.[36]

Seamus Woods was another of McNally's 'super gunmen'. Woods was described in a British intelligence report as 'the most dangerous man in Belfast'. Born in 1900 near the village of Ardglass on the east coast of Ulster, Woods' mother was an intense nationalist, a supporter of the Gaelic Athletic Association and Irish language movement, who refused to allow any item not made in Ireland into the family home. Her children were brought up with the hope and expectation that they would become revolutionaries. Woods moved to Belfast and, together with McCorley, quickly became the spearhead of the IRA in the city. One of his first 'jobs' for the IRA in Belfast was to organise the burning of the tax offices where he was employed as a trainee accountant. Other Belfast IRA officers, men such as Joe McKelvey, had a longer pedigree of republican activism. But none of these leaders were as lethally effective as Woods and McCorley.[37]

In the 1918 UK general election Sinn Féin won a majority of seats in Ireland and took control of many councils in local elections nearly two years later. From 1919 to 1921 the IRA waged an insurgency that drained the British government of money, troops and police urgently needed elsewhere in the empire. IRA assassinations or murders led to reprisals by the police and the military. Some were systematic and sanctioned, such as the burning of houses belonging to republican families. Others were chaotic, drunken and murderous – police discipline began to break down.

Republican courts steadily replaced those of the crown; taxes were no longer paid to the British government. Its writ had broken down in much of the country. Prime Minister David Lloyd George and the Sinn Féin leader Éamon de Valera agreed to a truce that came into effect on 11 July 1921. The subsequent Anglo-Irish Treaty was signed in London in the early hours of 6 December.

The Free State would raise its own revenue, police force and army – but it would still be a dominion within the British empire, nominally loyal to the crown and linked to the wider imperial legal system. (Appeals could be made to British judges, members of the Privy Council in London.) The treaty fell far short of the all-island Irish republic envisaged in 1916 and split the republican movement. Éamon de Valera refused to support it, as did a substantial part of the IRA.[38]

Loyalists in six-county Northern Ireland, which remained a devolved part of the United Kingdom, were also enraged by the treaty. Colonel Fred Crawford, who in 1914 had been the UVF's principal gun runner, recalled that Craig seemed 'to be very anxious and hard hit over this awful betrayal. I never knew such gloom to hang over Ulster before. Even in the days of the U.V.F. from 1912 till 1914 at no time was there such gloom as at present. Then there was the excitement of activity but now it is a question of sitting tight and waiting for the last blow to fall.'[39]

The British government's release of 130 northern IRA internees in mid-January was also profoundly shocking for Belfast's unionists. Uncertain about the British commitment to Northern Ireland, loyalists saw the creation of a new Irish National Army – led by former IRA insurgents – as an existential threat. Ulster unionists had not been included in treaty negotiations but were expected to participate in a somewhat ambiguous all-island Council of Ireland between the two governments in Dublin and Belfast and a mechanism to redraw the border, possibly in the Free State's favour. They had already sacrificed three counties – Cavan, Donegal and Monaghan – from the province of Ulster in order to secure a larger Protestant, unionist majority in what became Northern Ireland under the Government of Ireland Act of 1920. They would not give anything else to a Dublin government.[40]

Irish republicans believed that the new government in Belfast, headed by Prime Minister Sir James Craig, was a brittle edifice. The twelve nationalist and republican MPs refused to recognise the Northern Ireland parliament, which was opened by King George V at City Hall in June 1921 – it was hoped that a 'statelet' crudely assembled on sectarian lines would prove an embarrassment to the British government and an economic liability.[41] The fifty-year-old Craig, a former banker, veteran of the Boer War and the scion of a whiskey distilling family, was a capable organiser but notably lacked the charisma of Sir Edward Carson, the brilliant barrister and erstwhile leader of Ulster's resistance to home rule.

Although Protestants constituted two-thirds of Northern Ireland's population, two of its northern counties – Fermanagh and Tyrone – had Catholic (largely nationalist) majorities. So too did Northern Ireland's second city of Derry. Michael Collins sought to heal the rift between republicans over the treaty by covertly organising a 'northern offensive' that would test British resolve and possibly even topple Craig's government. The IRA in the north escalated its campaign of arson and killing in Belfast in the weeks after the treaty.[42]

The large-scale military offensive in the North failed to materialise. Acrimony between the two sides of the IRA frustrated plans for the May operation. But rumours of a massive invasion from the South swept across loyalist Belfast, feeding paranoia and violence. Sectarian atrocities such as those inflicted by Catholic insurgents on English and Scottish Protestant settlers in seventeenth-century Ulster loomed large in the loyalist imagination. Incidents of IRA violence towards Protestants in the South of Ireland were reported in graphic detail in the Belfast press.[43] The four months after the Anglo-Irish Treaty saw an intense wave of atrocity. Much of the violence was perpetrated by the undisciplined Ulster Special Constabulary (USC), a largely part-time police force that had absorbed loyalist paramilitary groups. It was in the context of this violence that the McMahon murders occurred.

On the day of the murders, Richard Mulcahy, the provisional government's minister for defence, sat down at his desk to consider what had happened in Belfast. Mulcahy concluded that the Special Constabulary – paid for by the British government – were now murdering Catholics with impunity. He wrote a letter to the government warning that 'the implications of the present situation in the North-East' meant he was unsure whether the treaty could be saved or whether renewed war against the British was now necessary. The National Army stepped up planning for the few 'northern offensive'.[44] Mulcahy was torn. He wanted the treaty to work, to continue building the new Irish state. But he also wanted revenge.

On 22 June 1922 two IRA volunteers, Reginald Dunne and Joseph O'Sullivan, shot dead Field Marshal Sir Henry Wilson on the doorstep at his Belgravia home. Wilson, who had recently retired as the head of the British Army, was now an MP for North Down and a security adviser to the Northern Ireland government. The London IRA had received orders to kill Wilson as a reprisal for the 'whole-sale massacres of Irish nationalists in Belfast'.[45]

Joe O'Sullivan's sister recalled that he 'had broken down and sobbed when he read of the murder of the McMahon family in Belfast. Then he straightened himself up and said: "Someday we'll have our revenge on those who planned the pogroms."'[46] Shortly before his execution, Reggie Dunne wrote a statement blaming Wilson for the 'Orange terror' in Belfast, especially his support of the USC – 'the principal agents in his [Wilson's] campaign of terror'.[47]

Belfast atrocities, most notably the McMahon murders, and the vengeful assassination of Henry Wilson were the sparks that lit the Civil War in Ireland, a conflict that would last from 28 June 1922 until 24 May the following year.[48] The British cabinet, angry and fearful after such an audacious murder in the heart of establishment London, quickly blamed the anti-treaty IRA for Wilson's murder. Lloyd George demanded that Collins move against them or else the British Army would re-commence operations in the South of Ireland. Six days after Wilson's killing, the National Army commenced operations against the IRA, shelling the Four Courts building which functioned as the anti-treaty headquarters in Dublin city centre.

In February 1924 Minister for Defence Richard Mulcahy returned to the question of responsibility for the McMahon murders when he circulated a military intelligence memorandum to his cabinet colleagues. In it was a description of the activities of the purported leader of the 'murder gang' that carried out the murders. The memorandum became known as 'the Nixon Memo' after its subject, District Inspector (DI) John Nixon of the RUC.[49] According to the memo, Nixon's gang was made up of long-serving regular police officers that carried out successive atrocities. This gang not only killed innocent Catholics but revelled in gruesome acts of torture – such as castration – before death.

The McMahon murders were not only an atrocity but a seismic event that cursed Irish politics for decades. They were quickly recruited to make polarised political arguments. In London the *Spectator* concluded that only the vicious Sinn Féin party could have carried out such a horrific atrocity. Echoing the theory advanced by the police, the magazine claimed that the family had been 'done to death by Sinn Féin gunmen' disguised as policemen. Death was the price of the McMahons' purported British loyalty; a rumour existed that the McMahons had refused to sign some 'Republican pledge'. The *Spectator* provided no evidence for its claims but they served to poke a finger in the eye of Irish republicans.[50]

For the Irish government in Dublin the absence of a specific motive underlined the savage bigotry of the perpetrators and their supporters. Loyalist murderers had been recruited as policemen, with the connivance and protection of the unionist government. It did not matter that many part-time policemen never harassed or harmed their neighbours. The violence of some – and the too-frequent lack of disciplinary action thereafter – was a reminder that Northern Ireland was a 'cold house for Catholics'.

The murder of Henry Wilson spelled the end of the Lloyd George government's attempts to fundamentally restructure Northern Ireland's police. There was now little appetite in Westminster for a confrontation with Craig and his cabinet. Among Catholics, the almost wholly Protestant 'B' Specials were the most resented manifestation of a unionist government that systematically discriminated in favour of Protestants when it came to public services and employment. For four decades, grievances against the 'B' Specials grew – Catholics exchanged tales of petty insults and occasional violence inflicted by neighbours who held a grudge against them or were simply 'bitter' (bigoted).[51]

The failure to intervene and reform the Special Constabulary in 1922 proved disastrous. In 1969 images of the 'B' Specials once more indiscriminately opening fire in residential streets in Belfast brought back haunting memories of violence for those who could remember the 1920s or had heard their parents or grandparents talk about 'the pogrom'. A year later the British government disbanded the USC. It was too late; a disastrous new cycle of violence had already begun.[52]

CHAPTER TWO

Belfast's Descent

BEFORE THE PARTITION OF THE island in 1920, Belfast was Ireland's fastest-growing and largest city. Its population had spiralled upwards from just under 100,000 in 1851 to nearly 350,000 at the start of the twentieth century. The city's thriving shipyard, engineering and textiles industries attracted more and more migrants from the city's rural hinterland. 'Belfast, with its industrial clamour, its new red brick that screams at you and its electric trams that fly faster than the trams anywhere else,' observed the writer Robert Lynd, 'has made itself, too hastily, and when it lies silent through the fear of God on the morning of the seventh day, you see that is as yet an industrial camp and not a city.'[1]

A rush of migrants brought new slums. These snaked out westwards and northwards from the city. Hundreds of thickly populated alleyways streamed into major thoroughfares. Some hastily constructed suburbs, like those along the Falls Road, became quickly associated with territory or a 'camp' held by one political 'side' or the other. Cramped 'kitchen-houses' with two rooms per family abutted smoke-filled, deafening workplaces – workers grew accustomed to shouting to make themselves heard, the ironically labelled 'Belfast whisper'. Poverty was widespread across the city but Catholics were much less likely to hold skilled, well-paid jobs, including when it came to public employment. Apprenticeships

27

were hard to come by in a city where Protestant associations acted as gatekeepers to skilled employment.[2]

Belfast's Protestant majority was being steadily eroded, but not overwhelmed, by Catholic migration. By 1920 just under a quarter of the city's population were Catholics. The Lagan river divided the predominantly Protestant east from the more mixed west and north of the city.[3] The relative boom-time of the city's war economy had given way to a recession and hunger. Life expectancy for both sexes was not much over fifty; infant mortality was higher than the British average and Catholics were disproportionately affected.[4]

The colour that relieved the graft and grime of Belfast's streets came in the form of its football clubs, political associations and the shimmering beauty of Belfast Lough, bounded on both sides by the tumbling hills of counties Antrim and Down. And once a year different groups of factory or mill workers would also elect 'a queen' from among them. 'Courtiers' would dress a young woman in lace and garlands of flowers and set her on an improvised cart or 'throne' to be paraded through the streets. Local writer Frederick McGinley described the grace of such scenes amid the stacks and the smoke. But the fate of Belfast's impoverished 'queens' was fixed: 'Notwithstanding their youth, beauty and charm their reign was short. They were old at forty-five; dead shortly after.'[5]

Journalist James Kelly recalled clambering up the mountains overlooking west Belfast to pick blackberries and drink the stream water on late summer days in the years before the cataclysmic 'pogrom'. It was here in June 1795 that a group of Belfast radicals – consciously acting out enlightenment ideals of aesthetics and political liberty – stood on top of a mountain crag, swearing 'never to desist in our efforts until we had subverted the authority of England over our country, and asserted our independence.' Among them was the future leader of the United Irishmen rebellion of 1797–98, Theobald Wolfe Tone. And it was on this site – also known as McArt's fort – that Belfast IRA volunteers would sleep while 'on the run' in the 1920s.

Kelly sketched the view of Belfast from McArt's Fort as he saw it as a child:

> the dim outline of the Scottish coast faintly traced on the horizon. Little coasters chugged slowly up the Lough towards the harbour-mouth where the skeletons of great ocean-going liners rose amidst the giant gantries of the shipyards. Over the sea the sky was clear and blue but over the city a pall of smoke hung menacingly. It was thickest over that part of the city where the mill chimneys crowded close together marking the slums in which the workers dwelt.

Belfast was a grand city of empire. Its sprawling new Baroque city hall in Donegall Square, decorated by the same craftsmen who fitted the *Titanic*'s lounges and saloons, was unveiled in 1906. But there was a sickness in Belfast, what Kelly called 'an ugliness of the spirit', which would eventually destroy his young life as he knew it.[6]

The annual Twelfth of July demonstration by the Orange Order – to commemorate Protestant King William of Orange's victory over the Catholic-supported armies of James II in 1690 – brought with it the threat of sectarian violence. A quickening beat of Orange drums would reverberate around the city while Catholics mounted a watchful guard at street corners to prevent attacks on their homes.

IRA officer Thomas McNally recalled as a boy watching the barricading of the streets near the Falls Road. The women dug up 'kidneys', the small, rounded Belfast cobblestones that were a weapon of choice during every riot in the late nineteenth and early twentieth centuries. Among his earliest memories were 'riots, police baton charges, calling out the military – more charges – the reading of the Riot Act; some unfortunates, usually innocent people, shot; Orange processions,

Catholic counter-demonstrations with huge bonfires on each side; provocative arches … torch light processions'.

After running battles between Catholic residents and loyalists, the police, supported by the British Army, would intervene to separate the two factions. McNally remembered hussar soldiers on horseback charging down his street, 'using their lances where the opportunity afforded'. Normally rioting subsided once the cavalry arrived. But Catholics resented the beating of residents defending their own streets, tying ropes across the streets to unseat the hussars and emptying the contents of chamber pots from upstairs windows on police or soldiers on the street below.[7]

More occasionally, such as during the 1907 riots, the poor of Belfast would unite to protest against social conditions and the refusal of Belfast's bosses of industry to bargain with trade unions. In that year a Kerry-born RIC constable called William Barrett had briefly led a short-lived police mutiny in sympathy with the strikers and demands for higher wages. The result was the same – British cavalry units sent into Belfast slums to reinforce a wavering RIC, protests and violence suppressed.[8]

During riots roads were dug up and barricades such as upturned carts were manned by vigilantes to prevent mobs from gaining access to parts of the city. Holes were cut in the walls of houses so that people could have multiple escape routes if they came under attack.

The geography of violence in Belfast during the period was also extremely intimate. Most attacks occurred within the congested, working-class streets near the city centre. York Street and North Queen Street in north Belfast was the most murderous area of Belfast.[9]

Gaining access to the docks or the city centre could be perilous. A visitor arriving at Belfast's docks at the wrong time could find themselves pitched into a riot. Sailor James McClune, a veteran of the great First World War naval battle at Jutland, was stabbed by a mob seconds after he disembarked from his ship in July 1920.[10]

The city's political leaders and police chiefs could hear the violence and smell the burning. Waring Street, the headquarters of the RIC's Ulster Division (and later the RUC), was a few hundred yards from York Street. City Hall in Donegall Square was close to Joy Street and the Markets areas immediately to the east – some of the oldest Catholic settlements in the city. The Grosvenor Road to the west was a faultline between the loyalist Sandy Row and the nationalist Falls Road.

Policing Belfast had been one of the RIC's greatest challenges. In 1865 the Belfast borough police had been dismantled due to its partisanship and incompetence. A commission of inquiry found that it was almost entirely Protestant and that many police officers were members of the Orange Order.

The imposition of the RIC on a Protestant majority city that wanted to keep its own police service meant that a wary or even overtly hostile relationship between the police and working-class loyalist areas endured into the twentieth century. Loyalists frequently portrayed the RIC as a 'hostile agency', made up principally of rural Catholics who showed little liking for Protestant Belfast.

Suspicion over the policing of Belfast cut both ways. When sectarian riots broke out in 1884, the city's Protestant magistrates were quick to swear in temporary special constables. Catholics regarded special constables as the Protestant mob in uniform, whereas unionist politicians believed that they were instrumental in restoring order.

In February 1886 the Conservative MP Randolph Churchill (father of Winston) visited Belfast to campaign against a Home Rule Bill for Ireland. Churchill spoke to a packed Ulster Hall, finishing his speech with an adaptation of Thomas Campbell's epic poem *Hohenlinden* (switching 'Munich' for 'Ulster'):

> The combat deepens. On ye brave
> Who rush to glory or the grave!

> Wave, Ulster, – all thy banners wave,
> And charge with all thy chivalry.

The speech electrified loyalist Belfast. The choice of Campbell, a poet sympathetic to the French revolution, was deliberately provocative – Churchill was daring Ulster to defy the writ of the British government.

Four months later, and days before the vote on the Home Rule Bill (it was defeated), loyalists employed at the city's Alexandra Dock attacked their Catholic co-workers. Some jumped in the water and swam to safety; others escaped using makeshift rafts. James Curran, a seventeen-year-old docker, drowned. Rioting broke out at his funeral on 6 June. Several pubs were attacked, burned and looted. After loyalists surrounded and attempted to burn a police barracks in the Shankill Road area – with seventy-two policemen inside – RIC constables fired indiscriminately from the barracks onto the street, killing seven people and wounding many more. Of the thirty-two people killed during the rioting, twenty-four were shot by the police. More than 340 police were injured, mostly by kidneys flung by rioters.

Belfast's unionist leaders were furious, complaining that the police were out of control. The RIC was temporarily withdrawn from the loyalist Shankill Road and assurances were given that the police would behave differently in the future. This was a serious blow to the RIC's reputation and morale in the city. The police had effectively 'lost the contest of wills'.[11] It was a lesson in the politics of street violence that loyalists did not forget.

Gangs in the city often fractured on sectarian lines. Both goaded and fought with the police. As a teenager in Edwardian Belfast, the poet Thomas Carnduff joined 'the Pass Gang' in south Belfast: 'We were as tough a crowd of young bucks as could be found in the city. Our particular aversion was Catholics. We ambushed them, jibed them, slaughtered them when opportunity came our way'. Other loyalist gangs included 'the Forty Thieves', 'the Bushrangers' and the feared 'Bogey Clan' in north Belfast.

Catholic gangs included 'the Cronje Clan', named after General Piet Cronjé who defeated the British at a number of battles during the Boer War in South Africa. The 'Cronjies' wore black-and-white checked flat caps. Rival sectarian gangs would sometimes meet on 'the Bog Meadow' between the Shankill Road and Falls Road to fight it out with fists and stones. A childhood education in street fighting – including the knowledge of every corner and bolthole in a gang's patch – was invaluable for those who picked up a revolver instead of a kidney in Belfast during 1920–22.[12]

The six counties of what became Protestant-majority Northern Ireland were spared from much of the violence – IRA assassinations, robberies and police reprisals – that erupted elsewhere in Ireland during the first months of 1920. First Battalion, Norfolk Regiment, the resident garrison in Belfast, had also been stationed in Belfast before the First World War. But aside from a few officers and non-commissioned officers,[13] the sixty-seven Norfolk officers and 1,063 soldiers who arrived in Belfast in 1919 were unfamiliar with the city. The regiment had suffered nearly 6,000 fatalities at the front. Those that left Belfast in 1914 – cheered by thousands of shipyard workers as they sailed past the newly constructed *Britannic* (sister to *Titanic*) – were more likely to have died or been wounded and disabled than to have survived the war. In the spring of 1920, Belfast still seemed strangely calm compared to the violence of Dublin and Cork – the Norfolks regarded themselves as fortunate to have been sent to Belfast. On 26 June the regiment provided the guard of honour for the unveiling of the new *Titanic* memorial by the Viceroy of Ireland, Field Marshal Lord French.[14]

Tensions in Belfast built steadily over the summer as news of IRA violence came north. The civil wars expert Stathis Kalyvas has described how, in times of state weakness or disorder, a majority population can be tempted to go on the offensive, to use violence as a means of pre-emptive deterrence against a looming threat from a sizeable minority group in its midst. A rival group that makes up approximately one-third of a population is likely to experience such an attack since it is large enough to pose a threat, but not so large as to sow doubts about the success of a 'trial of strength'. If the power of the minority seems to be on the rise, then the temptation for the majority is to strike sooner than later, to use atrocities as 'an instrumental tool to convey the credibility of their coercive capacity and, thus, prevent civilians from providing information and support to their rivals'.[15]

At the Orange Order's traditional demonstration on 12 July 1920, Edward Carson went on the offensive. Carson stirred up loyalist fears and anger, telling loyalists that they should not wait for the 'same bondage and slavery as the rest of Ireland'. He struck out at the British government for failing to suppress Sinn Féin – if London was incapable of protecting them then they should mobilise the UVF and 'take the matter into our own hands'.[16]

Eight days later an RIC police commander, Colonel Gerald Smyth, was shot dead by the IRA in Cork City. Smyth was from a well-known Ulster Protestant family. The news outraged Belfast's loyalists who turned on their Catholic workmates and 'rotten Protestants' – those who belonged to 'unpatriotic' socialist movements or were simply believed to be insufficiently 'loyal'. An RIC report described how loyalists who were employed at Workman and Clark's shipyard – 'the wee yard' – invaded the 'big yard' of Harland and Wolff looking for Catholic workers: 'A regular hunt-up took place, as a result of which Roman Catholics were badly beaten and thrown in the water. Some of these had to swim long distances to save their lives'.[17]

Some counter-expulsions of Protestants took place in Catholic-owned firms or where Catholics made up the majority of workers. In

October 1920 the Expelled Workers' Relief Committee reported that 8,140 workers had been removed from their jobs. Approximately one quarter were Protestants, 2,000 were women and 1,000 were Catholic ex-servicemen. Most were unskilled labourers. Over 30,000 dependants also faced hunger and deprivation.[18]

Loyalists were following the 1886 template but on a larger scale. And this time there was no prospect of a swift return to work and an end to violence. The stakes had changed – the future of an independent Ireland and that of the new Northern Ireland were in the balance.

So too had the means of violence. Even before 1914 unionists and nationalists had imported large amounts of rifles, revolvers and explosives. The end of the First World War meant that Ireland, like the rest of Europe, was awash with black-market opportunities to acquire surplus weapons and ammunition from demobilising military units. A long-serving policeman in north Belfast reflected that the city had left behind its 'stone age' – the time of the kidneys or cobblestones – for 'the "boyos" of the present day with their rifles, grenades and revolvers'.[19]

The Sinn Féin response to the expulsions was to organise committees across Ireland to boycott Belfast goods and services. Unionists set up an Ulster traders' defence association which implemented a counter-boycott against the South of Ireland. The resulting economic self-harm, exacerbating a global depression, placed more fuel on the bonfire of grievances.[20]

Shooting soon broke out in a city full of veterans. Trenches were dug and street barricades manned. By July 1920 the IRA had also established a sizeable presence in Belfast (approximately 500 'volunteers').[21] Eleven Catholics and eight Protestants were killed over ten days; many more were injured. The police called for assistance from the British Army's resident battalion – 1 Norfolks.

Catholics in west Belfast were angered by the Norfolks' excessive violence during the summer of 1920. Nine people were killed during riots and shooting on 22 July alone. A detachment of Norfolks arrived on the Falls Road during the afternoon with orders to seek out and engage snipers in the area. They opened fire at the roofs of houses in and near Kashmir Street, from where they believed gunmen were firing. A soldier shot dead Brother Michael Morgan as he looked out of a window of Clonard Redemptorist Monastery. (The British Army claimed that snipers were firing from the monastery.)[22]

The Norfolks were also deployed on the same night in the east of the city. A group of thirty soldiers led by Lieutenant John Woodthorpe beat back a loyalist mob who were attempting to burn St Matthew's Catholic Church and a nearby convent in the Short Strand area. The bushes in front of the church were doused in petrol and set on fire. A nearby pub was broken into – after looting its contents a group of men threw a piano from the top of the building onto the street below. (A poem composed to mark the loyalist victory at this 'Battle of Seaforde Street' especially celebrated the looting of spirit groceries: 'The whiskey it was flying, and damn it, it was grand. Instead of paying two bob a glass, you had a bucket in your hand.')

Woodthorpe sent for reinforcements. His men held the line, shooting dead two Protestant men, William McClune and James Stewart. Several soldiers were wounded by missiles, including kidneys, thrown by the crowd.[23] A military lorry on the Newtownards Road was attacked by a mob who threw stones and bottles – the group of soldiers and police trapped inside lay flat on the bottom of the lorry to avoid injury. A few Norfolks soldiers then opened fire from the lorry, killing two Protestant women, Nellie McGregor and Ann Weston.[24]

The Norfolk soldiers quickly won the admiration of the commander of the British Army in Ireland, General Nevil Macready, for being 'quite as ready to shoot Orangemen as Shinners'. But from the autumn of 1920 onwards the Norfolks were regarded with suspicion and even hatred by much of the loyalist populace. The Minister for Home Affairs, Sir

Richard Dawson Bates, professed to believe the rumour that the regiment was biased against Protestants due to an apparent connection with the Duke of Norfolk, the most senior Catholic nobleman in England, and requested they be replaced. When Prime Minister James Craig complained to the British government that the military response to loyalist violence was heavy-handed, since 'in no case could the initiation of outrages be traced to the Orangemen', General Macready told Field Marshal Henry Wilson that this was an 'outright lie' and praised the 'unbiased' Norfolks.[25]

The Norfolk Regiment were known as 'the Holy Boys'. This nickname dated back to the regiment's experiences in Spain during the Napoleonic Wars of the early nineteenth century when Spanish soldiers confused the 'Britannia' symbol for that of the Virgin Mary. The regiment's temperament resembled the landscape of its county, predictable and well-ordered. The Holy Boys' motto was 'Firm' and they were proud of their reputation for discipline.[26]

The Norfolks were eventually reinforced after the 'truce' of July 1921 when Macready sent 1st Battalion, Seaforth Highlanders to Belfast. The Highlanders' 'patch' was centred on the Catholic Falls Road area in west Belfast, Police District 'B'.[27] Other units of the British Army – such as 1st Battalion, The Essex Regiment at Carrickfergus or 1st Battalion, Somerset Light Infantry across Belfast Lough at Holywood – were called upon when violence flared in Belfast. But it was the Holy Boys who were persistently in the frontline when it came to suppressing violence.

General Macready had formed a low opinion of Craig and the RIC when he served as the most senior military commander in Belfast in the months before the outbreak of the First World War. This was the height of the home rule crisis, when the UVF was importing large amounts of weapons and ammunition from Germany and some sympathetic army officers in Ireland were threatening to refuse any order to suppress loyalist Ulster. As in 1914, Macready told Wilson, the RIC in Belfast 'were perfectly useless to take any unbiased action'. Craig, his ineffectual cabinet and the head of the RIC in Ulster, Lieutenant Colonel Charles Wickham, were all 'terrified of their own people, and incidentally of losing their jobs'.[28]

After the July violence subsided, families burned out in the Catholic enclave of east Belfast made their way to the Falls Road area in the west of the city. Guarded by Norfolk soldiers with bayonets fixed to ward off further attacks, they walked slowly through the city centre – 'a sad procession of carts and coal lorries loaded down with furniture and pathetic little chattels saved from the wrecked homes of Ballymacarrett'.[29]

Worse was to come. On the afternoon of Sunday, 22 August 1920, IRA Volunteer Seán Culhane boarded the Dublin train at Belfast's Victoria station. As the train pulled into the town of Lisburn, a few miles south of the Belfast, Culhane saw that many of the houses near the station were on fire. The streets were a 'seething mass of fire, while great clouds of red tinted smoke hung overhead'.[30]

Hours earlier Culhane had been part of an IRA 'squad' who shot dead DI Oswald Swanzy as he left Lisburn's Christ Church Cathedral. The IRA blamed Swanzy for the murder of the Sinn Féin lord mayor of Cork, Tomás Mac Curtain, gunned down by a police reprisal gang five months earlier. In the hours after Swanzy's death, a loyalist mob rampaged through the streets of Lisburn, burning Catholic businesses and homes. Loyalists posed for photographs outside the ruins of the burned Catholic presbytery. The *London Illustrated News* reported that the destruction was 'suggestive of Ypres or Arras' during the war.[31]

The violence spread to Belfast where another attempt was made to burn St Matthew's Catholic Church. Off-duty soldiers and local residents fought off the initial attack. The mob set fire to Catholic houses in nearby Seaforde Street and Foundry Street. A six-year-old Catholic girl was reported to have been doused in petrol. Her mother managed to beat back her attacker before the child could be set alight.

Catholics working at the nearby Coal Quay were attacked by loyalist shopworkers and beaten with iron bars and tools used for punching through iron plates.[32] A total of twenty-two people were killed and more than 300 seriously injured during the riots that followed Swanzy's death. Hundreds of families abandoned their homes.[33]

Much of Belfast's Catholic community was sharply opposed to the IRA's offensive in the city, worrying about the economic cost and the loyalist response. Unlike in the rest of Ireland, large numbers of northern Catholics continued to favour charismatic West Belfast nationalist MP Joe Devlin, 'Wee Joe', his Irish Parliamentary Party and the Ancient Order of Hibernians (AOH) movement over Sinn Féin. Seamus Woods believed that only 25 per cent of the Catholic population were 'in sympathy with the IRA', less than 10 per cent of the overall population in the city. Others were indifferent. During the truce some Belfast Catholics – 'believing for the moment that we had been victorious and that the Specials and UVF were beaten' – rushed to join Sinn Féin and the IRA (and were known as 'trucileers' by the old guard). But Belfast IRA intelligence officer David McGuinness estimated that 75 per cent of the Belfast population remained hostile to the IRA.[34]

The 'Hibs' was a fraternal organisation that had emerged from agrarian secret societies like the Ribbonmen and the Molly Malones in the nineteenth century. Often seen as the nationalist equivalent of the Orange Order – dedicated to Catholicism and given to parading with banners and bands on 'their day' (St Patrick's Day and St John's Eve on 23 June) – the Hibs gave the Irish Parliamentary Party a powerful economic and social network, not least due to their links and investments in banking and insurance companies.

In 1920 the Hibs moved to build up its own paramilitary force, sometimes called 'the Knights'. The National Secretary of the AOH and the Nationalist MP for Armagh, John Dillon Nugent, reported that he sent 'huge quantities' of arms and ammunition from the rest of Ireland to north-east Ulster. Hibs' violence was generally defensive; small numbers of ex-soldiers gathered on the streets to prevent loyalist incursions into Catholic areas.[35] Some of the Hibs' arsenal ultimately ended up in the possession of the IRA, either given freely by disillusioned Hibs, by those seeking to enrich themselves, or seized by force.[36]

The tempo of IRA burning and assassinations – encouraged by IRA general headquarters in Dublin – empowered younger, more radical IRA volunteers. Roger McCorley was enraged when an IRA volunteer tipped off Catholic bishop Joseph MacRory about a plan to burn Belfast city centre in revenge for the burning of Cork by members of the RIC Auxiliary Division in December 1920. (The operation had been ordered by Michael Collins but was cancelled after MacRory met with IRA leaders in Dublin and 'pointed out the serious consequences and the probability of the entire nationalist population being exterminated' if it went ahead.) Even so, the IRA's arson campaign across Belfast inflicted a staggering amount of damage over the next eighteen months. Factories, mills, cinemas, draperies, distilleries and railway goods yards were all repeatedly burned.[37]

Despite the energy of the IRA's young leaders and the arming of Hibs' veterans, by early 1921 it was evident that Belfast's armed loyalists easily outnumbered nationalists in men and arms. The new unionist government in Belfast ensured that much of the UVF was incorporated into the USC, a 20,000 strong auxiliary police force formed in the autumn of 1920.[38]

The establishment of the USC was a response to two immediate concerns of Prime Minister David Lloyd George's government in London. The first was that 'public bands' of men, many of them war veterans, had begun to spring up in different parts of Ulster. By August 1920 the UVF had also been reactivated.

Fearing a repeat of 1914 when Ulster appeared to teeter on the edge of rebellion, the establishment of a Special Constabulary was supposed to give the British administration in Ireland some control over these previously autonomous paramilitary forces. The second pressing reason was that the manpower of the Special Constabulary eased the strain on an overstretched British Army and RIC.

General Macready opposed the formation of the Special Constabulary, arguing that it would 'probably sow the seeds of civil war' in Ulster.[39] Even Lieutenant Colonel Wilfred Spender, whom Sir James Craig put in charge of reorganising the UVF in the summer of 1920, confided to the British Army's commander in Belfast that 'arming small bodies of men in the manner suggested will only lead to more trouble and excitement, more nerves and consequently more attacks'.[40]

In the autumn of 1920 battalions of the old UVF were rebranded as 'B' Specials units; the officers and non-commissioned officers in both organisations were often the same. The original intention was that the Special Constabulary would defer to, and take instruction from, the regular RIC. But the RIC itself was riven with internal suspicions. It was also much smaller than the USC. (The total muster of the regular RIC in Northern Ireland was 2,324 in November 1921.) Erstwhile Ulster volunteers, albeit now wearing police uniform, often resisted taking orders from Catholic sergeants from places like Cork or Kerry in the South of Ireland.

The Special Constabulary was initially divided into three parts. The 'A' Class was a full-time uniformed force who were relatively well-disciplined compared to the 'B' Class. Recruits could expect to be posted away from their native counties. The 'B' Specials were locally recruited and part-time. In the early months of their formation they did not always patrol in uniform but wore armbands.

Plans for a part-time 'C' Special Constabulary were also rolled out in 1920. It was initially envisaged that the 'C' Class would be open to older men past the normal age of military or police service or those who could not give up the time required to serve as a 'B' constable. However, the new 'C1' Class established in 1922 was designed to be a quasi-military territorial force, one which prioritised the recruitment of ex-servicemen, had a greater arsenal of weaponry and could deploy rapidly across Northern Ireland. By the summer of 1922 the police in Northern Ireland numbered 1,100 RUC, 5,500 'A' Specials, 19,000 'B' Specials and 7,000 'C1' Specials, a combined figure of 32,600 men for a population of just 1.2 million.[41]

A lull in rioting and killing in early 1921 gave way to a more intense IRA offensive and loyalist reprisals during the summer. Shortly before midnight on 9 July 1921 the IRA attacked a police lorry on Raglan Street in west Belfast killing one policeman, Constable Thomas Conlon, a Catholic from County Roscommon in the west of Ireland, and wounding two others. Among the wounded was Constable Edward Horgan, also from the west of Ireland and who had served in the Irish Guards in the First World War. IRA officer Seán Montgomery described the attack: 'A shout in a southern brogue, "Halt, hands up!" [IRA Volunteer] Joe Donaghy was using a Peter the Painter 12 rounder [revolver]. He opened fire, three Policemen fell, one killed and two wounded.'

Another IRA account claimed that the police lorry was carrying a 'murder gang' – the policemen had their faces blackened, carried revolvers and were drunk. The RIC said the lorry was part of a routine patrol to enforce the curfew. Conlon and Horgan were never named in any republican intelligence report as members of a suspected murder gang. (On the contrary, Conlon was described by Seán Montgomery as a reliable source of intelligence for the IRA.)[42]

The next day – hours before the start of the truce of 11 July and formal negotiations between Sinn Féin and the British government – loyalist Belfast exploded. Hundreds of Catholics were burned out of their homes, and fifteen peopled died of gunshot wounds (ten Catholics and five Protestants).[43]

In the weeks after the truce a former Sinn Féin organiser and IRA commander from south Ulster, Eoin O'Duffy, was appointed as the

BELFAST'S DESCENT

republican truce liaison officer for Belfast. The RIC city commissioner, John Gelston, agreed to allow O'Duffy to operate his own republican police force in the city. IRA volunteers armed with revolvers stood guard outside O'Duffy's headquarters in St Mary Hall's in Belfast city centre.[44]

Rather than reducing IRA attacks, O'Duffy deliberately escalated its campaign of arson and assassination in the autumn of 1921. Attacks by loyalists on Catholics in Belfast in the weeks after the truce triggered O'Duffy's new campaign. In a few days of rioting at the end of July loyalist arsonists destroyed fifty-eight Catholic houses in the city; another 103 were badly damaged.[45]

O'Duffy's arrival in Belfast also coincided with that of DI John Nixon. O'Duffy had already tried to kill Nixon when the latter was based in Fermanagh, as DI for Lisnaskea district in the south-east of the county, in late 1920. The IRA had, to Nixon's disgust, infiltrated the RIC barracks in the village of Tempo – with the assistance of several Catholic constables – and killed Sergeant William Lucas.

A Protestant from a loyalist background, the outnumbered Lucas showed remarkable courage. After being shot twice, he fell to his knees outside the barracks before attacking his assailants with a pocketknife. He died ten days later. Nixon claimed that O'Duffy left him a note in the barracks warning him not to carry out any reprisals for the attack. Nixon offered a curt public reply at the inquest into Lucas' killing: 'I am the District Inspector, and I care no more about the Irish Republican Army than I do about a dog in the street.' He then struck the table, shouting, 'Never! Never!' Before O'Duffy could arrange an assassination attempt, Nixon left Fermanagh to take up his new command in Belfast.[46]

DI Nixon was aware that he was top of O'Duffy 'kill list' and took additional security measures. (Even so Belfast IRA commander Seamus Woods claimed that he came close to killing Nixon on one occasion.)[47] Nixon also had his nemesis in his sights; the IRA reported it had intelligence that Nixon ordered his men to 'do in' O'Duffy in Belfast.[48]

43

Born in 1877, Nixon was an unforgettable figure in the damp, soot-filled streets of north Belfast – tall, broad and – for the police – unusually overweight. He had a sallow, rounded face, a small mouth and moustache and prominent bags under hooded and narrow eyes. His booming voice was memorable – even among the ringing noise of an industrial city. So too was his 'soft' Cavan accent amid the cut tones of Belfast. Nixon was a policeman who had risen from the ranks rather than being directly appointed to DI as an RIC 'officer'.[49]

The fate of his family and friends – left on the wrong side of the border where they were exposed to IRA raids on their homes – weighed heavily on John Nixon. His Cavan-born wife was also dying. Nellie Moore had married John Nixon in June 1920 and moved with him to Belfast. The couple resided at 'Derna', a comfortable house on the Crumlin Road in the north-west of the city. Just over a year later, aged thirty-five, she succumbed to tuberculosis and 'exhaustion'.[50] It was too dangerous for Nixon to bury his wife in their native county; Nellie was interred instead near the home of her sister in County Fermanagh in Northern Ireland.[51] The life of his brother, Detective Sergeant Sam Nixon of the Dublin Metropolitan Police, was also in danger; in March 1922 Sam Nixon wrote a letter to the British government stating that he would likely be murdered if he was not quickly moved from Dublin. His fears were well-grounded – Michael Collins' assassination 'squad' had been planning to kill him for months, but like his brother, the security-conscious Sam Nixon was difficult to find.[52]

John Nixon's 'C' District was a largely working-class loyalist district in west Belfast, centred on Brown's Square Barracks just off the Shankill Road. The area also contained a large Catholic minority, including around Stanhope Street, just to the north of Brown's Square. Nixon's patch also included part of the mostly Catholic Ardoyne and Marrowbone areas of north-west Belfast, policed by a head constable based in Leopold Street Barracks. To the immediate south and south-west of the Shankill Road and Nixon's district lay the majority nationalist, Catholic 'B' District centred on the Falls and Springfield Roads.

In late 1921 John Nixon was commended by police headquarters in Belfast for suppressing the IRA in west Belfast.[53] Several Catholic constables who served under Nixon had a very different opinion of his command. They gave statements to Sinn Féin representatives that pointed to a collapse in discipline in 'C' District. They claimed that some policemen drank alcohol in Brown's Square Barracks and were inebriated when on duty. Special constables also used the four-storey Brown's Square Barracks to shoot wildly into nearby Catholic streets.

With the exception of 'C' District's Ardoyne and Marrowbone areas, much of the rest of north Belfast was commanded by DI J.J. McConnell, based at 'D' District headquarters in Glenravel Street. Loyalists increasingly resented McConnell's determined efforts to suppress their activities, which included reprisal attacks and the burning of Catholic houses. On 28 June 1921 Colonel Fred Crawford complained in his diary about the excessive number of Catholic police officers in the city, many of whom he believed were in league with Sinn Féin.[54] His primary target was DI McConnell, whom he suspected of harbouring Sinn Féin sympathies. Twelve days later McConnell was shot in the leg – he identified the shooter as a 'B' Special.[55]

Crawford's suspicions were correct. McConnell was working with Sinn Féin; he even provided ammunition to the IRA which he deposited in a convent for collection.[56] McConnell's decision to actively take the side of republican insurgents was symptomatic of the decay within the RIC during the last year of its existence, as old standards and regulations were ignored, and political factions drove a wedge between the ranks. Many Catholic constables felt they had no future in the RUC, which was to come into existence on 1 June 1922, either because of discrimination within the police or a reluctance to serve the new Northern Ireland.[57]

Nixon for his part came to especially resent those Catholic constables at Leopold Street Barracks whom he believed 'were in sympathy with the IRA'. But only a few Catholic RIC constables chose to give information directly to the IRA. Although some, like McConnell, switched sides during the dying days of the RIC, their behaviour was not typical. Norfolk Regiment intelligence officers reported that the Leopold Street police, led by a decorated Catholic head constable called William Brennan, were very reluctant to pass on intelligence to *anyone* outside their barracks (including Nixon). Their suspicions that such information could be misused for murder proved to be well-founded.[58]

According to Fr Bernard Laverty, a Catholic priest based at St Patrick's Church on Donegall Street (a few hundred yards from Brown's Square Barracks), there were sixty-nine Protestant constables and eleven Catholics in Brown's Square. Laverty's contacts in the RIC told him that 'a number of notorious murderers' were serving constables in the barracks.[59] A Catholic constable called Patrick Flanagan claimed that he received death threats after he intervened to stop four Protestant constables who were firing indiscriminately into a Catholic district. A Protestant constable instructed another to type up Flanagan's death notice within the latter's hearing. Special constables in Brown's Square were also said to have threatened to throw Catholic policemen out of the upper-storey windows, claiming that they were Sinn Féin sympathisers.[60] Nixon was observed drinking while on duty. (He had never been disciplined for drunkenness.)[61] Constable Michael Furlong said he saw Nixon smashing the windows of a Catholic house with a sweeping brush in May 1921 – a policeman eventually grabbed Nixon by the neck and forced him to stop.[62]

On 10 July 1921, the day before the truce took effect and in the aftermath of the IRA's fatal Raglan Street ambush of the RIC, Constable Flanagan alleged that Nixon and some of his men shot up Catholic houses on the Old Lodge Road. Special constables then dragged out two Catholic men and beat them. Flanagan saved one of the men –

'unconscious and practically naked' – from being lynched by locking him in a cell; he later brought him to hospital. Nixon made no attempt that night to stop the burning of Catholic houses and the looting of pubs in 'C' District.[63]

During the same month British officials arrived at an uncomfortable conclusion: the police, specifically the 'B' Class of the Special Constabulary, were instigating rather than suppressing sectarian violence. (The full-time 'A' Specials were seen as reasonably effective, their being more closely under the control of the RIC.)

The army had been forced to confront police indiscipline in Ireland before. During the burnings in Cork in December 1920, soldiers from 2nd Battalion, South Staffordshire Regiment fired over the heads of the drunk Auxiliaries and eventually 'rounded up and forced them [the police] back to Barracks'.[64] But tensions and violence between the police and the army in Belfast were now on a scale never experienced. If a de-escalation in Belfast during the 'truce' agreed by London and the Sinn Féin leadership was to work, then loyalist paramilitaries-turned-policemen had to be demobilised. On 1 September Sir John Anderson, Under-Secretary for Ireland, instructed the military to act as the sole police authority in the city.

The RIC and the Special Constabulary in Belfast were now to work solely under the instructions of the 'Competent Military Authority', namely Colonel Commandant George Carter-Campbell, commander of the British Army's 15th Infantry Brigade, or his designated officers in the various police districts. Carter-Campbell quickly ordered the 'B' Specials off the streets.[65]

Northern Ireland's Minister for Home Affairs, Sir Richard Dawson Bates, was dismayed, telling his ministerial colleagues that, although the 'B' Specials were 'a very undisciplined body', they were the only force over which – until now – the unionist government had some control. The city's loyalists were furious. They believed that the 'B' Specials, far from being a hindrance, were instrumental in quashing Sinn Féin activities in the city.[66]

On 2 September 1921 Carter-Campbell met with the Northern Irish cabinet to discuss Craig's proposal for the military to introduce large-scale internment and searches for arms in the city. When Carter-Campbell insisted that a more hard-line approach 'should be done without regard to either side and that if SF quarters were searched Orange quarters should be equally searched', Craig and his cabinet told Carter-Campbell that they could not endorse such an approach and withdrew their request.[67]

Carter-Campbell's health rapidly deteriorated in Belfast. General Archibald Cameron took over command of the city – and Ulster – in mid-October. (Carter-Campbell died two months later.)[68] Some questioned whether Cameron who had spent much of his career in the Black Watch – known as one of the most Presbyterian of Scotland's regiments – was right for the role. He told a government official that 'he loathed all Roman Catholics collectively and individually'. (The same official was reassured to learn later that Cameron hated all religions equally.)[69]

In November 1921 James Craig persuaded Lloyd George to allow for a transition of police powers to his new government on 22 November 1921. He promptly ordered the redeployment of the 'B' Specials back onto the streets. General Cameron viewed Craig's insistence on redeploying the 'B' Specials back into some of the most volatile parts of Belfast – against military advice – as a capitulation to the mob.

Shortly after Cameron's arrival in Belfast he met Dawson Bates, Wickham and a representative of shipyard workers whose name he believed was 'Byers' at the Ulster Club. (This may have been William Byers, who was associated with the militant Ulster Protestant Association.)

Belfast journalist James Kelly described Dawson Bates as 'buck-toothed, white moustache stained yellow from chain smoking … a little spindly individual with bent shoulders whose appearance belied his reputation as the "strong man" of the cabinet.[70] Cameron and his superior Macready were similarly damning. Macready wrote that Dawson Bates was 'an excitable ass'. He also did not spare Wickham, who he called 'a rotten man … one of the type who is always trying to scrimshank from his regiment. I do not know how Craig got him, but the young man is simply out to feather his nest and get a job as IG [Inspector General] of Craig's Constabulary.'[71]

During the meeting at the Ulster Club, Byers complained about the British Army's withdrawal of the 'B' Specials from Belfast and more recent attempts by Cameron to exclude them from parts of the city. He warned Cameron – either the 'B' Specials were empowered to go after the IRA or loyalists would take matters into their own hands. Cameron recorded his reaction in a letter to General Macready: 'I'm afraid I lost my temper with him (Byers) … What the advocates for their [the 'B' Specials'] employment hope is that they will go and murder some of the opposing side.'[72]

Fourteen people died the day after the Northern Irish government assumed police powers; ten were Catholics. One of the fatalities of the violence during the end of the November was forty-three-year-old Margaret Millar who lived in Dock Lane in the north of the city. Her son had been shot dead in June of that year and her daughter blinded in a separate bomb attack.[73]

The military were now in uncharted territory – which civil power should General Cameron ask for instructions, Lloyd George's government or that of Craig? General Macready summarised Cameron's dilemma in a letter to the Chief of the Imperial General Staff in London, Field Marshal Henry Wilson. Events could shift very quickly in Belfast. What to do if a new inferno suddenly took hold?

> The Government in England could not give him [Cameron] orders in sufficient time to meet emergencies nor, I presume, could he

look upon the Ulster government as the 'power' to call upon him to act in aid of the civil power. To do so would, in my opinion, put grave responsibility on the soldier man, because it is no good birking [*sic*] the fact that in some cases the Orangemen are as much in fault over these Pogroms as the SF [Sinn Féin], and I believe the position of any wretched soldier would be absolutely impossible.[74]

Macready informed Wilson that it was also 'quite possible' that Craig's government would be ousted by a more extreme faction – what he described as the 'Labour' movement within loyalism – placing the army in an even worse position. To protect the reputation of the British Army, the best option would be to hand over internal security responsibilities entirely to the police. But that would lead to even more atrocity, and Catholics would be the principal victims.[75]

In the end Cameron played for time. Craig and Dawson Bates believed that the police should have primacy, and call upon the military for assistance (or send them back to barracks) as they saw fit. Cameron made it clear that, unless his superior – General Macready in Dublin – ordered him to do so, he would not implement any changes to the 'present procedure' of military command over the police. But some police, not least DI John Nixon, sensed a shift in the balance of power and began to obstruct rather than take orders from the army.

Cameron also did what he could to thwart the 'B' Specials. He delayed handing over UVF weapons that had been stored in Tamar Street and which Craig's government had authorised the police to use. And, although the 'B' Specials were once again permitted to redeploy in Belfast, Cameron continued to insist they were excluded from certain, predominantly Catholic, parts of the city such as the Ardoyne and Marrowbone areas in the north of the city.

The British Army's stance irritated Craig and his ministers who accelerated their plans to introduce new legislation that would give them unambiguous powers when it came to internal security. This would eventually culminate in the Civil Contingencies (Special Powers) Act, which came into force on 7 April 1922.[76] The intervening period, November 1921 to April 1922, saw the military-police relationship break down in much of Belfast.

In late 1921 Dawson Bates passed on a series of complaints made by members of the Special Constabulary, including by Colonel Fred Crawford and west Belfast 'B' Specials commandant David Fee, about the conduct of the Norfolk Regiment. These included the purported bayoneting of a boy named Colin Livingstone and soldiers 'dragging fathers into the streets in night attire, thus terrorising children'.

It was also alleged that soldiers from the Norfolk Regiment threatened to shoot the inhabitants of Trafalgar Street in Sailortown in the north of the city. Crawford claimed that the Norfolks told residents that, 'We won't leave an Orange bastard about York Street.' Lieutenant Colonel Clement Yatman, a staff officer at military headquarters in Belfast, told Dawson Bates that the allegations were 'greatly exaggerated'. Loyalists in the area verbally abused the soldiers, calling them 'English bastards'. Their intention was to provoke the Norfolks.[77]

John Nixon had initially worked closely with Captain Harry Papworth, the Norfolks' intelligence officer, organising raids and co-ordinating intelligence gathering. The relationship soured towards the end of 1921 when a conflict broke out between the Norfolk Regiment and the 'B' Specials. Nixon recalled that at this point, 'I was obliged to take the part of the Special Constabulary against some officers of the Norfolk Regiment.'[78] A Catholic policeman in 'C' District described Nixon's furious reaction to 1 Norfolk officers when they attempted to give orders to the police around this time – 'the military officer be damned. I am in charge of this district.' The Norfolks were also enforcing a greatly resented military curfew in parts of loyalist north and west Belfast.[79]

Nixon and the 'B' Specials were especially enraged by their continued exclusion from parts of the city. In January 1922, at an inquest into the murder of a Protestant couple in Ardoyne, Andrew and Lizzie Anderson, Nixon blamed the Norfolks for these 'avoidable' deaths – if the special constables had been present in Ardoyne they would likely have saved the Andersons' lives.[80]

According to British military intelligence, several groups of loyalist paramilitaries were closely linked to, or tolerated by, the police. Some were conducting intelligence work, others were involved in reprisals, including murder, and some were doing both. The Orange Order set up an espionage network run by a former soldier called Alfred Lusted, who operated in Nixon's 'C' District. Lusted also co-operated with the military, passing on intelligence about suspected IRA activities.[81]

On 15 June 1921 Colonel Fred Crawford was nearly shot by one of these intelligence 'agents'. As part of this duties as commander of the Special Constabulary in the south of the city he had just completed a round of inspections of his 'B' men on his bicycle when he spotted a man watching him from the entrance of the city's Botanic Gardens. As he cycled over to question him, the man pulled out a revolver and pointed it in Crawford's direction. Crawford noticed that he was drunk and slowly pointed out his Special Constabulary armlet. Eventually his would-be-killer lowered his weapon and told Crawford that he was a former naval officer who was now working undercover for Major Carteret Leathes, the Special Constabulary's head of intelligence. Crawford eventually helped the dishevelled 'agent' home to his lodgings.[82]

Fred Crawford was also guilty of indulging in amateurish intelligence work. He had an adolescent love of intrigue and secret societies. In early 1921 Crawford claimed that he was approached by a senior officer in police headquarters in Belfast and asked if he could 'set up a such a force of two hundred ... armed with Webley revolvers, .38 calibre'.[83]

Crawford's ostensibly clandestine Ulster Brotherhood – also known as 'Crawford's Tigers' – were anything but discreet. Crawford called a public meeting for recruits. Two hundred volunteers were sworn in at the Ulster Unionist Party's headquarters and weapons handed out. Crawford submitted receipts for expenses, claiming he and his Tigers continued to report directly to police headquarters in Belfast, who approved of his initiative even if British officials in Dublin Castle did not.

Crawford and his men produced fantastical reports – including one that suggested the IRA had designed a secret code of signals which involved touching the lapels of their jackets in a certain way. A respected unionist and magistrate was also reported as sheltering IRA men and a cache of arms.[84] Crawford was in favour of summary reprisal shootings against suspected 'Sinn Féiners'. He acknowledged that such a policy was 'drastic' but necessary; these killings would be 'justifiable and right in the eyes of God and Man'.[85] But Crawford also admitted that he struggled to control his men. He feared that a general, indiscriminate massacre of Catholics in Belfast could lead to an equivalent response against Protestants in the South of Ireland.[86]

The hard-line unionist MP William Coote also believed that loyalist reprisals were a logical response to the British Army's hesitant approach towards the IRA in Ulster. The army and the RIC, Coote argued, should have adopted a policy of official reprisal against IRA sympathisers in the city as they did elsewhere in Ireland. (In the province of Munster, reprisals included the burning of suspected republicans' houses and the holding of 'drumhead' courts martial where IRA volunteers were shot dead within minutes of being captured.) Another unionist MP, Thompson Donald, recommended a 'three for one' policy – three Sinn Féin supporters should be shot if a policeman was harmed.[87] For the British Army, however, the difference between Belfast and Munster was that in the latter the IRA were responsible for the majority of violence.

In Belfast it was loyalists, including some members of the police, who were doing most of the killing.

The Ulster Imperial Guards was the largest and most capable paramilitary organisation in Belfast. The 'Imps' were born out of the Ulster Ex-Servicemen's Association. The hostile *Irish News* speculated that the organisation took its name from 'the Kaiser's famous corps of goose-steppers'.[88] The Ulster Ex-Servicemen's Association had, since its inception in 1920, excluded Catholics. It stood for 'Protestantism, loyalty, and no surrender'. Robert Lynn, the unionist Westminster MP and editor of the *Northern Whig*, served as vice-president of the association. He warned its members that they would need to mobilise to resist Sinn Féin or they risked being governed by that 'Spanish American Catholic Jew – de Valera'.[89]

The key organisers of the Imperial Guards were Robert Boyd, secretary of the veterans' group and Richard Tregenna, a sailor turned plumber, a leading trade unionist and a vice-president of the Ulster Unionist Labour Association (UULA). Unionist leader Edward Carson had established the UULA in 1918 as a means of countering nationalist and socialist influence in the trade union movement.

Any notion that the UULA could be easily controlled and organised by the unionist elite was quickly shattered after the end of the First World War. In September 1920 thousands of loyalist shipyard workers gathered near Belfast's docks to protest against the government's failure to mobilise or arm loyalists to take on the IRA in the city. One of the speakers, unionist councillor and trade unionist Alex McKay, addressed them as the 'gentlemen of the Imperial Guard'.

Loyalist labour had a complicated, often antipathetic, attitude to 'fur-coated' unionism. Two leading members of the UULA, John Gordon (a future UULA MP) and Joseph Cunningham (a future UULA senator), refused to join the UVF after its formation in 1913, seeing it as too elitist and conservative. (Gordon had openly 'mocked their [the

UVF's] drilling by parading up and down with a broomstick.)[90] Some jettisoned their previous associations with socialism in the 1920s – John Gordon became involved in the right-wing British Empire Union and was appointed as a junior minister at the Ministry of Labour in Belfast. Others, like Richard Tregenna, continued to cleave more closely to their radical labour principles – with a markedly anti-Catholic, Orange tinge.[91]

Threats to act unilaterally melted away after the formation and deployment of the Special Constabulary. The subsequent withdrawal of the 'B' Specials and loyalist suspicions over the truce prompted a resurgence in loyalist paramilitary murder. Before his departure Carter-Campbell reported that William Coote MP was one of the orchestrators of the militant response, warning that 'the [loyalist] tail is beginning to wag the dog.'[92]

Although the Imps had support from hardliners among the city's business and media elite, the working-class origins of many of the Imps' leaders alarmed Craig's government. The British Army's commander in Belfast, General Cameron, warned General Macready that the Imps' leader Robert Boyd was a 'regular kind of Bolshevist' who was trying to blackmail the British government at the point of a gun. The Imperial Guards, Cameron wrote, were 'out to dominate the Govt. and the country in accordance with their own wishes.'[93]

Ex-servicemen used the UULA to demand jobs and better living conditions. Rather than taking orders from the officer class, they now demanded a say in the running of the new Northern Ireland. The establishment of the Imps in the autumn of 1921 was supported by more extreme unionist MPs, men like William Coote, and those who relied on the UULA for their electoral support, including Harry Burn and William Twaddell, the respective Westminster and Northern Irish Parliament MPs for West Belfast, as well as William Grant and Tom McConnell, who represented North Belfast.

Tregenna viewed the Imps as a militant check against republicanism – and any deal or treaty that did not completely separate the six counties from the rest of Ireland. But he also loudly stated his demands for employment, better working conditions and housing in Belfast. His threat of force against the government was an explicit one. He advised his men in the Imps to 'join the B Force and to get confidence along three yards of steel. And if Sir James Craig and his £3000 a year Cabinet don't like it, turn them around that way ... and we will put men there who believe in it.'[94]

The Imperial Guards parade on Armistice Sunday, 13 November 1921, was the first time that Craig's government and the police appreciated the scale of paramilitary mobilisation that had taken place over the previous two months. Nine 'battalions' made up of several thousand veterans wearing their medals marched to religious services around the city. The North Belfast Imperial Guards parade was led by Major Gerald Ewart, who was also the 'B' Specials commandant for that part of the city.

Ewart was a scion of Belfast's business elite and a hardliner in his politics. He was also a friend of the late DI Swanzy – he had been at his side in Lisburn when Swanzy was gunned down in Lisburn.[95] However, the most dynamic and influential leader of the north Belfast Imps was Captain Samuel Waring, a former professional soldier who had been promoted through the ranks. Under Waring's command were three decorated former senior non-commissioned officers who had served in the Royal Irish Rifles and the Special Constabulary. Each commanded a company of Imps.[96]

The parade in west Belfast was led by William Coote, William Twaddell and Harry Taylor. Taylor was a shopkeeper on the Shankill Road, a local magistrate and 'B' Specials commander. Robert Lynn MP was sick and so could not attend but sent a message of support. Another leading supporter of the Imps who paraded in west Belfast was

Councillor William Bickerstaff, a Shankill meat-curer, publican and the 'B' Specials station commandant at Brown's Square Barracks.[97]

Thousands marched to Townsend Street Presbyterian Church off the Shankill Road where Rev. William McCorkey read from the Book of Nehemiah: 'And I said should such a man as I flee?'[98] Another minister told the Imps that the scars on their bodies from the First World War were testament to their defence of the liberties guaranteed by their Protestant faith. In east Belfast William Steele, a former Royal Inniskilling Fusiliers sergeant, led the Imps on the parade, while Captain Thomas Mayes, late of the Royal Irish Rifles, marched at the head of the south Belfast battalion. It was a formidable show of force.

Three days later the Imperial Guards met again; companies of Imps filed into Wellington Hall in the city centre where they were addressed by William Grant, former dock worker, trade unionist and North Belfast MP and a vice-president of the UULA. It was rumoured that Prime Minister Lloyd George planned to impose an all-Ireland parliament on Ulster. Grant mocked the British cabinet including Winston Churchill 'of Celtic Park fame (laughter)' for their perfidy. (In 1912 Churchill addressed a home rule meeting that was relocated – due to loyalist protests – to the nationalist sportsground of Celtic Park.) Ulster, Grant warned, would not accept the writ of the British cabinet in case of such a betrayal.[99]

According to the political scientist Paul Staniland, governments have four options when it comes to engaging with an emerging paramilitary group – suppression, containment, collusion, or incorporation.[100] The Imps' leaders had initially refused to meet with the Ministry of Home Affairs. William Lyons, Grand Master of the Orange Order in Ireland, stepped in to help. Lyons convened a meeting of the Orange and Black Loyalist Defence Association and asked both Colonel Goodwin, the commander of the Special Constabulary, and the leadership of the Imperial Guards, to attend.

At the meeting, Colonel Goodwin stressed his manpower shortages in the Special Constabulary and his wish to absorb the Imperial Guards. The Imps agreed to help. In late 1921 Prime Minister James Craig's government announced its intention to incorporate the Imps into the new 'C1' Class of the Special Constabulary. In March 1922 the Belfast Imps, among them the city's most dangerous loyalist paramilitaries, were recruited *en masse* as 'C1' special constables.[101]

A few days before the McMahon murders, hundreds of men who belonged to the York Street Battalion of the Imperial Guards – including the McMahon family's most deadly enemy – were 'marched into a hall in York Street'. There they were reviewed by Colonel Goodwin, and many were selected for service in the new 'C1' Constabulary. Captain Sam Waring, formerly a commander of the Imps in north Belfast, was appointed to serve as adjutant of the North Belfast Regiment of the 'C1' Constabulary.[102] Waring was not an exception. Other Imps took up similar leadership roles; John Kelly, one of Waring's deputies, was promoted to command a 'C1' Constabulary detachment in west Belfast.[103] Sam Waring reported that in north Belfast alone he was responsible for the recruitment of over 2,000 'C1' Class constables.[104] Murderers now wore the uniform of His Majesty's police.

According to Wickham, the 'C1's were formed with a single purpose in mind – 'the absorption of a dangerous independent Orange force which was organising itself for action'.[105] General Cameron's senior intelligence officer in Belfast reported that the Imps planned to 'get rid of Wickham and [Belfast City Police Commissioner] John Gelston and force their nominees on the Government'. The Imps also rejected the betrayal of Ulster loyalists in the 'lost counties' of Cavan, Donegal and Monaghan. Robert Boyd had made 'a wild speech' in which he claimed that, after the incorporation of the Imps into the 'C1' Specials, they would then 'march [across the border] to Monaghan'. General Cameron predicted that the Imps would eventually 'run up against the Army and I hope get a severe lesson'.[106]

Long-standing tensions between the Special Constabulary and the British Army escalated quickly during this period. When a speeding 'B' Specials vehicle ran into a military patrol in Cromac Square in the city centre, a group of soldiers gathered around the special constables to take revenge. An officer intervened and eventually managed to move the constables out of the area.[107] In March 1922 General Macready reported to Secretary of State for War Laming Worthington-Evans that loyalists, not republicans, were now the main challenge for the British Army in Northern Ireland – 'the balance for making trouble is due to the so-called Protestants'.[108]

The IRA was watching. Roger McCorley noted the collapse in relations between the Special Constabulary and the soldiers. On one occasion, when he and his men were preparing an attack on a Special Constabulary lorry carrying supplies, a British Army sergeant in command of the military escort spotted McCorley. He then ordered his men to move on 'and in passing he said to us, "We are moving off now and you can do what you like with them."'

McCorley recalled that, 'This new attitude of the British troops in Belfast seemed to spread and in the later fighting which took place there, they kept as much as possible out of our way when we were attacking the Special Constabulary.' In March 1922 when loyalists, including 'B' Specials, attacked the Catholic Falls Road area, IRA volunteers reported that neither they (the IRA) nor the soldiers fired on each other but worked together to push back the loyalists. (There is no account of soldiers fighting alongside IRA volunteers on the British side.)[109]

A special constable told Colonel Crawford that he and other loyalists were confident that they would soon deal with the young soldiers: 'We will eat them up. Most of us have been in the late war and the military are only schoolboys and would be nowhere with us.'[110]

Many of the Norfolks may have missed the First World War, but they were professionals. Rather than the rushed sequence of training and mobilisation for the war in 1914, the young soldiers had been exposed to longer periods of exercises and marksmanship expected of a professional army. Instead of yielding when confronted by determined and armed loyalist veterans, the Norfolks held fast.

Soldiers, especially the Norfolk Regiment, saved lives. That was the clear memory of James Kelly growing up in Catholic west Belfast during the 'pogrom':

> One of the odd, almost folk, heroes of the time was a dashing young Englishman, a lieutenant of the Norfolk Regiment ... [who] sported a small, clipped moustache and had a public schools' accent with a dry laugh which earned for him the nickname 'Ha-ha'. Women, terrified by some inexplicable shooting incident, used to cry out with relief 'Oh thank God, here comes Ha Ha.'[111]

The same officer – possibly the ever-conspicuous Lieutenant Robert Scott – was also singled out by republicans. (Scott was out to dominate his 'patch' of west Belfast. He had as little time for the IRA as he had for loyalist paramilitaries.) Graffiti that read 'Haw Haw Beware!' appeared on a gable wall on Albert Street, near the Falls Road. The following night the IRA received a daubed response below the original message: 'Haw, Haw doesn't care!'

Bob Scott patrolled the dark, smoke-filled alleys of Belfast wearing an eye-patch and carrying 'little Willie', the .303 Lee-Enfield rifle he had modified by shortening the barrel for urban combat. (Its effectiveness was doubted by other Norfolk officers, but it made a terrific noise when fired.) Loyalists, the part-time '"B" men' of the USC and republicans all came to loathe and fear him.[112]

John McCoy, a senior IRA officer in Ulster, recalled that Lieutenant Scott moved through the streets of Belfast with an Irish wolfhound by his side and a revolver in his hand. Scott interrogated McCoy on one occasion in 1920 and later visited him in the military hospital in Belfast in the middle of the night after McCoy was shot by police near the border: 'He was standing over me at the side of the bed when his dog sniffing at my face on the pillow wakened me. When I looked up I saw the officer and his dog. The officer's one good eye was boring into mine … I had been roused so suddenly and looking into this one piercing eye, I got a scare.'[113]

Scott was ruthlessly impartial. When a Catholic shopkeeper broke curfew, opening her door and stepping out on her doorstep, Scott pointed a revolver and threatened to blow her head off. That was typical of his personality. (Years later when commanding 2nd Battalion, Royal Norfolks on the Indian-Burmese frontier during the Second World War, Scott commended a soldier for killing two Japanese prisoners – he had saved Scott the trouble of 'cutting their throats'.)[114]

On 7 January 1922, on the day the Anglo-Irish Treaty was ratified by the Irish parliament, Dáil Éireann, Eoin O'Duffy – who had voted in favour – wrote a letter to the Belfast IRA instructing its commander that 'a state of war existed' [against James Craig's government] and 'to regard the truce as non-existent'.[115] O'Duffy was appointed as chief of staff of the new Irish National Army in February 1922. Joe McKelvey, the newly appointed commander of the IRA in Belfast, was determined to further escalate operations in the North. So too was Seamus Woods. Both men would later lead different factions of the IRA in Belfast – Woods, McCorley and many of Belfast's most active IRA volunteers joined the National Army; McKelvey took the side of the anti-treaty IRA and was executed by the Free State government during the Civil War.[116]

British military intelligence about the IRA in Belfast rapidly improved in the final months of 1921 and the beginning of 1922. The Norfolks' intelligence officer Captain Harry Papworth compiled long lists of IRA volunteers and their addresses 'from a most reliable source'. (Much of this information was accurate.)[117] Arrests of IRA volunteers fed loyalist paranoia, bringing home to the city's loyalist population what Lady Lilian Spender – Wilfred's wife – described in her diary as 'the horror that crawls in our midst'.[118] William Coote MP, fearing a plot to unite Northern Ireland with the south, warned Prime Minister James Craig not to 'soil his garments' by negotiating with Sinn Féin. Bombings became more frequent and even more indiscriminate – explosives such as Mills bombs were thrown into crowded streets where families were gathered.[119]

The Norfolks struggled to respond to the surge in killings. The return of the 'B' Specials brought the British Army directly into conflict with Belfast's police. Initially soldiers hesitated when responding to reprisals carried out by the Special Constabulary and by the Imperial Guards. IRA officer Seán Montgomery remonstrated with a sergeant – the soldier apparently did not know he was talking to an officer of the IRA – for not stopping the shooting of two barmen as they left work at Patrick Madden's pub off the Crumlin Road on the night of 9 January. According to Montgomery the soldier replied that 'it was not his duty' to intervene to stop police crime. (Montgomery suspected that he was afraid.)[120]

Between November 1921 and April 1922 at least six members of the Imperial Guards were killed during fighting in Belfast.[121] A Norfolk soldier who made a name for himself during street battles against the Imps in Belfast was Lance Corporal Reggie Turner. The son of bootmakers in Norwich, Turner grew up within sight of the flint and limestone spire of the city's Norman cathedral. In October 1920, at the age of eighteen, Turner joined his county regiment.

By late 1921 Turner was in the thick of combat in Belfast, leading a section of eight men, part of 'C' Company, 1 Norfolks. On 2 January Turner was ordered with his section to Sailortown in the north of the city. Loyalist snipers were at work throughout the afternoon, firing from Garmoyle Street. Turner moved with his section towards the fire but was unable to locate the gunmen.

Turner then sent his men back to cover and 'went sniping on my own'. He located Imp sniper Alex Turtle, from Tiger's Bay in the north of the city, and shot him dead. Turner gave his account of what happened at the inquest into Turtle's death:

> I very nearly got shot by four men who repeatedly fired at me. The deceased fired at me but missed and I returned the fire and hit him. This was the only casualty I know of in that locality. I fired from Garmoyle St. and hit the man at the corner of North Ann St. He had a rifle and was about 15 yards away from me. After firing I saw the man fall to the ground, I saw his comrade pick his rifle up, he aimed at me with the intention of firing, and I ran straight across the road into cover behind the corner of Trafalgar Street.

Turtle was shot in the neck. He bled to death within minutes. The distance of the exchanges of shots – only 15 yards – gives an insight into the conditions of urban combat in Belfast at the time.[122]

The Imps' response came a few hours later. At 7 p.m. eighteen-year-old Private Ernest Barnes, also of 'C' Company, 1 Norfolks, was standing sentry with a group of soldiers at the corner of North Queen Street and Sussex Street in north Belfast. Local residents warned the soldiers to take care since a sniper was nearby. The Norfolks went looking for the gunman. As they entered Sussex Street, Barnes and the other soldiers could hear the sound of men calling to each other in the darkness. The streetlights of North Queen Street meant that the Holy Boys were visible from Sussex Street, which was in darkness, but they in turn could not see the gunmen who were now hunting them.

Later intelligence indicated that Private Barnes was now the target of the Imps' most feared sniper, Jordy Harper, a veteran of the First World War. Harper's first shot missed; Barnes' corporal raised his rifle and replied. Jordy Harper then coolly advanced through the fog towards the soldiers, firing twice before disappearing down nearby Dale Street – one of these rounds fatally wounded Barnes in the chest.[123]

The Norfolks were quick to publicly express their anger over Barnes' death. Their commanding officer, Lieutenant Colonel Francis Day, announced that the regimental band would no longer play at public functions in the city.[124] Unionist leaders in north Belfast recognised the potential public relations damage posed by the killing of Barnes. The North East Belfast Unionist club on York Street – key supporters of the Imps – organised a collection for Private Barnes' mother who lived in the village of Fakenham in Norfolk.

UULA Councillor David Jones wrote a letter to Mrs Barnes telling her that the loyalists of Belfast knew that her son 'was doing his duty as a British soldier and we are extremely sorry that his bright and promising career has been so untimely ended'.[125] Mrs Barnes replied to Jones, asking him to 'kindly convey our thanks to the loyalists of York Street for [their] sympathy'.[126] She appeared to be unaware that her son's 'untimely' death was at the hands of a well-known north Belfast loyalist.

James Craig's government fully anticipated an IRA 'invasion' of Northern Ireland in early 1922. Rumours of IRA imminent plots and movements circuited through the streets of Belfast. The killing of four 'A' special constables on 11 February – on a train briefly transiting through provisional government territory in County Monaghan on their way to Enniskillen from Belfast – accelerated the cycle of loyalist reprisals in Belfast.[127] That night notices went up around Belfast announcing a 'monster meeting' of the Ulster Imperial Guards – 'Come and protect yourselves before you are taken from your homes. The rebels are violating your border.'[128]

Violence became even more intense – an Italian ice-cream seller was shot on York Street. Catholic ex-soldiers who had been seriously wounded in the war were moved from military hospitals after they received a threatening note which began – 'You and your sneaking dogs of Papish cunts must go.'[129]

In early February the British Army handed over 20,000 UVF weapons to the Northern Irish government. There could not have been a worse time to do so. (Many were old, if not unusable, but the risk of some of these weapons being used for murder was obvious.) Newly recruited members of the 'C1' Class of the Special Constabulary were tasked with guarding the weapons at Tamar Street – one of these men quickly siphoned arms to his brother, Robert Craig, a leader of the Ulster Protestant Association (UPA) gang responsible for many loyalist murders in east Belfast.[130] During a 48-hour period between 13 and 15 February, thirty-one people were killed.

The Norfolks were concerned that the police, notably John Nixon, were carrying out murders based on military intelligence. On 13 February Captain Papworth witnessed IRA snipers firing from several doorways on Unity Street in north Belfast. He wrote down the numbers of the houses and passed them directly to DI Nixon.[131] Two nights later loyalists threw bombs into the same houses that Papworth had identified to the police. A resident told the Norfolks' intelligence officer that special constables had carried out the attacks during curfew hours.[132]

The Norfolks also came under attack from special constables in Nixon's district. On 7 February twelve Norfolk soldiers were pinned down by fire directed at them by the police. Whenever a soldier tried to cross the street they were fired on by a nearby 'B' Specials post.[133] Loyalists blamed the Norfolks for the death of Imperial Guard Ben Lundy six days later. The next day a Norfolk soldier, Private Arthur Dickinson, was shot in the knee near the Old Lodge Road.[134] Norfolks' intelligence indicated that 'John Hermon 50 Old Lodge Road and his son have a revolver and an automatic and ammo for both weapons. They are both B Specials and both bad.'[135] Members of the Special Constabulary also claimed that two days after the killing of Lundy, the Norfolks shot

Hector Stewart, a 'B' special who was fatally wounded by a bullet wound to the neck near Hanover Street in the west of the city. Some special constables threatened to kidnap soldiers in revenge.[136]

On the morning of 14 February a popular and well-known loyalist, William Waring, was shot dead. Waring was the custodian of Belfast's largest Orange Hall on Clifton Street. He was also the uncle of Imps commander Captain Sam Waring. He was killed by a sniper from the Catholic Stanhope Street area as he returned to the hall with a cup of milk for two cats he kept there. His murder predictably outraged the Imps and precipitated a new bout of reprisals.[137] Captain Papworth wrote a report on Waring's funeral and its aftermath:

> I heard remarks passed by some of the followers that they would have a 'Roman' before they went to bed and at 2000 hrs Mr [Edward] Ryan RC was shot by an Orange gunman, the bullet lodging in his stomach. The troops who were in the vicinity came on the scene and were on the verge of firing on a man who they saw running up the Shankill Rd, when the police from Brown's Square got between them and their object and he made good his escape.[138]

Loyalists blamed Lieutenant Scott: '[They] have been heard saying nasty things about the officer with the patch over his eye, what they will do to him, if they get him on his own.'[139]

The month of March opened with a new round of burnings of homes in west and north Belfast. Catholics were again disproportionately affected. In west Belfast a sick, elderly woman was saved by her daughter who rushed her into the street in a wheelchair. Both women were then attacked by a mob who doused the chair-bound woman in paraffin. Before a match could be struck a neighbour intervened, beating back the woman's assailants until she was eventually removed to safety. The mob 'paraffined' three pigs instead.[140]

In the north of the city, a woman called Katherine Neeson was shot and mortally wounded while standing at her doorstep. A few days previously during a wave of attacks against Catholics in the York Road and North Queen Street areas, loyalists had thrown a bomb into the Neeson home on Little George's Street where Katherine lived with her husband Bernard, an expelled worker, and their three children. Witnesses to the murder saw a group of approximately forty men walking down Great George's Street. One of the men calmly walked towards Katherine and then shot her from a few yards away. Her killer boarded a nearby tram and made his escape. A crowd of men remained on the street. They prevented an ambulance crew from reaching Katherine, who lay bleeding on the hall floor for an hour and a half. She was nearly eight months pregnant with her fourth child. The ambulance crew eventually carried her out through the back yard of the house. Both Katherine and her unborn child were pronounced dead at the Mater Hospital soon afterwards.[141]

On the night of 7 March a group of Norfolk' soldiers, fighting from house to house along Wall Street near the Shankill Road, shot four young Protestant men. One of the men, Joseph Thompson, died of his injuries. That night a bomb was thrown by loyalists at a group of Norfolks, wounding four soldiers.[142] The Norfolks refused to back down. The next night a soldier shot dead Herbert Hassard in the north of the city.

Hassard was a decorated former Royal Irish Rifles soldier. He was also a member of the 'A' Class of the Special Constabulary and an Imperial Guard. He had two large tattoos on either arm, one of King William of Orange, the other of a Union Jack. The Norfolks regarded Hassard as 'one of the best Orange snipers in the York St. area and has been responsible for many of the casualties in it'. Some Catholic residents of the area claimed that Hassard was killed while sniping at children on Isabelle Street. Remarkably, despite evidence from military witnesses at the inquest that a soldier killed Hassard in the execution of his duty, a judge ruled that it was not clear who had fired the fatal shot, and awarded £100 to his father as compensation.

Hassard's death sent a shock of fury through the Imps. Captain Papworth reported that, 'The Orange mob in York St. say they will have 6 Norfolk soldiers for Hassard before Saturday.'[143] Three days later a gunman shot dead Lieutenant Edward Bruce, an officer of the Seaforth Highlanders. Dressed in civilian clothes, Bruce was walking with friends near the city centre when he was shot in his left eye, chest and legs.

RIC Sergeant John Murphy suggested that Bruce may have been targeted because he arrested two special constables in civilian clothes around the same time as Hassard's death. One of the men had an unlicensed revolver but city police headquarters directed that the charges be dropped. Murphy witnessed the special constable in Springfield Road Barracks behaving 'very vindictively' toward the Seaforth Highlanders officer. The failure to confirm whether Bruce was murdered by the Special Constabulary – as alleged by Catholic witnesses – or the IRA added to the soldiers' sense of isolation and vulnerability.[144]

Herbert Hassard's funeral was preceded by men from 1st Battalion (York Street) of the North Belfast Regiment of the Imperial Guards, led by their commander, a baker and former soldier called Charles McKinnon, his second-in-command Gibson Sewell and Sergeant Major Archie Boal. As the funeral party moved north along York Street, towards Carnmoney graveyard outside the city, groups of armed Imps entered Catholic houses and ordered the inhabitants to pull the blinds or shut their curtains as a mark of respect.[145]

At a place called Whitehouse on the outskirts of the city, the Imps siphoned petrol from a bread van and attempted to burn down a nationalist hall. (The local RIC intervened and helped to put out the fire.) A shop was also looted during the funeral procession. Then an Imp recognised a Catholic shop assistant called Hugh McAnaney and shot him. Lying wounded, his head cradled by his wife Mary, Hugh McAnaney asked for an ambulance. A mob surrounded the couple – a Protestant woman intervened and lay on top of Hugh McAnaney in an attempt to protect him. She was dragged away. A man was then heard to say, 'That will be alright,' after which he shot McAnaney in the head, killing him instantly. A Presbyterian minister who was with the funeral procession, Reverend Samuel Cochrane, told police he did not see anything.[146]

Episodic exchanges of fire between the Norfolks and members of the Special Constabulary continued throughout March and early April.[147] Battalions from other regiments sent to reinforce the Norfolks also quickly found themselves confronting hostile police as well as the IRA and loyalist paramilitaries. Private James Brown of 'A' Company, 1st Battalion, The Essex Regiment, was nearly kicked to death after he tried to disarm a 'B' Special who was firing indiscriminately into a Catholic street near York Street. The constable blew a whistle and a group of loyalists 'set on the soldier'. The intervention of a passing 'A' Class Special Constabulary patrol saved Brown from being lynched.[148]

On 23 March Lieutenant Fred Parkinson of 4th Battalion, Worcestershire Regiment, shot dead Special Constable Charles Vokes during riots near the city centre. Parkinson, in charge of a group of soldiers on the junction of North Street and Royal Avenue, suspected that Vokes was carrying a weapon. After initially refusing to co-operate, Vokes eventually put his hands up and allowed the soldiers to search him. They found a revolver in his coat. Hearing Vokes' protests, a loyalist crowd soon surrounded Parkinson and his men. Vokes made a run for it; Parkinson shot him dead. The Worcesters then ran back towards Belfast City Hall to escape the mob.[149]

Instead of acknowledging the scale of the problem between parts of the Special Constabulary and the British Army, Sir Richard Dawson Bates and the Northern Irish government continued to single out the Norfolks as a uniquely anti-loyalist regiment. Dawson Bates stated that General Sir Henry Wilson, Chief of the Imperial General Staff until

GHOSTS OF A FAMILY

February 1922, had issued orders temporarily replacing 1 Norfolks as the lead battalion in police districts 'C' and 'D', west and north Belfast. This is untrue.

After the bomb attack on Wall Street on 8 March soldiers from 1st Battalion, the Essex Regiment temporarily reinforced and relieved Norfolk soldiers at a few guard posts or 'pickets' in west Belfast. The Norfolks had been stretched by the violence of the preceding days. The nationalist *Freeman's Journal* wrongly interpreted this as a capitulation to the loyalist mob who had nicknamed the regiment 'the Pope's Bodyguard'.[150] The Norfolks' records show that there was never any withdrawal from large parts of the city – they remained in command of both police districts (C and D) throughout this period.

General Macready had considered removing the Norfolks from Belfast due to pernicious gossip about their Catholic sympathies. On 8 March Colonel Spender urged James Craig to ask the British Army to keep the Norfolks out of Protestant areas – 'the Protestant population and the police are both very hostile to the Norfolk Regiment'.[151] Macready was enraged. He vented in a letter to Field Marshal Henry Wilson on 14 March, blaming the Northern Irish government for leading the slander against the regiment:

> the Norfolks will probably be withdrawn, as the Orangemen have got up a pogrom against them simply because they happen to be called Norfolks, and as a matter of fact, have no more Roman Catholics than any other English regiment. But it will not be a bad thing if they take them away, although my own inclination is to leave them there and express myself freely to Dawson Bates and those of his kidney who started this here.[152]

Orders were given for 1st Battalion, Seaforth Highlanders to become the principal 'garrison' battalion, replacing the Norfolks in Victoria

Barracks in the centre of the city. The wives and children of the Norfolks returned to England in preparation for the battalion leaving Belfast and were replaced by the families of the Seaforths.

Then Macready changed this mind. The Holy Boys remained in Belfast for another six months and the Seaforths were instead accommodated in the Belfast War Hospital – a sprawling former lunatic asylum near the Falls Road.[153] The need for more troops to respond to the surge in violence was obvious.

Macready's change of heart may also have been influenced by King George V's continued close interest and bond with the Norfolks. (A whole company of the Holy Boys – the Sandringhams – had joined the regiment from the King's beloved Norfolk estate during the First World War and was nearly wiped out at Gallipoli.) Sending the Norfolks back to Britain prematurely could have been interpreted as an unacceptable loss of face to the British Army, and especially to the King's favoured regiment.

In March 1922 Macready ordered that patrols in Belfast should always be commanded by an officer. He was concerned that, since loyalists had begun systematically targeting British troops, small groups of soldiers led by a sergeant or a corporal might be tempted to commit a reprisal in Protestant areas.[154]

Lieutenant Colonel Francis Day never wavered during this period of intense political pressure. His subordinate in 1 Norfolks, Lieutenant Lionel Gundry-White, kept a diary in which he poured out invective in bad French about most people – their appearances and failings of character. Yet, besides Colonel Day's eyes being too close together, Gundry-White found little wanting in his commanding officer, extolling his politeness and cool intelligence.[155]

Slander against the Holy Boys had no effect on their operations in February and March of 1922. They continued to prevent police atrocities. For example, on 11 March a Norfolk patrol disarmed a regular RIC constable and a 'B' Special whom the soldiers believed were firing

GHOSTS OF A FAMILY

indiscriminately at Catholics. Meanwhile, the soldiers also continued to target the IRA, making a steady flow of arrests and weapons seizures.[156]

Five days before the McMahon murders, on 19 March 1922, the new commander of the British Army's 15th Infantry Brigade, Colonel Commandant Herbert Potter, wrote to his mother in England. He told her of the crimes he had seen in Belfast since his arrival the previous month. An incident that stood out was that of 13 February when a loyalist had thrown a bomb into the midst of a group of children playing with a skipping rope on Weaver Street, just off the York Road.[157]

Four girls and two women died in the Weaver Street attack – most of the victims died slowly and in great pain as shrapnel worked its way into their bodies. Many more were seriously injured and disfigured, including seventeen children. (A journalist described seeing one of the injured in the hospital, ten-year-old Barney Kennedy, standing sobbing beside the shredded body of his older sister Kathleen while he waited for doctors to treat his mangled arm.)[158]

Herbert Potter had been happy to take up command in a 'loyal' city, having served previously in the South of Ireland where 'nearly everyone is against us'. Now he believed 'there is nothing to choose between the two sets of murdering Christians'. Loyalists in the police hoped that the arrival of Field Marshal Henry Wilson to advise Craig would give the Special Constabulary a freer hand in the city. Potter was unimpressed both by the police – 'the fact of the matter is that nobody in the North of Ireland is fit to be a Policeman' – and by Wilson, whom he found to be distracted and prone to long, rambling monologues.[159]

In June 1922 the British government finally gave Prime Minister James Craig an ultimatum about the conduct of the Special Constabulary. On 3 June a concealed British Army sniper near the Newtownards Road in east Belfast shot dead two loyalists, Samuel Millar and Daniel Bruce. Military headquarters claimed the men were armed and had been shooting at residents in the Catholic Seaforde Street area. Immediately after the killings, a group of 'B' Specials in a Lancia car began to shoot up houses on Seaforde Street. A crowd of loyalists then surrounded some soldiers from 1st Battalion, Somerset Light Infantry, shooting two of them, Sergeant Mitchell and Private Burrows (both survived their wounds).[160] A Somersets officer who tried to intervene was thrown to the ground. General Cameron reported that the officer 'managed to regain his feet and wound one of his assailants, or he might have been murdered'.[161]

Instead of assisting his soldiers Cameron complained that the 'B' Specials drove past the wounded men and moved further down the street. A report by DI Richard Heggart that largely exonerated the Special Constabulary was dismissed by the military as a deliberate and inexcusable cover-up. (The politically astute Inspector General of the new RUC, Lieutenant Colonel Charles Wickham, moved quickly to distance himself from the initial investigation, rebuking Heggart after the rubbishing of his report in London.)[162]

DI Richard Heggart had risen through the ranks. He had a wiry build, a shock of dark hair, and deep-set eyes. His thin lips, shrouded by a large moustache, gave him an air of inscrutability. He had made his reputation during the Easter Rising when he had coolly refused to surrender the RIC barracks in Enniscorthy, County Wexford, after the town was briefly seized by armed volunteers during the Easter Rising. (Heggart and his men opened fire on the rebels; the 'siege' was lifted by the British Army after three days.) Heggart was appointed to command 'C' District in west Belfast in 1919, which he handed over to Nixon the following year.[163]

The British Army cared little for Heggart's Easter Rebellion fame. A British military intelligence report concluded that 'Crimes Special Branch' at police headquarters was not fit for purpose. It was noted that both Heggart and a senior RIC intelligence officer in Belfast, DI Ewing Gilfillan, had no military intelligence experience. As far as military intelligence officers were concerned, both Heggart and Gilfillan were stonewalling them.[164] Military headquarters in Belfast reported that it was 'more and more difficult to effect the exchange of even the most unimportant items of information'.

General Macready complained to Lloyd George's cabinet that the attack on the Somersets reflected the rot that had taken hold in the police: 'In Belfast, if anyone shoots an Orangeman they would be shot in return, no matter whether the Orangeman was committing a crime or not. The police in Belfast will not take action against Orangemen.'[165]

Macready's fears were well-founded. Loyalist Joseph Arthurs was arrested on military evidence for his part in the violence that led to the attack on the soldiers. He was acquitted by a jury the following month. Arthurs was eventually interned by the Northern Irish government, after he was suspected of murdering a forty-four-year-old woman, Mary Sherlock, in east Belfast in October 1922.[166] DI Reginald Spears described Arthurs as 'a criminal maniac ... one of the most fanatical gunmen in the city'.[167]

Secretary of State for the Colonies Winston Churchill told James Craig the police had 'failed signally in their duty' to assist the military. Churchill warned that police obstruction or attacks on the army could undermine future military assistance to Northern Ireland and have a bad effect on 'the temper of the troops themselves'. Sensing Churchill's anger, an uncharacteristically contrite Craig replied that there had been persistent problems with the calibre of officers who were in command of the Special Constabulary, a problem which he hoped London would assist in solving in the future.[168]

Churchill's rebuke of Craig over the Specials' behaviour towards the Somersets was the only time during the Belfast 'pogrom' that the British government, albeit implicitly, threatened to reduce military assistance if police indiscipline was not addressed by Craig. The threat had an immediate effect. But Churchill's outrage came too late, not least for the many victims of the Special Constabulary over the preceding two years.

Estimates of fatalities during the 1920–22 'pogrom' range from approximately 410 to just over 500 killed and 1,200 to 2,000 people wounded. Most of those killed or evicted from their homes were Catholics. Close to 8,000 people were forced out of their homes and 650 homes or businesses were burned. The majority of the killings occurred during the first six months of 1922. Most of the dead – perhaps as high as 80 per cent – were civilians who were not members of the police, military or any paramilitary organisation.

Protestants too were victims of widespread burning and murder (described by General Macready as 'a Sinn Féin pogrom' to counter that by 'Orange' extremists). The majority of Protestants killed – just under 200 people or 30 per cent of the total dead – were also civilians. Republicans burned many of Belfast's Protestant-owned businesses due to the perceived or real political affiliation of their owners and employees.[169] Something had broken in Belfast.

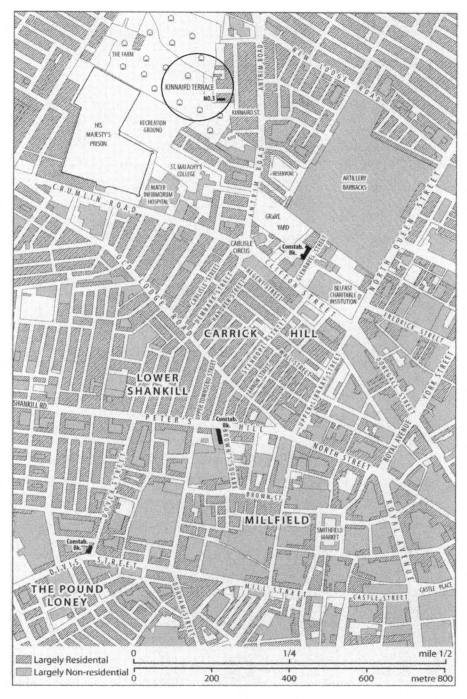

Street map including Kinnaird Terrace and the Antrim Road in North Belfast and Brown's Square and the Shankill Road in West Belfast. (Courtesy of Dr Tim Wilson)

Images of Owen McMahon and his sons John and Bernard as they appeared in newspapers at the time of their death. (*Sunday Pictorial*, 26 March 1922)

3 Kinnaird Terrace, the McMahons' home, a few hours after the murders. (*London Illustrated News*, 1 April 1922)

A group of Belfast IRA volunteers, c. 1921.
(Courtesy of the National Museum of Ireland)

A group of Auxiliaries c. 1920. (Courtesy of the National Museum of Ireland)

Members of the Ulster Special Constabulary with suspected IRA prisoners. (*Belfast Weekly Telegraph*, 10 June 1922)

Norfolk Regiment soldiers with civilians in the Marrowbone area early 1920s. (By kind permission of the Trustees of the Royal Norfolk Regiment Museum Collection)

DI William Lynn, police commander of 'D' District (north Belfast) in the early 1920s. (Courtesy of his son, private collection)

A pamphlet supporting John Nixon around the time of his dismissal from the RUC in 1924. (Courtesy of the Deputy Keeper of the Records, Public Record Office of Northern Ireland)

'An alarmed crowd running the gauntlet of the gunmen along York Street'.
(*London Illustrated News*, 10 September 1921)

York Road veterans, 24 November 1921, the day of the attack on Patrick McMahon.
(Courtesy of the National Museums of Northern Ireland)

IRA intelligence photograph of David Duncan, marked X, centre. The man marked X on the front right is James Turkington, a unionist city councillor who was described by the IRA as 'Ulster Labour, Vice President'. (Courtesy of UCD Archives)

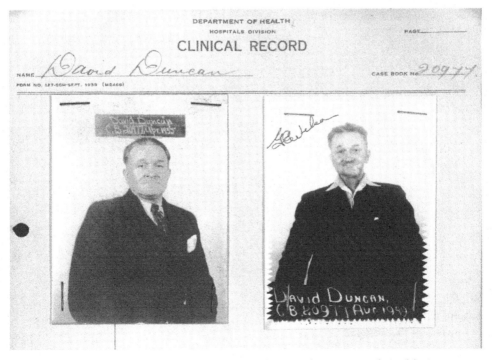

RG 10 270 David Duncan. Clinical Case File. Queen Street Mental Health Centre. (Courtesy of the Archives of Ontario)

An Orange parade in Toronto, 1931. (Courtesy of Toronto City Archives)

'Buck' Alec Robinson and UVF leader Gusty Spence photographed in the 1980s. (Courtesy of the Bobbie Hanvey Photographic Archives, MS.2001.039, John J. Burns Library, Boston College)

PART 2

CHAPTER THREE

Aftermath

SURVIVING PHOTOGRAPHS OF OWEN MCMAHON show a well-dressed, dark-haired man with a prominent jawline and a generous moustache. His friend T.J. Campbell described him as 'a decent, quiet, kindly soul'. Owen and his wife Eliza (née Downey) were the children of farmers. Both grew up near the village of Rathfriland, in sight of the Mourne Mountains in County Down. The McMahons' farm was bigger than most, but the family were by no means wealthy.[1]

Born in 1864, Owen was one of seven siblings (six boys and a girl) who survived to adulthood. All of the brothers moved to Belfast, where they formed a formidable business partnership, each buying, leasing and managing a string of pubs in the city. They also owned several grocery shops and spirit groceries across the city. Owen's acquirement of the Great Eastern Bar on the Newtownards Road in 1900 was a statement of confidence and ambition. Formerly owned by the Protestant Pritchard family, the Great Eastern was a thriving pub in the heart of loyalist Belfast. In 1905 Owen transferred ownership of the Great Eastern to his brother Bernard. Two years later he purchased the Capstan at 100 Ann Street in the city centre from a Protestant publican called Mary Swanton.[2]

The Capstan would become Owen McMahon's business headquarters until his death. Owen and his brothers Patrick and Daniel ran several bars and spirit groceries in nearby North Street. In 1912 Patrick sold a pub on the Albertbridge Road in the east of the city to Alexander McBride (a republican later murdered by police in 1921), and consolidated his business interests in the north and centre of the city, buying out his brothers' interests in the North Street pubs.

Patrick was more flamboyant and erratic than his brothers. He was known in Belfast and in Dublin as a high-stakes gambler. By the early 1920s, he was in financial trouble; he was forced to hand over one of his Belfast properties to clear a debt with a building society. He also owed money to the Ulster Bank and several businessmen who had invested in his pubs.[3]

Despite his financial troubles, at the time of the murders of his brother and nephews, Patrick ran the popular Century Bar and the Old North Street House on North Street. He had also acquired a pub in the docks area of north Belfast, as well as several pubs in the city centre, including one on Belfast's main shopping street, Royal Avenue.[4]

Another brother, Tom, ran a bar, the International, at nearby 1–3 York Street, a billiard hall on the same street, as well as pubs on Cromac Street and Grosvenor Road. Tom was close to his brother John, who owned a pub on Henry Street – also in the city centre – and another on the Crumlin Road, one of Belfast's western arteries. Daniel McMahon extended his business interests into south Belfast. In 1917 he bought the Balmoral at 687 Lisburn Road from a Protestant publican called Samuel Cahoon.[5] Like the Great Eastern, the Balmoral was an ocean liner among Belfast's flotilla of pubs. Perhaps the most surprising McMahon purchase was in September 1910 when Bernard McMahon took over two pubs in the North Street area formerly owned by William Bickerstaff – later the commander of the 'B' Specials at Brown's Square Barracks under DI Nixon.[6]

Owen McMahon had an array of other business interests, including investments in livestock.[7] Before moving to 3 Kinnaird Terrace in the north of the city, Owen and his family spent some years living and working in the Great Eastern Bar. Owen's 'quietness' about his Irish nationalism was not only wise for his safety and that of his family; it was also necessary if his business was to thrive in such an area. His directorship of Glentoran Football Club was an astute means of endearing himself to the east Belfast community.[8] So too were the McMahon brothers' subscriptions to the Ulster Prisoner of War Fund in 1918 – Owen, Bernard, Patrick, John and Daniel all publicly advertised their donations. (Only Tom is missing as a contributor.)[9] Owen was also an enthusiastic supporter of cycling and boxing and a horse-racing enthusiast – sports that transcended Belfast's social and sectarian divisions.[10]

By 1920 – with the exception of the indebted Patrick – the McMahon business empire was thriving. The brothers were used to sporadic sectarian trouble in the city. But the next two years saw a rampage of violence against publicans and spirit grocers. Long-standing criminals cloaked their violence in political colours. Most pubs in Belfast were owned by Catholics. The breakdown in law and order meant that publicans were easy targets for those looking to settle a sectarian score, steal alcohol or money, or do all three at the same time.[11] By March 1921, of the approximately 400 licence holders in Belfast, half had been put out of business due to robberies, intimidation or arson.[12]

The McMahons were battered by robberies and assaults during this period. Bernard McMahon submitted three claims for extensive damage to his premises and stock.[13] Patrick was raided on three occasions.[14] On 22 December 1920 two men, Robert Browne and Sam O'Neill, robbed the Century Bar on North Street. After arriving in a large group at the bar, ordering a drink and refusing to pay, Browne and O'Neill jumped over the counter. Browne threw a bottle of whiskey at the barman, Patrick Brierty, while O'Neill stole nearly £20 from near the register.

As the group of men made their escape, Brierty lunged at O'Neill, tackling him to the ground and holding him there until the police arrived. Browne ran away down North Street with Patrick McMahon's bar manager in pursuit; an off-duty police constable also gave chase and tackled Browne to the ground. Browne appealed to bystanders, shouting that he was from the Shankill Road. No help came; Browne and O'Neill were both arrested.[15]

Patrick McMahon was awarded £85 – worth just under £3,500 a century later – in claims for damages to his property in October 1921. During the same month he was assaulted by Alexander O'Donnell and Hugh Lavery, who followed him from his bar, the Imperial, and tried to rob him of his watch. (The police quickly chased after and arrested both men. Lavery was convicted of attempted robbery and given a four-month prison sentence; O'Donnell was sentenced to a year in prison for another robbery.)[16]

On 28 November 1921 it was the turn of Daniel McMahon. At his pub on the Lisburn Road, four gunmen forced the seventeen-year-old barman, James Devany, to empty the till. On the way out, one of the men turned and shot the boy in the chest (he survived his injuries).[17] (Another public house owned by Daniel McMahon, on Castlereagh Street in the east of the city, had been burned during the August riots of 1920.)[18]

Owen, not least due to his sporting patronage, was the best known of the McMahons. He served on the board of management of the Belfast and Ulster Vintners' Association from 1902 until his death. Both Owen and Eliza would have believed themselves fortunate to move away from the political cauldron of the Newtownards Road to a quiet street in the north of the city.

Despite the turmoil of the previous two years, in March 1922 the McMahons appear to have been a happy, prosperous family. Owen's estate was estimated to be £31,000 (just under £1.5 million in 2024). Owen and Eliza had eight children. Bernard and John both worked in their father's business; Pat and Frank were cutters in men's tailoring establishments. Like most parents of the time, the McMahons had also endured bereavement. A son, Daniel, had died in 1919 aged fifteen as a result of acute appendicitis.[19]

Kinnaird Terrace may have been somewhat removed from the fulcrum of violence a few streets away, but the family were still attuned to violence potentially reaching their doorstep. When she heard the crash at the door in the early hours of 24 March, Eliza McMahon sat up and immediately remarked that it was a bomb. Their turn for a raid, or worse, had arrived.[20]

In the wake of the McMahon murders, Belfast's Catholics doubled down on defences to prevent any police raids or incursions during curfew hours. The following day the detective branch of the police attempted to raid the Marrowbone area. They were met with well-organised resistance. According to a military intelligence report: 'On the arrival of the police cars, whistles were blown, women and children screamed and shouted, and a brisk fire was opened from all directions on these.' The police fired back, expending more than 200 rounds of ammunition. Police from Leopold Street Barracks, who had not been informed of the raid, arrived on the scene and were nearly shot by their own colleagues.[21]

On 28 March Joe Devlin MP rose in the House of Commons to speak about his friend Owen McMahon. Devlin told the House that members of the Special Constabulary were responsible. He went on to point out that such men were paid by the government in London and asked why MPs were 'prepared to subsidise and pay for hired assassins who are bringing the blush of shame to our cheeks'. He singled out the new 'C1' Class, noting that he and other law-abiding Catholics were defenceless against them: 'There is nothing to prevent them breaking into my house any night. I do not carry arms.' Devlin demanded that martial law be declared, and control of the police be taken away from the Northern Irish government.[22]

Winston Churchill publicly defended the performance of the Special Constabulary. In private, however, he was profoundly alarmed by military reports of murders committed by the Specials. At a meeting in London on 28 March, Churchill warned the Northern Irish prime minister that if he refused to reform and discipline the police then London could declare martial law.

Rocked by English outrage over the McMahon killings, Craig had momentarily lost his poise. He signed a new agreement on 30 March with Michael Collins. In it Craig agreed to restructure the Special Constabulary, recruiting more Catholics to its largely Protestant ranks. These constables would be used to police Catholic areas. Those accused of serious crimes such as murder could be tried by non-jury courts. Craig also made a commitment to set up an independent commission to investigate outrages, including alleged murders by the police. Finally, the pact also underlined Craig's commitment to establish a commission to recommend possible revisions to the border.[23]

Under this new 'Collins-Craig Pact' the provisional government agreed that all IRA activities in Northern Ireland should now cease. The *Church of Ireland Gazette*, the newspaper of the all-island Anglican Church, heralded the agreement – 'The prayers of the Irish people have been answered ... All good Irishmen will thank God for the settlement which these two men, with their respective colleagues, have reached under the helpful auspices of the British Colonial Office.'[24]

Such high Church optimism made no impression on loyalist Belfast. Loyalists feared that any mechanism to revise the border would lead to significant losses of territory on the part of Northern Ireland – many districts near the border had large Catholic majorities. The 'B' Specials commandant for west Belfast, Harry Taylor, informed the British Army that unionists had now 'lost faith' in James Craig.[25]

Loyalist militants like William Coote believed that Catholics were too disloyal and could not be relied upon to serve as a sizeable part of any police force in Northern Ireland. Eight days after signing the pact James Craig changed his mind. He wrote to Winston Churchill telling him that he would have to renege on the commitment he had made to fundamentally restructure the Special Constabulary. (Craig also sent Churchill a copy of parliamentary speeches by Coote and other Northern Irish MPs to underline the threat he faced from his loyalist flank, especially on reform of the police in Belfast and on possible changes to the border.)[26]

Craig now announced that under his premiership no part of Northern Ireland would be transferred to the Free State, even if recommended by a boundary commission. Churchill protested, pointing out that London was paying for Northern Ireland's defence while at the same time Craig's government was refusing to abide by the Anglo-Irish Treaty and the wishes of the British government.[27] Craig was unmoved and unimpressed. In a letter to Dawson Bates he complained about the British government's excitable reactions to reports of atrocities in Ireland: 'They get clean off the rails and require nursing like children.'[28]

In Dublin the provisional government's minister for external relations, Charles Gavan Duffy, offered an alarming assessment of why the pact was doomed: 'Craig, though himself pacifically inclined, is too weak or too nervous to assert himself against the domination of the combined Orange extremists and Orange militarists in Belfast, so that today we have a perfect example of military dictatorship [the Special Constabulary] in that area.'[29] By establishing such a large, undisciplined force as the Special Constabulary, Craig had handed a political veto to armed extremists.

Collins' promises also brought no respite to Belfast; within hours of the pact being signed, the IRA embarked on another round of burnings of unionist-owned businesses.[30] Collins himself was also not acting in good faith to implement the agreement. At a meeting with leading northern nationalist and republicans less than two weeks after the signing of the pact he advocated a renewed campaign of arson since unionists 'think a great deal more of property than they do of human life'. The following day, 12 April, his nominated representatives met with unionists at a short-lived, failed 'conciliation committee' in Belfast.[31]

The dreadful shock of the McMahon murders had quickly given way to a crescendo of murder and violence over a six-day period, from 27 March to 2 April. The IRA intensified its attacks on policemen. The Norfolk Regiment also reported an influx of Catholic men into the Stanhope Street area whom they suspected were IRA volunteers.

On 31 March a bomb was thrown into a house beside Brown's Square Barracks owned by Francis Donnelly, a Protestant, killing his two-year-old son, Francis junior, and mortally wounding another son, Joseph, aged twelve. (Francis and his eleven-year-old daughter, Mary Ann, were also wounded in the attack). Lieutenant Eric Hayes, who had taken over as the Norfolks' intelligence officer, reported that loyalists appeared to have targeted the house due a rumour that Donnelly's Catholic brother-in-law was in the IRA. Such talk was borne out of local malice and sectarian ill-feeling towards this 'mixed' family – there was no intelligence to back up loyalists' claims.[32]

At 10.30 p.m. on the same day, two special constables in civilian clothes were recognised after alighting from a tram near the Catholic Short Strand area of east Belfast. Special Constable Thomas Hall, a veteran of the First World War, was beaten and shot in the abdomen, dying a few hours later. (His companion, Special Constable Andrew Moody, was also badly assaulted and shot but survived his wounds.)[33]

At 10.15 p.m. the following night RIC Constable George Turner was shot dead while standing at the junction of Woodford Street and the Old Lodge Road, not far from DI Nixon's Brown's Square Barracks. A witness called James Girvin told Sinn Féin investigators that Turner had fired a shot up nearby Park Street; a group of soldiers who were nearby

AFTERMATH

returned fire, killing the RIC constable. Loyalists were convinced the Turner had been killed by the IRA.

There was an immediate police reaction, as captured by Norfolk Regiment reports:

> At 2255 two men, one in police uniform with rifle and the other in plain clothes, blue suit, tweed cap and burberry, entered the house of WILLIAM SPALLEEN [*sic*] and shot him dead in his bedroom. The [grand]son of this man aged 12 years was in the room with his [grand]father and states he would be able to recognise these men.[34]

Twelve-year-old Gerard Tumelty also provided an account of the killing of his grandfather, William Spallen, to Sinn Féin representatives. The family had buried Spallen's wife, Ellen, earlier that day. Gerard was in bed with his grandfather when he woke to the sounds of gunfire. He then heard the sounds of footsteps coming up the stairs. His grandfather hurriedly reached for money, a sum of £20, which he vainly hoped would buy him his life:

> The man in plain clothes asked my grandfather his name and he answered, 'William Spallen.' He then raised his revolver and fired three shots at my grandfather. Before he fired and when I saw the revolver I said, 'Don't shoot my [grand]daddy shoot me,' and he replied, 'Lie down or get up and get out or I will put a bullet in you' and immediately he shot my grandfather. This man snatched money which was in my grandfather's hand and both men then ran away.[35]

On the way out of the house, Spallen's murderers warned his daughter, also called Ellen, not to follow them or they would 'blow her brains out'. She replied, 'Blow them out. You have blown out all the brains I

87

care about.' She ran upstairs where she found her son cradling William Spallen's body.

William Spallen's stepson lived across the street. Daniel McGrath described how a young boy, one of the Gray family who lived at 9 Arnon Street, came to his house to tell him what had happened. McGrath ran to 15 Arnon Street where he saw his stepfather's body. As he returned to his house he was stopped by an army officer who ordered him off the street. McGrath protested that his father had been shot, to which the officer replied – 'Don't worry, I know the man who did all this.'[36]

The Norfolk Regiment reported that Joseph Walsh was the next to die; his young son Michael was also mortally wounded:

> About 2300 hours six or seven men entered No. 18 Arnon Street by both front and back ways and shot Joseph Walsh in his bed. With him in bed there were his three children, Bridget aged 2, Michael aged 7 and Frank aged 7 and they were all wounded, one seriously. The man's wife states that some of the men were in police uniform and some in *mufti*. They had flash lamps and fired four of five shots. She cannot recognise any of them.

The killing went on through the night, with further attacks in nearby Stanhope Street:

> At 2340 hours JOHN [*sic*] MCCRORY[37] of No.15 Stanhope street was shot [dead] in the yard of No. 11. William Kitson who also lives at No. 15 states that a party [of] gunmen came to the door and demanded admittance and that he and McCrory left by the back door. McCrory got over the wall, but he hadn't time and he concealed himself in a sack in the yard [that] was used by the raiders as a stand to enable them to fire over the wall at McCrory. Kitson states that he was the man they were after as he

had received his death warrant (which he handed into the Brigade office). These men were not in uniform. He can recognise one of them and thinks they were police.[38]

It seems unlikely that a murderer could stand on, but not notice, William Kitson. Kitson's other account, which he gave to the Sinn Féin investigation, omitted such a claim. In it Kitson recalled that he hid with his children in his yard under 'old coverings'. He then saw McCrory attempt to flee through a hole that linked Kitson's house to 13 Stanhope Street. He was followed by 'four or five men' who confronted him in the yard of No. 13. After cornering McCrory, one of the men shouted:

> 'Hands up, you bastard.' John McCrory then said: 'All right, son. I never done hurt nor harm to nobody.' The armed man then said: 'Not so much of your sonning, get them up, you bastard.' And fired three or four shots … Someone shouted from the street, 'Here is the military.' All the men then ran away. The armed man was Constable Gordon of Brown's Square barracks. After they went I got up and saw John McCrory dead.

Kitson then went outside to the street to tell soldiers from the Norfolk Regiment what had happened. He saw Constable Henry Gordon standing by a policy lorry nearby. Some soldiers then helped him carry Joseph McCrory's body inside.[39]

Bernard McKenna, a sailor who had returned from sea only a few days previously, was murdered minutes after McCrory in nearby Park Street. According to a Norfolk Regiment report: 'At 2345 hrs three men, one in police uniform, two in mufti with C Special arm bands entered No. 26 Park Street and shot Bernard McKenna in his bedroom. His wife states that the men were drunk, that they fired three shots – doubtful if she can identify any of them.'[40]

The Sinn Féin investigation produced a statement signed by Catherine Hatton who lived at No. 9. She was visiting the McKennas when she saw Constable Henry Gordon with three other men – two were in plain clothes (one more than the Norfolks' report) – come into the house, go up the stairs and shoot dead Bernard McKenna. Norfolk Regiment soldiers arrived at the McKenna house when one of the plain-clothes murderers was still inside. He had returned to the scene of the murder and was attempting to force Catherine Hatton into one of the bedrooms. She recalled that when the Norfolks opened the door he 'immediately ran out down Stanhope Street and fired towards the military, one of whom replied by firing. I then said to the military, "That was one of the murderers who had murdered the man upstairs" … they answered if they had known they would have blown his block off.'[41]

Six Catholics died in what was called the 'Arnon Street Massacre'. Four – William Spallen, Joseph Walsh, Joseph McCrory and Bernard McKenna – died as described in reports written by 1 Norfolks' intelligence officer, Lieutenant Eric Hayes. Michael Walsh, Joseph's son, died in hospital five days later. An eight-month-old boy, Robert Walsh – Joseph's nephew – was shot dead during indiscriminate shooting on Alton Street during the morning of 2 April.[42]

Lieutenant Hayes believed he knew who was responsible for the first four murders: '[The] murders are undoubtedly the work of the police as a reprisal for the murder of Const. Turner. All these men form part of the Brown's Square contingent and if the troops on duty can identify any of them if should be possible to get hold of the actual murderers.'[43]

Belfast IRA officer Seán Montgomery recalled that some IRA volunteers were present in the area at the time of the murders but that they did not open fire due to the numbers of police. Montgomery also reported that the military intervened to try to stop the killings or at least arrest the perpetrators:

An officer of the Norfolk Regiment had the driver of a Police Car against the wall, and three soldiers with rifles at the ready to fire. He said to the Special that if he did not tell him [who the murderers were] he would give the order to fire. He [the driver] said that he had nothing to do with it, but that DI Nixon was in charge and the police had told the army they were going to raid.[44]

The Norfolks set up cordons around Arnon Street and the surrounding area to prevent more murders.[45] Reports from Belfast to the provisional government in Dublin noted a more aggressive approach by the military towards the Special Constabulary in the days after the killings. On 3 April an officer stopped a Special Constabulary lorry on Conway Street in the west of the city, ordering it to turn around or 'he would blow up their lorry'.[46]

Since the police had carried out the killings, Lieutenant Hayes collected witness statements from residents in the area. Locals recognised some of the perpetrators as either regular RIC or Special Constabulary who lived nearby.[47]

Evidence collected by the Irish government placed Henry Gordon at the centre of the Arnon Street and Stanhope murders. Ten days after the murders Sinn Féin leaders in Belfast produced a secret report for the provisional government. Constable O'Donnell from Glenravel Barracks had come forward to implicate Henry Gordon. O'Donnell was on duty in the Stanhope Street area on the night of the murders. After the killing of Constable Turner, Gordon asked him if he was going to take part in the reprisals. O'Donnell refused. Gordon then took out his revolver and ordered him to leave.

O'Donnell had joined the police nearly twenty years before. There were no blemishes or commendations on his unremarkable police record. By his account, he had originally wanted to follow procedures and formally complain to his superiors. In the days after the murders, he met with District Inspector George Williams at Belfast police headquarters. But he found Williams to be evasive, refusing to give assurances that he would investigate Gordon's alleged involvement in murder.[48]

The Nixon memo – the 1924 Irish military intelligence report on atrocities perpetrated by DI Nixon and his 'murder gang' – suggested Constable George Turner was shot by other policemen so they would have an excuse to carry out the 'Arnon Street massacre'. It claimed that Henry Gordon then entered the day-room at Brown's Square Barracks, picked up the sledgehammer he used in the McMahon killings and asked for volunteers. One constable objected. Undeterred, Nixon, Gordon 'and the remainder of the gang, accompanied by a number of "B" Specials, went into Arnon Street in an armoured Lancia, riddled the nationalist houses, beating and kicking women and children, and murdered seven persons. Some were shot, others had their brains dashed out with the sledgehammer.'[49]

There was no medical evidence to suggest that anybody in Belfast was beaten to death with a sledgehammer in early April 1922. The Nixon memo contradicts the Sinn Féin investigation undertaken by Dr Russell McNabb in the hours after the murders. McNabb was the senior medical officer for the IRA's 3rd Northern Division; his medical practice was attached to the Mater Hospital. In his evidence Constable O'Donnell also made no reference to Henry Gordon wielding a sledgehammer – instead he threatened him with a revolver.

The Sinn Féin report is more detailed and precise than the Nixon memo produced nearly two years later. It stated that Constable Turner was caught in the crossfire after a gun battle broke out between the Special Constabulary and the military – the latter fired the fatal shot. (The British Army's account of Turner's death does not mention this – Lieutenant Hayes reported that an IRA unit from outside the area was responsible.)[50]

The Sinn Féin investigation also reported that the police responsible arrived in armoured cars and came from the direction of the Old Lodge Road. This contradicts the Nixon memo's assertion that the attackers, led by Nixon and Gordon, came directly from Brown's Square Barracks, which was situated to the south of the Arnon Street. Local resident John Swindles recalled seeing a crowd of armed civilians and some policemen – approximately 100 – moving from east to west, towards the Shankill Road, shortly before the murders. However, he also saw a Lancia car outside Brown's Square Barracks which 'made no attempt to interfere with the crowd carrying arms'.

This evidence from Swindles and other Sinn Féin sources does not exonerate Nixon's men, including RIC Constable Henry Gordon, from involvement in the murders. Military intelligence, namely reports by the Norfolk Regiment, strongly pointed to Brown's Square police participation in the violence. However, it does suggest a chaotic scene of special constables (including from the 'C1' Class of the Special Constabulary) and possibly civilians arriving from different locations and joining in the assault on the Arnon Street area during a night of intense rioting and violence.

The Sinn Féin report went on to describe the violence inflicted upon the victims of the attacks. There is no mention of a sledgehammer being used to kill Joseph Walsh – his head was shattered after being shot at close range. In one house the raiders failed to find any men but proceeded to smash up the front room, including breaking a religious statue – the infant of Prague. A girl asked the raiders: 'Do you know there is a God above?' A gunman responded: 'God is on French leave.' Several women were beaten during the attack, including being hit by rifles.[51]

For some policemen the perceived collective 'guilt' of the Stanhope Street as a republican area was enough to justify atrocity. Less than two weeks before the Arnon Street killings DI Nixon told the British Army that Stanhope Street had been 'denuded of men', implying that this was because the IRA 'are going to make trouble again very shortly'.[52]

Nixon evidently believed that Stanhope Street was so saturated with IRA volunteers that most of its menfolk moved in and out of the area according to IRA operational requirements. The Norfolks were more sceptical. Lieutenant Hayes acknowledged that there was a significant IRA presence in the area, which was bolstered by an influx of outsiders from time to time. But many locals did not support Sinn Féin, Hayes concluded, preferring to rely upon the military as a means of defence against loyalists and the police.[53]

None of the Arnon Street victims were leading republicans in the area. Why were they targeted? Media reports emphasised McCrory's and Walsh's military service during the First World War. Both had served in the Royal Irish Rifles – Walsh was with the 6th Battalion in Salonika. McCrory had moved with his wife into William Kitson's house at 15 Stanhope Street after being forced out of their home in nearby Campbell Street by loyalists. (William Kitson also served in the Royal Irish Rifles during the war.)

The *Irish News* concluded that loyalist violence was now so mindless and indiscriminate that even men who had spent time in the British Army were no longer safe.[54] However, instead of assuming that they would be spared because they were veterans, the men may have been targeted *because* of their military service. It was widely known that ex-British soldiers – once they had allayed suspicions and proved their commitment to the republican cause – were valued by the IRA for their marksmanship.

Intelligence gathered by 1 Norfolks indicated that ex-British soldiers were playing a key role in the Stanhope Street IRA. IRA Volunteer John 'Armoured Car' Morgan was arrested at a house in Stanhope Street in November 1921. Morgan was a former gunner, ex-Royal Field Artillery. Information from workmen indicated some suspicious activity in 11 and 13 Stanhope Street. (The latter was the home of William Kitson, although here is no evidence to suggest that Kitson was an important republican in the area.)[55]

In the days before the Arnon Street killings, intelligence seized at Sinn Féin headquarters in St Mary's Hall and elsewhere in Belfast revealed the names of some prominent IRA leaders. For example, IRA Belfast Brigade officer and British Army veteran Charles McWhinney, with an address at 25 Stanhope Street, was arrested on 21 March 1922. Another suspected IRA officer was believed to live next door to McWhinney, at 27 Stanhope Street.[56]

In the paranoid atmosphere of Belfast 1922, military veterans who had served together in Flanders, Gallipoli or Salonika found themselves on opposite sides of a sectarian street war. Military experience and proficiency marked a man out as both familiar and suspect. This was especially the case if you lived in an area – Stanhope Street – where republican snipers were frequently active.

Groups of raiders behaved differently. Some did not hesitate to smash their way into a house and kill at close quarters. Others knocked on doors and appeared more nervous or uncertain when it came to opening fire. George Murray described how five men in police uniform and two in civilian clothes knocked at his door 12 Arnon Street. Upon entering, a man placed a revolver to his head: 'Then he asked me my name and I gave it to him. He then said, "Get the child out of your arms." Another of the same party said, "I will do it." I then went to leave the child down when a shot was fired going over my head, and striking the wall of the fireplace making a hole as large as my hand. They then all left.'[57] Murray survived.

Some of the murderers of Arnon Street, those wearing 'C' Specials armbands and dressed in civilian clothes, were clearly anxious not to be seen or apprehended by the military. By contrast the *sangfroid* of Constable Henry Gordon is remarkable. Here was a man who was confident that the Norfolks could not lay a hand on him.

Three days after the 'Arnon Street massacre', Lieutenant Hayes wrote a report for his superiors. The military had now reached a vital watershed moment. Police murder could no longer go unpunished, 'In my opinion it is <u>extremely important</u> [original emphasis], if we wish to retain the confidence of the RC population to push the inquiry into the Saturday murders right to a definitive conclusion.'[58]

Initially it seemed that the RIC, through City Commissioner Gelston, would co-operate with the military and investigate allegations of police murder in the Arnon Street area. Gelston ordered DI William Lynn to take over the investigation. In the days after the killings, Lynn worked closely with the Norfolk Regiment, telephoning Gelston from military headquarters to update him on his investigation. He also assisted the military in planning searches of the area. On 5 April Lynn moved into Brown's Square Barracks to arrange a parade of policemen for possible identification by witnesses to the murders.[59]

According to Bishop MacRory, relying on Catholic police sources, Nixon refused to turn his men (RIC and Special Constabulary) out on parade.[60]

A Sinn Féin secret report – drawing on the evidence of Catholic constables – stated that a notice for such a parade was posted in Brown's Square Barracks on the morning of 5 April, scheduled for 4 p.m. the same day. Upon seeing the notice Henry Gordon turned to a group of special constables, 'Look at that, it's a nice thing that we'll have to parade before the whores of Stanhope Street. There's one certainty I won't be there.'

When Joseph Walsh's widow came to the barracks that afternoon the parade did not take place. On her way out, Margaret Walsh saw Henry Gordon standing near the door – 'There's the man who murdered my husband.' A group of policemen grabbed her and pushed her out into the street. There she was further assaulted, this time by a mob – 'She was severely mauled, and blood was flowing from her face when she succeeded in regaining the shelter of her own house.'[61]

Another witness, William Spallen's stepson, Daniel McGrath, immediately left Belfast with his wife and three young sons. He joined the National Army in Dublin, serving in the Dublin Guard under the command of Commandant (later General) Patrick O'Daly. McGrath was wounded during fighting to seize the Four Courts garrison from the anti-Treaty IRA in late June. O'Daly's Dublin Guard acquired a notorious reputation for atrocity in County Kerry – it was a terrible irony that McGrath, like many other Belfast men who fled their homes during the 'pogrom' and enlisted in the National Army, found themselves fighting in the cruellest and most violent theatre of the Civil War.[62]

The Arnon Street murders bore some resemblance to the McMahon killings. A sledgehammer was used to batter in the door of Joseph Walsh's house. Victims were shot in their homes, as opposed to being taken away and killed more discreetly elsewhere. Some of the killers were dressed in civilian clothes; others wore police uniforms.[63] The victims were shot at very close range. The killing of Joseph Walsh, who was lying in his bed with his children, was exceptionally gruesome, even relative to the violence of the period.

There are also some differences to the McMahon murders – the attack at Kinnaird Terrace was directed towards a single family and executed in a matter of minutes; the five perpetrators then ran from the scene before the arrival of police from Glenravel Barracks. By contrast, the Arnon Street atrocities were carried out by a large group who entered successive houses over a prolonged period. The murderers did not fear the regular RIC, who did nothing to impede the attacks (and were strongly suspected to have been complicit in them). The only opposition they faced was from the British Army.

CHAPTER FOUR

A Terrible Victory

THE FACT THAT THE IRA did not immediately respond to the McMahon and Arnon Street murders with an atrocity of their own was seen by some as a sign of defeat rather than restraint. Andrew Magill, a senior official at the Ministry of Home Affairs, wrote that the McMahon murders 'sent a shiver of horror through everyone in Belfast'. But they also had a macabre usefulness: 'I would not like to say that it [the McMahon murders] put a stop to the outrages of the [IRA] gun men, for that would be too dreadful a thought, but it undoubtedly made them pause, as they realised they were up against a party just as sanguinary and evil disposed as they were themselves.'[1] Loyalists, Magill believed, had outbid republicans in an auction of terror.

News of other horrific crimes perpetrated by the Special Constabulary also circulated in the city. In the days after the Arnon Street killings an armed special constable was reported as having attempted to rape two women in a home in Joy Street near the city centre. After residents complained to the RIC, a group of special constables returned to the street on 13 April. Witnesses said they smashed windows and fired shots at houses.[2] A local defence group was mustered, firing on the special constables – who later claimed they were on a routine patrol. Special Constable Nathaniel McCoo was fatally wounded.[3]

Attempts by the Norfolk Regiment to prevent more attacks in April 1922 meant that loyalists turned their fire on the soldiers instead. Lieutenants Ian Lywood and Lionel Gundry-White were ambushed by loyalist snipers as they walked along Hartley Street, not far from Brown's Square. Lywood tried to run for reinforcements but was shot in the leg. Lying wounded on the street, he heard a man call out – 'Good shot!' – to a sniper concealed in a house.[4]

On 18 April loyalist gunmen shot and wounded intelligence officer Captain Harry Papworth and Private James Grant when they intervened to stop rioting and burnings in the Marrowbone area. (Grant's wounds were serious; he was shot in the chest and neck but survived.) A Norfolk soldier then shot and killed William Johnston, an ex-soldier who the military claimed had fired on Grant. Despite the Norfolks' actions, nearly all the houses on a single street, Antigua Street, were burned or ransacked and more than fifty families were made homeless.[5]

On 4 May a group of women on Stanhope Street pleaded with the soldiers not to leave the area, since the special constables from Brown's Square were drunk and threatening to burn them out of their homes. According to a Sinn Féin report, 'The women of this street, remembering the massacre in Arnon St of 1st April and apprehending a similar occurrence last night, became frantic with fear and simply refused to let the soldiers go off duty ...' The Norfolks then arrested a drunk special constable and ordered other constables to leave the area.[6]

The murder of thirty-seven-year-old Protestant postman Robert Beattie, shot dead while delivering letters in Ardoyne on the morning of 13 May, precipitated a brutal and very public loyalist reprisal. Beattie was a well-known Orangeman, a veteran of the north Belfast UVF and the British Army. Enlisting in the Royal Irish Rifles at the outbreak of the First World War, he was wounded on the first day of the Battle of the Somme in 1916. He later served with 2nd Battalion, Royal Irish Fusiliers

(2 RIF) in Salonika in the eastern Mediterranean, rising to the rank of quartermaster sergeant.

As Beattie's funeral passed through Belfast city centre, a group of armed loyalists broke off from the procession and opened fire on passers-by whom they had identified as Catholics, wounding several. William Madden, a Catholic and an ex-Royal Navy sailor, was delivering fruit to a shop on North Street. He was questioned by one of the funeral party about his religion. When he refused to answer, he was shot in the chest at point-blank range. Loyalist violence in the city centre continued for at least half an hour, terrifying shoppers and local residents. William Madden was murdered on one of Belfast's busiest streets. But no witnesses came forward and nobody was ever charged.[7]

The Norfolks struggled to stop further loyalist shootings and arson in the Ardoyne and Marrowbone areas. After one gun battle in which soldiers wounded a loyalist sniper, a man was seen firing from Ballycarry Street while holding a white flag at the same time. Shots were frequently exchanged between the Norfolks and the Special Constabulary. Some Protestant residents complained that the soldiers were firing from the Sacred Heart Catholic church on the Oldpark Road.[8] Catholics in the area reported that a Special Constabulary lorry in the area drove around emblazoned with chalk graffiti – 'Papish blood is sweet.'[9]

British Army commanders kept up their efforts to enrol Catholics in the Special Constabulary in Belfast. Meetings were held between officers and senior members of the Catholic clergy – the latter promised tentative support for police reform. The provisional government in Dublin initially supported Catholics becoming special constables – as long as they could police their own areas. Eoin O'Duffy said that 'the cream of the IRA' in Belfast should join the force.

Bishop MacRory saw many obstacles to restructuring the police. He warned the government in Dublin about the scale of loyalist opposition to Catholic enrolment in the Special Constabulary. James Craig might be shot by loyalist paramilitaries if he delivered on the pact. MacRory also told the British military that Catholics would not join while John Nixon remained as DI in the city.

A serious blow to the military's plans to reform the Special Constabulary was the introduction of the draconian Civil Contingencies (Special Powers) Act on 7 April 1922. It quickly became known to nationalists as the 'flogging bill' in reference to one of its many controversial provisions to put down 'sedition'. The city's Catholics would not enrol in a new Special Constabulary if organisations and symbols of Irish nationalism could be outlawed. Five days later Lieutenant Hayes offered a bleak assessment of the prospects for implementing the Collins-Craig Pact. He also explicitly blamed DI Nixon: 'I think there is very little chance of any agreement being reached in the area so long as DI Nixon and his specials are allowed to carry on their present campaign of terrorising the RC population.'[10]

Colonel Wickham's stated plan for Catholics to make up a third of the RUC also floundered. A committee to examine the future of policing had been set up in early 1922. Some Catholic representatives, including a senior officer of the IRA, Frank Crummey, took part in proceedings. But at a meeting in April the newly appointed director of security in Northern Ireland, Major General Sir Arthur Solly-Flood, stated that he and the government would not accept the one-third proposal. (Craig had made clear that Solly-Flood would have precedence over Wickham when it came to the structure of the new RUC.)

Shortly after this meeting Frank Crummey was arrested and later interned. A Catholic priest, Fr Hugh Murray, also withdrew from the committee. Loyalists had attempted to kill him. He wanted no further role in discussing Northern Ireland's new police force.

James Craig wrote to Collins at the end of April to assure him that he was committed to forming some kind of 'Catholic Police Force' in Belfast. But loyalist violence and that of the IRA, including the 'northern offensive', meant that relations between both governments plummeted in the weeks afterwards. Co-operation on policing came to nothing.

Craig also reneged on his commitment to establish a commission of inquiry into the murders of the McMahons and other atrocities. In June he told Lloyd George that he took 'grave exception to an inquiry appointed by the British government'; he had consulted his own cabinet and was withdrawing his consent. Such a mechanism, he protested, would 'defeat the ends of justice' since it would revive recent 'Dublin Castle methods', such as making unfounded allegations about police complicity in atrocities. The exchange underlined both Craig's antipathy towards the departing British administration in Ireland and his determination to scupper a future role for London to investigate police violence in Northern Ireland.[11]

Michael Collins had agreed to allow a commission to investigate atrocities in the twenty-six counties as well as in Northern Ireland (led by a British military officer with representatives from both governments in Belfast and Dublin). But Prime Minister David Lloyd George also turned against the idea of an inquiry. Sir Stephen Tallents, a senior official sent to Belfast to advise on the British government's future policy towards Northern Ireland, warned that the adverse findings of this commission could 'inadvertently encourage northern Catholics in their refusal to recognize the Northern government'.[12]

By the end of May the British Army in Belfast was rapidly losing confidence in its ability to reform the police and suppress Special Constabulary violence. The RIC in Nixon's district made no attempt to enforce the curfew in Protestant areas. The British administration in Dublin Castle was being steadily dissolved; RIC headquarters and command structure had practically ceased to exist pending disbandment and the establishment of the new RUC on 1 June. And since the introduction of the Special Powers Act, soldiers were more hesitant about firing on the Special Constabulary. They believed they could no longer rely upon London (or Dublin Castle) to overrule Craig's government and reaffirm military security primacy.[13]

Charlotte Despard, a seventy-five-year-old Irish republican and the sister of the former Viceroy of Ireland, John French, gave an account of the British Army's despondency in her diary after a meeting with the Norfolks' commanding officer, Lieutenant Colonel Day, at the end of May. Day told her he was 'helpless' to act decisively against the police. He advised her to petition James Craig's government instead. Although Day 'liked the Specials as little as we do ... he had to obey orders'. As for the loyalist murder gangs, Despard concluded – 'No efforts made to bring the murderers [to justice] although several of them are well known. Trustworthy evidence is at hand, but it is refused. The guilty escape and the campaign of murder goes on.'[14]

Remarkably, Despard, despite her well-known republican and socialist views, secured a meeting with Richard Dawson Bates. Being the sister of Lord French was enough to push open the doors of the Ministry of Home Affairs at Donegall Square. Dawson Bates may also have believed that Despard had a message from the Irish government – she was known to occasionally have the ear of Michael Collins.

Despard had been widowed young and lived with Maud Gonne MacBride, a republican activist who inspired some of W.B. Yeats' most famous poems. (Her husband, John MacBride, led the Irish Brigade that fought on the side of the Boers against the British in South Africa and was executed for his part in the Easter Rising in 1916.) Like her companion, Despard cared little for drawing-room niceties. She enjoyed skewering powerful men opposed to her causes.

Dawson Bates opened the meeting by asking Despard what he could do for her. Despard listed the sectarian crimes she had witnessed, waving away the minster's interruptions – 'Two or three times he tried to stop me. I made him listen.' Eventually Dawson Bates broke in – 'Every law-abiding citizen has our protection,' he protested. 'How about the ex-soldier I saw on Saturday, whose little child was barbarously murdered at his door? Is there no justice for him?' Despard fired back. Dawson Bates turned his back on her. Despard aimed a few final words and then departed.[15]

As part of the 'northern offensive', the Belfast IRA, dressed in police capes and coats, launched a bold raid on the RIC's Belfast headquarters in Musgrave Street on 18 May. Their objective was to seize armoured cars kept at the barracks. However, a guard quickly raised the alarm and the attack was called off after a brief exchange of fire.[16] The following day saw a sharp escalation in IRA arson attacks – unionist-owned warehouses, spirit groceries and a cinema were all burned.[17]

Loyalists in north Belfast responded with a new round of shootings and burnings. Three armed loyalists broke into the house of the Murray family on Spamount Street in north Belfast, firing at Charles Murray and other members of the family. Somehow none of the bullets hit their targets; Charles Murray then attacked the men with an axe. The three men fled the house just before soldiers from the Norfolk Regiment arrived. A Protestant woman, Mary Donaldson, was killed in the crossfire as the Norfolks pursued the gunmen up the street.[18]

On 22 May the IRA shot dead unionist MP William Twaddell in Belfast city centre. The attack was carried out by two volunteers against the wishes of the IRA's Belfast command – Seamus Woods was furious.[19] Woods' anger was not simply due to the insubordination of those who carried out the attack without any orders. He also correctly feared a new explosion of sectarian violence if a high-profile unionist political figure, one closely associated with the Imps, was murdered, and that Catholics would pay an even heavier price.

As was so often the case, the most vulnerable were killed first. Charles McMurtry, a Catholic 'rag picker' in the docks area of north Belfast, was attacked and killed by a mob. And a sixty-three-year-old Protestant gravedigger called James Telford was shot dead while walking through the Falls Road area with his granddaughter. A witness described how he was shot and fell to the ground. A man then approached and, stooping over Telford, shot him for a second time. (His granddaughter was not injured.)[20]

During the next few days there was an exodus of Catholics families from the York Road/Shore Road and the Stanhope Street/Arnon Street areas. More than 100 families were forced to leave Weaver Street.[21] Charlotte Despard found the presbytery of St Patrick's Church on Donegall Street 'full of frightened looking women with babies in their arms. [I] heard that an Orange mob was gathering in a catholic street close by. Terrible things have happened in this quarter. Some streets have been swept clean of Catholics altogether. Over the houses from which they have been expelled the Union Jack is waving.'

Despard went to a nearby street where she spoke to the widow of a British soldier. The Special Constabulary had raided her house. Finding no one inside, they burned the house anyway. Despard also went to see the aftermath of rioting and shooting in Ardoyne. There she was greeted by crying women, shattered windows, doors pulled off their hinges and broken children's toys in the street:

> Many men were standing about, resentment and despair on their faces. The women looked as if they had suffered until they could suffer no longer. They were near collapse. One weeping woman with a baby in her arms, whose husband had left the day before to take two of the children to a place of safety, showed me where a bullet had passed through the house, nearly grazing her. She stood trembling. As she stood there a special [constable] came up, 'What have you there?' he said, clutching the front of her dress. 'My breast', she answered.[22]

Successive British Army reports indicated that the Special Constabulary were out of control, driving around in lorries and firing indiscriminately

GHOSTS OF A FAMILY

into Catholic residential streets. Lieutenant Harold Watling described one such incident on 31 May:

> Protestant crowds collected in the Old Lodge Road and egged on the Specials who fired into RC streets at random even when no target presented itself. They fired along Upper Library St., Arnon St., and Stanhope St. They began at about 1700 hours. The Protestant mob set fire to houses in Peter's Place and killed a man and woman there, neither of whom have yet been identified.

The victims of the St Peter's Place attack were John Jennings, an old and blind Protestant man, and a young Catholic woman called Jane Doran. The next day loyalists broke into the house of a Catholic woman, Mary McElroy, and her daughter, Rose, on the Old Lodge Road, murdering them both.[23] When Colonel Fred Crawford went to the aid of a wounded woman lying face down near Brown's Square Barracks, 'the hooligan element started to menace me'. He left the area hurriedly – he said he had to meet his son before he left for England – but urged some local women to call an ambulance. The injured woman, Lizzie Donnelly, had been shot in the groin and later died of her wounds.[24]

The following day loyalists attempted to burn Susan McCormick alive at a house in the Donegall Pass area of south Belfast. After throwing her to the ground, kicking her in the head and body, a group of men threw petrol over her and lit a match. She somehow survived the attack. Her attackers had been looking for her employer, a Catholic doctor.[25] She was taken to the Mater Hospital where her extensive burns were treated; many of her teeth had also been kicked out during the attack.

Three days after Susan McCormick's admission, the Mater Hospital came under attack. For forty-five minutes during curfew hours doctors and patients cowered beneath windows as bullets spattered the building. The hospital authorities sent a telegram asking King George V to intervene and secure military protection for the building. The military, it was claimed, no longer patrolled the city streets at night. (The appeal seems to have worked, at least for a time – a military picket was placed on the hospital until the end of the month.)[26]

Looting broke out, including on the loyalist Shankill Road. John Nixon and some policemen from Brown's Square arrested ten men who had broken into a pawn shop. One of Nixon's men then shot dead a Protestant boy, John Kane. A mob surrounded the barracks, shouting that Nixon and his men were 'murderers'. Only the arrival of the Norfolk soldiers broke up the mob and freed the police from what had turned into a dangerous siege.[27]

By June there were increasing signs of British Army demoralisation in Belfast. Colonel Commandant Potter complained that on the day of Field Marshal Henry Wilson's funeral a group of nationalists on Stanhope Street waved the Irish flag in the direction of loyalists on the Old Lodge Road, 'In the evening they hastily sent out for protection and military patrols worked all night.'[28] Resented by all sides and lacking support from London, military discipline began to fray. A soldier from the Somerset Light Infantry was reported to have written: 'Look up you bastards – Wilson will be avenged this week.' He was arrested by the military after Catholics reported the graffiti to an officer.[29] A Catholic civilian, Thomas Mullaney, was shot during an argument with a sentry near the city centre in disputed circumstances – two soldiers stated that Mullaney put his hand in his pocket as if to draw a revolver.[30]

Other incidents included a complaint by two ex-servicemen in west Belfast who claimed that soldiers smashed up Catholic homes on Norfolk Street after receiving reports that snipers were operating there. An officer was overheard saying that 'it was damned nearly time they were out of Norfolk Street and to get the IRA to protect them'. Norfolk Street was in the Seaforth Highlanders area of operations; a few days earlier Seaforth reinforcements who were marching from the docks to the Belfast War Hospital were caught in a crossfire between loyalist and republican gunmen. A young highlander, Private Cole, was wounded in the back.[31]

Catholic residents also reported that a group of soldiers from the Seaforth Highlanders operating in the Falls Road area took to wearing Orange lilies on their uniform. An agitated Norfolk soldier was arrested by a military patrol on Wall Street – it was believed he was going to take revenge on the residents there (possibly for loyalist attacks on the Holy Boys a few months earlier). Retribution went both ways; 1 Norfolks soldier Private George Deane was shot in the wrist by an unidentified gunman while walking off-duty near the Shankill Road.[32]

The collapse in late May of the 'northern offensive' punctured morale within the IRA's Belfast units. A brief occupation of the border village of Belleek in Fermanagh was easily pushed back by a British Army counter-attack. Preparations in the days before the offensive had been complicated by mounting tensions between pro- and anti-treaty factions within the IRA. (Much of the Belfast IRA was pro-treaty; Seamus Woods took over command of 3rd Northern Division.)[33] Following the outbreak of the Civil War, Michael Collins' government needed British military supplies to defeat the anti-treaty IRA.

Since early 1922 the Belfast IRA increasingly dedicated much of its limited manpower and arsenal for the defence of Catholic areas. In west Belfast thirty-two volunteers operated a continuous twenty-four-hour reaction force. The IRA also established more than twenty pickets in the Falls Road area. Each was provided with electric torches to signal a warning of any 'enemy' incursions.[34] Michael Collins authorised the establishment of 'Belfast City Guard', a force of seventy-two men commanded by some of Belfast's most efficient (and lethal) volunteers.[35]

The police had netted a huge intelligence haul (and a sizeable amount of explosives) after the raid on Sinn Féin headquarters at St Mary's Hall in the city centre on 18 March 1922. Many of the individuals named on the carefully administered lists of IRA officers were either arrested, interned or fled the city.[36]

A leading Sinn Féin representative in Ulster, Louis J. Walsh, argued that the IRA had to abandon its campaign in the North. In a letter to Bishop MacRory, Walsh wrote that offensive actions should always have been unthinkable given the predictable scale of loyalist reprisals; the IRA should have confined itself to acting as a 'defensive force'. He complained that he and other critics were dismissed by republican hard-liners as 'white flaggers', and the result was to have a number of people 'murdered and hunted from their homes.'[37]

Dr Russell McNabb preferred to raze Belfast to the ground – 'If we are going to be cleared out of Belfast we are going to leave no Belfast.'[38] IRA intelligence officer Frank Crummey objected to those in Sinn Féin who now wanted young IRA volunteers 'to die in the last ditch'. Sinn Féin and the IRA were two distinct entities. Crummey bitterly noted that a lot of political types talked of war but never put themselves in the firing line – 'Our people are more dispirited and cowed than they have been in the memory of anybody … the whole of Stanhope Street area is deserted, and our poor people are huddled in the Falls area and sleep on the floor.' It was, Crummey said, up to the IRA's commanders to decide what to do.

IRA officer Joseph Murray described the organisation in the North as 'a lost legion'. Despondency had set in – 'The National Spirit amongst the people is practically dead at the moment.'[39] The only option after the failure of the last-ditch May 'northern offensive' was to cease the IRA's campaign in Belfast. According to Seamus Woods, 'We stopped burning and that really saved us, for the Civil War broke out below and if the Orangemen had been quick they could have wiped us out.'

The contest of violence was over. The Special Constabulary had extended its control over the city – operating from requisitioned pubs and spirit groceries such as the Beehive Bar on the Falls Road or Fearons on the Oldpark Road. (The latter was a command post for the Ardoyne and Marrowbone areas. It was sandbagged and a Union Jack flew from the rooftop.)[40]

Craig's government and the RUC now had primacy over internal security in Northern Ireland, not the military – an authority that would remain largely unchallenged by successive governments until the outbreak of the more recent Troubles in the late 1960s. The government in London offered some funds for unemployment relief and the rebuilding of housing burned down during riots. Reform of the RUC was dropped. The British Army, in a display of cold pragmatism, shelved its earlier protests and adapted to the new reality of providing aid to the police as requested by the Northern Irish Ministry of Home Affairs.[41]

The British government did push back on General Solly-Flood's wilder plans in order to bring police spending until control.[42] Northern Ireland's security advisor wanted to build up the police force to a total number of 42,500 – including nearly doubling the size of the 'C1' Class Constabulary. The 'C1' Class would also be equipped with artillery and heavy armour – completing their transition into 'Ulster's Army'.

Solly-Flood also corresponded with the head of the Royal Air Force, Sir Hugh Trenchard, sending plans to the Air Ministry for the establishment of an Ulster Air Force under the command of the police which could undertake 'offensive bombing operations at a later stage'. The suggestion was quickly shut down by Churchill. It was 'not the business of the Ulster Police to have an Air Force'.[43]

Stephen Tallents warned the government in London that the 'C1' Specials – 'a territorial military force in all but name' – was 'a dangerous weapon', one that could turn on the British government in a time of crisis. Dawson Bates was the 'least competent' of all the government ministers. A conflagration, consuming ever more British resources, would easily break out if the government did not approach the reduction or disbandment of parts of the Special Constabulary in a careful way.[44]

RUC Inspector General Charles Wickham secretly backed Tallents. He went behind Craig's back to sound the alarm in London about the potential threat of the 'C1' Class. It was still a body 'stained with politics'. If there were serious future differences between the British government and Craig's government, Wickham believed it was 'more than likely that the rank and file of the Force would refuse orders from their imperial officers'. Wickham was warning of a possible mutiny.[45]

In 1922 General Solly-Flood's estimated costs for the Special Constabulary came to more than £5 million, which he proposed should be paid by the British government. By January 1923 he was gone – effectively dismissed for incompetence and profligacy – to Wickham's considerable approval. His office had been successfully infiltrated by an agent of the IRA (and subsequently that of the Free State government). Ex-soldier Pat Stapleton had previously served alongside another clerk and IRA spy, James Tully, at British Army headquarters in Victoria Barracks; both men had passed on valuable intelligence on military and police operations until the end of 1922 when, under suspicion from the RUC, they moved to the Free State.[46]

The overall cost of the Special Constabulary from 1922 to 1923 exceeded £2.6 million (approximately £125.6 million a century later), most of which was paid for by the British exchequer. For the British cabinet this burden was far too high for a largely part-time police reserve in a small part of the United Kingdom – at a time of economic crisis and when total British defence spending globally was just over £105 million.[47] Under pressure from London, Craig reduced overall annual expenditure to £1.5 million – cutting down the size of each class of the Special Constabulary.

In early 1924 the new Labour government of Prime Minister Ramsay MacDonald was determined to disband the 'A' and 'C1' Class of the Special Constabulary. Craig's protests to London were rebuffed by the Secretary of State for War, Stephen Walsh MP. Walsh, the son of Irish immigrants, was a largely self-educated former miner and trade unionist. He had the backing of the military, who wanted little to do with Craig's force. Walsh and his successors stopped short, however, when it came to reforming the 'B' Specials, who remained an almost wholly-Protestant entity.[48]

In December 1923 Colonel Wickham was the guest of honour at a dinner at the Orange Hall on the Shankill Road to celebrate the west Belfast 'B' Specials' victory over the IRA. Sir Joseph Davison, High Sheriff of Belfast, chairman of Belfast City Council's Police Committee and County Grand Master of the Orange Order in Belfast, paid tribute to John Nixon and the police – regulars and Special Constabulary – who served under him in 'C' District: 'It was due to them that there was now in the city of Belfast an era of peace.' Nixon had beaten the hated O'Duffy who had been 'driven out of Belfast'.[49] Wickham – fully aware of the crimes committed by the police in 'C' District including the Arnon Street killings – responded by warmly congratulating the 'B' Specials for their service.[50]

Craig also tried to appease his loyalist critics. His government announced the building of a large, three-story 'recreation building' for the North East Belfast Unionist Club – headed by William Grant MP and situated at 229 York Street. This was the area where anti-government feeling among the Imps was strongest. (The building was paid for out of the Belfast Unemployed Relief Fund.)[51]

In 1923 DI John Nixon was made a Member of the Most Excellent Order of the British Empire (MBE) for his role in suppressing the IRA in Belfast. West Belfast's 'B' Specials commander Harry Taylor was also awarded an MBE. Both men's supporters were disappointed. According to Captain Thomas Mayes, 'DI Nixon was the man who put O'Duffy out of Belfast, and for that he got the lowest honour they could give him.'[52]

Nixon was not mollified by his gong; his behaviour towards his superiors became even more erratic and insubordinate in the months afterwards. In July 1923 he demanded that he be promoted, writing a letter to Wickham – quickly leaked to the press – in which he ludicrously claimed that 'C' District had been 'more orderly than other Districts'. Nixon went on to make a more sensational claim. His district would have been even more peaceable but for the actions of John Gelston, the RIC's city commissioner who had conspired with the Norfolk Regiment and the parish priest in Ardoyne to exclude Nixon and his men from the area. The military had also excluded the police from the Stanhope Street area for a time but this order was rescinded following the intervention of Craig's security supremo General Solly-Flood after his arrival in Belfast in April 1922.[53]

In August 1923 Colonel Wickham was informed that Nixon had received a financial 'gift' from a businessman as a demonstration of gratitude and admiration on the part of loyalists on the Shankill Road. The collection was organised by 'B' Specials sub-commandants at the Shankill and Brown's Square Barracks. Among the subscribers were the managers of bank branches in 'C' District. Wickham ordered Nixon to return the gift. Rather than comply, Nixon brazenly asked Wickham to reconsider before eventually relenting and returning the money.

A more confident government and police command would have sacked Nixon. But both were afraid of Nixon's support among the Special Constabulary and within militant loyalism. Officials in the Ministry of Home Affairs believed that Nixon personally leaked his July 1923 letter of complaint to Wickham. Nixon's supporters, especially those in the Special Constabulary and the Orange Order, were indignant that their champion had not been promoted. A unionist minister, Robert Megaw, warned that some 'organisations' with 'immense membership ... were determined to go to all extremes on behalf of Nixon, and to bring about a removal of the Inspector General [Wickham] and the D.I.G. [Deputy Inspector General John Gelston].'[54]

Sir Joseph Davison, a pawn-shop owner on the York Road and Belfast's leading Orangeman, was a key supporter of Nixon and helped to finance his campaign for promotion.[55] He convened a meeting in north

Belfast to agree a strategy to lobby the government. The meeting resolved to send two senior Orangemen, Samuel Waring and Thomas Mitchell, to meet with Craig and Dawson Bates and reprimand the government. A separate deputation from the UULA also met with Dawson Bates, demanding that Nixon be promoted so that he, as a loyalist police officer risen from the ranks, would 'represent Labour' in the RUC.

Unionist labour was in revolt; its leaders, including William Grant MP, James Turkington and Samuel Waring, sent a long list of complaints to Craig. They pointed out the failings of the police to protect loyal citizens and their property, including the murder of William Twaddell MP – 'the greatest friend the working man ever had'. They contrasted the honourable Twaddell with the extravagance and incompetence of Englishmen, accusing Colonel Wickham of misusing RUC vehicles to bring his friends to tennis parties and General Solly-Flood of setting up a large and inefficient intelligence branch.[56]

Other petitions, especially those from Orange lodges in the city, were more sinister, threatening to overthrow the government if Nixon was not given senior rank. Dawson Bates even received death threats for his 'disloyalty'. A prominent Belfast Orange lodge criticised City Commissioner John Gelston for his purported 'Roman Catholic tendencies' and accused him of giving the IRA an 'open license' during the preceding two years.[57]

William Coote MP accused the government of trying to dismiss Nixon. Only his intervention, and that of his loyalist allies, stopped Dawson Bates and Wickham from doing so. Coote was a friend; he had known Nixon since he was a boy in County Cavan, on the very frontier of Ulster. Nixon, he said, was a man of proved resolve: 'When they [Craig's cabinet] slept soundly in their beds, Mr Nixon, like a man, attended to the work which settled the trouble.'[58]

Coote was right. James Craig's government had considered dismissing Nixon in the summer of 1922. General Solly-Flood suggested that Nixon should be removed for insubordination, but that Craig should first consult with certain 'organisations'. Craig refused since this would set a precedent, potentially handing a veto to the Orange Order over future public appointments or dismissals.

Dawson Bates penned a damning memorandum on Nixon for Craig. Nixon had become 'mixed up in politics … In his District he has also allowed the feeling to develop that there is only one law that for Protestants, and in consequence the Protestant hooligan is allowed to interpret in his own fashion the laws of the country'. Nonetheless, Dawson Bates recommended keeping Nixon so as not to make 'a martyr of him'. Craig agreed; Nixon stayed.[59]

Concerns within Craig's government over Nixon's behaviour escalated further during the autumn of 1923. At 10.15 p.m. on Monday, 4 September thirty-four-year-old publican John Shevlin shut up his bar on the Oldpark Road in the north of the city. He was accompanied by his brother James. Both men had good reason to be concerned about their safety. They had just moved to a predominantly loyalist area, taking over the running of the pub three weeks previously. Two days beforehand, James overheard men pointing at him and his brother, saying, '[They] won't be long coming out of that place'. Now, after walking a few yards, John Shevlin was stopped by three men who drew revolvers and shot him point-blank.

The badly wounded Shevlin stumbled from the footpath into the street where he was run over by a passing tram. When the police arrived at the scene they found John Shevlin lying with his leg trapped under a carriage. He was still alive. After fifteen minutes the tram was eventually jacked up, and Shevlin taken to the city's Mater Hospital. It was too late. He was pronounced dead on arrival.

DI Nixon appeared at the inquest and told James Shevlin he would 'leave no stone unturned' until he found his brother's killer.[60] However, the Ministry of Home Affairs appeared to believe that Nixon may have been in some way implicated in the murder and/or its cover-up. Robert

Megaw, parliamentary undersecretary at the ministry, wrote a report for Prime Minister James Craig about the incident following an urgent meeting with City Commissioner John Gelston about the case.

According to Gelston, 'a protestant gang' had murdered Shevlin to send a message to the government following cuts to the 'B' Class of the Special Constabulary and the removal of armed guards who were protecting MPs William Coote, William Grant and John Gordon. Megaw told Craig that he was shocked by such an allegation – 'I can hardly think it so' – but then went on to discuss the 'problem' of DI Nixon, 'The misfortune in regard to our chance of capturing the murderers is that Nixon is the DI in charge and his probable complicity with unrest in the neighbourhood ties his hands.' Megaw then crossed out 'unrest', replacing it with 'certain civilians'.

A few hours before John Shevlin's murder, Nixon told the policemen of the police Orange lodge – the Robert Peel Loyal Orange Lodge (LOL) – that he would no longer adhere to the regulations of the police code with respect to passing on confidential information if a detective in his district, Sergeant Kelly, was not removed. It seemed a troubling coincidence, one which Megaw also reported to Craig.[61]

Craig sent an immediate response to Megaw:

> Thank you very much for your kindness in reporting further on the subject of the Oldpark murder. I feel strongly that if N. is to be removed or transferred it should be done at once, otherwise your Ministry will be subject to very severe attack at a later date, as all the circumstances will be forgotten. I feel sure [Sir Richard Dawson] Bates will consider this aspect of the case.[62]

Stephen Tallents, the British government's Northern Ireland trouble-shooter, gave his own views on Nixon's complicity in the loyalist campaign of terror against Belfast's Catholics to his superior, John Anderson:

> With reference to a matter which I think you will remember my
> mentioning to you about Nixon when last I was in London, I
> gather that he is likely to have been mixed up with various affairs
> of the kind and probably with that one. But I am told that he is
> not of sufficiently intrepid a temperament to take part himself in
> the perpetration of acts for which he would fearlessly assist to lay
> plans.[63]

Seamus Woods, now a National Army officer, maintained an extensive intelligence network in Belfast. At the end of September 1922 he reported a shift in Craig's government against those 'who had been given unlimited powers during the [loyalist] terror campaign notably DI Nixon and all his staff'. Now that the IRA campaign was over, Nixon and his men were surplus to requirements. After he was passed over for promotion, Nixon threatened Wickham and City Commissioner Gelston, telling them that 'their lives were no long safe'.

According to Woods, the 'Nixon gang' had renewed their campaign of murder, including shooting up Catholic areas in an attempt to provoke the IRA. But elements of the Special Constabulary had moved against Nixon and his men – 'In a particular area last week in Belfast the Official Specials returned the fire of some of Nixon's gang; this is a great change in Belfast.'[64]

The murderers of Shevlin had crossed a line. Shevlin was popular in the city. Belfast City Council passed a motion condemning the murder and offering sympathies to the family. But still Craig's government prevaricated. Rather than directly confronting Nixon on the question of discipline and even conspiracy to murder, the government waited for other grounds on which to act against him.

Their opportunity arrived in January 1924 after Nixon was elected as the Worshipful Master of Robert Peel LOL. Before partition the British Administration in Dublin Castle had banned police membership of any 'political association', which included the Orange Order. That decision was reversed after the establishment of the RUC – at least when it came to the Orange Order and other affiliated 'loyal orders'.

The officers and committee members of Robert Peel LOL were among Nixon's most devoted supporters, including Head Constable John Giff, Sergeant Alex Sterritt and Constable Henry Gordon. Among the lodge's (and Nixon's) political patrons were Sir Joseph Davison, Robert Lynn MP and Richard Tregenna. Other supporters of the lodge included Councillor William Bickerstaff and George Huey, both 'B' Specials commanders and connected to the UULA. Robert Peel LOL concentrated James Craig's most dangerous and powerful loyalist critics in one place. He was quick to see the threat.[65]

In early January Colonel Wickham was informed that John Nixon and some members of the lodge had made speeches about political matters, including warning against any revision of the border under a prospective Boundary Commission. He issued a circular on 17 January reminding serving police officers not to make political speeches. Nixon's response was to double down. On 29 January he gave a speech at a Robert Peel lodge meeting in Clifton Street Orange Hall in which he said that the Free State military had encircled Northern Ireland with arms provided by the British government but, 'if the loyal men in Ulster stood together and did what they said they would do ... not an inch of Ulster soil would be yielded'.

Nixon's west Belfast ally, 'B' Specials commander Harry Taylor praised Nixon for his 'not an inch' exhortation (a rallying cry taken up by hardline unionists throughout the twentieth century). Two MPs, Harry Burn and William Grant, were also present. Burn made a speech in which he warned the lodge about traitors within, 'what they had to fear in Ulster was not Romanism, but rotten Protestantism'.[66] After Nixon's speech was reported in the press, Wickham moved immediately to suspend him from duty. He then summoned Nixon to a meeting in his office on 21 February,

A TERRIBLE VICTORY

during which Nixon refused to answer questions. A misconduct hearing was scheduled but the journalists who had reported on the Robert Peel lodge meeting and were called as witnesses did not show up.

Nixon now made a sensational claim: that the nominated president of the court of inquiry, County Inspector Frederick Britten, was part of a conspiracy against him. He could produce a witness who had overheard County Inspector John McNally say that Britten had called Nixon 'the companion of the scum of the Shankill Road' and that the government was waiting for an opportunity to serve him his 'deserts'. The conservation took place in December – before Nixon's alleged offences – at the Victoria Hotel in Newry, County Down.

McNally hit back, telling Wickham that he had stayed at the hotel on 5 December 1923. He met District Inspector Thomas Fletcher in the dining room for dinner. Also in the room, at another table, was Samuel Williamson, a travelling salesman and ex-RIC sergeant. Williamson worked as a clerk at RIC headquarters in Dublin but was dismissed from the RIC for forging commendation letters. This was the so-called witness in Nixon's 'fairy story'. Both McNally and Fletcher were southern Irish. Britten was English. These were exactly the type of officers that Nixon felt were unfairly promoted above him.

The Ministry of Home Affairs cancelled the court of inquiry, citing intimidation by Nixon and his supporters.[67] Prime Minister James Craig asked the Governor of Northern Ireland, the Duke of Abercorn, to travel to Belfast to sign a formal order to dismiss Nixon. Abercorn consented but was furious to discover that, as he travelled on a ferry from England to Belfast, the Minister for Home Affairs Sir Richard Dawson Bates was heading in the other direction. Dawson Bates had contrived to avoid putting his signature on the order to fire Nixon – alongside that of Abercorn – knowing that it would prompt an angry response from loyalists. Samuel Watt, the permanent secretary of the Ministry of Home Affairs, signed the order on 28 February. Officials in London considered stripping Nixon of his MBE but backed down following advice from Craig and his ministers.[68]

Wickham moved quickly to transfer a number of Nixon's men out of Belfast. Henry Gordon was relocated to rural north Down. It was an unpopular decision among the rank and file.[69] Gordon resigned and emigrated to California – he received a certificate of 'good character' for his RUC service.[70]

Mass protest meetings were organised in the wake of Nixon's dismissal, including by the Orange Order.[71] Alex Agnew, a Shankill loyalist and trade-union leader, addressed one such meeting. Nixon, he said, was a unionist but crucially he was also for the working man: 'It was all very well to go out with the big drum and the Union Jack, but when it came to Saturday night Union Jacks would not fill their bellies (Applause).' At a packed meeting at the city's Ulster Hall, Nixon was greeted on the platform with a rendition of 'For He's a Jolly Good Fellow'.[72]

Nixon's old friend William Coote could not contain his anger. In the Northern Irish parliament, he delivered a withering condemnation of Craig for his treacherous behaviour. Government minister Herbert Dixon claimed that Coote suffered a stroke as he cited the biblical verse, 'Whom the Gods wish to destroy they first make ...' Coote died a few months later.[73]

British government officials worried that Northern Ireland might 'turn [militant] labour'. Nixon was supported not only by trade unionists but by leaders of the Orange Order like Sir Joseph Davison, ex-Imperial Guards and 'B' Specials commanders such as Harry Taylor and William Bickerstaff. The only option for Craig was to remind unionists of the enemy outside the gates, that the Free State was plotting against Northern Ireland and unionists needed to stay united. Craig was convinced that 'a tap of the big [Orange] drum would restore substantial unity at once in the reach of the Government party in the counties'.[74]

Nixon was a symbol more than a leader. He was a poor orator.[75] However, the perception that he was the man who defeated the IRA in Belfast – and his working-man, loyalist labour sympathies – were enough for him to secure a seat on Belfast City Council in elections in August 1924. The ever-versatile ruling Ulster Unionist Party embarked on a strategy of co-option. Nixon agreed to be put forward as the party's candidate for the Belfast North constituency in the 1925 Northern Irish parliamentary elections. This association with official unionism blunted Nixon's appeal to voters and he was not elected, largely due to working-class dissent over the government's economic record (as well as a large Catholic, nationalist minority vote in the constituency).[76]

Nixon's short-lived co-option meant that he had squandered the potential of leading a mass populist movement in Northern Ireland energised by disenchanted ex-servicemen, policemen and trade unionists, similar to those on the European continent. Nonetheless, in 1929 Nixon was elected to the Northern Irish House of Commons, this time as an independent unionist MP for Woodvale (in west Belfast), a seat he held until his death in 1949. Nixon's much-used election pitch was that he was against 'Red Tape, the Broken Covenant, and Betrayal of Cavan, Monaghan and Donegal, Big Jobs and Salaries for Lawyers and Members of the Government and their Officials'.[77]

Nixon remained popular with some of the rank of the file of the RUC, constantly championing increases in police pay and benefits. But he lost none of his resentment towards its leadership. When in 1944 the head of RUC Special Branch, DI William Moffatt, met with Nixon to discuss a corruption case Nixon subjected him to 'a barrage of insult'. Moffatt wrote in his diary that 'it is impossible to imagine the mentality of the person who recommended such an uncouth boor for the position of D/I in the RIC'.[78]

Between 1929 and 1937 Nixon voted with the government on only fourteen occasions.[79] He insisted on wearing a heavy overcoat in the parliamentary chamber and a sombrero hat. He used to throw down his large black notebook with a crash, which, according to James Kelly, 'invariably sent a shiver along the Government benches, for generally his information on local scandals and misconduct was on target, mostly gleaned from his police connections'. He especially enjoyed taunting the long-serving Minister for Home Affairs Richard Dawson Bates, who resigned in 1943, damaged by allegations levied by Nixon that he received corrupt payments from a Belfast property developer. Nixon was also an early and unrelenting critic of appeasement of Germany, attacking the former cabinet minister and the cousin of Winston Churchill, Lord Londonderry, for his close ties to Berlin. (His old nemesis Eoin O'Duffy was a supporter of the Nazi regime.)[80]

Nixon's record as a ruthless police commander between 1920 and 1922 may have been an electoral asset. But for the rest of his life he was widely believed to have been responsible for the McMahon murders. Occasionally whispered rumours burst out into the open. In August 1925 the *Derry Journal* published a letter from James Gillespie, a former RIC sergeant and now a resident of the Irish Free State. Gillespie – who never served in Belfast – claimed that Nixon, Head Constable John Giff and a police officer he called McNaghten were all 'trying to avoid the ghosts of a certain family' who had been murdered in Belfast.

'McNaghten' appears to refer to a Catholic police officer, Constable Patrick Naughten, who served in the Irish Guards during the First World War. An attempt had been made to kill Naughten and his family when a bomb was thrown into their house off the Ravenhill Road in east Belfast on 5 May 1922. Nobody was hurt; local republicans blamed loyalists for the attack.[81]

Nixon sued for libel. In evidence he swore that he 'took no part in the McMahon murders'. He was represented in his case against Gillespie and the *Derry Journal* by the attorney general of Northern Ireland, Richard Best. Nixon's legal team set out the appalling gravity of the charge made by Gillespie. This was not a murder but the 'massacre of a whole family ... There had been something Oriental in the savagery of the McMahon massacre – the blotting out of the males of one family. It was a crime which shook the whole community and burned deep and broad into the public mind.'[82] The perpetrator remained a mystery. Nixon said he suffered from 'mental agony, distress and fear' as a consequence of the malicious rumours. The court found in favour of Nixon who was awarded £1,000 in damages.

Two court officials subsequently accused Nixon of trying to illegally interfere in the jury selection for his libel trial. During an encounter in a Belfast street, Nixon had handed them lists of jurors he wanted to hear his case. Nixon stated that he had made a mistake but told the court that 'his life was at stake and that it was vital for him to prove his innocence'. The Lord Chief Justice of Northern Ireland, Sir Denis Henry, criticised Nixon for his 'carelessness' but did not jail him for contempt of court.[83]

Ten years later Nixon again sued for libel. This time the defendant was the publisher of the memoir of an IRA officer. Derry-born Charles McGuinness claimed to have been a polar explorer and a customs officer in the Soviet Union. He had served in the British Army before switching sides, fighting with Boer insurgents in South Africa and later with the IRA. (He would join the International Brigades on the republican side of the Spanish Civil War.) Metheun and Co. of London published McGuinness' autobiography *Nomad* in 1934, selling several hundred copies. Commenting on the 'Belfast pogrom', McGuinness wrote that:

> The wiping out of the McMahon family of Belfast, father and sons, who were in no way affiliated with the IRA will for ever remain as a stain on the well-spattered escutcheons of Ulster. One man, who has since been elevated to Parliamentary honours was charged

GHOSTS OF A FAMILY

with the order of execution of the McMahons, and is luckier than he knows to be alive today.[84]

Northern Ireland's attorney general again represented Nixon – Sir Anthony Babington told the court in February 1935 that Nixon was gravely ill and unable to attend. The libel case proceeded without him. Nixon nonetheless requested that Colonel Wickham and Robert Lynn, the former unionist MP and the editor of the *Northern Whig*, give evidence to the court to support his case. RUC headquarters did not directly decline the request for Wickham to attend but rather opaquely replied saying that a senior officer would be present in court to address any police matters relating to the murders.

Babington laid out Nixon's case on similar grounds to those of the previous libel trial. The crime was the worst 'massacre' that Belfast had seen in its recent history. The culprits were as yet undiscovered and 'to lay the responsibility for it at the door of any person was the most horrible charge that could be made ... They were murders for which anyone could yet suffer the supreme penalty.' To be called the McMahons' murderer was 'to be held up now and hereafter to the hatred and contempt of all citizens for all time'.

Nixon also called Head Constable John Giff, who had served with Nixon in Brown's Square Barracks, and Robert Pakenham, the former Head Constable of the Special Constabulary detachment at Court Street Barracks, as witnesses. During his summing up, the Lord Chief Justice, Sir William Moore, told the court that the murderers of the McMahons were 'a disgrace'. He hoped 'their conscience, please God, will visit them yet'. He then awarded John Nixon £1,250 in damages.[85] Nixon's libel victories did nothing to diminish rumours that he had murdered the McMahons. For Catholic Belfast – and the Irish government – Nixon and his 'Brown's Square gang' had already been found guilty.

124

CHAPTER FIVE

The Brown's Square Gang

SHORTLY AFTER 1 A.M. ON 24 March 1922 Constables Alex Sterritt and Henry Gordon made their way on foot to Carlisle Circus. There they entered a corporation hut and picked up a sledgehammer. Holding it before them, Sterritt, Gordon and three other police officers struck out up the nearby Antrim Road before turning off towards Kinnaird Terrace. Wielding the sledgehammer, the group smashed their way into the McMahons' home: 'All the male members of the party were taken into the drawing room and placed against the wall. One lad of 14 years succeeded in hiding himself under a Chesterfield [couch], but the remainder were shot one after the other.'

This was the account given by RIC Constable Michael Furlong to the IRA, reproduced in the Nixon memo. Of all the RIC constables suspected of being part of Nixon's murder gang, Henry Gordon's name was repeatedly passed to Sinn Féin investigators by relatives of victims and other policemen. IRA intelligence even suggested that Gordon was a roving hitman, turning up in different parts of Ireland to murder IRA volunteers.[1]

Gordon was born into a dying milieu. His father was the land steward on a succession of gentry-owned estates. His first home was at Glynwood in County Westmeath in the Irish midlands, an estate famed

125

for its herd of cattle, and which passed to ten-year-old Travers Dames-Longworth – close in age to Henry Gordon – in 1907.[2]

The Gordons later moved to County Leitrim, where they lived on the lushly wooded grounds of Lord Harlech's estate on the banks of the River Shannon. Harlech's tenants demanded better conditions and the purchase of their holdings. As a child Henry Gordon experienced land agitation and even occasional violence. Joining the police offered a much more secure livelihood than the fading prospects of his father's employment.

Henry Gordon enlisted in the police aged nineteen on 4 August 1914. Six months later he volunteered for war service. Gordon was an outstanding soldier and finished the war as a sergeant in 2nd Battalion, Irish Guards. He suffered a wound to the head at Passchendaele on the western front in 1917 but appears to have fully recovered.[3] By the time Gordon returned to Ireland, the 'big house' at Glynwood had been burned to the ground. A second County Westmeath home owned by Travers Dames-Longworth, who also served in the Irish Guards during the war, was burned soon afterwards.[4]

Gordon recommenced his RIC service in Belfast. In early 1920 he was sent to train new recruits to the RIC at Gormanston Camp near Dublin – the force was being rapidly expanded to counter IRA violence, recruiting the Auxiliary Division and the infamous 'Black and Tans'. Gordon returned to Belfast and 'C' District in the summer of 1921.[5]

On 12 February 1922 a young Catholic man called William Tennyson was found lying dead in a street near Brown's Square Barracks. During the subsequent inquest the Tennyson family's lawyer, Alex Lynn, asked DI Nixon whether Constable Henry Gordon was on duty on the night of the murders. Lynn then alleged that evidence had been concealed and that Gordon was directly implicated in the case.

Lynn stopped just short of calling Gordon a murderer but was nonetheless removed from the court after he condemned the RIC – 'they ought to send to Scotland Yard or some other place which would do something to bring the assassins to justice'. DI Nixon angrily objected to Lynn's outburst. Gordon was 'one of his best men', he protested, and had saved a number of lives on the night of Tennyson's death, but witnesses to his heroism were too afraid to come forward.[6]

A surviving photograph of Henry Gordon shows a thin-lipped, broad-shouldered man with a large nose and a sweep of brown hair. He is wearing a carefully knotted tie, a blazer, and is staring directly at the camera with his grey eyes. He exudes the authority of a man who has done well in the army. On his jacket lapel is a masonic pin. Gordon, vilified in Catholic Belfast, was extremely popular within the police. In 1923 his fellow constables elected him to serve on Northern Ireland's Police Representative Body.[7]

Henry Gordon was one of a group of tough Belfast policemen who were sent to trouble spots. Another was Alex Sterritt. The son of a farmer, Alex Sterritt was born in 1884 near Milford in north Donegal. Powerfully built and nearly six feet tall, he joined the RIC at the age of twenty-two and was stationed in Belfast from the summer of 1912 onwards. There he worked as a plain-clothes constable under Nixon, making successive arrests of IRA volunteers in 'C' District, including IRA officer Charles McWhinney of Stanhope Street in early March 1922.[8] In the summer of 1922 Sterritt was given a financial reward for his excellent police service at the instigation of DI Nixon and General Solly-Flood.[9]

According to Stephen Tallents, Sterritt was 'the real force behind Nixon'. Somewhat surprisingly Tallents reported that Alex Sterritt and his brother William – also a police constable – enjoyed good relations with the IRA in their home district of Donegal, which now lay in the Free State: 'During a recent visit to their family home across the border the Sterritt brothers entertained to a "big night" all the leading republicans of the district. But the interpretation of this incident is not clear.'[10]

The commander of the local IRA battalion was Neal Blaney, a resourceful anti-treaty leader who had continuously targeted loyalists in the Milford area. Blaney claimed that he had established a business relationship during the Civil War with a loyalist from whom he bought a large quantity of UVF rifles for use against the National Army.[11] Such a relationship may not only have been about money. Henry Wilson and other loyalist extremists hoped that the anti-treaty side would topple the provisional government since that would destroy the Anglo-Irish Treaty and possibly lead to British reoccupation of the twenty-six counties.[12]

Nixon, Gordon and Sterritt – all located at Brown's Square Barracks – were the three members of the RIC identified by the Norfolk Regiment as being behind a campaign of murder and terror in Belfast. In April 1922 Lieutenant Eric Hayes submitted an intelligence report of a suspected attack by what he called the 'Brown's Square Murder Gang'.

Shortly after midnight on 9 April a Crossley tender containing two uniformed men and several in plain clothes drove up Flax Street and turned into the largely Catholic Havana Street area of north Belfast. There the lorry stopped and a group of plain-clothes men inside debussed. The lorry returned to the Crumlin Road and was not seen again. The plain-clothes men then went around the back of a house and attempted to enter it. A group of terrified women inside the house shouted to their neighbours for help. Lieutenant Hayes described how 'men turned out with arms and opened fire on the raiders who returned the fire … finally the raiding party retreated across waste ground in the direction of the Marrowbone where it is believed they picked up their car'.

The intended target may have been John O'Kane, resident at 65 Havana Street, who was a volunteer in the Ardoyne Company of the IRA. Hayes concluded: 'This party [of raiders] is probably the party from Brown's Square which always appears when murders of RCs are carried out or attempted.' In the days afterwards a deputation of residents, led by the local Catholic priest, petitioned the British Army to keep a patrol in the area at all times and to permanently exclude the Special Constabulary from entering Ardoyne.[13]

Eight days after the Ardoyne 'battle', Lieutenant Hayes wrote another report on the Brown's Square gang. Loyalists in north Belfast had been firing from Ballycarry Street into the predominantly Catholic Marrowbone area. On 19 April Norfolk soldiers discovered a group of police led by DI Nixon in a Lancia armoured car 'wandering about in Ballygarry [sic] Street in a very mysterious manner. Plain clothes constables Stirret [sic] and Gordon, who are stated to be members of the Brown's Square Murder Gang were there'. Nixon told the soldiers that he was there to arrest Protestant looters and that he had fired shots in order to stop rioting in the area. Hayes did not believe Nixon's explanation: '[Nixon] has seldom if ever been known to arrest or in any way interfere with Protestants during the riots ... It is possible that this party were occupied in causing isolated RC householders to leave the district by force'.[14]

Of the twenty-six members of the regular police identified in Sinn Féin reports or testimonies as belonging to the police murder gang, only six were from Northern Ireland.[15] The rest were from what became the Irish Free State, including Brown's Square's Head Constable John Giff and Head Constable Robert Pakenham. (Only three were Catholics: Sergeant Christy Clarke, Sergeant Patrick Clancy and Constable Matthew Maher.)[16]

A veteran of the 1886 Belfast riots, Head Constable John Giff was in his late fifties during the 'pogrom'. Even by RIC standards he was an exceptionally large and imposing man. In 1913 he was promoted to head constable and served in Kilkenny, close to his birthplace and family in the south-east of Ireland, before returning to Belfast four years later. He had an outstanding police record.

Head Constable Robert Pakenham, like Henry Gordon, grew up on a landed estate in the west of Ireland. Pakenham's father, a former soldier in the Connaught Rangers, worked as a gamekeeper on an estate in County Mayo in the west of Ireland. After labouring on the estate for a time, Robert Pakenham joined the RIC at the age of twenty-two in 1895. Pakenham moved to Belfast in 1904 and was promoted to detective sergeant. In the early 1920s he was in charge of the Special Constabulary at Court Street Barracks, near the Crumlin Road and in Nixon's District.[17]

Nixon, Gordon and Sterritt all had strong family connections to 'lost Ulster', those counties left out of Northern Ireland. Their relatives in Donegal and Cavan had signed the Ulster Covenant and drilled with the UVF. The radicalism of these men, contemptuous of a Belfast establishment that had 'thrown to the wolves' loyalists (and police dependents) in their native counties, chimes with the experiences of frontier peoples in other parts of Europe at this time. The number of military veterans in the group of policemen named in IRA reports is also striking – these men had become accustomed to the violence of war; they adopted an uncompromising approach on the streets of Belfast.[18]

Constable Andrew McCloskey of Leopold Street Barracks told Sinn Féin investigators that many of the police murderers under Nixon's command worked as plain-clothes constables. These men were 'out for the purpose of shooting IRA men and failing them, shooting any Catholic'. He named these constables as Henry Gordon, Berry Preston, William Sherwood, Thomas Topping and Thomas Haire. With the exception of Haire, all these men were ex-Irish Guards. (Sherwood grew up near the Harlech estate in County Leitrim – both he and Henry Gordon were also close in age.)[19] Sergeant John Murphy of 'B' District, himself an Irish Guards veteran, identified three more constables, ex-Irish Guardsmen – Sergeant Patrick Clancy, Constable Alexander Earl and Constable Edwin Caldwell – whom he said were also responsible for murders.[20]

Sinn Féin intelligence reports offered different motives to explain the Nixon gang's murder campaign. According to a commission established by Sinn Féin to investigate police atrocities – the 1922 Commission – Nixon was 'a religious fanatic' who frequently preached in the police mission. His bigotry also brought him material benefits: 'It was mainly [due] to this that he owes his promotion.' Alex Sterritt was reported as being a failed policeman – 'a dud' – until the murder gang was formed: 'though still a constable, he is [now] looked on as a man who wields great power'.[21]

The first Brown's Square reprisal, according to the Nixon memo, was the murder of three republicans – Edward Trodden, John McFadden and John Gaynor – on 26 September 1920 in revenge for the killing of a police constable a few days earlier. A party of RIC under County Inspector Richard Harrison left Springfield Road Barracks in 'B' District, separated into three groups and proceeded to shoot up the Falls Road and Kashmir Road areas of west Belfast. Harrison and a group of men then moved to the house of Edward Trodden, a forty-year-old barber and an unsuccessful Sinn Féin candidate in that year's Belfast Corporation's elections. They entered the house where they pulled Trodden out of bed, dragged him downstairs by the hair and shot him dead in his backyard.[22]

The 1922 Commission report stated that Trodden's murderers were Constable Alex Sterritt, Constable Berry Preston and a policeman called 'Norton'.[23] Head Constable Giff, Sergeant William Reid and Constable James Glover killed McFadden. Giff's party also went to the house of John Gaynor and shot him dead in his bedroom. Sergeant Patrick Clancy and Constable William Reid did the shooting while Giff held Gaynor's parents at gunpoint in the family kitchen.

According to the Nixon memo, Giff then bayoneted Gaynor's body, fired shots into other rooms in the house and threatened the victim's mother after she refused to tell him the whereabouts of her other son.

The British Army created a 'secret file' on the killings. (This is now missing.)[24] An inquest found that McFadden and Trodden were killed unlawfully by 'unknown persons', whereas Gaynor was lawfully killed

GHOSTS OF A FAMILY

while resisting arrest. Commissioner Gelston reported that Gaynor had been shot while rushing towards a policeman with the intention of seizing his rifle. Belfast IRA commander Seamus Woods claimed that he acquired a copy of a sworn statement in which Constable James Glover admitted to shooting Gaynor, but in self-defence. (Glover was killed by the IRA on 10 June 1921.)[25] In the House of Commons, Joe Devlin angrily accused the government of ignoring police murder.[26]

Nixon was still in Fermanagh during this period so cannot be held directly responsible for these first murders.[27] RIC County Inspector Richard Harrison, lead liaison with the Special Constabulary, also had a good alibi. On 26 September 1920, the day of these murders, Harrison was on special duties in the south-west of Ireland – sent to County Clare after a series of police murders – where he remained for over a month before returning to Belfast.[28]

The Nixon memo goes on to state that this '[murder] gang was given over to Nixon' after his arrival to command the city's 'C' District on 1 November 1920. Just after midnight on 27 January 1921 the gang attacked again. The trigger for reprisal was the IRA's killing of two RIC constables a few hours earlier. Three men entered a boarding house at 1 Bray Street in the west of the city and shot dead a twenty-six-year-old chemist called Michael Garvey. An RIC constable called Thomas Gillan saw Harrison, Nixon and Pakenham in a Ford car driving down the Shankill Road near Bray Street in the minutes after the shootings. (The 1922 Commission report instead implicates Nixon, Constables Alex Sterritt and Berry Preston.)

The murderers' intelligence was correct; their victim was a volunteer in the IRA. Michael Garvey had put his chemistry skills to use while serving in the engineering company (bomb-making) of his local IRA battalion.[29]

Margaret Morgan, Garvey's landlady, gave evidence at the inquest that three men carried out the killing; one was clearly wearing a police uniform and a helmet. Another wore a hat with black veil extending down to his waist so as to obscure his features. The third man she did not see clearly. After the men left the house, Morgan pulled down the window and shouted, 'You murderers, you have murdered the boy!' The killers joined five other men and stood on the street ignoring Margaret Morgan's shouts until they were picked up by a brown-coloured lorry a few minutes later. The murder was reported to the nearby Leopold Barracks. DI Nixon arrived shortly afterwards and took charge of the murder scene.[30]

According to the Nixon memo, the next victims of the murder gang were Patrick and Daniel Duffin, both prominent members of the west Belfast IRA. Hugh McShane, an IRA officer, recalled that at the time of their deaths the Duffin brothers were in the early stages of planning an operation 'to disrupt the water supply at Aldergrove [Royal Air Force] Aerodrome'. The two brothers were shot in their house at Clonard Gardens near the Falls Road on 23 April 1921.[31]

The inquest file contains evidence from the dead men's older brother John. The Duffin family heard a knock on the door of their house at 11.50 p.m. Patrick, who was due to get married a few days later, came upstairs and asked John what to do. John told him to open the door as he thought it was a police search for weapons. It was better to comply than resist. John then heard a voice telling his brother to 'Put up your hands!' followed by the sound of shots being fired. He looked down and saw a man in a fawn coat wearing a tweed cap but could not make out his face.

The next morning John Duffin went to the police to report the murders. The killers had left a dog in the house. DI John Ferriss went to the Duffins' residence and took the dog away. A doctor who examined the bodies of the two brothers in the kitchen gave evidence that both had been shot in the chest.[32] The Nixon memo named Sergeant Christy Clarke, Sergeant George Hicks, Constable Caldwell and Constable

Golding [*sic*] as the gang members who carried out the killings. Hicks fired the fatal shots, using a silencer.

There are some contradictions in republican accounts implicating Sergeant Christy Clarke in the Duffin murders. One claimed that Sergeant Clarke left his dog in the Duffins' house after the killing of the two brothers. However, the 1922 Commission report suggested that the dog belonged to Constable Thomas Earle and that Sergeant Hicks, Constables Haire, Earle, Golden, Cooke and Glover were responsible for the Duffin killings. There was no mention of Christy Clarke or Constable Caldwell.[33]

The Nixon memo concluded that the murder of the Duffins was a reprisal for the shooting and wounding of DI John Ferriss, the forty-five-year-old Catholic district inspector recently appointed to take charge of 'B' District in west Belfast. This is impossible. Ferriss was not shot by the IRA until the following month. He was attacked and wounded as he left a meeting with a parish priest at St Paul's Church on the Falls Road.[34]

The more likely instigators of the Duffins' murders were policemen from the RIC Auxiliary Division. The Auxiliaries or 'Auxies', largely made up of demobilised officers of the British Army, had a limited presence in Ulster. They were mostly deployed in the three other Irish provinces. But Auxiliary units occasionally travelled to Belfast for supply, logistical reasons or to go on leave.

The Auxiliaries had many close connections to the regular RIC and the Special Constabulary in Belfast. Thomas Stewart, a native of County Antrim and a cadet from 'Q' Company – a unit later implicated in murders in Belfast – had recently been sent on attachment to the Special Constabulary in the city.[35] Constable Henry Gordon had been stationed at the RIC depot at Gormanston from 9 November 1920 until 8 June 1921 before the murders of Kerr, Halfpenny and McBride.[36] Alexander McCabe, a cousin of DI John Nixon and a neighbour of Henry Gordon's family in County Cavan, served in the Irish Guards. He was attached to

'F' Company of the Auxiliaries, which quickly gained a reputation for reprisals and murders. He transferred to the RUC in Belfast in 1922 and remained in the police until his retirement in 1954.[37]

IRA officer Joseph Murray recalled that the arrival of 'P' Company from the Auxiliary Division in late April 1921 spread fear among republicans in the city. A response was required: 'We concluded that this company of Auxiliaries had come to the city to clean up and wipe out the IRA and that the morale of the rank and file, together with the morale of the nationalist population, was in danger. We then mobilised a party of about twelve men armed with hand grenades and revolvers.'

Roger McCorley and Seamus Woods searched the city during 23 April but failed to locate any of 'the Auxies'. As night fell McCorley and Woods called off the attack. Minutes later, Woods, McCorley and Joseph Murray were walking home along Donegall Place – Murray on one side of the street, the two IRA commanders on the other – when they caught sight of Auxiliaries John Bales and Ernest Bolam ahead of them:

> I made an effort to cross the street to join Woods and McCorley when a tram came between us, and stopped. I ran around the tram and as I did so I heard four or five shots. When I passed the end of the tram I saw two Auxiliaries lying on the ground and saw McCorley disappear around the corner of Castle Lane.

Bolam was killed in the first shots. Bales made it across the street, pursued by McCorley and Woods who shot him multiple times – Bales died the following day in hospital. A passing detective constable fired a number of shots after the fleeing IRA men; none hit their target. (A pedestrian and a woman travelling on the tramcar were wounded in the cross-fire.)[38]

Seamus McKenna, a tough and dedicated leader of the IRA's 1st Battalion in Belfast, recalled the Auxiliaries' response to the killings:

'There was something like twenty-two of them in the hotel that night. They had come from Sligo for a rest cure in Belfast. When the RIC contacted the hotel and told the Auxiliaries of the shooting, they dashed out and, guided no doubt by RIC, raided public houses in the Catholic area nearest the shooting.'[39]

A more drastic Auxiliary reprisal soon followed. IRA officer Seán Montgomery had been part of McCorley and Woods' group. He was stopped by an auxiliary who ordered a passer-by, who also happened to be an IRA volunteer, to search Montgomery. If the auxiliary had known who they were they would have been shot on the spot – 'ten minutes later the Falls Road was full of the RIC and Auxiliarys [*sic*]... the RIC murder gang and some Auxiliaries were sent up to Clonard Street and shot dead the Duffin brothers'. Montgomery went with a group of IRA volunteers to ambush the police when they returned to the Duffin house but missed the visit by DI Ferriss by a few hours.[40]

Sergeant Christy Clarke knew that the IRA were determined to kill him. A native of Offaly in the Irish midlands, he continued to live in west Belfast with his wife and eight children. He did, however, take some precautions, wearing a bullet-proof vest and varying his routine. He had spent most of his two decades of police service in Belfast; his wife Alice was from the city. Clarke was well-known in Belfast's popular greyhound racing and hare-coursing scene, acting as a timekeeper during races at Celtic Park.

On 13 March Christy Clarke attended the funerals of two Catholic RIC constables who had been shot dead. His wife also attended the burial at Milltown Cemetery and noticed two men following her husband. She attempted to reach him as he left the cemetery, before he boarded a tram, but could not push her way through the crowd.

As Clarke alighted from the tram on the Springfield Road, both he and Constable Edwin Caldwell were surrounded by a group of IRA volunteers who opened fire. A bullet hit his protective vest. He was subsequently shot five times – in the legs, shoulder and head. IRA officer Patrick McCarragher then turned his revolver towards Caldwell and pulled the trigger – the gun jammed. Caldwell ran but McCarragher chased after him, put him up against a wall and again pulled the trigger. The revolver still would not fire. Roger McCorley recalled that Caldwell did not draw his own weapon: 'The policeman [Caldwell] was so scared he was not able to move at all with the result that McCarragher got away in spite of the jammed gun.'[41]

After his death the nationalist *Irish News* reported that Christy Clarke was exceptionally popular on the Falls Road.[42] Local Catholics had saved Clarke's life some months previously. On 27 August 1921 Clarke questioned two young Protestant men called William Campbell and James Brown who were acting suspiciously outside Magee's pub on the Springfield Road. Brown pulled out a revolver and fired at Clarke but missed. A crowd then set upon the men, beating them severely, before Clarke intervened and arrested his would-be-murderers. Such accounts complicated the picture drawn by the IRA of the police sergeant as a serial murderer.[43]

The Nixon gang were also implicated by republicans in three reprisal murders in the early hours of 12 June 1921. Two days previously Roger McCorley, Seamus Woods and at least four other IRA volunteers shot dead Constable James Glover on the Falls Road in west Belfast. Glover, standing by a cinema near Cupar Street, was struck by six bullets at close range, four in the back, one in the jaw and another in the neck. His companions Sergeant James Sullivan and Constable Hugh Sharkey were also wounded in the attack.[44]

The first of the victims of 12 June was Alex McBride, a thirty-two-year-old Belfast publican who lived in north Belfast. According to the Nixon memo the driver of a Crossley tender was told to report to Nixon at 11.20 p.m. on the night of 11 June. The driver was told that Constable Glass was replacing him for the night. Glass then drove Nixon to the

Crumlin Road in the north of the city where they picked up a group of policemen. The lorry was subsequently stopped at a curfew checkpoint manned by Constables James McDonald and John Rogan near the Sacred Heart Catholic church in Ardoyne. Nixon was accompanied by Head Constable Giff, Sergeant Reid, Constables James Russell, Glass, Sterritt, Gordon and Norris. Two other constables are named – 'Caher' and 'Hare'. These are likely to be references to Constables Joseph Carr and Thomas Haire.[45]

The gang arrived at McBride's spacious residence at 8 Cardigan Drive, just off the Cliftonville Road, at approximately 1 a.m. Elizabeth McBride opened the door. Nixon told her that he was bringing her husband to the barracks for questioning. Alex McBride was taken out of the house in his nightclothes. Minutes later Elizabeth heard the sound of shots. Her husband's body was discovered the next morning. Nixon then brazenly called back to the house the following day to commiserate with Elizabeth on the death of her husband. (The 1922 Commission report says nothing about Nixon speaking to Elizabeth McBride during her husband's abduction or what followed. It does, however, add a detail that rosary beads were found in Alex McBride's hands when his body was found.)

Evidence originally given at the inquest offered a very different account of the murder. RIC Constable David Boyd testified that he discovered McBride's body on a lane leading from the Crumlin Road to the Ballysillan Road in the north-west of the city at 4.30 a.m. on 12 June. McBride was dressed in a nightshirt; he was also wearing trousers, a waistcoat and a hat. (There is no mention of rosary beads in Boyd's report, although Boyd did find some business receipts in the dead man's pockets.)

Elizabeth McBride's evidence to the inquest recalled that after 1 a.m. she saw a large open-top lorry park up outside her home. The men inside appeared to be in uniform. The majority 'were wearing soft caps, hanging on one side, the remainder had dark caps as worn by the police'. Alex McBride opened the upstairs window and asked them what they wanted. He was told to 'open the door'. He went downstairs and then returned accompanied by two police officers wearing a uniform of 'a lighter shade'.

One of the men had a fair moustache; someone spoke with an English accent. They told Alex McBride to get dressed. McBride asked them why they were taking him away, to which one of the men replied that they needed for him for 'identification purposes' at the nearest military barracks. McBride asked them if that was the Antrim Road Barracks. One of the men then turned to the other, saying, 'Where are the nearest barracks?' The other replied, 'I think Holywood.'

Elizabeth pleaded with the men not to take her husband. Instead, four or five other men came up the stairs and escorted the hurriedly dressed McBride outside. Elizabeth went upstairs and from the window watched the lorry drive away. Some minutes later she heard two shots fired followed by a brief pause and then five more. A Royal Army Medical Corps doctor, Lieutenant James Loughridge, certified that McBride was shot multiple times, including in the head and chest.[46]

The evidence given by Elizabeth McBride complicates the attribution of her husband's murder to the RIC. The regular RIC did not wear 'soft caps, hanging on one side'. Neither did the military who wore caps or helmets. The Auxiliary Division of the RIC wore sloping berets. Elizabeth McBride's description of the men who abducted her husband bears no physical resemblance to DI Nixon. One spoke with an English accent. Neither knew the location of the nearest (military) barracks, wrongly presuming that it was in the County Down village of Holywood. The men who abducted Alexander McBride appear to have been a mixture of Auxiliaries and other police.[47]

After killing McBride, the Nixon memo stated that the murder gang then went to the home of Malachy Halfpenny at 21 Herbert Street in Ardoyne. Halfpenny had served as a gunner in the Royal Field Artillery

GHOSTS OF A FAMILY

in the First World War. He had recently found work as a postman and was a member of the Ancient Order of Hibernians. Constables Gordon and Sterritt dragged him from his bed. Halfpenny put up a struggle but Gordon and Sterritt eventually pulled and pushed him into a Crossley tender. Halfpenny's body was found the next morning in waste ground in the Ligoniel area; it had been thrown across a barbed wire fence and was 'riddled with bullets'.

The memo added that residents reported hearing Halfpenny moaning in agony for nearly twenty minutes. He had been shot seventeen times, the soles of his feet had been pierced with a bayonet and he had been castrated. It noted that, 'Head Constable Giff always used a bayonet on his victims, as he considered it prolonged his agony and he didn't believe in giving them an easy death.'

The Halfpenny family found themselves under attack again on the day of the funeral. As Malachy Halfpenny's coffin proceeded through north Belfast, the police struggled to hold back a loyalist mob which threw stones and swore at the mourners.[48]

At the inquest, Lieutenant Loughridge related that he found four wounds on Halfpenny's body, one through the right arm between the shoulder and the elbow, another through the right wrist and another through the right thigh including an entrance and exit wound. The last wound was directly above the right ear; a bullet severed the temporal lobe of the brain. The last injury was the cause the death; the victim died within seconds of being shot. He could not have cried out in pain for hours. Loughridge made no mention of wounds to Halfpenny's feet or castration.[49]

Although Malachy Halfpenny was a former soldier and a Hibernian, he does not appear to have been a member of a paramilitary group. His murder may have been another case of mistaken identity. The Halfpennys at no. 21 lived a few steps away from the Bradley family at no. 20. A few months earlier Hugh Bradley had been named in

140

police intelligence reports in relation to an attack on a police officer. Such suspicions were correct; IRA records confirm that Bradley was a volunteer in 'A' (Ardoyne) Company of the 1st Battalion of the Belfast Brigade.[50] British military intelligence also indicated that Hugh's father, Charles, was one of the IRA's leaders in the Ardoyne area.[51]

Neighbours, on the alert for incursions by 'murder gangs', heard the arrival of the lorry on Herbert Street. Some opened their windows and screamed out warnings and cries for help. Witnesses told the *Irish News* that they heard some of the men in the lorry speaking in Belfast and English accents.[52]

Winifred Halfpenny recalled that at 1.10 a.m. there was a knock on the door of the family house. She opened the window and saw a vehicle similar to those used by the curfew patrols. She then saw three men approach her house. One was wearing a police cap; the other two men were wearing 'soft grey caps' and trench coats. She asked whether they were the military and received the reply: 'It is alright, come down and open the door.'

On the doorstep Winifred saw a man – broad, thick set, clean shaven, with a thin nose and lips, Belfast accent – wearing 'a khaki cap with black glazed peak and shiny top [with] goggles on the cap's peak'. He was also dressed in a 'short khaki … double-breasted coat with brass buttons' … 'the same as a mounted soldier'.

This was not a description of a regular Belfast RIC policeman. It more closely resembled a driver from the RIC Transport Division. The man went straight for her brother saying, 'This is the man we want' and dragged him across the floor to the door, slamming it behind him. The lorry then left, moving towards the Crumlin Road. A few minutes later the family heard the sound of shots close by.

The Halfpennys' neighbour at no. 20, Annie Bradley, corroborated much of Winifred Halfpenny's statement, adding that the lorry or vehicle looked like those used by the Special Constabulary. She also said that she heard a man speaking in an 'English accent' but added that she thought that 'it was put on'. Another neighbour, James Davey, reported that he saw a Crossley tender lorry with about fourteen men in it. Davey believed these men may have been dressed in civilian clothes except for the driver, who was possibly a special constable.

James Davey saw Malachy Halfpenny being dragged from his house into the street, put in the lorry and then heard the sound of a whistle. The men then 'reassembled and got into the motor' and moved off. The lorry stopped at the nearby Ardoyne fire station before moving on down the Woodvale Road. Another witness told the inquest that he saw a body lying just beside the Ardoyne fire station around 10 a.m. the next morning and reported it to nearby Ligoniel RIC station.[53]

Constable James Glover's brother Samuel lived at Ardoyne Fire Station.[54] Malachy Halfpenny was shot outside Samuel Glover's house at Ardoyne fire station on 12 June, the night before James' funeral. The reprisal message could not have been clearer.

At the inquest DI Nixon asked Head Constable Robert Dinsmore to account for all police vehicles under his control in Musgrave Barracks on the night of the murders. Dinsmore gave the court details of the movements of all Belfast RIC Crossley tenders on the night of the murders. He admitted that one vehicle was missing a licence plate – it had just been made available and was required urgently for use due to the breakdown of another lorry.

Nixon then asked him whether there were more Crossley tenders 'other than those in your charge' in Musgrave Barracks between 11 and 14 June 1921. Dinsmore replied that twenty-one other vehicles were in Musgrave Barracks on the night of the murders which were not under the command of the Belfast RIC and that these left the city on 13 June at 2.30 p.m. to return to Gormanston Camp near Dublin. He told the inquest that, unlike the dark green regular RIC vehicles, Auxiliary Division Crossley tenders were a pale blue colour.

The next witness examined at the inquest was a former Royal Navy lieutenant who was part of a detachment of Auxiliaries stationed at Musgrave Barracks from 11 until 13 June. Temporary Cadet Eric James served in 'Q' Company. At the inquest he was described as second-in-command of an Auxiliary platoon – approximately eighty to ninety men.

James told the court that he had two vehicles out on patrol until 12.15 a.m. His men then remained in Musgrave Barracks for the rest of the night, except for Officer Cadet Lee who had leave to spend the night with his wife elsewhere in the city. James confirmed that Lee was 'short, and was lame at the time'. Accompanying James and his men was a detachment from the RIC Transport Division, Gormanston Camp, who were also based in Musgrave Barracks on the night of the murders.[55]

Constable Alex Sterritt was also called to give evidence at the inquest. He told the court that he was on duty that night 'suppressing riots' in the York Street area during the early morning of 13 June. Sterritt's presence in 'D' District is somewhat exceptional since he was assigned as a plain-clothes detective constable to Nixon's 'C' District. Sterritt sent his RIC vehicle 'of the usual dark green colour' back to Musgrave Street Barracks between 1.30 and 2 a.m.

Robert Pakenham told the court that all his special constables and their vehicles were back at Court Street Barracks – close to where the murders took place – by 12.45 a.m. John Giff also gave evidence that none of his men at Brown's Square Barracks were near any victims' houses in the early hours of 12 June. Nixon followed Giff and Pakenham onto the witness stand and told the inquest hearing that the IRA often impersonated the British military or the police, citing an incident where they overpowered Belleek RIC station in 1920 dressed in British Army uniforms.

The final victim was William Kerr, a twenty-six-year-old hairdresser who lived on the Old Lodge Road. Kerr was a member of the Hibernians. His brother was a regimental sergeant major in the British Army.[56]

That made no difference. Kerr was abducted from his house at just after 1.20 a.m. His body was found near the Springfield Road in the western outskirts of the city at 6.40 the same morning. According to the Nixon memo, as well as being shot many times his arms and legs had been broken, 'evidently with butt end of rifles'. This account of torture also features in the 1922 Commission report. The report adds that his abductors stood outside Kerr's house discussing whether they would go and 'do in' another victim who lived nearby.

At the inquest into William Kerr's death, his wife and his sister Alice, who was staying with the family, gave evidence that the family was asleep when they heard a knock on the door of the house. William Kerr got up and put on his trousers while Alice lit a candle and opened the door.

A fair-haired man with a thin moustache, about six feet tall, blue eyes, wearing a Highland soldier's regimental hat, khaki trousers and a long dark coat with black buttons – 'like a policeman's coat but not an RIC coat' – and goggles on his cap pushed past Alice and ran upstairs. He told William Kerr that he was arresting him for 'identification' purposes. He had an English accent. Kerr's wife concluded that he was a 'Black and Tan'. Both women told the police that they would recognise the man in uniform again. Two other men also entered the house; Kerr's wife believed that they were special constables but that they were dressed in civilian clothes.[57]

On the way down the stairs, Alice Kerr grabbed the man in uniform by the elbow and asked him to take her instead. He laughed. Undeterred, Alice warned: 'If anything happens to my brother I can identify you.' The man replied simply: 'You won't see him again.' He then left the house and pushed William into a lorry on the street. A group of eight or ten men, all dressed in civilian clothes, were waiting outside. One of these wore a trench coat, a handkerchief over his nose and mouth and carried a revolver. Alice ran after them. The man with the handkerchief over this mouth turned and said in a Belfast accent: 'If you don't get in I will put a bullet in you.'

At seven that morning Alice Kerr walked across the city to Musgrave Street Barracks and demanded to speak to a district inspector. She was told to come back two hours later. While waiting outside the gates she saw a police lorry emerge from the gates. Alice looked directly at the driver. He was the same tall, fair-haired man from the night before. Catching Alice's eye, her brother's killer turned up his coat and looked away.

Lieutenant Loughridge gave his evidence at the inquest. He made no mention of William Kerr's arms and legs being broken or dislocated. Kerr was shot multiple times, including in the neck, torso and legs. A bullet also passed through his foot. (This may be the source of the rumours about one of the victims being bayoneted in the foot.)

Lieutenant Colonel William Freeston of the Somerset Light Infantry, the president of the board of inquest into the murders, questioned police witnesses at length, remonstrating with those who he felt were being evasive. Colonel Commandant Carter-Campbell requested the police to organise an identity parade of constables from Gormanston who were in Belfast at the time of the murders. The RIC stalled, made excuses and ultimately took no action.[58]

What Auxiliaries Officer Cadet James did not tell the court was that, upon their arrival in Belfast, the Auxiliaries immediately began terrorising the Catholic population in the city. At 9.45 p.m. on the night of 10 July a lorry sped up the Falls Road. Auxiliaries inside fired sporadically as they moved along the road. People on the street panicked; some of the old and young tripped and were trampled on by those trying to seek cover.

A lorry of Auxiliaries then seized three men and drove from the Falls Road to the corner of Ashmore Street where a cheering loyalist mob beat the prisoners. The first to be thrown from the lorry was an elderly man. He was kicked repeatedly in the head. An ex-soldier – who showed the Auxiliaries his discharge papers in an appeal for mercy –

was also brutally assaulted. Some residents intervened and prevented the two men from being beaten to death. The third prisoner tore free from the mob and ran to safety.

The Auxiliaries were also present during rioting in west Belfast on 14 June 1921 after the funeral of 'A' Class Special Constable Thomas Sturdy who had been shot dead two days previously. Loyalists were enraged by taunts and the waving of republican flags during the funeral procession; fighting broke out in the area between crowds from the Shankill and Falls roads. Sandbags were filled by ex-soldiers on both sides and snipers took to rooftops. Among those killed was William Fraser, a twelve-year-old Protestant boy who went to look for his sister Becky and was shot in the face by a sniper from the Falls Road area. (His two brothers had previously drowned trying to save a friend who had fallen through the ice while skating on the frozen Springfield dam.)

A Protestant ex-soldier called Hugh McAree rushed out to help; he was shot in turn and fell beside William Fraser. A passing lorry of Auxiliaries picked up McAree and the boy – both were still alive – and brought them to the Royal Victoria Hospital; Hugh McAree and William Fraser were pronounced dead shortly after arrival. The *Irish News* reported that, while at the hospital, the Auxiliaries 'waved their revolvers in a threatening attitude at groups of people who fled panic-stricken.'[59]

Colonel Commandant Carter-Campbell kept pushing for an investigation into the murders. He asked his staff to consider if the military officers on the inquest board, including Colonel Freeston and Lieutenant Cuthbert Hiatt of the Norfolks, could organise an identity parade and compel the police to participate. This was not legally possible; the police still had discretion over criminal investigations and only the RIC could order an identity parade. Nonetheless, British officials in Dublin Castle pressed ahead with plans to hold an identity parade in Gormanston Camp.

The British Army evidently suspected that Auxiliaries based at Gormanston Camp and their accompanying RIC drivers were guilty of murder in Belfast. But the RIC was stonewalling the army. So too were the solicitors representing the families of the victims – Halfpenny, Kerr and McBride – who advised their clients not to further incriminate the police. The British Army and officials in Dublin Castle asked Alice Kerr to travel to Gormanston Camp for an identification parade. She refused to go, as did her sister-in-law. Winifred Halfpenny was also not available; she had left the country. The families of murder victims were understandably terrified that they might be targeted again. Dublin Castle and the British Army ultimately let the matter drop.[60]

It should have been possible to identify the tall, English-accented, Glengarry wearing man with goggles who abducted William Kerr. The goggles worn by this man and the abductor of Malachy Halfpenny suggest that both men were drivers, further narrowing down a potential list of suspects from the police temporarily based at Musgrave Barracks. DI Nixon tried to frustrate investigations by suggesting that the IRA may have dressed up as policemen and carried out the killings. Obstruction and a lack of initiative on the part of Nixon meant that it was left to British Army officers at the inquest to interrogate police witnesses at length on their movements on the night of the murders.[61]

A month after the murders of 12 June 1921, the Belfast IRA reported that a group of Auxiliaries attacked a Catholic-owned shopkeeper in the city, firing shots and threatening another man.[62] Citing intelligence from a police source, Belfast IRA officer Tom McNally recalled that, although the regular RIC carried out some of the first police reprisals during the 'pogrom', later murders were perpetrated by gangs of recently recruited police or 'Tans' – not long-serving member of the RIC.[63]

The Nixon memo ignored evidence given by the families at respective military inquests. These testimonies offered a more complicated picture of who was responsible for the reprisal murders in Belfast during curfew hours. It also overlooked the conclusions of the contemporaneous Sinn Féin investigation into the McMahon killings – that the Special Constabulary and not the regular RIC were responsible. The selective exclusion of some accounts corresponds with a general preference of the Free State government to place blame for horrific police reprisals principally on regular, long-serving police officers. Some in the government may have sincerely believed that constables Gordon and Sterritt were the perpetrators; they had earned their reputations for violence. However, accusing RUC officers rather than part-time special constables also landed a bigger propaganda blow against the Northern Irish government.

The first claim that a senior police officer – a thinly concealed reference to Nixon – led the gang that carried out the McMahon murders was published on 19 June 1922 in the *Weekly Irish Bulletin* (*Belfast Atrocities*). The *Bulletin* was an official propaganda publication of the new Irish state. Its aim was to win attention and sympathy from the world's press for the nationalist victims of the 'pogrom'. The prose of the *Bulletin* was deliberately lurid; it added in shocking details not found in Sinn Féin investigations, witness statements or other murder reports. It was the *Bulletin* that published the false account of Joseph Walsh being sledgehammered to death – 'his head battered to pulp' – adding that Walsh's murderers then threw the family's crucifix and rosary beads in the fire.[64]

In the case of the McMahon murders, according to the *Bulletin*, citing an unnamed source, Mary Downey's evidence 'tallied in all particulars with the description of District Inspector [deleted name] one of the chiefs of the murder gang'.[65] If this was supposed to refer to Nixon – and it seems most likely – then the *Bulletin's* source is obviously mistaken. Nixon was 5ft 9 inches in height; he was somewhat overweight and had a fleshy face. But he was not clean-shaven (he had a prominent moustache during this period).[66] And he was also almost forty-five years old, ten to fifteen years older than John McMahon's description, and spoke with a soft Cavan brogue, not with a Belfast or an English accent.

The Nixon memo repeated many of the *Bulletin*'s claims. The single source cited by the Nixon memo as evidence for the involvement of Nixon's men in the murders was forty-three-year-old Constable Michael Furlong. The memo did not include any direct testimony by Furlong. Furlong was based in Leopold Street, near Ardoyne in the north-west of the city; Carlisle Circus and Antrim Road were not part of his normal 'beat'. He does not appear to have personally witnessed a key event, one repeatedly used as evidence to implicate the regular RIC's involvement in the McMahon's murders – the taking of the sledgehammer by Constables Gordon and Sterritt from the hut at Carlisle Circus in the minutes before the attack at 3 Kinnaird Terrace.

Furlong gave an earlier statement to Sinn Féin investigators only a few hours before the McMahon murders. He had spent all of his nearly two decades of police service in County Antrim, including fifteen years in Belfast. His record is unremarkable until the Belfast 'pogrom' – no decorations, commendations or punishments. He had his nose broken and face cut during rioting in January 1921. Two months later he was commended by a judge for breaking up a juvenile gang that had plagued Ardoyne with robberies and violence. His evidence also led to the conviction of a loyalist rioter, John Presdee. Although a special constable who was on duty at the time swore to Presdee's innocence, Furlong's account was corroborated by other RIC constables.[67]

Furlong said that he was severely reprimanded by DI Nixon for confiscating two unlicensed revolvers in the possession of a 'B' special constable called Adair. Nixon, together with Adair, then confronted Furlong in Nixon's office at Brown's Square station: 'Nixon told me I was a blackguard and that if I didn't stop my blackguardism he would get me out of his district in 24 hours ... I should not have seized these revolvers.' A humiliated Furlong handed back the revolvers to Adair. Aside from Nixon breaking the window of a Catholic house with a brush, Furlong did not witness Nixon directing or participating in violence. Curiously,

Furlong also testified that when Nixon was not present in the barracks some Protestant constables seized their opportunity and went up to the top of Brown's Square Barracks to snipe into the nearby, largely Catholic, streets. Constable Myles Kehoe claimed that special constables at Brown's Square sometimes opened fire on the nearby streets at 3 p.m., the time when Head Constable John Giff and Sergeant William Reid left the barracks to go for dinner. Some reprisals were tolerated or even encouraged, but not, it seems, indiscriminate shooting from the barracks.[68]

Many policemen only came forward to offer information to Sinn Féin after the signing of the treaty and the announcement that the RIC would be disbanded. Policemen from the South of Ireland urgently needed to make their peace with the new government in Dublin. Some accounts of violence – given to Sinn Féin representatives in the city – contained obvious exaggerations, but these do not appear to have been challenged by the provisional government. For example, Constable William Duffy of Mountpottinger Barracks claimed that he had personally ordered the military to shoot at a Protestant mob on the Newtownards Road during rioting in the summer of 1920. The British Army had killed twenty-nine and wounded many more. Many loyalists were secretly buried as a way of concealing the incident.[69] Duffy's narrative is clearly fantastical; there are no official or unofficial records to back up this scale of British Army violence on any day in east Belfast.

Rather than insisting that Nixon was present at reprisal murders, IRA commander Seamus Woods stated that Nixon always made sure he was deliberately absent (echoing the view of British official Stephen Tallents). In a conversation with Ernie O'Malley, a former anti-treaty IRA leader and author, Woods gave a very different account of Nixon's involvement in the McMahon murders to that presented in the Nixon memo: 'I came down from Belfast as a result of the McMahon murders [for a meeting in Dublin]. Curfew was at 12 in Belfast and at 1230 the murder took place. Nixon, the District Inspector, must have closed a blind eye. He personally didn't ill-treat prisoners.' He also said that Nixon offered him a drink after Woods was released from internment in 1923.[70]

Nixon repeatedly frustrated or blocked investigations into crimes committed by policemen under his command in 'C' District. Many of these were perpetrated by members of the Special Constabulary or the RIC Auxiliary Division. Some appear to have been carried out by the RIC, including by Constable Henry Gordon. However, the killings took place in 'D' District so whether Nixon winked or closed his eyes or not, other police officers, such as DI Lynn and the city's Special Crime unit, were far more pivotal when it came to policing the immediate area around Kinnaird Terrace and investigating the murders. Nixon's 'gang' was not the only reprisal force in Belfast. There were other loyalist killers in Belfast who had their own motives and an even greater capacity for atrocity.

CHAPTER SIX

Taking a Delight in Killing

THE BODY OF FORTY-THREE-YEAR-OLD JANE Rafferty was found face down on her kitchen floor. Shortly after 9 p.m. on 17 September 1922 four men entered her home at 11 Andrew Street. Jane was one of the few Catholics who lived in the row of terraced houses, located just off York Street. Her husband, a Protestant sailor in the Merchant Navy, was away at sea. Her children were not in the house at the time of her death. She was very much alone. After being beaten and abused for some minutes – clumps of hair were found beside Jane's body – one of her attackers shot her dead.

The RUC believed that Jane Rafferty was killed by her neighbour, a twenty-year-old Protestant man called Alec 'Buck' Robinson who lived a few doors down on the same street. Robinson had also served in the Merchant Navy for a time. He was heard boasting: 'I have put another spy out of the way. I put three thro' her head.' A British military intelligence report noted that Jane Rafferty may have given the RUC intelligence about the whereabouts of a cache of loyalist weapons.[1]

Jane Rafferty was the third and final Catholic victim of murder in the York Street area on Sunday 17 September. Earlier that day Robinson was seen in the company of twenty-two-year-old former soldier, 'C1' Special Constable William Nesbitt who lived next door to Robinson on Andrew Street. Later interned, Nesbitt was described in a police intelligence report as 'an outlaw of the worst type' who also 'delighted in taking the lives of Roman Catholics or any other person who would cross his path'. Police believed that Nesbitt shot dead Thomas McCullagh, a labourer, near York Street on the same day as the murder of Jane Rafferty. He and Alec Robinson were then believed to have targeted James McCloskey, a sailor on a few days' leave, who was shot dead on his doorstep on Marine Street, not far from Andrew Street.[2] Although regarded as one of the most sadistic gunmen in the York Road district, Nesbitt could be ruled out of any lists of suspects when it came to the McMahon murders. On 19 March 1922 he was arrested after firing shots with a revolver during a riot; he was still in police custody five days later.[3]

Alec Robinson had the face of a streetfighter – a broad nose, a downturned mouth, a large forehead and small blue eyes. Like Nesbitt, he was a policeman, a member of the 'C1' Constabulary. He was also politically connected. His aunt was married to the unionist MP for North Belfast, William Grant, a supporter of loyalist paramilitary groups including the Imperial Guards and the UPA.[4]

Before he became an MP in June 1921, Grant had been a leading figure in the paramilitary Ulster Brotherhood or 'Tigers' established by Colonel Fred Crawford. A month after his election he was shot and wounded in the shoulder on York Street. Nationalists claimed Grant was leading an attack on a nearby Catholic street when he was fired on; unionists said he was on his way to ask the military for help. A cheer went up when the Belfast MP was hit.[5]

Alec Robinson was not the only suspected gang leader in north Belfast with influential connections. Edward Leathem, a close ally of Sir Joseph Davison and the Worshipful Master of York Road Loyal Orange Lodge, was among those who frequently criticised a breakdown in law and order in Belfast in 1922. His brother George was regarded by the British Army as being among the most notorious loyalist paramilitaries in north Belfast, responsible for a series of sectarian attacks in the York Road area.[6]

Alec Robinson was recruited into the police through his involvement in Belfast's boxing scene. (One of the 'C1' Constabulary's key officers in north Belfast, Captain William Pinder, was also a main organiser of boxing matches in the city.) He boasted that he received a personal commendation from the Lord Lieutenant of Belfast, Viscount Pirrie, for his service.[7]

A few months before he joined the Special Constabulary in early 1922 Robinson was convicted of assaulting a Presbyterian farmer with a hammer after a dispute on the outskirts of Belfast over rabbit trapping. (He served a two-month prison sentence.) According to the RUC, Alec Robinson was responsible for several murders. A report noted that Robinson 'was a dangerous gunman and leader of a murderous gang, and actually takes a delight in killing. He is suspected of killing and wounding many people all over the city and makes no secret of it, as he openly boasts of doing so.'

Robinson preyed on the weak. The RUC strongly suspected that one of his victims was fifty-six-year-old Catholic, Peter Mullan, who worked as an attendant at the Crumlin Road cinema. On the night of 29 August 1922 Robinson and his companions attracted attention after arriving late at the cinema and noisily taking up their seats in the darkness although the programme had been running for some time. After the lights were switched on at the end of the showing, Peter Mullan moved down the aisle to clean up. A man, identified as Robinson, stepped forward and shot Mullan in the head.[8]

Robinson and William Nesbitt were suspected of murdering publican Patrick Lambe at his bar – the Blacksmith's Arms – on York Street on 13 February 1922 (the same day as the nearby Weaver Street murders). Paddy Lambe's killer shot him at close range in the chest before calmly walking out the door. A few weeks later, on 27 February, Robinson was seen throwing a bomb from a tram which severely wounded two men and a ten-year-old boy on Curtis Street near the city centre.

Robinson and Nesbitt were was also believed to have killed Catholic policeman, Sergeant Martin Bruen, during a robbery of a pub on York Street on 13 April 1922. A native of County Leitrim, Sergeant Bruen had provided a statement to the provisional government in which he identified Robinson's uncle, William Grant MP, as the leader of a loyalist mob, supported by Head Constable Pakenham and the Special Constabulary of Court Street Barracks, who attacked Catholic residents in north Belfast.[9]

On 6 October 1922 the RUC finally arrested Alec Robinson for murder. Ten days later the Ministry of Home Affairs issued an internment order for Robinson. Shortly afterwards the Minister for Home Affairs, Sir Richard Dawson Bates, received 'a peace offer' through a loyalist intermediary called Annie Armstrong, who owned a pub on Peter's Hill in the Shankill Road area. Armstrong offered 'an assurance from the boys of Shankill, Newtownards [Road] and York Street districts there will not be a shot fired or a bomb thrown or any other act of intimidation if [George] Scott and Robinson are released'.[10]

Colonel Henry Toppin, a senior official at the Ministry of Home Affairs, arranged to meet Annie Armstrong. He asked her to find out whether Robinson had any relatives in Canada so that he could be sent there. Rather than charging Robinson, the new commander of 'D' District, DI Cornelius O'Beirne, ordered his release and that of two other internees, leading members of the east Belfast UPA, Joseph Arthurs and Frederick Pollock, on the condition that they leave Ireland for at least two years. A report on Robinson stated that, 'At the urgent request of his friends he was released on 11th November to allow him to go to England.'

At the inquest into the killing of Jane Rafferty a police witness misleadingly claimed that it was 'a most mysterious crime, and that no facts could be found about the affair at all'. George Scott and Annie

Armstrong's son Herbert were given a one-month suspended sentence for the illegal possession of arms.

The Northern Irish government paid for the fare of Robinson, Arthurs and Pollock, and gave each man a small sum of money from the Secret Service account to support them on arrival in England. RUC Head Constable Peter Fallon, a Catholic from the west of Ireland, accompanied the three men during 'the deportation to Great Britain', reporting that he left Robinson in Sheffield, Pollock in Leicester and Arthurs in London before returning to Northern Ireland. Arthurs, Fallon concluded, was a devious type but former 'C1' Constables Robinson and Pollock 'seemed chastened' by their brief internment and would honour their commitment not to return to Northern Ireland.

Alec Robinson returned to Belfast a few weeks later and was arrested and reinterned. Senior police officers again discussed sending him to Canada or to his relations in America. O'Beirne joked that Robinson 'would be a very useful citizen in [crime-ridden] Chicago'.[11]

In July 1923 DI O'Beirne suddenly recommended Robinson's unconditional release. He purported to believe that the man he described as a near-psychopathic killer a few months previously had now learned 'a useful lesson'. Robinson was now no longer 'any danger to the peace'. His uncle William Grant MP had successfully lobbied the government for his release. O'Beirne, a Catholic ex-army officer, adapted his views accordingly.

Contrary to O'Beirne's strained optimism, Robinson quickly burnished his reputation for violence. He eventually did leave Belfast for Canada. Arriving at the port of St John in New Brunswick on 8 April 1928 he declared that he intended to become a farmer. Instead, he travelled to the cities of Chicago and Toronto where, as predicted, he became involved in mob violence and crime before returning to Belfast in the early 1930s.

Robinson was centrally involved in sectarian riots in Belfast in 1935, forcing Catholic families to leave the Docks area in the north of the city.

He carefully promoted his image as a crime boss, dressing like a Chicago gangster – slouched hat, sharp suits, rings on every finger – while showing off a pet lion, which he had somehow acquired from Dublin Zoo.[12]

Small, baby-faced, blond and blue-eyed, George Scott, the other loyalist named by Annie Armstrong, was regarded by the RUC as 'one of the principal gunmen' in Belfast, responsible for many of the hold-ups and shootings of publicans in the city. A former Royal Navy sailor, he was a serving 'B' special constable until his dismissal from the police in August 1922. Scott was also a close friend of twenty-three-year-old Royal Irish Rifles veteran John Williamson. Both men were suspected by police of murdering two-year-old Francis Donnelly and his twelve-year-old brother Joseph on 31 March. People who had witnessed Scott's crimes – such as the shooting and wounding of two barmen in Murray's spirit grocery on the Oldpark Road on 28 August 1922 – were reported as being too terrified to give evidence against him. Scott was eventually interned on 10 November 1922. (He was released eight months later.)[13]

James Craig's government interned sixteen loyalists from April 1922 until May 1923. (A total of 649 suspects – overwhelmingly republicans – were interned during the same period for various lengths of time.)[14] George Scott's friend John Williamson was also interned. He had previously been convicted of assaulting an RIC constable at the end of 1920, as well as a number of other violent offences, serving a year in prison with hard labour. In early 1922, a few weeks after his release from prison, he joined the 'C1' Special Constabulary. Williamson was a leading UPA gunman, writing that he and his comrades in the UPA had 'stood by our guns ... when the Shinners threatened to wipe out the Protestants in Belfast.'

John Williamson could not have been present at 3 Kinnaird Terrace in the early hours of 24 March. He was arrested hours earlier after the discovery of two rifles and a quantity of ammunition at his house on Fortingale Street near the Shankill Road. Like George Scott, Williamson was interned in November 1922. One of the people who strongly recommended his internment was Constable Alex Sterritt who testified that Williamson was 'a dangerous mobman'.[15]

Williamson claimed to have been recommended by his superiors in the 'C1' Constabulary for 'secret service' work under Lieutenant Colonel Maldwyn Haldane, a former senior Security Service (MI5) intelligence officer. This new intelligence service was the short-lived creation of General Solly-Flood. The Ministry of Home Affairs asked for corroboration but were told that Williamson's commanding officer 'preferred not to write' but would pass on information orally to the minister. In the summer of 1923 Williamson was released after he gave an undertaking to emigrate to Canada.

The UPA's spectacularly ill-suited motto was *Pro Rege, Lege, Et Grege* (for the king, the law and the people). Its leaders were motivated by crude sectarianism. The UPA's headquarters was situated in Hastings public house on the Newtownards Road. There, two of its leaders, Robert Craig and Thomas Pentland, indulged in sadistic acts such as administering floggings with a cat-o'-nine-tails over a gymnast's pommel horse. After the IRA campaign subsided in the summer of 1922, the RUC moved to arrest and intern Craig, Pentland, and four other members of the east Belfast UPA.[16]

The arrest and internment of the twenty-seven-year-old Craig was a delicate matter for the police and the Ministry of Home Affairs in Belfast. Craig had until recently been employed as a police agent by ex-MI5 officer Colonel Haldane's intelligence service. Craig's supporters complained that the government was attempting 'to use the Orange ladder and then kick it away'.[17] The Minister for Home Affairs, Sir Richard Dawson Bates, ordered the release of Craig after less than a year, following public protests and petitions from unionist MPs.[18]

Part of Craig's leverage over the police and the Ministry of Home Affairs stemmed from the intelligence he passed on about potential loyalist threats to Craig's government including from an east Belfast UPA leader called Robert Simpson. An RUC report described Simpson as 'the most desperate and dangerous gunman on the Protestant side in this side of the city. He was chairman of the notorious UPA murder gang and its leading light.'

Simpson was arrested at his home – with seven rounds of ammunition in his pocket – in east Belfast on 26 March 1922, the day of the McMahon funerals. The RIC commander of 'E' District, DI Reginald Spears, believed that Simpson was responsible for the murder of fourteen Catholics up to that point. As he was being led away Simpson calmly turned and told Spears that he would kill him one day.[19] Robert Craig, the police's agent inside the UPA, informed the government that he was working to dissuade the UPA from marching to Prime Minister James Craig's offices to protest against Simpson's arrest.[20]

Simpson had influential friends. Sam McGuffin, the unionist MP for Belfast Shankill, protested to Dawson Bates that Simpson was 'a law-abiding citizen'. However, he concluded his letter with the cryptic sentence – 'It is a little difficult to explain matters in a letter, but if you would do me the favour of calling, I should be very pleased to lay the facts before you.' A petition for Simpson's release was also signed by the lord mayor of Belfast, Sir William Coates. Other petitioners included unionist MPs William Grant, Thompson Donald and Harry Burn.[21]

Simpson, for his part, made no secret of his sectarianism during his internment hearing – 'I will always hate Roman Catholics.' He also admitted that he broke the law but that it was 'to assist the Crown Forces in my own way' and that, 'I may have used the gun, but I did it for the benefit of Ulster.'[22] Simpson told Dawson Bates that he had followed the advice of Colonel Fred Crawford 'who extorted us [the UPA] to extremes.'[23] After he served a sentence for ammunition offences, Simpson was interned in February 1923 for fourteen months.[24]

There was a considerable overlap in membership between the UPA and the Imps. However, it was the latter who alarmed the IRA most. In January 1922 the IRA's senior intelligence officer in Belfast, Frank Crummey, reported that the most dangerous 'murder gangs' operating in the city were those of the Imperial Guards who 'had been doing all the gun work during the recent disturbances'. Now acting as policemen, the erstwhile Imps were permitted to march in formation and carry arms openly, even when not on duty, as long as they had their police identification on them.[25]

Jordy Harper, the Imperial Guard suspected of killing Private Barnes, lived on Grove Street, close to Alec Robinson. Four months before the death of Barnes, Harper was arrested and charged with the attempted murder of a Catholic woman, Catherine Kearney, who lived on Vere Street, close to Harper's home. Kearney had testified against one of Harper's friends in a court case in March of that year.

On 14 August 1921 Catherine Kearney was walking home when she saw a visibly drunk Harper on the street waving a revolver. Somebody pointed out Kearney to Harper. He immediately raised his revolver and fired in her direction. His intended victim took cover in a doorway. Harper, thinking she had gone home, went to Catherine Kearney's house where he was met at the door by her mother. Mrs Kearney said that Harper 'swore by the man above that he would come in either before curfew or after it and that he would neither use hands nor feet on her but would give her the contents of what was in pocket'. Mrs Kearney was not intimidated. She told Harper she knew his mother and father and that he should go away home. Harper was found not guilty by the court.[26]

A few months later Jordy Harper provided an alibi that helped clear an Imperial Guard, James Galbraith, who was accused of the attempted murder of a boy called Patrick McGurnaghan on Vere Street on 24 November 1921. A young Protestant woman, Minnie Park, shouted, 'All right, Galbraith, you will not get away with that'. She then rushed over to help the boy. Park testified to the court that she 'saw him [Galbraith] perfectly'. Harper contradicted Minnie Park, saying that he and Galbraith were part of the guard of honour at the funeral of Imperial Guard and ex-Royal Navy sailor Bertie Phillips at the time. Two other Imps, ex-Royal Navy sailor Barnsley Sloan and James McMichael, provided the same alibi. (Galbraith was found not guilty of attempted murder but was convicted of the robbery of a spirit grocery owned by a Catholic woman on Vere Street.)[27]

Although many of the Imps were veterans, the 'C1' Class Constabulary also accepted younger recruits like Alec Robinson. A particular hotspot for street fights between Norfolk soldiers and young loyalists was the Malvern Street and Ariel Street area, just to the north of the Shankill Road. It was here on 22 March – thirty-six hours before the McMahon murders – that the Norfolks arrested Thomas Johnston, a nineteen-year-old 'C1' Special, who the soldiers claimed belonged to 'the Orange murder gang'.

A young Protestant woman, Esther McDougall, saw Johnston open fire at residents on Stanhope Street and throw a bomb at Catherine Hatton's house at no. 11. (Hatton was a victim of an attempted rape nine days later during the Arnon Street reprisals.) McDougall shouted at Johnston that she would 'tell the soldiers'.

Lieutenant Cuthbert Hiatt was on duty in nearby Wall Street when he heard the bomb explode and ran in the direction of a plume of smoke rising over Stanhope Street. There he found nineteen-year-old Esther McDougall who gave a description of Johnston and another man. Hiatt set off up nearby Cavour Street, where he saw Johnston and fired a shot over his head. Johnston turned and bolted into a nearby house. Hiatt discovered a tunnel at the back of the house, leading onto another street.

The Norfolk officer gave up the chase, but some minutes later he saw Johnston standing in a nearby street. This time Johnston was caught by surprise; Hiatt made his arrest. Johnston informed the military that he was a 'C1' Special.[28] Esther McDougall and Lieutenant Hiatt both gave evidence against Johnston in court in early May. The jury could not agree; Johnston was not convicted of the bombing offence, although he did receive a sentence of three months' hard labour for stealing from a pub on the nearby Old Lodge Road.

Esther McDougall was now a loyalist target – she received a letter telling her she would be killed. On 24 May loyalist gunmen attempted to shoot her in west Belfast but wounded a companion instead. Two days later they succeeded; Esther McDougall was shot dead outside her Stanhope Street home.[29]

Splits emerged between those in the police in Belfast who wished to arrest and even intern members of the Special Constabulary who were suspected of murder, arson and robbery and those that objected to arrests and prosecutions. DI Richard Heggart wrote a report on one such man, 'B' Special Constable Samuel Ditty. Ditty was a former soldier who had served in the Royal Irish Rifles and was involved in fighting during the 1916 Easter Rising. He was severely wounded in France shortly before the 1918 Armistice. He was still only twenty-two at the time of his arrest on 28 November 1922.

Heggart and his men had successfully infiltrated Ditty's gang. However, prosecuting its members was almost impossible – 'Such a reign of terror exists of this gang that people are afraid to identify them.' DI Nixon also vouched for Ditty, describing him as an 'exemplary' policeman: 'the internment of Ditty is the greatest wrong and injustice that ever came under my notice'.[30] But Nixon acknowledged that he did not know Ditty very well. Ironically, given his own furious desire for advancement, he blamed Heggart's lead detective in 'C' District, Sergeant John Magee, for acting out of malice because he had missed out on promotion.

A 'B' Specials meeting, attended by District Commandant Harry Taylor was held in west Belfast to protest against Ditty's arrest. The assembled policemen sent a letter of protest to Minister Richard Dawson

Bates.[31] Ditty also received support from a former senior Royal Irish Rifles officer, the MP for West Belfast at Westminster, Colonel Philip Woods, who testified to his innocence and 'excellent character'.[32]

Despite such political pressure, Heggart reassured his superiors that he had made no mistake. Ditty was interned – but only for six months – along with another member of his gang, David Taylor. Andrew Scott was also recommended for internment, but this was revoked since he was only sixteen years old. Other gang members identified by Heggart, including Thomas McIlwrath and Norrick Herst, were neither charged nor interned. Another suspected gunman was still a child and could not be named or interned because of his age.[33]

Heggart also moved against 'B' Special Constable James Mulgrew – another 'well-known gunman' attached to Brown's Square Barracks. Mulgrew was interned on New Year's Day 1923 after the attempted murder of the Catholic owner of a spirit grocery, Daniel Bradley, near the Shankill Road. He had previously been convicted for assaulting a tram conductor in February 1921 but continued to serve in the police.

Harry Taylor again vented his contempt for 'the authorities' – Wickham and Dawson Bates – who ordered his constable's internment, stating that 'no single man did more on behalf of our Northern Parliament' than Mulgrew. Taylor reminded the government that, as a former member of the UVF Special Service Section, Mulgrew had been a bodyguard to James Craig and Edward Carson. Lieutenant Colonel Horace Gaussen, the commandant of the Special Constabulary in Belfast, also appealed for Mulgrew's release.[34]

Mulgrew had other supporters including Robert Lynn MP and DI Nixon. Loyalist pressure on Craig's government had some effect. Mulgrew and a man called Daniel Traynor – also suspected of being involved in the attempted murder of Bradley – were released on bail less than two months after their initial arrest and subsequent internment. Taylor promptly reappointed Mulgrew to the 'B' Specials at Brown's Square.

(He served in the police for a further eleven years and campaigned for John Nixon during elections to the Northern Ireland Parliament.)[35]

Giving evidence in public against loyalists was self-evidently dangerous. During 6–8 October 1921 a loyalist gang held up and robbed multiple spirit groceries and bars in the York Road area. Eyewitness testimony from Patrick Connolly, a Catholic described by the *Irish News* as 'a man of powerful physique and engaging personality' who ran a spirit grocery near the York Road, led the police to Robert Martin, Joseph Gault and Joseph McKee. Martin was released but another three men – William Fannon, George Elliott and Bertie Phillips – were subsequently arrested.

On the evening of 22 November 1921 Patrick Connolly was having his dinner in a back room when a group of men entered his shop. Connolly went out to serve them; the men opened fire and Connolly was fatally wounded in the abdomen. The following day Bertie Phillips was fatally shot in the throat near York Street. (IRA officer Seán Montgomery claimed that he killed Phillips.)[36]

When Elliott, Gault and McKee were brought to trial for Connolly's murder, a witness refused to testify. Patrick Connolly's statement, given before his death, was ruled as inadmissible. The charges were dismissed due to 'want of evidence through death'.[37]

Men like Jordy Harper, James Mulgrew, Alec Robinson, George Scott, Robert Simpson and their gangs were all capable of extreme violence. Without a greater understanding of motive, knowledge and opportunity, it is impossible to know who or which group – RIC, Special Constabulary, paramilitaries – should be treated as the principal suspect or suspects for the attack on the McMahon family. To uncover the grievances, capabilities and networks of the man who should be regarded as the lead suspect for the McMahon murders it is necessary to move from Northern Ireland in 1922 to 'the Belfast of Canada' – the city of Toronto – in the late 1930s.

PART 3

CHAPTER SEVEN

The Notorious David Duncan

OF ALL THE LOYALIST GANG leaders in Belfast, none was as complex, charismatic and dangerous as the decorated military veteran and leader of the Imperial Guards in Belfast David Duncan. Duncan's accounts of his service in the British Army, the RIC Auxiliary Division, the Special Constabulary and the French Foreign Legion were selective and self-laudatory. In reality, Duncan's military and police service was marked by paranoia and sudden acts of extreme violence. He charmed, lied and betrayed with ease. And, despite confessing to murder, he was never sentenced to a day in prison. Duncan was not alone – there were other former soldiers in north Belfast with grudges to settle. Among them was Boer War veteran Alick Kennedy, who also suffered from a severe psychiatric illness.

In June 1923 David Duncan was the focus of significant press attention when he appeared in court to sue the Dublin newspaper *The Freeman's Journal* for libel. *The Northern Whig* described him as a well-dressed former British Army officer with 'a fine service record'. The previous summer *The Freeman's Journal* had published an article on loyalist attacks on Catholic-owned pubs and spirit groceries in north Belfast, most recently Patrick Blaney's business on the York Road. Blaney and his wife had been upstairs in the living quarters above their spirit

167

GHOSTS OF A FAMILY

grocery when a bomb smashed through the window, rolled along the floor and exploded a few yards away from where the couple were sitting. Patrick Blaney suffered extreme lacerations to the face and shoulder.[1]

The source for the article was Michael Collins' brother-in-law and publicity officer, Patrick O'Driscoll, who kept in touch with the IRA intelligence network in Belfast. The information on Duncan was distributed by the Irish government's publicity bureau and republished by *The Freeman's Journal*. It stated that prior to the attack on Blaney 'the notorious David Duncan, an adjutant of the Imperial Guards, who runs the York Road in the interests of Protestantism, was noticed making himself conspicuous in the neighbourhood of this shop'.

Duncan claimed that he had received a written death threat in the days after the article was published. The Irish cabinet was advised that O'Driscoll would be 'a very bad witness' to send to Belfast since he had relied upon IRA intelligence, evidence that would be readily dismissed by a Belfast court.[2]

Duncan was awarded £150 in damages – the equivalent of nearly £6,500 a century later. The Irish government paid the amount in addition to Duncan's legal fees and those of *The Freeman's Journal*.[3] It was a remarkable victory for a man who, by his own account, had organised 'a loyalist uprising' in Belfast during the preceding year.[4]

David Duncan was born on 19 February 1891, the youngest of six children, to Joseph Duncan and his wife Ellen (née Stranaghan). Both his parents were from the rural County Down hinterland to the south-east of Belfast. His father worked as a blacksmith. At some point the couple moved to Belfast, possibly to find jobs for their older children. Leaving school at the age of twelve, David was initially employed as an office boy in Workman, Clark and Co., one of the shipbuilding yards, and later worked at the soft drinks manufacturing firm Cantrell and Cochrane's.[5]

On 17 January 1907 Duncan, a month short of his sixteenth birthday, lied about his age in order to join the British Army, enlisting in his local regiment, the Royal Irish Rifles.[6] After a period of training in Aldershot in England, Duncan sailed with 1st Battalion, Royal Irish Rifles (1 RIR) for Burma. For more than two years the Royal Irish made up the garrison at Alexandra Barracks in Maymyo, the Upper Burma town where the writer Eric Blair (George Orwell) trained as a colonial police officer two decades later. In 1912 Duncan's battalion were sent to Kamptee in central India. Duncan joined the military orange lodge, the Rising Sons of India LOL 703. The battalion then moved to garrison the South Arabian colony of Aden a year later. It was from here that 1 RIR – made up of nineteen officers and 999 other ranks – sailed for England at the outbreak of the First World War.

On 6 November 1914 Lance Corporal David Duncan arrived with the rest of 1 RIR to join the British Expeditionary Force in France. He was wounded ten days later, shot in his left arm at Rue Tilleloy near Neuve Chapelle, hours after 1 RIR had moved to the front lines for the first time. He was relatively fortunate. He missed the Battle of Neuve Chapelle in March 1915 when most of 1 RIR were killed or wounded.

After recovering in hospitals in Glasgow and Dublin, Duncan was posted to 6 RIR. This battalion was distinctive from others formed by the regiment during the First World War, many of which were assembled according to UVF regiments. It was raised in Dublin, attached to 10th (Irish) Division rather than 36th (Ulster) Division, and contained many Catholics as well as Protestants. Duncan did well in his new battalion; he was promoted to sergeant.[7]

In the summer of 1915 David Duncan sailed with 6 RIR from England to take part in a new offensive against Ottoman troops at the Gallipoli peninsula on the Dardanelles straits of the Anatolian peninsula. The men looked wide-eyed at the phosphorescence that lit up the Aegean Sea as their troop ship slipped passed shadowy Greek islands on their way to the front.[8]

In early August the New Zealand and Australian Division were directed to attack a pivotal ridge called Chunuk Bair on which Ottoman general Mustafa Kemal Pasha – the future Ataturk, founding father of the Turkish Republic – and his forces were dug in. The 6 RIR, who had been detached from 10 Irish Division to reinforce the assault, were ordered up to a flat plateau called 'the Farm' on 9 August.

A subsequent history of the Gallipoli campaign captures the horror with which New Zealand officers observed the fate of the Irish soldiers. The towering Chunuk Bair ridge loomed above 6 RIR. The Farm '… projected from the hillside like a terraced tennis-court or cricket field … any attempt to cross the terrace was deadly'. A group of Maori soldiers watched horrified, as a captain from 6 RIR prepared his men to cross the exposed Farm and attack the Chunuk Bair ridge: "'Surely you won't do it – it can't be done," said an officer of the Maoris … "I'm going – I've been told to," was the reply. He led forward the men round him, and according to the testimony of the Maori officer, none came back.'[9]

Captain Francis Eastwood from 6 RIR also gave an account of the annihilation of half of his company at the Farm:

> I led it in. There was not a falter, they followed us like one man, soon catching me up and we tore forward like driven birds. A mine did not explode at our feet but shrapnel, machine guns, rifle fire poured into us, a sort of enfilade fire as the man on my left seemed to take the lot … Once the volley was over, there was no more firing, as every man was lying flat in the long grass … The order was again shouted down the line. I shouted, 'Go.' About seven men arose out of the original hundred and I was hit in the wrist. Fortunately or not, as they got it later, the second half of my company did not come in.[10]

Eastwood's men barely fired a shot. Yet their courage was staggering to those who watched. After the war, bodies of 6 RIR soldiers were found within 25 yards of the crest of the ridge.[11]

Lieutenant James Pollock, in charge of 6 RIR's machine-gun post, witnessed the destruction of his battalion from a nearby ridge. He and some survivors beat off an initial Turkish counter-attack. But they were running low on ammunition and had almost no water left. They received a report of an imminent massive Turkish assault down the ridge. Instead of withdrawing, Pollock and his men waited. He wrote a scribbled entry in his diary – 'My End.'[12]

Just before dawn the following day the survivors of 6 RIR at the Farm heard the roar of Mustafa Kemal's men. Thousands of Turkish soldiers poured down the hill. Other British battalions broke and fled. The Irish Rifles held their position, standing up in their trenches to meet the first waves of Turkish soldiers and fighting with bayonets, fists and rocks for nearly two hours. Eventually what remained of the battalion were ordered to withdraw.

The 6 RIR had arrived at Gallipoli on 6 August with twenty-eight officers and 912 other ranks. Four days later the battalion was reduced to just over 300 men led by three officers (Captain Eastwood, Lieutenant Pollock and Sergeant Duncan were among them).[13] This was the most catastrophic moment in David Duncan's military career, a horror that left its mark on the survivors. The battalion was eventually reformed and reinforced. After their withdrawal from the failed offensive at Gallipoli at the end of 1915, 6 RIR was sent to the Salonika front between modern-day Greece, Bulgaria and North Macedonia. Expecting a major Bulgarian offensive, 6 RIR were ordered to defend the Rendina gorge on the eastern fringe of the front in early 1916.

The push never came: 6 RIR casualties were low; their rations were supplemented by fish from Lake Beshik. Salonika was far from the thirst, dysentery and fire of Gallipoli. However, the abuse of alcohol – easily sourced from local villages – was a persistent problem for 10 (Irish) Division, as it was for others.[14] Duncan was again promoted, this time to company quartermaster sergeant major, in charge of the battalion's stores and supplies. In April 1916 he transferred to the Royal Irish Fusiliers (RIF), received an officer's commission as a second lieutenant, and joined 2 RIF in Salonika – a unit mostly tasked with repairing roads and defences – where he served as a transport officer.[15]

By Duncan's account, he was thrown from a horse in June 1917. He was unconscious for more than half an hour and suffered from 'a deep scalp wound'. His war service deteriorated rapidly. (Duncan claimed that he began to hear voices after this injury.)[16] Duncan's narrative of his own mental decline is somewhat unconvincing; no records exist to corroborate his account of brain trauma. Instead of a head injury, in 1931 Duncan attempted to claim compensation for a wound to his knee, which he suffered in May or June 1917. He made no mention of a head injury in his application. When Duncan was first hospitalised, he told doctors that his delusions and paranoia began after he was accused of murder in January 1922. He then changed that account in favour of his war-service injury in later consultations with psychiatrists.[17]

Rather than believing that Duncan's mental illness was caused by a fall from a horse, the most senior psychiatrist at Ontario Hospital Dr J.R. Howitt concluded that 'the balance of evidence' was against Duncan's illness being related to war service.[18] The most likely accelerant of Duncan's physical and mental deterioration was his alcoholism. By his own account, in October 1917 Duncan was reported for being drunk while on duty and sent back to the regimental depot in Ireland. His timeline appears to be wrong. The 2 RIF war diary records that Duncan was sent to England for hospital treatment in August of that year. The reason for his hospitalisation is not given. Duncan's service file has not survived. He could be highly selective and manipulative in his descriptions of his past. But disciplinary issues related to alcohol abuse and mental deterioration would explain why he was sent to England – he appears to have been punished by having to start his commission as an officer again; his previous service would not be recognised.[19]

Duncan returned to active duty in France on 15 February 1918. A month after his return to the front, he was disciplined because of his drinking and ordered back to England. There the Officers' Medical Board decided that Duncan was 'war worn' and he was asked to resign his commission and leave the British Army. During his libel trial, Duncan claimed that he left the army because he could not afford to live on the salary of a second lieutenant, a complaint more commonly heard from the petulant son of an aristocratic family than a professional solider recently commissioned from the ranks. (The *London Gazette* recorded that Duncan gave up his commission in the Royal Irish Fusiliers on 30 June 1918.)[20]

David Duncan travelled back to Belfast where he attempted to work for a time as a welder. He lasted less than six months: in the spring of 1919 he was back in military service, enlisting in the Royal Fusiliers – an English regiment with its headquarters at the Tower of London – and was given the relatively junior rank of corporal. The Royal Fusiliers were assembling two battalions – the 45th and 46th, each comprising 700 men – to aid the anti-Bolshevik forces, the 'Whites', in the Russian Civil War. The aims of Winston Churchill, the Secretary of State for War and Air, in early 1918 had been to 'strangle Bolshevism in its cradle' and get Russia back in the war.

After the armistice a war-weary British public was increasingly sceptical of the Russian campaign. The Allies had sent enough troops to prolong the Russian Civil War but not to win it. After months of stagnation and Red Army counter-attacks, Lloyd George's government decided to establish a 'North Russian Relief Force' (including the two Royal Fusiliers battalions) for a major offensive near Archangel. If a breakthrough was not made in the summer of 1919, then the Allies would withdraw and hand over the front to the already demoralised Whites.[21]

The soldiers recruited for 45th and 46th Battalions, Royal Fusiliers were mostly volunteers – veterans described as 'the pick of our fighting men'. Some, like Duncan, had served as officers during the war. But discipline was a problem, especially in the 150-strong D Company, 45th Battalion, made up of Scottish and Irish volunteers. Its commander, a former Irish rugby international from Dublin called Captain Esmond Martelli, was an alcoholic. On 1 July, two months after arriving in Russia, Martelli was arrested for drunkenness and sent back to England where he resigned his commission and left the army.[22]

The north Russian front was extremely porous; the Bolsheviks used local guides to move through undefended swamps and forests and surprise the British from the rear.[23] By the time Duncan arrived in Archangel in May 1919 British soldiers looked upon their Russian allies with extreme wariness if not outright fear and contempt. Desertions and betrayals by White soldiers were common; the Allies had taken a risk by allowing large numbers of Bolshevik prisoners to switch sides and serve in 'White' units.

On 7 July 1919 Russian soldiers in a unit called Dyer's Battalion mutinied, killing nine British officers and two non-commissioned officers. The mutineers then reportedly cut the heads, hands and feet off the dead bodies.[24] A fusilier recalled that two companies of 45th Battalion were sent to kill or capture the mutineers.[25] When they arrived at the camp:

> The Russians were drunk and firing their rifles in the open at anything. We opened fire with our Lewis guns and had them chasing around like rabbits in an attempt to get through the main entrance. Here they were met with the bayonet, by the Australian company.[26]

Of those mutineers arrested, twelve were selected for execution. This was a botched affair; only four were killed in the initial burst of fire. Captain Edward Alfrey of the 45th Battalion helped to finish off those 'left kicking at their posts'. One man, an 'uncannily cool and collected' sergeant, had not been hit. He defiantly ripped off his blindfold and shouted 'Long live the Bolsheviks' before he was shot dead.[27]

Two weeks later a company of Whites were discovered to be plotting to kill their officers. An Australian soldier recalled that a group of Polish soldiers shot every tenth man in the mutinying company.[28] An American officer described how when the First Archangel Regiment refused to go to the front, British soldiers fired on them in their barracks. Thirteen men from the Archangels were also executed; the British placed a machine gun behind the Russian soldiers selected to make up the firing squad – 'they would be shot if they did not shoot the mutineers'. The execution was carried out. The remaining soldiers agreed to go the front where they promptly deserted.[29]

Horrific accounts of atrocities committed by the Red Army, including the castration of wounded American soldiers while they were still alive, fuelled an intense sense of fear among the Allied soldiers, providing the context for occasional atrocities against suspected or proven mutineers.[30] When a drunk White Russian officer blurted out over dinner with officers from the French Foreign Legion that his men were planning a mutiny, legionnaires 'carried him out and put his feet to the fire until he had betrayed the names of the affected Russians'. Captain Alfrey recalled that 'the officer, who was quite badly burned, had to be killed'. The legionnaires then went directly to the White Russian camp and shot the suspected mutineers.[31]

By August 1919 Lloyd George's government had effectively given up hope of an allied victory on the north Russian front. A full withdrawal was decided; in September the evacuation of Allied forces was largely complete. David Duncan was sent home shortly before the rest of his battalion. He was hospitalised on his return at the British Red Cross Hospital at Netley. Meanwhile, the 45th and 46th Battalions of the Royal Fusiliers were disbanded. He travelled to Dublin after his discharge from Netley in the autumn and was released from military service on

2 December 1919. Fifteen days later he married Sarah Cockrill, the daughter of a recently deceased north Dublin jeweller. The forty-five-year-old Sarah was seventeen years older than her new husband.[32]

Once more a civilian, Duncan briefly moved into the Cockrill family home at 8 Whitworth Terrace in Drumcondra in north Dublin, before accepting a place on a course in County Wexford for veterans who wished to go into farming. Duncan failed to settle in Wexford. He stood out, recalling that the local IRA sent him two threatening letters accusing him of being an 'Orange spy'.[33]

By the autumn of 1920 Duncan was back in Belfast. On 29 September Duncan and a man called Robert Halliday attacked a group of Catholic potato-pickers who were returning in a lorry to their homes in the Markets area of the city after working in the countryside. As the lorry passed the Ropeworks factory in east Belfast a woman shouted, 'Here's the Fenians coming.' A crowd of men then gathered and threw bolts, rivets and stones. A woman was badly injured.

A man in the lorry, Patrick Catney, recognised David Duncan and Robert Halliday and gave a statement to the police. Catney said that he had worked with Duncan and knew him well. Duncan and Halliday were sent for trial on 14 January 1921; a jury found them not guilty.[34] Patrick Catney was later brutally assaulted while working on the Albertbridge Road in east Belfast; he was beaten by a group of men and then stabbed repeatedly – he survived the attack.[35]

Three days after his acquittal David Duncan joined the RIC Auxiliary Division. He was posted to 'N' Company stationed at Trim in County Meath. On 9 February N Company raided a shop in Robinstown owned by a loyalist, Richard Chandler. During the raid goods were looted and members of the family assaulted. Duncan's erratic behaviour and alcoholism were mostly ignored among the heavy-drinking Auxiliaries. (He was only fined once for poor discipline.) But in late September 1921 Duncan overstayed his leave while in Belfast. He was arrested and sent to Auxiliary Division headquarters in Dublin. There he was summarily convicted of misconduct and dismissed from service on 20 October 1921.[36]

Duncan returned to Belfast where he promptly joined the Ulster Imperial Guards. He moved into a house on Harrisburg Street off the York Road, which was listed in the 1921/1922 Belfast Street Directory as being in the possession of Joseph Duncan, David's older brother and the family member he most trusted. Joseph, a blacksmith, continued to live with his family at 44 Spamount Street.[37]

Belfast republicans noted Duncan's return to the city. IRA intelligence reports claimed that Duncan played a leading role in a group called 'the Cromwell Clubs', which had been set up, and were directed from, Ulster Unionist Party headquarters at the city's Old Town Hall. Sergeant William McCartney of Musgrave Barracks was believed to hand out lists to members of prominent republicans and nationalist businessmen for targeting.

The source of much of this intelligence was John Harkin, a former soldier and Irish Parliamentary Party councillor in Belfast. Harkin identified David Duncan as a leader of a Cromwell Club. When Harkin visited Dublin on a business trip at the end of October, he recognised Duncan on Dame Street and saw him enter Dublin Castle. Duncan's journey south was likely less conspiratorial than Harkin suspected – he believed that Duncan's trip may have been relevant to the operations of the Cromwell Clubs. In reality, Duncan was in Dublin for his disciplinary hearing prior to his ultimate dismissal from the RIC Auxiliary Division.

The Cromwell Clubs were just another, more sinister, nickname – given the notoriety of the seventeenth-century Lord Protector in Ireland – for what became the Imperial Guards. Seán MacEntee, a leading Belfast republican who had recently moved to Dublin, forwarded Harkin's report to Sinn Féin president Éamon de Valera. MacEntee, whose father had served as a nationalist councillor with Harkin on

Belfast City Council, did not use the term 'Cromwell Club' but instead highlighted David Duncan as 'one of the leaders of the new organisation' and suggested that the IRA's intelligence department 'give this matter particular attention'.

MacEntee also sent a photograph, originally published in the 1 November edition of the *Belfast Telegraph*, with an 'X' marked above Duncan, who is seen standing in front of a column of men on Canning Street, just off York Street. Also marked in the photograph is James Turkington, a vice-president of the UULA, a Belfast city councillor and secretary of the Ulster Workers' Trade Union, a breakaway and proudly loyalist trade union.[38]

Duncan quickly established himself as a leader within 1st Battalion (York Street) of the north Belfast Imperial Guard. He commanded the 'Imps' guard of honour at the funeral of Walther Pritchard. He also likely played a prominent role in the guard for the funerals of Imps and military veterans Herbert Hassard and Robert Beattie during which Hugh McAnaney and William Madden were killed. (Duncan would have known Beattie well from their service – Beattie as a quartermaster, Duncan as a transport officer – in 2 RIF in Salonika.)[39]

Certain leaders, charismatic and feared men like David Duncan, could quickly impose their authority on other loyalists, even amid the chaotic street fighting, burnings and robberies. On one occasion a group of loyalists boarded a tram stopped on the Shore Road in north Belfast, singled out a Catholic passenger, Thomas McCaffrey, and shot him. Some members of the York Road Special Constabulary were nearby. When a constable raised his rifle and aimed it at one of the gang, a witness recalled that 'a man came out of a public house opposite and getting into the line of fire put up his hand. At the same time another man who was standing beside the Specials covered them with a revolver and ordered the rifle to be lowered.' The constabulary complied. The Imps had such power and command.[40]

THE NOTORIOUS DAVID DUNCAN

In 1921, at a time when many Catholic publicans were leaving the York Road – the broad avenue that extended northwards from inner-city York Street – for fear of being shot or burned out, Patrick McMahon saw an opportunity and moved in. He took over the lease at 215 York Road from a Protestant spirit grocer called John Wilson and moved into a flat above the spacious shop.[41]

At 6.40 p.m. on 24 November 1921 two gunmen attacked Patrick McMahon at his spirit grocery at 215 York Road. Patrick was behind the counter when two men entered carrying revolvers. They demanded money from the till; McMahon handed over £6 and the men left. A few minutes later he was warned by a neighbour to shut the doors of the shop as he was now in even greater danger. McMahon described in a statement to the court what happened next:

> I opened the door and looked out. I saw a man with a revolver standing just outside the door. He did not say anything. He fired three shots at me. There are two glass panels [either side of the] door. These shots came through the door. I stooped down and the shots went over my head. When I went to push the door the prisoner [David Duncan] fired the shots through the glass. I had a good view of the man. The gas was lit in [the] kitchen and the light flashed in his face when I opened the door.[42]

The account of McMahon handing over the day's takings and then being targeted requires explanation. If the money was gone, then why attempt to shoot or murder him? The men who had stolen the money must have recognised McMahon and passed on information that he was present to McMahon's would-be-murderer. The obvious excitement or commotion in the street suggests that his attacker made it clear that he was going to kill McMahon; somebody had enough time to warn his intended victim.

GHOSTS OF A FAMILY

Why would loyalists particularly wish to harm Patrick McMahon? McMahon had recently taken over a business previously managed by a Protestant family at a time when Catholic families on the same road were being forced out of business following attacks by loyalist gangs. Moving into a previously Protestant-owned business would have been seen as an act of defiance in Duncan's territory.

McMahon was far from alone in being targeted; several other Catholic publicans were also marked out for death in York Road/Street, part of a sectarian purge of Catholic businessmen in the area. The night before the attack on Patrick McMahon, a publican at 183 York Street called Joe Cosgrove heard a knock at the door of his bar shortly after closing. When Cosgrove went to open the door, he was confronted by 'two or three armed men' who opened fire. One bullet hit him on the shoulder; another shattered his elbow.[43]

Intelligence gathered by the IRA suggests a motive for why Duncan – among the other gunmen and paramilitary leaders in North Belfast – attacked Patrick McMahon. An IRA report on the Special Constabulary compiled in July 1922 noted that Duncan, 'ex-B&T [Black and Tan] lives with H. Black, York Street, Adj. in Imp. Gds.'[44] Henry Black was a grocer and a loyalist whose shop at 213 York Road was right beside that of Patrick McMahon. During the 1920s Henry Black and his father Thomas appear to have converted the premises into a pub called the Volunteer.

Although Duncan is recorded in military records as living at 44 Harrisburg Street, he appears to have moved a lot (possibly to avoid being targeted by the IRA). His address was later recorded by the RUC as being on Seaview Street – also off the York Road.[45]

The precise reason for why Duncan might have wanted to kill Patrick McMahon is not clear, beyond a general sectarian campaign of violence in the city. But, if the IRA's intelligence is correct, he clearly had every opportunity to watch and nurture a grievance against McMahon.

His daily proximity would explain why he was recognised so quickly by Patrick McMahon as his would-be murderer.

David Duncan was accused of murdering James McIvor the day after the attack on Patrick McMahon. McIvor was a shopkeeper who traded on Little Patrick Street, just off York Street. Duncan would repeatedly state that McIvor was an IRA commandant in Belfast. (There is no evidence to substantiate Duncan's allegation. McIvor is not included in the IRA's membership rolls for Belfast.)[46]

Two witnesses came forward to identify Duncan as one of two men who shot McIvor. Daniel Loughran was sipping a cup of tea in his house opposite McIvor's at around 4.45 p.m. He could see McIvor smoking at his shop doorway and conversing with a customer. Duncan and another man approached, pushed McIvor back into the shop, pulled out revolvers and fired several shots, hitting McIvor in the chest and abdomen. Duncan's companion was considerably taller and ran from the scene 'like a greyhound'.

Another witness, a Catholic ex-soldier called Bernard Monaghan, testified that he had served with Duncan in 6 RIR at Salonika. Monaghan saw Duncan and another man on Little Patrick Street firing five or six shots into McIvor's shop. He ran away as he feared his former comrade might 'give him one too'.

During the subsequent trial Duncan's barrister claimed that Monaghan was motivated by sectarian malice since he and the accused 'did not dig with the same foot'. Monaghan responded: 'When you are soldiering together that doesn't matter'. He also admitted that he did not know at the time whether to report the shooting to the IRA or the police. After co-operating with the police he worried about the possibility of 'being plugged too'. Monaghan's intense fear of Duncan, despite their experience soldiering together, was obvious. A customer who was shot in the leg while speaking to McIvor at the time of the attack, a Protestant woman called Margaret Knocker, did not give evidence at the trial. Another witness in the shop, a Mrs Mulholland, also did not provide a statement.[47]

A British Army intelligence report – not revealed to the court – indicated that Duncan also attempted to murder another publican. At 9 p.m. on 3 December, eight days after the McIvor murder, James Kelly closed his spirit grocery on Lawther Street in north Belfast. Shortly afterwards he answered a knock on the door and saw two men. One immediately drew a revolver and shot Kelly at close range. A bullet struck him in neck; he was also wounded in the face but survived the attack. He gave the military a description of the two men – a very tall man and another shorter, stockier man wearing a trench coat (the second man fired the shots). The Norfolks' intelligence officer Captain Papworth concluded that these were the same two men who had killed McIvor.[48]

Duncan was never charged for this attempted murder. At the end of December 1921, shortly before the arrest of Duncan for the attempted murder of Patrick McMahon, DI Lynn recorded in his diary that he was also making 'inquiries' about the attack on James Kelly.[49] But without a witness to testify in court, Lynn could not add this crime to Duncan's charge sheet. Kelly may have been reluctant to co-operate with police given the pattern of reprisals against those who assisted with the police investigations into loyalist killings. British Army intelligence reports are full of the names of alleged perpetrators of attacks on Catholic businesses and residents. But these men were very rarely arrested or charged by the police. Witnesses who spoke to the British Army often refused to co-operate with the police or to testify in court. Patrick McGurnaghan, the young boy shot on the same day as the attack on Patrick McMahon, was a key witness in the trial of a loyalist, Thomas Saunders, accused of shooting and wounding Catholic shopkeeper Sarah Bannon in the face in March of that year. Although the badly injured McGurnaghan survived, he did not testify against Saunders.[50]

Patrick McMahon did provide evidence to the RIC, which led Head Constable William Love directly to David Duncan who was arrested on 4 January 1922. On learning of the charge Duncan replied: 'I know nothing about it, Head.' The confidence shown by Patrick McMahon gave courage to others. Witnesses to the McIvor murder now came forward. Six days after his arrest for the McMahon attack, Duncan was also charged with the murder of James McIvor.

The case against Duncan divided the police. DI William Lynn appeared on the side of the prosecution. A sergeant under Lynn's command, William Robb, also gave evidence, but for the defence. Robb claimed that Duncan offered vital assistance to the police in the York Road area. Sergeant Robb's evidence was backed up by a local Presbyterian minister and prominent loyalist, Reverend Samuel Cochrane.[51]

Newspaper reports in the unionist press adopted a sympathetic tone towards Duncan. The *Northern Whig* described him as a 'respectably dressed' former officer with a fine war record.[52] Duncan's barrister, James Williamson KC, called a witness who claimed that Duncan was a mile away on the day of the murder. Williamson also informed the court that Bernard Monaghan had recently been arrested for shouting 'Up the Rebels' and breaking windows on Royal Avenue in Belfast city centre.

Williamson concluded the case for the defence by telling the court that, as a former officer, his client was used to discipline and controlling men. Duncan was 'not the class of man to commit such a crime'. Rather he was 'a member of a volunteer corps called the Imperial Guards – a non-official body composed entirely of ex-servicemen, for the purpose of aiding the civil authorities, and again and again he had marched at the head of his men up York Street'.

In summing up the McIvor murder case Mr Justice T.W. Brown said that whoever killed McIvor was of 'the lowest breed'. He questioned why Bernard Monaghan did not give evidence to the police earlier, suggesting that it was due to his unfavourable character. He praised

David Duncan and the Imperial Guards for 'guarding property' and helping the police. He also pointed to Sergeant Robb's evidence in support of Duncan. The accused had several alibis for the time of the murder. If there was any 'doubt' in the jury's minds they should look to 'evidence of character'.

This was a risibly selective account of the role played by the Imperial Guards during the violence of late 1921 and early 1922, as the British Army could attest. Duncan's war record also showed that he had been forced to resign his commission because of a lack of discipline. Sergeant Robb's evidence in defence of Duncan's character was wilfully misleading. Nonetheless, the jury took eight minutes to find Duncan not guilty. The crown solicitor then dropped the McMahon shooting charge. Duncan, who had already been on bail, was free to go.[53]

Patrick McMahon's faith in the Northern Irish justice system proved disastrous. Duncan was cleared of all the charges against him. Expecting retaliation for his role in the trial, Bernard Monaghan left Belfast and joined the National Army in Dublin.[54] Patrick McMahon quickly vacated 215 York Road.

A few months later 215 York Road was back in Protestant hands – a publican called William Barriskill had taken over the lease. An Orangeman and a freemason, Barriskill's politics were known; he was a supporter of the unionist MP in the Northern Irish parliament for Belfast East, James Duff. He had previously worked in Belfast's linen mills. In the 1920s he became a successful spirit grocer.[55]

Patrick McMahon and Bernard Monaghan had every reason to be afraid. Although he did not directly name Duncan, Belfast IRA officer Seán Montgomery recalled in his memoirs that, 'There was a lieutenant in the Ulster [Imperial] Guard. That man's favourite was shooting Barmen about York Street and elsewhere and was blamed for shooting a girl out of Gallahers Tobacco Factory, York Street.'[56] The woman Montgomery was referring to was Nellie McMullan (22), shot dead on

16 May 1922 as a loyalist reprisal for the killing of Robert Dudgeon a few hours earlier. Dudgeon was a former Royal Irish Rifles soldier who worked in city hall and was popular in loyalist circles. At the inquest into his death it emerged that the military shot Dudgeon during rioting in the west of the city.[57]

Anybody trying to understand why Patrick McMahon had the courage and the connections to pursue a case against Duncan could have quickly alighted on a single explanation – there was only one Patrick McMahon who was a prominent publican and spirit grocer in Belfast. This was the brother of Owen McMahon, and Owen was the close friend of politicians, a man who was respected, and wielded influence, across the city. Patrick McMahon's challenge would receive a deadly answer.

Duncan also had a network of powerful men who protected him. His recent military and RIC Auxiliary Division service was anything but favourable. Nonetheless, this had not prevented his recruitment to the 'C1' Constabulary in March 1922 as part of a mass incorporation of Imperial Guards. Andrew Magill at the Ministry of Home Affairs offered the following description of how Duncan was initially selected for police service: 'Some hundreds of men were marched into a hall in York Street, Belfast, and were inspected by the Commandant of the C1 Division [Colonel William Goodwin], who selected a proportion of them for consideration as members of the C1 Force.'[58]

Days earlier the York Street Imps had been involved in the street lynching of Hugh McAnaney at the funeral of their comrade Herbert Hassard. Colonel Goodwin, a former commanding officer of 12th (County Antrim) Battalion of the Royal Irish Rifles, was recruiting policemen from one of Belfast's most murderous paramilitary groups. Goodwin did not know the north Belfast area and relied upon a local officer to direct him when it came to recruitment. That man was thirty-nine-year-old Captain Sam Waring. For Duncan, having Sam Waring's loyalty was essential and partly explains why, despite his deteriorating mental condition, he was able to operate so freely and with such authority in North Belfast.

Waring was, like Duncan, an *Old Contemptible*, a pre-First World War professional soldier. Born in Lisburn, he worked briefly as a ship's engineer for Harland and Wolff before leaving Belfast in 1900 at the age of eighteen and joining an English regiment, the Sherwood Foresters. (A battalion of the 'Old Stubborns' had been stationed in Belfast in the late 1890s.) Waring took to his new profession, climbing steadily through the ranks; he was promoted to sergeant in 1907. At the outbreak of the First World War Waring was commissioned as a lieutenant and posted to the Leicestershire Regiment. He was badly wounded at the Battle of Hooge in 1915. Although no longer fit for front-line soldiering, Waring joined what became the Royal Air Force where he served as a logistics officer.[59]

Sam Waring retired from military service with the rank of captain in early 1921. He then moved with his family to a house off the Antrim Road in north Belfast. Shortly after his arrival he was recruited by the Ulster Ex-Servicemen's Association as an administrator.

Waring's uncle, also called Samuel, was the assistant manager of the sprawling Crumlin Road mills owned by the Ewart family. Samuel Waring senior served as Joseph Davison's deputy in the Orange district of north Belfast and as the vice chairman of the Shankill Unionist Association. His brother William, the murdered caretaker of Clifton Street Orange Hall, was a close friend of DI John Nixon. Such connections, combined with his war record, explain why Captain Sam Waring was appointed as a senior commander of the Imps and subsequently adjutant of the 'C1' Class Constabulary in north Belfast.[60]

Waring was loyal to his men. On 28 June 1922 a forty-year-old 'C1' constable, former Imp and RAF serviceman called William Quinn was arrested by the RUC and charged with the illegal possession of explosives and a pistol. An inebriated Quinn had threatened to shoot a Catholic barman with a pistol. He gave his address as Louisa Street in north Belfast. Captain Waring gave evidence in court in support of Quinn. He claimed that Quinn was entitled to keep the revolver since his life was in danger. Quinn was convicted for illegal possession but did not receive a prison sentence. He was also accused of attempting to murder a woman, a friend of his wife, on Louisa Street, but that charge was dropped.[61]

Two days before the McMahon murders, RIC Constable Andrew McCloskey passed on an urgent message to Belfast's republican leaders:

> There is a man named Captain Waring in charge of the 'C' Specials. I have reason to believe that this man is one of the Organisers of the Murder Gang. He works this business with Fee, a rent Agent, on the Old Lodge Road. The Latter resigned last week and Harry Taylor, a Clothier on Peter's Hill has taken up his position in Command of the B Specials. These three men Waring, Fee and Taylor have been and are still organising the murders and massacres of Catholics. Waring is the leader of the gang.

Although from Donegal, McCloskey was an old Belfast hand; he had been stationed in the city for more than twenty years. In 1922 he was based in Leopold Street Barracks in 'C' District. McCloskey had a good, if somewhat unremarkable, record until the start of the Belfast troubles in 1920. He was fined four times in 1920 and 1921 for misconduct, including twice by DI Nixon. He did not spare Nixon in the evidence he gave to Sinn Féin. According to McCloskey, Nixon was also running a 'reprisal' gang: 'These are the old RIC. They are out for the purpose of shooting IRA men and failing them, shooting any Catholic.'

In terms of professional grievance, McCloskey had more reason to place the blame on Nixon. But he chose instead to underline the

GHOSTS OF A FAMILY

exceptional threat posed by Waring, Taylor and Fee: 'I haven't the least doubt but Waring and these two Assistants of his are bringing about most of the murders and shootings. If these three were got hold of most of the shootings would cease. There are others, but these three are the brains carriers.'[62] McCloskey's evidence was ignored when it came to writing the Nixon memo.

Waring relied on loyal former Royal Irish Rifles NCOs, men like forty-nine-year-old James Lyle, an Imps' company commander in north Belfast. Lyle had served as a sergeant in a seven-man machine gun detachment under the command of Lieutenant John Bowen-Colthurst during the 1903–4 British military operation in Tibet led by Colonel Francis Younghusband. Younghusband's force killed hundreds of Tibetans during this ill-matched, brutal campaign.[63]

In 1916 Captain Bowen-Colthurst and Company Sergeant Major Sergeant Lyle, both serving in 3rd Battalion, Royal Irish Rifles, were mobilised to suppress the Easter Rising in Dublin. Two days after fighting broke out in the city, Colthurst ordered the execution by firing squad of the pacifist, Irish nationalist and social campaigner, Francis Sheehy Skeffington and two journalists, Thomas Dickson and Patrick McIntyre.[64]

Colthurst praised Lyle for the assistance he gave him during the raid of a shop on Camden Street later that day that led to the capture of an Irish volunteer, Patrick Nolan. Some years later Nolan recalled what happened next: 'The sergeant in charge said I had better say my prayers as he was going to shoot me. He shot me alright.' Although badly wounded in the chest, Nolan survived. Lyle left the army in June 1916 with an 'exemplary' record and returned home to Belfast. (Colthurst was court-martialled, found to be 'guilty but insane' and, after a period of psychiatric treatment, emigrated to Canada.)[65]

In 1922 Lyle lived in Avoca Street, close to the western edge of the Bruce demesne. He was appointed as an 'instructor' for the 'B' Specials in north Belfast. Six days after the McMahon murders the IRA shot and badly wounded another James Lyle in an apparent case of mistaken identity – when the man, a mechanic from Dromore in County Down, confirmed his name his attackers drew their revolvers and fired six shots as he tried to escape. (Although seriously wounded, he survived.)[66]

Captain William Pinder was also a key figure in the 'C1' Special Constabulary in north Belfast. An Englishman who was two years older than Duncan, Pinder had been commissioned during the war as an officer in 3rd Battalion, Somerset Light Infantry, who were for a time stationed in Belfast. He and his family remained in Belfast after his retirement from the military shortly after the end of the war.

Pinder lived with his family at Lincoln Avenue, a few hundred yards from Kinnaird Terrace. A well-known amateur boxer, Pinder was employed by the Ulster Ex-Servicemen's Association as the organising secretary for north Belfast. He also joined the 'B' Specials before transferring to the 'C1' Constabulary in 1922, serving for a period as an intelligence officer.

Pinder worked closely with Harry Taylor, the 'B' Specials commander in west Belfast and with Major Leathes, head of intelligence for the Special Constabulary. Leathes and Pinder ran agents throughout the city. Leathes was an ex-Royal Irish Rifles officer who served as head of military intelligence in Belfast during the First World War. He was also in charge of the harbour's wartime defences and served as commanding officer of the Belfast Volunteer Defence Corps, a sort of wartime home guard. Leathes' former volunteer force in the docks area of north Belfast was largely incorporated into the Special Constabulary.[67]

Captain Edward Turner also held considerable sway among the veterans and loyalists in north Belfast. A veteran of the Boer campaign in South Africa, Turner re-enlisted at the start of the First World War, joining 9th Battalion, Royal Irish Fusiliers as a transport officer. He was awarded the Military Cross in March 1918. The following month he

GHOSTS OF A FAMILY

was shot in the chest and invalided out of front-line service. He later moved to Belfast where he married and settled down to his new trade as a publican. (A relation owned a pub on Peter's Hill, close to that of loyalist Annie Armstrong, the shop of Harry Taylor and Brown's Square Barracks.) Turner and his family lived at Cliftonpark Avenue, not far from the Antrim Road in north Belfast.

Turner appears to have played some role in the loyalist response to the IRA's campaign. When Councillor William Bickerstaff, the Brown's Square 'B' Special Constabulary commander, nominated Turner to a city council committee, Turner was praised for his defence of loyalists during 'the trouble'.[68] The Ministry of Home Affairs identified Turner as a key supporter of Nixon during the early 1920s. He subsequently led the official mourning party at the funeral of Nixon's father, representing the Orange Order and unionist councillors.[69]

Turner was especially active in the Ulster Protestant Voters' Defence Association, an organisation carefully monitored by the police and which included prominent loyalist critics of the government such as William Coote, Special Constabulary sub-district commanders like its chairman, George Huey, a jeweller who commanded the 'B' Specials on York Road, and Councillor James Turkington from the Shankill Road (photographed with Duncan leading the parade of Imps in late 1921).[70] Turner was also a leader of the city's anti-Prohibition movement – he steadily expanded his business interests in the 1920s, acquiring a number of public houses and spirit groceries in the city.[71]

Edward Turner was a supporter of the unionist MP Tom McConnell, whom he nominated as a candidate for the North Belfast constituency in the 1923 Westminster election. McConnell, known to his critics as 'the brewer', had many investments in the drinks and hospitality sector in Belfast – and was involved in a brewery business in the city. In 1922 the UULA launched a campaign to boycott Guinness and get their members to drink McConnells instead. (The proposal from John

THE NOTORIOUS DAVID DUNCAN

Andrews MP was roundly criticised by the rank and file: 'it would be necessary to put half a glass of whiskey into every pint to bring it up to the required strength.)[72]

David Duncan was closely connected to North Belfast's MP; he spoke on a York Road platform beside McConnell during his successful campaign in 1923. According to the *Northern Whig* newspaper Duncan was cheered loudly by the crowd. Duncan 'assured the large and enthusiastic audience that Mr McConnell's thoughts were ever with the ex-service men – the loyal men who had done their bit for King and country'.[73]

The Irish government believed that McConnell was an extremist. An intelligence report in mid-1922 referred to the North Belfast MP as a supporter of the 'Coote-ite Murder Gang'.[74] This view was shared by Fr Bernard Laverty, a priest at St Patrick's Church in North Belfast, who told Stephen Tallents that McConnell was 'a diehard leader [of a] murder gang'.[75]

Even if McConnell was not guilty of active support or involvement in a campaign of murder, he would have known about Duncan's reputation for violence. An uncompromising loyalist with a war record – in France as well as on the streets in Belfast – evidently played well. Men like Waring, Pinder, Lyle, Turner, Turkington, Huey and McConnell were all in prominent positions in north Belfast at the time that David Duncan was leading the most violent Imps faction. Like many others in positions of power they could have moved to stop Duncan. Instead, they directly recruited him.

Some in Belfast were quick to make money out of political instability and violence. In 1918, acting under the orders of Michael Collins, Dr Russell McNabb purchased nearly 250,000 rounds of .303 ammunition from Ulster volunteers with access to UVF stores. (A considerable amount of ammunition used in the subsequent War of Independence was of UVF origin.) The IRA also acquired some UVF rifles.[76]

Such intercommunal transgressions – loyalists co-operating with republicans to make money – were less common after the outbreak of violence in Belfast in the summer of 1920. However, some loyalists stood, indirectly at least, to benefit from the violence Duncan and his Imps inflicted on Catholic publicans, shopkeepers and businesses in the city. After twenty years of increasing trade in the pub and spirit grocery business, the years 1921–23 saw a sudden regression in Catholic ownership in areas where loyalist attacks on publicans had been most frequent.

The provisional government in Dublin concluded that there was a systematic campaign to remove Catholic publicans and spirit grocery owners from much of Belfast. Among the many reports of a sudden upsurge in threats and violence was one from William Barrett, the former leader of the 1907 police 'mutiny', who owned a spirit grocery on the Grosvenor Road near the city centre. Barrett was especially outraged that the police were responsible for much of the violence. He saw 'C1' Constable Herbert Scott push a notice under his door ordering him 'to leave or be shot or bombed out'. Scott had taken up residence nearby in the house of another retired Catholic RIC constable who had been intimidated into leaving by Scott and his gang.[77]

Some publicans tried to distance themselves from any public display of sympathies, including towards Catholic victims of the violence. IRA officer Russell McNabb alleged that James Murray was 'a fine example of one of these filleted Catholics. He is an extremely wealthy man, and mixes in the wealthy publican circle in Belfast.' The McMahons were, McNabb claimed, 'intimate friends' with Murray. But he did not attend their funerals nor did he close his business as a mark of respect – 'Furthermore, in order to openly disown any connection with the funeral he turned up at his shop in his luxurious Rolls Royce as the funeral was passing, and deliberately motored away from it.' Some days later, McNabb reported, Murray closed his business during the funeral of a special constable. McNabb was unsympathetic, but Murray was in an exposed position – he lived on Clifton Street, not far from the McMahons, and his pub had already been smashed up and looted.[78]

By 20 March 1922 seventeen Catholic traders left the York Street area after attacks and intimidation. Protestant publicans like James Brownlow, Alfred Moore, Thomas Harrison and Margaret Parsons steadily took over a string of pubs from Catholic families such as the Lambes, Gilmores, Cosgroves, McMullens and Donnellys.[79] George Turkington, a shopkeeper on Grove Street, just off York Street, and a supporter of UULA councillor David Jones, petitioned the government for the release of loyalist gang leader William Nesbitt, claiming that Nesbitt was the victim of a conspiracy by a 'Sinn Féin policeman'. Publican Annie Armstrong also appealed for Nesbitt's release, describing him as 'a trustworthy loyalist'.[80]

After he was shot by loyalists, Patrick Madden – who owned two lucrative pubs on the Crumlin Road and the Old Lodge Road – sold both his premises to William Dodds, who had recently entered the liquor and hospitality trade.[81] Elizabeth McBride – the widow of Alex, murdered in June 1921 – accepted a bid for her pub from a Protestant publican named Elizabeth Vance. A few months after the murders at Kinnaird Terrace, Owen McMahon's brother Daniel sold the prosperous Balmoral to Fred McNair.[82] Some of these sales may have been unconnected to loyalist violence, but it is very likely to have been a factor in at least some.

On 18 March 1922 Rose McMahon was serving customers in her sister's grocery shop – McCreeves – at 237 York Street when a crowd gathered outside. A man suddenly strode forward, raised a revolver and shot her twice, once in the chest and once in the arm.[83] Rose McMahon survived the shooting – after spending more than three months in hospital. Her sister Elizabeth McCreeve told Sinn Féin representatives in the city that she knew who the raiders were; she identified them to the police who 'advised' her to 'say nothing about it as otherwise she would run the risk of being shot'. She also pointed a finger directly at the Drennan family, who ran a grocery shop two doors down from the McCreeves.

McCreeve's testimony about the Drennans' alleged involvement in the killings in the area was sent to the provisional government. The Drennan brothers were members of the North-East Unionist Club on Brougham Street where they frequently attended meetings. (William F. Drennan nominated Herbert Dixon – later Lord Glentoran – as a candidate for the Westminster elections in 1923. Dixon had lobbied the government for the release of loyalist internees.) According to Elizabeth McCreeve:

> On their return from these meetings the hooligan element of the district congregate in the house apparently for instructions ... she overheard them say that "£5 and a white cap [immunity] was not enough for murdering a Catholic", from words it came to blows and "Specials" had to be called in to quell the dispute.[84]

Elizabeth said she saw the Drennans passing revolvers and ammunition from the back of their business to 'hooligans' who then carried out the shootings.[85]

It is difficult to corroborate McCreeve's testimony. She was clearly a business competitor with the Drennans and could have been motived by resentment. However, it is striking that during the attack on her shop, a few doors down from Patrick McMahon's premises and a week before the murders in Kinnaird Terrace, the gunman picked out a single principal victim among the customers and other staff in the shop – Rose McMahon. The attack may have been a case of mistaken identity or a belief that Rose and Patrick were related.

Some Protestant publicans were also targeted. William Armstrong a well-known publican with a range of business interests on the Newtownards Road and the Shankill Road was gunned down near his house in east Belfast just after 11 p.m. on 23 December 1921. His widow gave evidence which suggested he may have been murdered by men who were in a 'heavy' car. A passing driver saw a car with two red lights close to Armstrong at the time of the attack. As Armstrong walked towards his house – his children were hanging Christmas decorations in the front room – he was approached by a group of men who shot him four times, twice in the chest and twice in the back. The use of a motor car by the IRA to carry out an attack was unusual, especially at a time of local curfews and police checkpoints. Armstrong, who had recently purchased several pubs in the Shankill Road, may have acquired some powerful and dangerous enemies.[86]

Aside from Duncan, is it possible – among the already identified group of loyalist killers operating in Belfast in March 1922 – to identify longer-term grievances and more immediate trigger incidents which may have contributed to the attack on the McMahons? A grievance might place a victim in a perpetrator's sights but a trigger event, often a highly stressful incident or series of incidents, may prompt an individual to take some drastic action, in this case lashing out at a proximate target as a means of retribution. The stress of a trigger event may even allow the main perpetrator to persuade others to help settle his or her enduring sense of grievance (one not necessarily shared by the rest of the group).[87]

As already observed, for many of his accusers Nixon's fanaticism seems to be enough. Although he may have briefly served as a low-ranking IRA volunteer, Eddie McKinney, the McMahon's employee does not appear in police or military intelligence files in Belfast. The city was full of more promising middle-class or professional targets for reprisal. After the raid on St Mary's Hall, there was extensive intelligence available on IRA and Sinn Féin leaders and their supporters in Belfast. Among them was the family of Belfast IRA commander Seán MacEntee, who ran a pub near the city centre. Nixon also does not match the description given by survivors of the murders. And although they received support from the same networks, Nixon does not appear to have had a direct connection with David Duncan either.

Did Nixon experience a trigger event for wanting to carry out a spectacular killing on 24 March 1922? It was widely accepted at the time (and since) that the timing of the attack in Kinnaird Terrace was an immediate response to the killing of two 'A' Class members of the Special Constabulary earlier that day. Constables William Chermside and Thomas Cunningham were shot dead while on patrol on May Street during the afternoon of 23 May 1922.

Thomas Cunningham was twenty-two and from County Cavan. He had some connections to the Nixon family. Cunningham's mother was from Graddum near Ballyjamesduff – close to Nixon's family home – and his cousin appears to have been employed as a farm servant for a period on the farm of Nixon's late wife's family.[88] While any police killing is likely to have angered Nixon, it is unlikely that this rather loose Cavan connection to Constable Cunningham would have been enough to send Nixon into a murderous rage.

There was a strong suspicion within official circles, in Belfast and London, that Nixon colluded with the murderers of a Catholic publican, John Shevlin. Nixon could have been part of a cabal that sought to promote and then extract rent from loyalist business interests by attacking nationalist, Catholic-owned premises and their owners. For a district inspector, he was far too close to loyalist leaders in his district and had even publicly accepted a gift of money from them.

Unlike in the case of Shevlin, there is nothing in British government or military papers to suggest that Nixon was part of a conspiracy related to the McMahon and McKinney killings. His moral or even practical support for the killings cannot be ruled out, but there is no compelling evidence to suggest that he was the primary instigator of the McMahon murders.

Constable Henry Gordon certainly had experience of killing but it is difficult to find a motive for why he, Constable Alex Sterritt or other regular RIC Brown's Square constables, should have targeted Owen McMahon, unless they were directed to by others and responded unquestioningly.[89]

Another potential suspect, Head Constable Robert Pakenham, was based at Court Street Barracks, not far from the Bruce demesne and Kinnaird Terrace. The evidence given by Sergeant Martin Bruen suggested that Pakenham was very much on the side of loyalist extremists in north Belfast. However, Pakenham was more than ten years older than the description of the principal suspect. He spoke with a west of Ireland accent. And Pakenham also had no obvious motive to target Owen McMahon and his family for such an exceptional massacre.

There is of course the possibility of mistaken identity. A Patrick McMahon, unrelated to Owen's family, was an IRA volunteer in 'B' Company in west Belfast. But that does not explain why most of a family was murdered.[90] Past police reprisals during curfew hours had generally been more selective. The killers arrived in lorries and did not seem concerned about being interrupted, except perhaps by the military. Michael Garvey's killers chatted to a group of men on the street while they calmly waited to be picked up in a lorry. The hurried approach of the McMahon murderers, running away through the Bruce demesne on foot, suggests a different type of attack carried out by individuals who were anxious not to be intercepted by other police.

Captain Sam Waring and James Lyle are other potential suspects. They both lived close to the McMahons in north Belfast and were prominent in the Imps. A memorial service for William Waring was held at St Enoch's Presbyterian Church on 19 March. Three days later – two days before the attack on Kinnaird Terrace – the inquest was held.[91] The support offered by James Lyle to Captain Colthurst during the course of the Easter Rising in Dublin suggests that Lyle was an individual untroubled by, and involved in, murderous reprisal. However, there is no reason why Sam Waring or James Lyle would single out the McMahons for such extreme retribution. Neither men matched the physical description of the man who led the attack on the McMahons. Lyle was forty-nine years old in 1922 and surviving photographs of Waring show a tall, slim man with a moustache.[92]

There were many others in the city who were responsible for atrocity, men like Jordy Harper or 'C1' Special Constables Thomas Johnston and Alec 'Buck' Robinson. But again they also had no specific, identifiable grudge or motive to target Owen McMahon or his family and commit what was – even by the standards of the time – such an exceptional massacre. Alec Robinson – nineteen at the time of the murders – was too young to meet the description of the leader of the gang. Ex-soldier Sam O'Neill was acquitted of the robbery of Patrick McMahon's pub in January 1921. It seems unlikely that he would wait more than a year to organise a group to take such an extreme revenge against the McMahon family.

What about Brown's Square's 'B' Specials commandant, William Bickerstaff? He was involved in the grocery, pubs and spirit grocery trade. Did he want to move in on Owen McMahon's business? Or did he hold a grudge against a family related to the sale of pubs to Bernard McMahon in 1910? And then there is Bickerstaff's connection to Kinnaird Terrace via the Purdys. Were the McMahons being spied on by their neighbours?

The political scientist Stathis Kalyvas has written about the prevalence of 'malicious denunciations' during civil wars. Neighbours and/or competitors contract out grievances, dressed up as political intelligence, so that violent groups will rid them of their intimate enemies.[93] The Purdys were Presbyterians who came from the same small rural area as David Duncan's parents, just south of the County Down village of Ballynahinch. In 1920 Rosabell Purdy acquired a new public house – the Somme Bar – at 87 Peter's Hill, immediately across the street from Brown's Square police barracks. The occupier of the meat-curing business next door was William Bickerstaff.

The Purdys bought and sold other pubs during the time of the 'pogrom'. One of these was a pub on Earl Street, just off York Street in north Belfast. Another was a lucrative business at 97 Old Lodge Road, the former premises of a Catholic publican James O'Neill, who left after his pub was smashed up and looted by loyalists in July 1921. Rosabell Purdy was the registered owner of 97 Old Lodge Road for only a few months; she handed over the pub to Shankill publican James Armstrong – the brother of the murdered William – at the end of 1922. By 1924 it was owned by a tailor called John Morrison who put it up for sale in that same year.[94]

It is unwise to draw conclusions about the Purdys. They were loyalist publicans, business competitors of the McMahons, with a pub adjacent to Bickerstaff's premises and Brown's Square Barracks, and William Purdy had shown his political commitment by joining the Young Citizen Volunteers paramilitary group. But that in itself is not evidence of any intent on the part of the Purdys to harm their neighbours. However, in the paranoid atmosphere of the loyalist Shankill Road in early 1922, it is possible that a passing word by Rosabell Purdy or her son about the McMahons – the comings and goings of men like Eddie McKinney to visit their house or stay the night – could have planted a seed of suspicion in the minds of some very dangerous men like the special constables of Brown's Square.[95]

Bickerstaff was a leader of the 'B' Specials in Brown's Square. But he does not fit the description of the leader of the gang that murdered the McMahons. He was also more than ten years too old. Both Bickerstaff and the Purdys also do not appear to have had a pressing reason to single out 3 Kinnaird Terrace for a spectacular atrocity. And Rosabell Purdy cared for Eliza McMahon, Lily McMahon and Mary Downey in the immediate aftermath of the murders.

This leaves David Duncan. It is reasonable to presume that Duncan's reputation for ferocity, even by the standards of Belfast during that period, was earned. It would have been impossible for him to occupy a senior position in the Imps' most feared battalion without being involved in extreme violence. Duncan was a killer, with a potential grievance against the McMahon family.

Patrick McMahon was exceptionally courageous. Duncan would never have been arrested for the murder of James McIvor if Patrick McMahon had not first come forward to give an account of the attack on him the day before.

David Duncan experienced a series of trigger events in the days and hours before 24 March 1922. The arrest and trial, which could have resulted in Duncan's execution or life imprisonment, was self-evidently highly stressful. He later admitted that the trial caused a rapid deterioration in his mental state.

More bad news followed. On 22 March 1922, thirty-six hours before the McMahon killings, Duncan received confirmation from the British government that his military pension for the gunshot wound to his left arm was being terminated. (Military doctors estimated that the disability in his arm was now less than 5 per cent, far below the 20 per cent threshold for a pension.) Duncan was furious and campaigned unsuccessfully until his death to have the decision reversed.[96]

Around the same time as he had his pension revoked, the raid by the RIC and the Special Constabulary on St Mary's Hall on 18 March 1922 revealed that the IRA had recently been gathering intelligence on Duncan. A report on the Imperial Guards was dated from the day before the raid. Duncan's name and address was top of a list of Imps of interest to the IRA (other names included Joseph Gault, Jordy Harper and James Galbraith, who had all been implicated in recent murders). A confiscated Belfast IRA report was signed by an officer called Hugh O'Keeney. (Since O'Keeney was an unusual surname in Belfast, this intelligence may have placed the O'Keeney family under suspicion.) News of this IRA intelligence-gathering – uncovered by the Special Constabulary – would have exacerbated Duncan's paranoia.

Police also found a list of publicans and spirit grocers in the hall. The purpose of the list was not clear. However, it is possible that Owen McMahon and/or his brothers were included, and that this may have enabled Duncan to persuade his accomplices to target the McMahons.[97] It appears that Owen's brother Patrick left Belfast for a time in 1922. He sold some of his pubs in the city. Owen McMahon stayed; indeed, he was the only one of the McMahon brothers to list his profession as well as his personal residence in the Belfast directory for 1921/1922.[98] Loyalist paramilitaries made it their business to target those who denounced them to the police. If he could not locate Patrick McMahon, then Owen was also a candidate for retribution.

The McMahons seem to have known they were under threat in the weeks preceding the attack. Joe Devlin told the House of Commons that shortly before the murders, a special constable who lived near the family came to see the McMahons and offered to give them revolvers. The McMahons declined. Keeping weapons in the house could offer protection or bring suspicion if there was a raid. In his speech on the murders in the House of Commons, Joe Devlin focused his criticism on the 'C1' Class of the Special Constabulary, of which David Duncan was a member.[99]

If David Duncan did murder the McMahons and Eddie McKinney – and he seems by far the most likely suspect to have done so – how would he have convinced four other accomplices to join the attack on 3 Kinnaird Terrace? It is possible that some of the group thought they were on a raid rather than going to murder a family. John McMahon believed that only two men of the five opened fire. However, Duncan knew enough killers with few scruples, easily convinced of the McMahons' guilt in the wake of the St Mary's Hall raid or gossip picked up elsewhere.

GHOSTS OF A FAMILY

Duncan moved in the same circles as Jordy Harper, James Galbraith, Barnsley Sloan, Joseph McKee and Joseph Clarke. They were all Imps. The last three were listed in IRA intelligence reports as 'B' special constables. Joseph Clarke, who lived in Nelson Street, was described as 'a sniper'. Sloan and Harper had provided James Galbraith with his alibi for the attempted murder of Patrick McGurnaghan. A Norfolks' intelligence report suggested that Barnsley Sloan was acting as 'a scout' for Imps' sniper Alex Turtle when he was shot by Lance Corporal Turner. They were the type of men that David Duncan relied upon and sometimes led.[100]

In January 1922 Clarke, McKee and Sloan were charged with coercing a Catholic neighbour to leave her house with her children. Josephine Moan, the wife of a sailor who was away at sea at the time, recalled how the men – whom she had she had known since childhood – climbed over the wall into the yard of her house. Each of them carried a rifle. Clarke told Josephine Moan he was going to 'blow her brains out' if she did not leave the area. Sloan interrupted, saying – 'Don't let them out, burn them.'

Josephine Moan picked up her children and ran from the house. She returned with the police later that day; the house had been torched. After their arrests, the three men were granted bail. One of the two men who provided sureties for the bail of Joseph Clarke on 14 January 1922 was David Duncan's brother Joseph. All three men – despite Josephine's evidence and that of her aunt – were eventually found 'not guilty'.[101]

A few days after the McMahon murders an anonymous letter was pushed under a Catholic resident's door at Weaver Street. Written in pencil, the handwriting was rushed, lacking full stops or capital letters. Signed 'a friend' it opens – 'Dear sir or madam, The man who murdered Margaret Smith was James Johnston and Harry Spratt of 136 Cupar st and Harry Spratt of 185 lower argyle st[.] it was them who threw the bomb and done all the damage[.]' Margaret Smith was one

202

THE NOTORIOUS DAVID DUNCAN

of the victims of the Weaver Street bomb; she died from her wounds on 23 March.

The letter went on: 'it was Harry Spratt and James Johnston who murdered the McMahons[.] only two were armed 5 men altogether and laughing at the corner of the house they went into after they wiped the family out the whole family[.] In gods [*sic*] name these two men should be shot before they do much more murdering.' The writer then provides the two men's addresses again except this time the number 185 for Spratt is crossed out – possibly later by another hand – and 142 is written beneath. Both Argyle Street and Cupar Street were in west Belfast. The letter concludes – 'act at once and do not show this to the police' – before returning to Margaret Smith – 'they are laughing at Margaret smith dieing [*sic*] … may the lord rest mrs smith sole [*sic*]'.

Republican leaders in Belfast dismissed the letter as a crude attempt by the police to divert attention away from the 'real perpetrators'. The letter was likely delivered at night, during the official curfew hours when only the police and military were permitted to be on the streets. Weaver Street was a small Catholic enclave in the midst of an overwhelming Protestant part of north Belfast. Residents were constantly on the alert for loyalist gunmen; shootings were common. Delivering such a letter during the daytime would have risked revealing the identity of the bearer. Another possibility is that the letter was a crude attempt by a neighbour of both men to contract out a personal feud for the IRA to settle. But that seems unlikely. The hurried nature of the letter, the scrawled writing and repeated concern and anger over the killing of Margaret Smith, are peculiar.[102]

A week or so after the delivery of the anonymous letter, Harry Spratt was arrested for his alleged involvement in the sectarian murder of a young girl. Spratt, an ex-soldier, was also known as Harry Brett.[103] On 15 March Michael McCall, a Catholic labourer, saw Brett and another man called William Wilson near the ruins of Finnegan's pub that overlooked

203

Norfolk Street and the Falls Road. Wilson was armed with a rifle. McCall hurried to warn nearby residents. He was too late.

Another witness, John Crossey, saw Brett and Wilson knelt behind some rubble. Wilson fired two shots, one of which hit Mary Wilson, a four-year-old Catholic girl who lived with her family on Norfolk Street. Michael McCall ran out onto the street, picked up the child and brought her into her home. Her father described returning home to find his daughter's blood on the doorstep and some of her brains in the hallway. Brett (or Spratt) was arrested on 14 April. He denied any involvement in violence – 'the last firearm I had was in 1916 at the Somme'.

Both Wilson and Brett produced alibis and were acquitted by a jury. But jury trials in Belfast in 1922 were self-evidently unreliable, which is why the Northern Irish government introduced internment, initially for republicans and later – once the threat from the IRA had ebbed – for loyalists. It is not clear whether Brett was a member of the Special Constabulary. But instead of ignoring the letter the provisional government and its representatives in Belfast should have taken another look.[104]

Then there is the possible involvement of Alexander Kennedy. His great-grandnephew, Belfast Presbyterian minister, Reverend Brian Black, recently related the story of his family's 'black sheep'. The passed-down family tradition was that after the killing of William Waring – married to Alick's sister – 'there was a Catholic family that were taken out and murdered. This brought great shame on the family and so it was never talked about.' Alick Kennedy was exceptionally close to his brother-in-law, William Waring. William's daughter Violet said that Alick 'was the only one who stood up for her mother' after her father's murder. However, when Brian Black, then in his late teens, asked her about the McMahon killings, she ended the discussion: 'We don't talk about that.'

A former soldier, Alick had served in the Black Watch during the South African War, fighting in the disastrous defeat of the Highland Brigade at the hands of Boers at the Battle of Magersfontein.[105] In 1914 Alick had developed cirrhosis of the liver and was deemed unfit for war service. With many of its volunteers at the front, the UVF's North Belfast Regiment appointed Alick as 'armourer' at Dunmore House, responsible for the weapons and ammunition that were stored there.[106] In 1919 he suffered a stroke from which he nearly died. He physically recovered to a significant extent but his wife Dinah noted a change in his personality. He began to show signs of serious mental illness.

In January 1921 the War Office stopped Alick Kennedy's pension after he discharged himself from Hilden Hospital against medical advice. That decision triggered a spiral of self-harm and violence. On 19 February 1921 Alick Kennedy threatened to murder his wife Dinah at their home in Ritchie Street, just off York Street. He also tried to kill himself by drinking a bottle of iodine. He was sectioned as insane and sent for treatment at Purdysburn psychiatric hospital.[107] Doctors observed that his violent moods came and went; at other times he could be 'bright and cheerful'.[108]

In early 1922 doctors in Purdysburn reported some improvement in Alick Kennedy's condition and recommended his release to his family.[109] Dinah Kennedy wrote to protest, telling his psychiatrist that he was uncontrollably violent due to 'drink ... and the stroke on his brain'. She would give him the little money she had to keep her husband in psychiatric care. Alick was 'discharged to the care of his friends' on 7 February 1922 – the most violent period of the 'Belfast pogrom' and a week before the murder of his brother-in-law. He was later admitted to the Belfast Workhouse after Dinah refused to allow him back to the family home. (He died there on 19 January 1924 at the age of forty-one.)[110]

The Kennedy family home was close to the McMahon residence. The death of his father-figure William Waring may have unbalanced Alick, precipitating another bout of alcohol abuse and violence. It is impossible to know. It is also unclear if Alick Kennedy ever served in the Special Constabulary. He had no identifiable motive to single out and target the McMahons. It is possible that such a man, with a history of mental illness, could have been manipulated into joining the raid on 3 Kinnaird Terrace on 24 March. But the evidence is far from compelling.

It is more likely that the lingering family 'shame' and suspicion that hung over Alick Kennedy was a consequence of the sale of the Belfast UVF's ammunition to the IRA. Belfast publican and IRA volunteer Seamus Keaveney gave an account of how and where the IRA acquired such large amounts of ammunition from the UVF. In late 1917 he was approached by IRA officer Seán Cusack who asked him to lodge large amounts of money through his business bank account and then use it to pay Cusack's UVF contacts who had access to munitions. Keaveney described how he went to an 'Orange Lodge on the Antrim Rd' where he and others packed the ammunition into oat bags for transfer to a business in Dublin. At least some of Keaveney's account seems plausible: large amounts of UVF ammunition were stored on the Antrim Road, not in an Orange lodge but in the North Belfast UVF Regiment's Dunmore House headquarters.[111]

It would have been difficult to explain how – as the North Belfast UVF armourer residing in Dunmore House – he did not notice the theft of ammunition from late 1917 until mid-1918, feeding suspicions that he was complicit in the plot. Thomas McNally recalled that the IRA paid 'an ex-British armourer (non-Volunteer)' to help in the transfer and repair of arms.[112] Alick was notably excluded from any of the family death notices after the death of his brother-in-law William Waring.[113]

The throbbing pressures in David Duncan's mind – Patrick McMahon's complaint to the police, the discovery that he was on an

IRA target list and the withdrawal of his pension – do not fully explain the timing of the attack on the McMahons. Another trigger event was necessary. On the night of 23 March when the York Road/Street was full of talk of revenge, Captain Papworth presumed it was because of the killing of the two special constables: 'Great resentment was caused by the murder of the Specials, and the whole demeanour of the Loyalists changed, and threats of reprisals could be heard from gangs of loafers at the street corners in York St. With the arrival of curfew however they faded away and normal conditions prevailed at 2350.'[114]

The melting away of crowds of angry loyalists gave Captain Papworth and the Norfolks a false reassurance. In reality, plans were underway for the most notorious murders of the Belfast 'pogrom'. Loyalists on York Street and the Shankill Road were not just angry at the killing of the two special constables. One of their own had also just been mortally wounded. Seventeen-year-old Charlie Murdoch was shot near his workplace, a flax spinning mill, on Cupar Street in west Belfast at 3 p.m. on 23 March. He was not expected to survive and died the following day in the Royal Victoria Hospital. Tributes paid to Murdoch included from his 'comrades of Ariel Street'. Ariel Street was one of the most dangerous areas for the Norfolk Regiment in the Shankill Road area. The Norfolks had clashed with Murdoch before – he was arrested by an officer on 12 January 1922 and found to be in possession of a loaded revolver. (He never faced any police charges.)

Murdoch grew up just off Malvern Street, where his family still lived, but had recently moved to north Belfast, to Annadale Street. This street is adjacent to the Bruce demesne and yards from Kinnaird Terrace. It is also close to Joseph Duncan's house on Spamount Street.[115] After the murderers ran from the McMahon home into the Bruce demesne they were not seen again. Neither soldiers, police nor local residents reported seeing a group of five men, including one in civilian clothes, in the nearby streets in the minutes after the murderers' disappearance.

It is probable that the group that carried out the murders had a nearby location such as a house or a barracks in which to plan the attack and hide afterwards.

What about the descriptions of the gang given by the surviving members of the McMahon family? With the exception of one of the uniformed men, who John McMahon believed may have had an English accent, four of the party were reported as speaking with a strong Belfast dialect. That would appear to rule out Nixon, Gordon and Sterritt who all had distinctively softer, rural accents.

There was no doubt in John McMahon's mind that four of the five of his family's murderers wore the subtly distinctive uniform of the Special Constabulary known to the residents of the city. Except for their leader, this appears to exclude the 'C1' Special Constabulary who at that point normally wore civilian clothes and a Special Constabulary armband. It is more likely that these men were 'B' Specials. Their capacity for extreme violence was underlined a week later when the west Belfast 'B' Specials were implicated in the Arnon Street killings.

'B' constables James Mulgrew, George Scott and Samuel Ditty were marked out by police headquarters as being exceptionally dangerous. Special Constable George Scott was often on duty at Denmark Street, adjacent to Carlisle Circus and the Antrim Road. At 2.15 a.m. on 13 August 1922 he was arrested while wearing his uniform and armed with a revolver while not on duty. Scott had a reputation for targeting publicans, including during the autumn of 1922 when John Nixon was suspected of being behind an upsurge in violence.[116]

Before his murder, Sergeant Martin Bruen indicated that the Court Street special constables had conspired with a loyalist gang in the York Street area to carry out attacks on Catholics. It is difficult to know the exact identity of the four uniformed 'B' special constables who entered 3 Kinnaird Terrace on the morning of 24 March, but the range of main suspects, and their barracks, was not impossibly large.

THE NOTORIOUS DAVID DUNCAN

Similar attacks – on the O'Keeneys and the Shields families – occurred in the immediate aftermath of the McMahon murders, even if these did not result in the extreme and prolonged violence seen at Kinnaird Terrace (perhaps suggestive of Duncan's additional, more personal motive). This points to the likelihood of a gang based in and operating in the north of the city targeting the homes of wealthy Catholic publicans. And attacks on middle-class homes during the 'pogrom' were unusual.

There is some evidence that points to DI Lynn narrowing his investigation towards the York Street/York Road area. Lynn's diary entries are guarded, often lacking in detail. However, they reveal that he had a series of meetings in early April during his inquiries into recent 'outrages'. On 9 April, the next day, he recorded that he met with 'Adjt. Special Consy. in Henry St [RIC Barracks]', just off York Street.

The next day, just over two weeks after the McMahon murders, Lynn conferred at police headquarters with Commissioner Gelston. A few hours later he spoke with the commander of a special constabulary platoon in the York Road area. Immediately afterwards, Lynn had another meeting with Commissioner Gelston which lasted into the night. There is no record of what they discussed but Lynn's interest in the York Street/York Road area and his successive meetings on the same day with Gelston – days before the Sunday Express reported that there had been a breakthrough in the McMahon case, the police perpetrators identified – suggests that this was not routine conversation but related to his ongoing murder investigations.[117]

In terms of physical appearance, John McMahon described the leader of the group, the man wearing a civilian trench coat, as 'clean shaven, well made, about 30–35 years'. Mary Downey gave a more detailed description – 'a round, soft looking face and very black eyes, he was about 5 ft. 9 in. in height'. He spoke in a 'gruff voice', was clean-shaven and 'did not appear to be very young'. David Duncan was thirty-

209

GHOSTS OF A FAMILY

one at the time of the time of the murders, 5 feet 7 inches and a half, with dark hair and dark eyes. He also had a noticeably round and fleshy face – a feature also remarked on when he enlisted into the French Foreign Legion three years later.[118]

The police in 'D' District, including DI Lynn, were aware that Duncan was dangerous and even mentally unbalanced. The impact of adverse events on Duncan's mental state and actions can be seen in September 1922 after his application to join the RUC was rejected. Duncan approached a police sergeant on the York Road and told him he was going to shoot him. He also used 'very filthy and abusive language'. The sergeant attempted to arrest Duncan but was surrounded and threatened by a mob. The policeman fired two shots into the air and was able to make his escape.

In evidence in court, the sergeant said that he had been familiar with Duncan's erratic behaviour for some time: '[He] knew the prisoner had been a captain in the Army and that he had been gassed. He did not believe that Duncan was responsible at times for what he did.' Duncan's lawyer falsely claimed that his client had 'only one lung' due to his war service. (This was a lie, disproved by Duncan's military records, but the judge did not ask for such evidence.)

The presiding magistrate, James Roche, sentenced Duncan to serve a one-month prison sentence with hard labour, reduced from three months because of his 'previous good character' and excellent record in the British Army and the Auxiliaries. Initially Roche resisted Duncan's lawyer's appeals to have the sentence reduced. However, later that day Roche suddenly changed his mind. He recalled Duncan and told him he was going to impose a more lenient sentence – a fine of £3 and an undertaking 'to keep the peace and be of good behaviour' for a year.[119]

David Duncan either left or was removed from the 'C1' Constabulary towards the end of 1922 – possibly after the incident where he threatened

THE NOTORIOUS DAVID DUNCAN

to murder a police sergeant.[120] He found work as a toll collector for Belfast City Corporation. A year later he took a job as an attendant at the Union infirmary or hospital on the Lisburn Road in the south of the city. During his libel action he mentioned that his wife, Sarah, was living in Dublin, although he resided in Belfast. This is the only recorded mention of Sarah by Duncan after their marriage.[121]

On 18 September 1925 David Duncan arrived at the French port city of Dunkirk where he enlisted in the Foreign Legion of the French Army. His medical examination describes him as thirty-seven years old, barrel-chested, with a round face. Duncan informed the recruiting officer that he was not married (forbidden for recruits to the Legion). He was handed a small sum and a rail ticket to the port city of Marseille on the Mediterranean where he would join the depot of the Legion at nearby Aubagne. Possibly because of his family's connection with horses, Duncan was assigned to the recently established 1st Foreign Cavalry Regiment, which was headquartered at the coastal town of Sousse in French Tunisia.

Duncan saw some action in Tunisia, fighting to suppress tribal rebellions in the Atlas Mountains. His disciplinary record for his first eight months of service appears to have been acceptable. However, in April and May 1926 he lapsed into an episode of violent and erratic insubordination. He went on long drinking sprees in the town of Sousse, failing to return after his 'pass' expired and then resisting being escorted back to barracks. He was also punished, however, for showing compassion to another legionnaire who was denied food in the military gaol – Duncan was caught passing the man a piece of bread. On 17 June 1926 he was deemed unfit for further service in the Legion, not owing to his recent disciplinary record but due to a serious infection he had contracted in his mouth and teeth.[122]

David Duncan once more returned to Belfast. He rented a room on Frome Street, off the Newtownards Road in the heart of loyalist east

Belfast, and found work as a welder. In June 1928 Duncan married twenty-seven-year-old Emily Clements.[123] Emily's brother Matthew had served with Duncan in 6th Battalion, Royal Irish Rifles in Salonika.

Duncan was a bigamist. Sarah never divorced before her death in 1937, aged sixty-three, of heart failure. She was survived by her sister Mary, who was with her when she died. Sarah's death certificate recorded that she was a married housewife living in the same Dublin house she had briefly shared with her husband nearly two decades earlier. It is unclear whether Emily ever knew of her husband's other marriage.[124]

Duncan arrived at St John, New Brunswick, Canada on 5 April 1929. According to Duncan, Sir Joseph Davison paid his passage to Canada. He travelled in the most luxurious class – A1 – on his voyage aboard the *Duchess of Bedford*.[125] Like Alec Robinson a year earlier, he declared that he intended to become a farmer and then travelled on to the city of Toronto. Emily joined him in March of the following year.[126] Her brother Mathew also emigrated with his family to Toronto in 1929; the Clements lived in the same part of the city as the Duncans.[127] David quickly immersed himself in veterans' societies, the Irish Protestant Benevolent Society and Toronto's Enniskillen Loyal Orange Lodge 387.

Toronto was a place of opportunity, especially for Protestants from Ireland. Relative to population Irish Protestants were over-represented in the police and in other municipal jobs – the mirror opposite of American cities where Irish Catholics predominated. As in Belfast, being a member of the Orange Order could open doors for employment.[128] Duncan found work as a welder in an iron foundry, W.D. Beath on Symington Avenue in west Toronto. The Duncans and Clements arrived in Toronto in time to participate in the centenary celebrations of the founding of the Orange Order in Toronto – on 6 July 1930 15,000 Orangemen marched through the city, including the premier of Ontario.[129]

David and Emily moved into a comfortable home at 19 Uxbridge Avenue, a working-class suburb not far from W.D. Beath. Soon, however, his working hours at the foundry were reduced due to the Great Depression. It was not long before David Duncan's mind began to churn again. He was aggrieved at what he felt was his poor pay and the disloyalty shown by James Craig's government for the services he had rendered them during the years of what he called 'the Troubles'. He lay awake at night – he and his family were poor and hungry – listening to the freight trains that ground their way past his house on the grand trunk railroad.

Duncan set out his grievances in a letter to Prime Minister James Craig. He described his leading role in recruiting and running the north Belfast Imperial Guards, which were then incorporated into the 'C1' Constabulary in October 1922. Duncan told Craig that he had subsequently been 'arrested on the charge of shooting the Rebel Commandant John [sic] McIvor of Little Patrick Street, north Belfast'.[130]

By Duncan's account, he was the victim of a conspiracy: 'My object of this letter to you personally Sir James is that I believe there has been some underhanded work done where my work on your behalf and also on behalf of the government was concerned.' His loyal credentials, Duncan wrote, were impeccable and could be vouched for by Colonel Harold Charley, a former Royal Irish Rifles officer and 'C1' Special Constabulary commander, and Sir Joseph Davison, the head of the Orange Order in Belfast. The latter was 'fully aware of the work I carried out at that time [of the Troubles]'. He was appointed as an adjutant or recruiter for the Imps in north Belfast and his role was officially sanctioned by the Northern Irish government. Throughout the last months of 1921 'at the request of late Col. Goodwin [commander of the USC] and General Solly-Flood from the War Office, I continued to collect and enroll [sic] these men'.[131]

Duncan told Craig that he had been in the Orange Order's more elite Royal Arch Purple for more than two decades. Yet he had been rejected as 'unsuitable' for service in the RUC in September 1922. He had already petitioned both him and Lord Carson about this decision in 1929 but had not received any response. Duncan was, by his own estimation, 'victimised for my loyalty'.[132]

Craig's private secretary sent a short reply to Duncan: the prime minister was unable to help. The prime minister's office had taken advice from Andrew Magill, assistant secretary at the Ministry of Home Affairs. Magill observed that the dates given by Duncan for his 'C1' service were wrong – Duncan joined the 'C1' Class in March 1922, not in October of that year as he claimed.

Magill could find no record of Duncan's purported 'work' for Solly-Flood and Goodwin in late 1921. He made no mention of Duncan's claim to have worked with the Northern Irish government's 'War Office', possibly an allusion to the intelligence service run by the former MI5 officer Lieutenant Colonel Haldane. However, there is some truth in Duncan's account. In November 1921 the Northern Irish government had promised the Imps' leaders that many of their men would be incorporated into a restructured Special Constabulary in the coming months. Recruitment for the Imps was therefore linked to future amalgamation with the police.[133]

There was also a pattern of sending dangerous loyalist murderers across the other side of the Atlantic, as had been discussed by the police in several cases, including those of Alec Robinson and John Williamson. Journalist James Kelly also recalled that 'several known Orange gunmen, who had openly boasted of "notches" in their guns for the Sinn Féiners they had shot, were quietly provided with cash and one-way tickets to Canada'.[134]

In November 1931 David Duncan was let go by his employer. Unemployment levels in Toronto soared to more than 30 per cent. The Duncans had to leave their house and move to a poorer area in the east of the city. Soon Emily was pregnant with their first child. They were barely surviving on handouts – including from veterans' welfare organisations.[135]

THE NOTORIOUS DAVID DUNCAN

Duncan, like many of the city's Orangemen, was obsessed with the supposed infiltration of Irish Catholics into important public offices. The ordering of threats and the interests of the Toronto's Orange leaders were revealed when they passed a resolution to 'condemn all conspirators and assassins of the IRA, Communist, Fascist and other disloyal elements' and pledged their support to Prime Minister James Craig.[136] Orange brethren marched behind slogans like 'Keep Toronto British' and 'Ontario must be kept Protestant' while sponsoring schemes to get more Orangemen to migrate to Canada with their families. David Duncan favoured a more violent solution.[137]

CHAPTER EIGHT

The Patient by the Window

NEARLY THIRTEEN YEARS AFTER THE McMahon murders, on the night of 6 February 1935, a young woman in the east end of Toronto ran out of her house onto the street and screamed. She then ran into a neighbouring house, that of the Webb family. Barely able to speak, Emily Duncan told the Webbs that her husband planned to murder her and that he had their two young children in the family home with him. The Webbs immediately called the police.

Upon arriving at the Webbs' home, the police spoke briefly with Emily before then going to her house at 851 Craven Road. The constables called out to her husband that they were going to enter the house and that they had Emily's permission to do so. Forty-three-year-old David Duncan came to the door holding an axe and told the policemen that he would kill them if they tried to enter.

A group of policemen eventually kicked in the door. Duncan struck out with the axe but a police officer dodged his blow. It took four constables to overpower him but eventually David Duncan was wrestled to the floor and handcuffed. The children were unhurt. The police reported that he seemed quite paranoid – he believed 'someone is after him'. Duncan was brought before a magistrate who ordered his detention and examination at Toronto Psychiatric Hospital pending a further hearing.[1]

216

At the time of Duncan's arrest, Northern Ireland was getting ready for one of the most sensational libel trials in the city's history. The build-up and events of the trial were covered in detail by leading British newspapers and press agencies. John Nixon, now the MP for the Woodvale constituency, announced his plans to subpoena some of the most important political and security figures in Northern Ireland. County Inspector Ewing Gilfillan – the serving head of RUC Special Branch since 1922 and who had been involved in the initial investigation into the McMahon murders – was named by Nixon as a witness in the weeks preceding the trial.

In a press release published four months before the trial, Nixon declared that he would call witnesses to give evidence in court, clearing his name and proving that he was not responsible for the McMahon murders. Correspondence relating to the killings was eventually ruled out as inadmissible by the judge in the case.[2] But David Duncan was not to know of this on the date of his arrest on 6 February 1935, four days after Nixon had been granted a court subpoena ordering Sir Robert Lynn, the former unionist MP for West Belfast, to give evidence that Nixon claimed would exonerate him. Lynn had been vice-president of the Ulster Ex-Servicemen's Association and a key supporter of the Imperial Guards at the time of the McMahon murders. If any public figure could identify in court who was really suspected in loyalist circles of carrying out the murders it was Robert Lynn.

The prospect of revelations emerging from Nixon's infamous black notebook loomed large. Robert Lynn later told the court that he was very well-placed to hear rumours about who had carried out the McMahon murders in 1922 but he did not name any suspects in court. (The attorney general stated that 'he would not mention any names' during his questioning of witnesses – and Lynn appears to have followed suit.)[3]

February 1935 was a watershed moment in Duncan's life; he would end his life in a psychiatric institution. Nearly ten years before, Duncan had made another drastic decision – to join the French Foreign Legion. The legion was known as a place of refuge for those seeking to escape their past and start again.

The date of Duncan's departure to join the Foreign Legion was just days after John Nixon had accused the *Derry Journal* and James Gillespie of libel. On 4 September 1925, following an allegation of defamation by John Nixon's solicitor, the newspaper printed a 'fullest and unqualified apology' for the reference in Gillespie's letter to Nixon 'trying to avoid the ghosts of a certain family'.[4] Nixon stated that the letter had caused him 'unspeakable mental anxiety'; graffiti had appeared around Belfast identifying him as the McMahons' murderer. An apology was not enough. Nixon wanted exoneration – 'it was vital for me to prove my innocence' – which was why he initiated defamation proceedings. As in the case ten years later, Nixon's determination to clear his name risked shifting the focus towards other suspects, including the man who led the attack on 3 Kinnaird Terrace.

By the time the defamation trial began in Belfast three months later, ultimately finding in Nixon's favour, David Duncan was in the south of France. It is striking that on the only two high-profile public occasions when revelations about the McMahon murders threatened to emerge in public – where John Nixon publicly swore to clear his name – David Duncan made simultaneous, life-changing decisions.

Duncan had been mentally unwell for years. Emily Duncan told doctors that her husband 'had always been erratic and peculiar since she had known him'. As well as being an alcoholic, Emily said that he frequently 'talked and smiled to himself at night'. He had become increasingly paranoid and violent during the two or three months before his arrest. He repeatedly threatened to kill a heavily pregnant Emily with an axe. One evening Duncan came home drunk, refused to go to bed and talked about going downstairs to attack their neighbour who, he claimed, was harassing him. A terrified Emily went into early labour and gave birth to a son the following day.

THE PATIENT BY THE WINDOW

Reports by the psychiatrists who examined Duncan in the days after his arrest described their patient as 'most cooperative'. They were impressed with their patient's 'military bearing'.[5] Duncan was well-built and nourished with 'black hair, streaked with grey, and dark eyes'. He had the scars of gunshot wounds on his left arm and a smaller scar on his right arm. He also had tattoo marks on both arms and a larger King Billy tattoo on his chest. Duncan's brown suit was somewhat worn but he was described as clean and neat.[6] A medical examination showed a growth on his liver, which appeared to confirm reports of his alcoholism. His hospital file photograph shows a man with a round, wide face, a prominent chin and jaw and a downturned mouth.

Two weeks after Duncan's initial detention Dr Charles McCuaig wrote a report about his patient. Duncan appeared 'quiet and reserved' but persistently suspicious of other patients. He sat by the windows of the hospital, carefully observing people outside the hospital for long periods. He told McCuaig that 'members of the Royal Irish Constabulary of which he was a member have organized and are continually persecuting him … They put a "light ray" on his head which makes him feel queer. They also place animals of different kinds near his home which he considers quite abnormal. These animals make a terrific noise at times.' When the police called at the house on 6 February he thought 'they [his former police colleagues] were raiding him'.[7]

After Duncan lost his job as a welder, he had been occasionally employed by Colonel Baptist Johnston, a leading force in the Irish Protestant Benevolent Society in Canada. Johnston was known for his unyielding views on the cabalistic influence of Irish nationalists on North American politics. He once warned the unionist government in Belfast that they would not get a sympathetic hearing in New York: 'The Jews own it, but the Irish run it.'[8]

Johnston paid Duncan to investigate claims made by Irish Protestants in Toronto for assistance. According to a psychiatric report,

GHOSTS OF A FAMILY

on 6 February Johnston gave Duncan $3 for this work. Duncan gave $2 to his wife and spent the rest on wine. Drunk,

> [he] came home in the evening, talking in a loud voice and calling someone a coward, but there was no one in sight. He was very angry with his wife because the fire was nearly out and stated that his wife had done it on purpose ... He continued to shout about someone being a coward. He threatened his wife, stating, 'I'll kick your brains out – you're a traitor.'

Emily Duncan said that her husband confessed to her that he had killed an 'Irish Free State officer' in Belfast, a crime for which he had been tried and acquitted.[9]

David Duncan later denied to psychiatrists that he was a murderer or that he made such a confession to his wife. But he claimed that, since his trial for the attempted murder of the 'Free State officer', he had 'been followed by men who have interfered with his affairs in various ways'. Duncan told Dr John Dewan that his wife '"appeared nervous" of late and he feels that when he was out on February 6, 1935, his wife was affected by the power of those men which would explain the fact that she let the fire to get out. He thinks that his wife is working with his persecutors.'[10]

According to Duncan, the same men were responsible for his dismissal from his job. They used an invisible ray gun on him which caused 'a peculiar sensation in his right eye and side of head'. (Duncan's obsession with a ray gun may have been influenced by the immense popularity of the science-fiction Buck Rogers movie series in the 1930s.)

Duncan's 'persecutors', whom he initially described as members of the RIC, also gathered in the ravine near the railway track behind his house on Craven Road. He could hear them from his house at night taunting him. According to notes in his psychiatric file, he also heard voices on

THE PATIENT BY THE WINDOW

the street 'telling him to do filthy things which he would ordinarily never think of doing. He says he sometimes feels compelled to obey these voices, but at other times pays no attention them. He says, "they make it unpleasant for you if you do not obey them". Duncan blamed his persecutors for causing his daughter to fall sick – she contracted whooping cough in 1935 and polio two years later.

Sometimes Duncan's persecutors told him to commit sexual acts, other times it was to do something else degrading like picking up manure on the street or attacking somebody.[11] The voices were carried by electrical wires and radio. He had often called back at them and had gone into the ravine late at night to seek them out. Duncan's neighbours confirmed his erratic behaviour, including his frequent shouting at unknown antagonists near his home.[12]

Occasionally Duncan could ignore the voices, but at other times he felt compelled to comply. He began to hear the voices regularly after he was accused of murdering James McIvor in January 1922. His psychiatric file noted that, 'His condition appears to have followed after a rather anxious time, when he was accused of murder but acquitted.' Financial strain and Duncan's alcoholism then exacerbated his condition.[13]

Duncan enjoyed the occupational therapy at the hospital, played cards with other patients and slept well at night. However, he continued to hear voices. A month after his committal he changed his mind about the identity of his persecutors. He now told doctors that the voices he could hear were Irish republicans because of his leading role in putting down the IRA rebellion in Belfast. He told doctors that he had fought many enemies; he had been on the side of the 'Whites' against the Red Army and fought in the French Foreign Legion 'against Morrish [sic] tribesmen' in French North Africa.[14]

Four months later Duncan had a new enemy. This time it was communists who were conspiring against him. The one constant of Duncan's delusions was that the voices he heard always spoke with Irish

221

accents. He had fallen foul of communists in Belfast when he refused to take their side some years previously.

Duncan suffered from bouts of extreme behavioural change. According to Emily he could have relatively mild periods when he seemed content, even charming, to those around him. Emily described how he would help with the housework and doted on their two children, though his sense of persecution remained constant. He was, however, unable to cope with setbacks or rejection.[15]

Toronto's leading psychiatrists observed that Duncan was 'impulsive in his actions' and suffered from long bouts of hallucinations 'in both the visual and auditory fields'. He also experienced olfactory delusions (smelling things that were not real). Duncan showed 'absolutely no insight into his condition but is emphatic in stating that these persecutions are real'.[16] Consequently a magistrate declared Duncan 'dangerous and insane' and a warrant was issued to detain him at the Ontario Hospital (also known as the Ontario Provincial Lunatic Asylum).

Duncan's doctors concluded that their patient was a dangerous paranoid schizophrenic. His condition was deemed incurable since 'his delusions are fixed'. Stressful or emotional events would send him in an alcohol-fuelled spiral; he would also become extremely paranoid and violent.[17]

Duncan's fixation on those who slighted him, real or imaginary, is well documented in his medical files. He could also invent, or was susceptible to believing, fantastical assertions and conspiracies. One can imagine his possible reaction to finding out that he was on a list of IRA targets and the subsequent cancelling of his war pension in the days before the murders at Kinnaird Terrace.

The justification offered by Duncan for the killing of McIvor – he was an IRA commandant – was likely an invention in his own mind. DI Lynn described the targeting of McIvor, Patrick McMahon and James Kelly as part of a campaign of 'deliberate assassination' in north Belfast.

THE PATIENT BY THE WINDOW

Lynn had given evidence in court against Duncan for the attempted murder of Patrick McMahon. The objective was not violent robbery; it was the eradication of Catholic publicans and businesses in parts of the city. Loyalist justifications for opportunistic sectarian violence were easily concocted, especially by David Duncan.[18]

Reports by his psychiatrists emphasised that Duncan could be remarkably charismatic. He was often co-operative, warm and considerate in his relations with other patients and hospital staff. Then he would lurch into impulsive acts of violence, such as assaulting another patient who changed the radio station in the ward. He wrote to Canadian government ministers and local politicians asking them to intervene to have him sent home. Several made enquiries to the superintendent at the hospital, Dr John Howitt, asking if anything could be done for Duncan. The deputy minister for health for Ontario, B.T. McGhie, visited Duncan following petitions from members of his club. He found Duncan 'well educated, intellectual and still a good soldier', but also highly delusional, being convinced that 'outside influences when at their worst, absolutely control his thought and action either through violent ray wireless or other instrument unknown'.[19]

In 1936 Duncan contracted cancer of the mouth and was sent for surgery to Toronto General Hospital to have some infected tissue removed. While there Duncan charmed the surgeons so much that they concluded that he was sane and reported this to a senior official in the Ontario Department of Health. Dr Howitt politely remonstrated with the department reminding them that, 'paranoidal patients are often superficially quite well and their delusions are frequently concealed under favourable conditions'.[20]

Duncan was permitted occasionally to spend some time – a few hours – with his wife and children. During one of these visits home Emily again became pregnant, to the annoyance of unsympathetic officials in Toronto's social services department (the family were already

223

GHOSTS OF A FAMILY

receiving benefits). Emily repeatedly pleaded for her husband never to be discharged from psychiatric care as it was likely Duncan would try to kill her and the children.

Despite painful surgery and intermittent radiography treatment, David Duncan's cancer continued to worsen. Nonetheless, he unsuccessfully petitioned to be released from care so that he and his family could take up one of the 'small gardening farms' made available by the government. During a day visit home in November 1938 Duncan went to the ex-services club near his home and got drunk. When he arrived back at the house he threatened Emily. Once again, neighbours called the police; a policeman who arrived at the house was attacked by Duncan. Eventually two hospital attendants persuaded him to calm down, put him in a car and drove him back to the hospital. Duncan was never allowed home again.

During the summer of 1939, the Toronto-based *Globe and Mail* newspaper published two letters from Duncan in which he complained of the treatment of British Army veterans who were denied the same benefits as 'colonial' soldiers in Canada. Duncan told the newspaper that he had written to King George V, who had sent a letter from his 'royal train' to him and to Canadian government officials asking them to look into his case. Duncan and his supporters also petitioned the Canadian prime minister, William Lyon Mackenzie King, and Lord Londonderry in Belfast for an officer's pension, but these requests were refused. (Officially, because of his poor disciplinary record, Duncan had only held a temporary commission for a few months.)[21]

Duncan's public account of his life story – as related to the *Global and Mail* – was as self-laudatory and misleading as that given in court during his defamation action against the *Freeman's Journal* nearly sixteen years earlier. He exaggerated the extent of his war injuries, falsely claiming that he was 'a 25 per cent [disability] pensioner for two years, 1922–24' even though his war-related pension was terminated

224

in 1922 since he had largely recovered from his wounds. Duncan also claimed that doctors had cut away his left jaw during surgery and that he was suffering from severe disability in his shoulders and left arm. In reality surgeons had been far more precise in their treatment of his cancer, removing malignant nodules and a small part of his tongue.[22]

In the months before his death, David Duncan reverted to blaming Irish republicans for his misfortunes. He told doctors that during 'the Troubles' in Belfast in the early 1920s he had 'organised a Loyalist uprising' in Belfast. His British Army officer's uniform had been stolen during this period. The person who had it was now a member of the Toronto Police and was impersonating him. Irish republicans had infiltrated the hospital, recruiting staff so that they could keep him locked up under false pretences.

The same men had also caused his mouth cancer. Duncan warned that the political situation in Toronto was now very perilous. He told his psychiatrists to put him in touch with Dennis Draper, Toronto's infamously hard-line chief of police, so that he could tell Draper the extent to which 'these Sinn Féiners are harming the city'. Duncan also had a proposal for Draper – he, David Duncan, 'should be allowed out of hospital to prevent this'. He also cryptically remarked that, 'Someone has to be David Duncan while he has to be the tool'. Duncan would cleanse Toronto of Sinn Féin subversion. He wrote to Draper but never received a response.[23]

On New Year's Eve 1939 David Duncan died in considerable agony from the cancer that had steadily eaten away much of his face. He was forty-eight years old.[24] Aside from his wife and a Presbyterian minister, Duncan had no visitors in the months leading up to his death. His brother-in-law Matthew Clements never came to see him in hospital. The Last Post Society (a Canadian charitable society set up to assist war veterans and their families) covered the funeral expenses.[25]

GHOSTS OF A FAMILY

Despite or because of his mental illness, David Duncan was very selective in how he described his past. Doctors noted that he could be both dishonest and manipulative. Duncan never revealed in his extensive conversations with psychiatrists that he had been married twice. He gave a false timeline of when he was discharged from the Royal Fusiliers and Netley Hospital – claiming that it was in March 1920 – and omitted any mention of his marriage to Sarah Cockrill. He was careful not to speak too closely about acts of violence and murder for which there was strong evidence that incriminated him personally. He also made no mention of one of his principal accusers, Patrick McMahon. Duncan's name, which at one point inspired such terror in Belfast, and his secrets have been forgotten, replaced by newer nightmares.

EPILOGUE

WHEN THE SOLDIERS OF 1ST Norfolks boarded a ship on Belfast's docks on 22 September 1923 and sailed for England there was pointedly no civic reception, nor were there unionist dignitaries present to bid them farewell. Their battle against the police in Belfast has been forgotten.[1] They had suffered persistent casualties but only one fatality of a soldier killed in action.

In Belfast these young soldiers knew something that Prime Minister David Lloyd-George did not or wished to ignore. Murder was a festering infection that was seeping into the bloodstream of the city's politics. They tried to cut it out and reform the police. Their failure in 1922, undermined by the high politics of empire and a lurch away from Irish affairs in London, set the conditions for more than three decades of violence in Northern Ireland – the Troubles – at the end of the twentieth century.

Private Ernest Barnes is buried in Fakenham churchyard in Norfolk. His family chose a Celtic cross to mark his grave. Although patched with moss, the monument stands out in this remote corner of East Anglia. It is unclear if the Barnes family ever learned the identity of those who murdered their son and brother. His military rank and regiment are not recorded and there are no poppies or Remembrance Day cards on his grave. Etched on the memorial is a simple inscription: 'Ernest John Barnes. Killed on duty at Belfast on Jan 2nd 1922. Aged 19 Years. *At Rest.*'[2]

EPILOGUE

Some younger Norfolk officers and soldiers who served in Belfast also fought in the Second World War. Lance Corporal Reggie Turner, the soldier who shot loyalist sniper Alex Turtle, was commissioned as an officer and left the army in 1943. Promoted to lieutenant colonel, Robert Scott commanded 2nd Battalion, Royal Norfolk Regiment at the Battle of Kohima in 1944. He brought his adapted rifle from Belfast days, 'little Willie', with him. Clad in a filthy uniform, suffering from bouts of malaria and intermittently shouting abuse at the Japanese lines, Scott led successive assaults in the jungle mountains of Kohima until he and his men captured their objectives. Somehow he survived the war, dying in England in 1961 from injuries sustained in a high-speed motorcycle accident.[3]

Lieutenant Colonel Ian Lywood, who had been shot and wounded by loyalists in Belfast, was less fortunate. Lywood commanded 6th Battalion, Royal Norfolk Regiment during the defence of Singapore. His battalion was decimated during the Japanese advance and he was removed from command due to 'nervous strain'. Japanese soldiers bayoneted Lywood to death in hospital after the British surrender.[4] Former Norfolks intelligence officer Eric Hayes finished the Second World War as a major general and was present at the ceremony in September 1945 where Japan formally surrendered its Chinese territories.[5]

One of General Hayes' Royal Norfolk Regiment protégés and aides during the Second World War, General Ian Freeland, led the British Army back onto the streets of Belfast on 15 August 1969. Civil-rights demonstrations, demanding the end of discrimination against Catholics in Northern Ireland, had been attacked by loyalists. Violent protests quickly escalated. In Belfast, Catholic residents described seeing groups of 'B' Specials firing indiscriminately into houses. Loyalist mobs followed policemen into Catholic areas, burning and looting homes. Seven people were killed; hundreds were wounded – many were Catholics shot by the police. The street names were familiar. A new wave of troubles and

EPILOGUE

Operation Banner – the thirty-eight-year military operation in Northern Ireland – had begun.

As in the 1920s, the law was not seen to function equally. An editorial in the *Irish Press*, the newspaper of the largest Irish political party, Fianna Fáil, suggested that the McMahon murders set the template for 'the Protestant murder gangs' in the later Troubles. Loyalist terrorism was an effective political weapon. Once again, a British government was unwilling to deal 'too roughly with the assassins because they fear the Protestant backlash would be disastrous for the British Army'.[6]

At the end of 1969, as part of a series of reforms in Northern Ireland, the British government announced the creation of a new, largely part-time British Army regiment – the Ulster Defence Regiment (UDR) – to replace the Special Constabulary. As in April 1922, some nationalist leaders hoped that Catholics could join a reformed, cross-community security force. It soon became clear, however, that many of the leaders of the old Special Constabulary had been incorporated wholesale into the UDR.[7]

Although the British Army believed it was at war against the IRA, its relationship with loyalist paramilitaries was more complicated. Rather than fighting on two fronts, going on the offensive against the extremists from both communities, the British Army tolerated the largest loyalist terrorist group, the UDA – a legal organisation for most of the Troubles – and initially allowed its members to join the UDR.[8]

For much of the 1970s there were more than 14,000 full-time soldiers in Northern Ireland, the majority located in the Belfast area. Soldiers prevented many attacks, by loyalists as well as republicans. They were also responsible for atrocities – such as Bloody Sunday in Derry on 30 January 1972 in which fourteen unarmed civilians were fatally shot – that turned much of the nationalist population against the army (and some towards the IRA).[9]

Loyalists like Gusty Spence, leader of a terrorist group that – in a historical throwback for legitimacy – called itself the UVF, began the

EPILOGUE

new wave of killing in the mid-1960s. But it was a new generation of republicans that were responsible for most Troubles-related deaths. Loyalists formed ever-larger paramilitary groups and threatened to turn against the British Army if they did not do more to suppress the IRA or tried to impose a cross-community government in Northern Ireland. The UVF and the UDA emulated the violence of Alec Robinson. Murderous gangs like the 'Shankill Butchers' cut and rampaged their away across the city.

In May 1974 loyalist paramilitaries were at the forefront of the Ulster Workers' Council strike which collapsed the power-sharing executive established by the British government. Loyalist signalling of the costs of crushing loyalist dissent prompted uncertainty within the British government and resistance within the British Army to proposals to go on the offensive against loyalist paramilitaries such as the UDA. As during successive home rule crises, or in 1922 following the Collins-Craig Pact, loyalist mobilisation and terror worked, cowing the British government and delaying much-needed reform.

Evidence of collusion with loyalists – especially by some part-time soldiers in the UDR – deepened Catholic detachment from the state and energised violent republicanism. By the time of the paramilitary ceasefires and the 1998 Good Friday Agreement that finally established a cross-community government in Belfast, more than 3,500 people had been killed in three decades of violence.[10]

Eliza McMahon died at her home in north in 1937, fifteen years after the murder of her husband and four sons. She and her family had never moved back into Kinnaird Terrace after the murders, moving instead to a nearby house on the Antrim Road. Thousands of people again lined the streets of Belfast, bowing their heads as her coffin passed by on its way to the family plot at Milltown Cemetery.[11]

Nobody would ever be arrested for the murder of Eliza's husband and sons. DI Lynn had prosecuted David Duncan – for the murder of

James McIvor and the attempted murder of Patrick McMahon – and failed to win a conviction, despite the compelling evidence of Patrick McMahon and other witnesses. He had done his duty once.

The McMahons had been murdered in the wake of Duncan's trial and release – the possibility of a further revenge attack against the family was too obvious for a man of Lynn's intelligence to miss. Witnesses in other cases in his district had been shot and killed. After his investigations in the York Road area in early April 1922 – and his subsequent meetings with Commissioner Gelston – Lynn did not move to re-arrest Duncan. Like Eliza McMahon, he may have lost faith in Northern Ireland's justice system and wished to avoid further retribution against witnesses by not asking questions. The strain of policing Belfast never left William Lynn; he slept with a loaded revolver on a bedside table until his death in 1963.[12]

The McMahon family continued in business in Belfast. John McMahon never fully recuperated from his wounds but he helped as best he could to run the family's remaining pubs and spirit groceries. His uncle Bernard was one of Belfast's leading publicans until his death in 1958. (John and Leo McMahon both attended his funeral, as did their sister, now Lily Taylor.)[13] The other survivor of the killings, Michael McMahon, moved to Dublin where he married Bridie Nugent, daughter of well-known Dublin republican and former IRA officer Larry Nugent.[14] Owen McMahon's brothers and children stayed out of politics and said little about the night of 24 March 1922.

On 15 May 1974 a young man called Martin McAlinden was shot dead by British soldiers near the border town of Newry. McAlinden was a volunteer in the Official IRA. The British Army patrol surprised him and another republican, Colman Rowntree, at a ruined farmhouse where a large cache of explosives was later discovered. They were unarmed at the time of their deaths. By the British Army's account, upon being challenged, '[McAlinden and Rowntree] dived towards some sacking, and it was thought by the soldiers they were going for weapons'.[15]

EPILOGUE

Martin McAlinden was Owen McMahon's grandnephew. Martin's brother recalled that the shadow of the McMahon murders had hung over his and his siblings' lives. Their mother Anne – the daughter of Owen McMahon's only sister – was scrupulously law-abiding. But she could never respect or trust the RUC, who she held responsible for the murders of her uncle and cousins.[16]

In the 1960s ex-C1 special constable Alec Robinson was an inspiration to (and supporter of) the UVF. A loyalist celebrity during the Troubles, he frequently posed for photographs, including with UVF leader Gusty Spence. (According to Spence's biographer, the UVF leader had served in the Royal Ulster Rifles with Alec Robinson's son, whose middle name was 'DiVarco' – after Joseph Divarco, a Chicago gangster.)[17]

Towards the end of his life Alec Robinson gave an extended interview about his life. He boasted that when it came to violence in the city – 'I was one of the main men. I was the boss of loyalism.' He remained an unrepentant bigot, convinced that Protestants had gentler faces – you could tell a Catholic by 'looking at them'. He preferred the UVF, but the other, larger loyalist group, the UDA, were 'a lot of rats' who deserved to die.

Robinson had a fatalistic view of life and human agency: 'If you are going to live a wrong life you're going to live it; and if you're going live a good life you're going to live it.' Towards the end of the interview he broke down crying when he spoke about his mother: 'My mother brought some children into this world.' His mother was a midwife. What he meant by this is not clear.[18]

Robinson's notoriety, the fact that he had never been convicted of murder, motivated a new IRA 'super-gunman'. Brendan 'the Dark' Hughes was one of the most violent and feared IRA commanders in Belfast during the 1970s. He later admitted his role in – among other killings – the IRA bombings that murdered nine people and wounded hundreds more on 'Bloody Friday' on 21 July 1972 in Belfast city centre.

EPILOGUE

Brendan Hughes believed that 'Buck Alec' murdered his uncle and that, instead of being prosecuted, he had been protected and indulged by the Northern Irish government. Owen Hughes was travelling on a tram car on York Street on the evening of 4 March 1922 when it was held up by armed gunmen. A brief conversation took place before one of the men shot Hughes dead. His nephew's suspicions about Alec Robinson's complicity were also those of the police – the murder was listed as one of the arguments made for his internment in late 1922.[19]

In 2009 an Italian artist was commissioned to paint over a UVF mural in north Belfast with one of 'well-known and respected sporting, literary and artistic Northern Ireland figures'. It depicts, among others, Olympic gold-medallist Mary Peters and footballer George Best. Also on the mural is Alec Robinson and his pet lion. The man who police believed had viciously beaten and killed his neighbour Jane Rafferty, casually shot elderly cinema attendant Peter Mullan and vocalised his support for loyalist terrorists during the Troubles was described as 'a Belfast folk hero'.[20]

John Nixon's descendants have also been unable to escape the intergenerational damage of the McMahon murders. Nixon's awkward, lonely position in the Northern Irish Parliament was in contrast to his happy family life in north Belfast. On 11 January 1928 he remarried, to Kathleen 'Kay' Shannon who was nearly twenty years his junior. Remarkably the wedding ceremony took place across the border, in the Anglican parish church at Donaghmore in Kay's native Donegal.[21] The couple had two children, a boy and a girl.

At the time of his death in 1949, John Nixon lived with his family in a mansion called Woodvale House on the outskirts of west Belfast. His son, also called John Nixon, was a medical student at Queen's University Belfast; he married and later qualified as a psychiatrist, working for many years in Purdysburn Mental Hospital in Belfast where his patients included those scarred by sectarian violence decades earlier. According

EPILOGUE

to his family, Dr Nixon steered clear of politics and was appalled by the intolerance of Ian Paisley.

At the outset of the Troubles in the late 1960s, Dr Nixon moved his family out of his late father's home to Malone Park, an upper-middle-class suburb in south Belfast. He then converted Woodvale House into a psychiatric clinic. That did not spare him or his family from the violence of the Troubles. According to his daughter, in one incident near Belfast city centre he and other passers-by tried to save the life of an IRA volunteer who had blown off his own arm while handling explosives. The family received death threats following a media interview Dr Nixon gave in which he described himself as 'a man of peace'. After a bomb was discovered at the family home, Dr Nixon decided that he had to get his family out of Northern Ireland.

In 1972 the Nixons moved to Norwich where Dr Nixon worked as a consultant psychiatrist until his death ten years later. Norwich is one of the most distant cities from Belfast in the UK. (Ironically, and perhaps unknown to Dr Nixon, it was also the home of the British Army regiment that had such a bitter relationship with his father.)[22]

David Duncan is buried alone. His simple headstone in the military veterans' plot of Prospect Cemetery in west Toronto is inscribed with his former military rank – 'Lieutenant David J Duncan, Royal Irish Fusiliers, Royal Irish Rifles, British Expeditionary Force'. His grave lies close to the main war memorial in the cemetery, with the Canadian maple leaf flag flying nearby.

Duncan was survived by his wife and two children. Emily received little sympathy from the local authorities and charities who offered meagre assistance after her husband's hospitalisation. (She was criticised for her slovenly housekeeping.) At one point Emily suffered some form of mental breakdown requiring weeks of hospital treatment. The Duncans lived in worsening poverty in ever-smaller houses in Toronto's poorer suburbs.

EPILOGUE

Even while confined to Ontario Hospital, David Duncan exerted control over his wife. She occasionally refused to visit him, did not want him to be released, but always seemed to relent under Duncan's threats and manipulation. Duncan's day visits home to his family were as disastrous as Emily feared – he got drunk and attacked the police before being returned to hospital – but she felt compelled to allow him home.[23]

After her husband's death, Emily was released from her sentence of domestic terror. Duncan's children, aged under seven at the time of his death, grew up without any memories of their father's violence before he was declared insane. They at least were spared.

The ripple effects of the McMahon murders did much to foster future conflict in Ireland. But they also marked the family of one of Ireland's most remarkable peacemakers, law professor and President of Ireland, Mary McAleese. On the night of the killings, three young sisters, Mary, Norah and Sarah Jane McDrury, were renting rooms in one of the houses at Kinnaird Terrace. Originally from rural Roscommon in the west of Ireland, they were good friends with the McMahon family. Immediately after the murders they fled Kinnaird Terrace and moved to Ardoyne where they established a series of businesses including a spirit grocery. Their nephew – Mary McAleese's father, Paddy Leneghan – joined them and worked as a barman before acquiring his own pub, the Long Bar on the Crumlin Road.

It was in Ardoyne that Paddy Leneghan met his wife Claire. It was also there that Mary McAleese experienced the horror of sectarian attacks on her family and friends. Her brother suffered near fatal wounds during a loyalist attack in which he was beaten and stabbed with a bottle. In 1972 loyalists bombed her father's bar. A television cameraman who rushed to the area found Paddy Leneghan standing outside his shattered pub holding the lifeless body of a young woman called Olive McConnell.

235

EPILOGUE

As president from 1997–2011, Mary McAleese and her husband Martin were critical interlocutors with loyalist paramilitaries. UDA commanders, armed with a Northern Irish flag, a Glasgow Rangers scarf, champagne and a bouquet of flowers, visited the presidential residence Áras an Uachtaráin in Dublin in 2003. The following year they agreed to an indefinite cessation of violence.[24]

Although out of office, Mary McAleese's peace work continues. Some loyalist leaders want to end the UDA and UVF ceasefires. Loyalists never decommissioned their weapons after the Troubles and have threatened a new campaign of violence if post-Brexit divergences between Northern Ireland and Great Britain are not addressed.

Britain's loyalist dilemma has not gone away. The UDA and UVF count their memberships in thousands. On 25 March 2022 – a century and a day after the McMahon murders – loyalist terrorists targeted Ireland's foreign minister, Simon Coveney, during a visit to north Belfast. The British government does not consider loyalist terrorism a threat to UK national security. Consequently, while significant intelligence resources are dedicated to targeting small numbers of 'dissident' republican paramilitaries, countering loyalist terrorist groups is not an MI5 priority.[25] The ghosts of Kinnaird Terrace are with us still.

BIBLIOGRAPHY

MANUSCRIPT AND ARCHIVAL SOURCES

Archives of Ontario, Toronto (AOO)

RG 10-270, Queen Street Mental Health Centre patients' clinical case files

Bodleian Library Special Collections, University of Oxford

MS. Eng. c. 2803, AP Magill Papers, A.P. Magill Unpublished Memoir

Churchill Archives, Cambridge University (CHAR)

CHAR 22/12, Official, Cabinet, Irish Committee

CHAR 22/13, Papers of Sir Winston Churchill, Official, Cabinet, Irish Committee, 1 July–17 October 1922

General Registry Office of Ireland, Dublin (GROI)

Birth Certificates

Marriage Certificates

Imperial War Museum, London (IWM)

Department of Documents

HHW 2/2F and 2/2G, Private Papers of Field Marshal Sir Henry Wilson Papers, 1920–1922

LAWG/3, Private Papers of Lieutenant Colonel Lionel Arthur Gundry-White, 1919–1945

Land Registry of Northern Ireland, Belfast (LRNI)

Memorials, Belfast, 1923

Library and Archives Canada, Ottawa (LAC)

Canadian Immigration Service, Passenger List and Border Entries

Militia and Defence personnel files (1870–1948)

Library of Congress, Washington DC

Reports of the White Cross Society and American Committee for Relief in Ireland

BIBLIOGRAPHY

Military Archives of Ireland, Cathal Brugha Barracks, Dublin (MAI)

Bureau of Military History, Witness Statements
Civil War Operational and Intelligence Reports
IRA Membership Rolls
Irish Military Census, 1922
Michael Collins Papers
Military Service Pensions Collection

Museum of the Foreign Legion of France, Aubagne (MFLF)

Records of Service

National Archives of Ireland, Dublin (NAI)

1901/1911 National Census of Ireland
Ancient Order of Hibernians, Board of Erin Minute Books
Department of the Taoiseach
North East Boundary Bureau

The National Archives of the United Kingdom, Kew (TNA)

AIR 5, Air Historical Branch Papers
BT 395, Database of World War II Medals issued to Merchant Seamen
CAB 21, Cabinet Office and predecessors, Registered Files (1916 to 1965)
CAB 23, War Cabinet and Cabinet, Minutes
CO 904, Dublin Castle Records
CO 906, Colonial Office, Correspondence and Papers of the Irish Office
HO 184, Irish Constabulary Records
HO 267, Imperial Secretary to the Governor of Northern Ireland, Correspondence and
    Papers
WO 32, War Office and successors, Registered Files (General Series)
WO 35, Army of Ireland, Administrative and Easter Rising Records
WO 363, War Office, Soldiers' Documents, First World War 'Burnt Documents'
WO 372, Service Medal and Award Rolls Index, First World War
WO 373, Recommendations for Honours and Awards for Gallant and Distinguished Service
WO 374, War Office, Officers' Services, First World War, personal files

National Army Museum, London (NAM)

1966-02-68, Recollections of Acting Sergeant E S Virpsha, North Russian Expeditionary
    Force 1918–1919

National Library of Ireland, Dublin (NLI)

Art Ó Briain Papers

BIBLIOGRAPHY

Copies of statutory declarations by Belfast Catholics
Correspondence between C.B. Dutton and the Belfast Catholic Protection Committee
Diary of Charlotte Despard, May–July 1922
Seán O'Mahony Papers

Orange Heritage Museum, Schomberg House, Belfast (OHM)
Minutes of the Orange and Black Loyalist Defence Association

Police Museum of Northern Ireland, Belfast (PMNI)
Diary of District Inspector William Henry Moffatt
District Inspectors' Records

Princeton University Library Special Collections, New Jersey (PULSC)
Brigadier General Herbert Cecil Potter Papers

Public Record Office of Northern Ireland, Belfast (PRONI)
File series
ANT/1/1, Antrim Quarter Sessions
ANT/1/2, Antrim General Assizes
AUS/1, Registered General Files Series
BANK/1/1, Belfast Bankruptcy Court
BELF/6/1, Belfast Coroner's Court
BELF/6/5, Belfast Spirit Licenses
CAB/6, Unregistered Subject Files
CAB/9/B, Ministry of Home Affairs
CAB/9/G, Military and Police 'G' files
CRCT/3, Belfast Crown Court
D623, Abercorn Papers
D627, Montgomery Papers
D640, Private Papers of Colonel F.H. Crawford
D1288, Cunningham Papers
D1327, Ulster Unionist Council
D1581, Pollock Papers
D1633, Diary of Lady Lilian Spender
D4555, Royal British Legion of Northern Ireland
FIN/18, Treasury Division 'A' Registry Files
HA/5, Ministry of Home Affairs, General 'H' Files
HA/20, Ministry of Home Affairs, Private Office
HA/32, Ministry of Home Affairs, Secret Files
HOS/28, Mental Hospitals, Belfast District

BIBLIOGRAPHY

MIC150/1, July 1920–September 1936 Journal of District Inspector W. Lynn
PM/1, Correspondence, First Series
PM/2, Prime Minister's Office, Correspondence
T3580, Frederick McGinley Papers

Registry of Deeds of Ireland, Dublin (RODI)
Registry Index for Belfast, 1920–1924

Royal Fusiliers Museum, Tower of London (RFM)
RFM.ARC.571, Unpublished Memoir of Major E.M. Alfrey, Russia, May–October 1919
RFM.ARC.573.1, Typescript memoir of an unnamed Fusilier sent to North Russian Front

Royal Norfolk Regiment Museum, Norwich (NWHRM)
Intelligence Reports, Belfast, 1921–1922
Officers' Biographies Book

Royal Ulster Rifles Museum, Belfast
Copy of the War Diary of 1st Battalion, Royal Irish Rifles, 1914–1915

Sherwood Foresters Museum, Nottingham
1909 Annual
The Old Stubborns regimental journal

Staffordshire Regiment Museum, Lichfield
Questionnaires Regarding Service in Ireland, 1920–1923

State of California Public Records
Marriage Certificates
Death Certificates

The Parliamentary Archives, Houses of Parliament, Westminster (TPA)
Lloyd George Papers

Tomás Ó Fiaich Library, Armagh
Cardinal Joseph MacRory Papers

Toronto City Archives, Toronto
Neighbourhood Workers' Association Riverdale District Association records
Toronto Police Service, Police Crime Indexes, 1929–1933

Toronto Reference Library Special Collections, Toronto
L35, Toronto Loyal Orange County Lodge fonds

Ulster Folk and Transport Museum, Cultra (UFTM)
Sound Archive

University College Dublin Archives (UCDA)
Desmond and Mabel Fitzgerald Papers
Michael Hayes Papers
Ernest Blythe Papers
Seán MacEntee Papers
Richard Mulcahy Papers

CORRESPONDENCE AND INTERVIEWS
Email correspondence with DI William Lynn's son, 8 October 2023
Interview with Reverend Brian Black, Belfast, 2 June 2022
Interview with the granddaughter of John William Nixon MP, England, 4 February 2023
Interview with Norah Glynn, grandniece of Owen McMahon, and Joe Glynn, Dublin, 9 August 2022

PRINTED PRIMARY SOURCES
Books and Pamphlets

Aiken, Síobhra, Mac Bhloscaidh, Fearghal, Ó Duibhir, Liam, and Ó Tuama, Diarmuid, *The Men Will Talk to Me: Ernie O'Malley's Interviews with the Northern Divisions* (Dublin: Merrion Press, 2018)

Campbell, David, *Forward the Rifles: The War Diary of an Irish Soldier* (Dublin: Nonsuch, 2009)

Campbell, T.J., 'Pogroms: 1857–1935', *Capuchin Annual* (1943), pp. 456–67

Campbell, T.J., *Fifty Years of Ulster: 1890–1940* (Belfast: *Irish News*, 1941)

Carnduff, Thomas, 'I Remember', *The Bell*, 5/4 (1943)

Carnduff, Thomas, 'The Orange Society', *The Bell*, 17/4 (1951)

Carnduff, Thomas, *Life and Writings*, ed. Peter Gray (Belfast: Lagan Press, 1994)

Grayson, Richard (ed.), *The First World War Diary of Noël Drury, 6th Royal Dublin Fusiliers* (Woodbridge: Boydell, 2022)

Kelly, James, *Bonfires on the Hillside: An Eyewitness Account of Political Upheaval in Northern Ireland* (Belfast: Fountain Press, 1995)

Kelly, James, 'The Pogrom', *Capuchin Annual* (1943), pp. 480–5

Kenna, G.B., *Facts and Figures of the Belfast Pogrom, 1920–1922* (London: Forgotten Books, 2018)

Londonderry, Marquis of, *Ourselves and Germany* (London: R. Hale, 1938)

Macready, C.F.N., *Annals of An Active Life: Volume II* (London: Hutchinson, 1925)

BIBLIOGRAPHY

McAleese, Mary, *Here's the Story: A Memoir* (London: Penguin, 2020)
Moloney, Ed, *Voices from the Grave* (London: Faber and Faber, 2010)
Ramsden, John, *The Box in the Attic* (London: Shoot Raw, 2019)
Sturgis, Mark, *The Last Days of Dublin Castle: The Dublin Castle Diaries* (Dublin: Irish Academic Press, 1999)

Newspapers and Magazines

The Anglo-Celt
Ballymena Telegraph
Ballymena Weekly Telegraph
The Belfast Gazette
Belfast News-Letter
Belfast Telegraph
The Bellshill Speaker
Cabar Feidh – Seaforth Highlanders
Church of Ireland Gazette
The Daily Telegraph
Derry Journal
The Dublin Evening Telegraph
Eastern Daily Press (Norwich)
The Fermanagh Herald
The Freeman's Journal
The Globe and Mail
The Guardian
The Hibernian Journal
The Irish Ecclesiastical Record
Irish Independent
The Irish News
The Irish Protestant and Orange and Black Magazine
The Irish Press
The Irish Times
Irish Weekly and Ulster Examiner
Larne Times
The Light Bob Gazette – Somerset Light Infantry
Lisburn Standard
The London Gazette
The Londonderry Sentinel
The Manchester Guardian
The Northern Standard
The Northern Whig
Mid-Ulster Mail

Portadown News
Portadown Times
The Scotsman
The Spectator
Sunday Independent
The Times
Toronto Star

OTHER MEDIA SOURCES

Rebel Heart, first broadcast on BBC television in 2001 [available via DVD]

BBC Radio Ulster, 'The District Inspector', *Year '21*, first broadcast 18 June 2021, available at https://www.bbc.co.uk/programmes/p09lw4dh [accessed 5 February 2023]

PRINTED SECONDARY SOURCES

Books and Articles

Baker, Joe, *The McMahon Family Murders and the Belfast Troubles* (Belfast: Glenravel, 1995)

Barton, Brian, *The Government of Northern Ireland, 1920–1923* (Belfast: Athol Books 1980)

Bene, Kriszrián, 'Changes in the Composition, Equipment and Tactics of the 1st Foreign Cavalry Regiment of the French Foreign Legion during the Indochina War', *Nation and Security*, 16/2 (2023), pp. 114–26

Bennett, Huw, *Uncivil War: The British Army and the Troubles, 1966–1975* (Cambridge: Cambridge University Press, 2023)

Bew, Paul, *Ireland: The Politics of Enmity 1789–2006* (Oxford: Oxford University Press, 2007)

Bew, Paul, Gibbon, Peter, and Patterson, Henry, *Northern Ireland 1921–1996: Political Forces and Social Classes* (London: Serif, 1996)

Black, Robert, *Honours and Medals Awarded to the Royal Ulster Constabulary GC, 1922–2001* (Belfast: Royal Ulster Constabulary George Cross Foundation, 2015)

Black, Robert, Forrester, Hugh and White, Stephen, *Marking the Sacrifices and Honouring the Achievements of the Royal Ulster Constabulary GC* (Belfast: Royal Ulster Constabulary George Cross Foundation, 2022)

Bowman, Timothy, *Carson's Army: The Ulster Volunteer Forces* (Manchester: Manchester University Press, 2012)

Boyd, Andrew, *Holy War in Belfast* (Belfast: Pretani, 1987)

Bourke, Joanna, 'Shell-shock, Psychiatry and the Irish Soldier during the First World War', in Adrian Gregory and Senia Pašeta (eds), *Ireland and the Great War: A War to Unite Us All* (Manchester: Manchester University Press, 2002), pp. 155–70

Buckland, Patrick, *James Craig* (Dublin: Gill, 1980)

Burke, Edward, 'Loyalist Mobilisation and Cross-Border Violence in Rural Ulster', *Terrorism and Political Violence*, 24/22 (2022), pp. 1057–75

Burke, Edward, *Ulster's Lost Counties: Loyalism and Paramilitarism since 1920* (Cambridge: Cambridge University Press, 2024)

BIBLIOGRAPHY

Cohen, Stanley, *States of Denial: Knowing About Atrocities and Suffering* (Oxford: Blackwell Publishers, 2001)

Coogan, Tim Pat, *Michael Collins: A Biography* (London: Head of Zeus, 2016)

Cunningham, Niall, 'The Social Geography of Violence During the Belfast Troubles', *CRESC Working Paper Series*, Working Paper No. 122 (The University of Manchester, March 2013)

Davenport-Hines, Richard, *Titanic Lives: Migrants, Millionaires, Conmen and Crew* (London: Harperpress, 2012)

Devlin, Paddy, *Yes We Have No Bananas: Outdoor Relief in Belfast, 1920–1939* (Belfast: Blackstaff Press, 1981)

Falls, Cyril, *The History of the First Seven Battalions: The Royal Irish Rifles in the Great War Volume II* (Aldershot: Gale and Polden, 1925)

Farrell, Michael, *Arming the Protestants: The Formation of the Ulster Special Constabulary and the Royal Ulster Special Constabulary, 1920–27* (London: Pluto Press, 1983)

Feeney, Brian, *Antrim: The Irish Revolution, 1912–1923* (Dublin: Four Courts Press, 2021)

Ferriter, Diarmaid, *A Nation and Not a Rabble: The Irish Revolution, 1913–1923* (London: Profile, 2015)

Fleming, N.C., *The Marquis of Londonderry; Aristocracy, Power and Politics in Britain and Ireland* (London: Tauris, 2005)

Follis, Bryan, *A State Under Siege: The Establishment of Northern Ireland* (Oxford: Clarendon Press, 1995)

Garland, Roy, *Gusty Spence* (Belfast: Blackstaff, 2001)

Gerolymatos, André, *An International Civil War: Greece, 1943–1949* (New Haven, CT: Yale University Press, 2016)

Glennon, Kieran, *From Pogrom to Civil War* (Cork: Mercier Press, 2013)

Glennon, Kieran, 'The Dead of the Belfast Pogrom – Counting the Cost of the Revolutionary Period, 1920–22', *The Irish Story*, 27 October 2020

Glennon, Kieran, 'The Dead of the Belfast Pogrom – Addendum', *The Irish Story*, 20 January 1922

Gordon, Dennis, *Quartered in Hell: The Story of the North American Expeditionary Force* (Missoula, MT: Doughboy Historical Society, 1982)

Gray, John, *City in Revolt: Jim Larkin and the Belfast Dock Strike 1907* (Dublin: SIPTU, 2007)

Haines, Keith, *Fred Crawford – Carson's Gunrunner* (Donaghadee: Ballyhay Books, 2019)

Hart, Peter, *The 2nd Norfolk Regiment: From Le Pardis to Kohima* (Barnsley: Pen and Sword, 1998)

Hepburn, A.C., *Catholic Belfast and Nationalist Ireland in the Era of Joe Devlin, 1871–1934* (Oxford: Oxford University Press, 2008)

Hezlet, Arthur, *The 'B' Specials: A History of the Ulster Special Constabulary* (London: Tom Stacey, 1972)

Higgins, Francis, *Religion, Riots and Rebels: The Incredible History of Brown's Square Belfast* (Belfast: Belfast Lad Publications, 2021)

BIBLIOGRAPHY

Hughes, Brian, *Defying the IRA? Intimidation, Coercion and Communities during the Irish Revolution* (Liverpool: Liverpool University Press, 2016)

Jeffery, Keith, *Field Marshal Sir Henry Wilson: A Political Soldier* (Oxford: Oxford University Press, 2006)

Jordan, David, *The History of the French Foreign Legion: From 1831 to Present Day* (Guilford, CT: Lyons Press, 2005)

Kalyvas, Stathis, *The Logic of Violence in Civil War* (Cambridge: Cambridge University Press, 2006)

Kalyvas, Stathis, 'Fear, Preemption and Retaliation', in S.M. Saideman and Marie-Joelle Zahar (eds), *Intra-State Conflict, Governments and Security: Dilemmas of Deterrence and Assurance* (Abingdon: Routledge, 2008)

Kemp, P.K., *History of the Norfolk Regiment* (Norwich: Soman-Wherry Press, 1953)

Lynch, Robert, *The Partition of Ireland 1918–1925* (Cambridge: Cambridge University Press, 2019)

Lynch Robert, 'The People's Protectors? The Irish Republican Army and the Belfast Pogroms, 1920–1922', *Journal of British Studies*, 37/2 (2008), pp. 375–91

Magill, Christopher, *Political Conflict in East Ulster, 1920–1922* (Woodbridge: Boydell, 2020)

Mann, Michael, *The Dark Side of Democracy: Explaining Ethnic Cleansing* (Cambridge: Cambridge University Press, 2006)

Marley, Laurence, 'The McMahon Murders: Class and Killing in Belfast', in Darragh Gannon and Fearghal McGarry (eds), *Ireland 1922: Independence, Partition, Civil War* (Dublin: Royal Irish Academy, 2022), pp. 109–13

McGaughey, Jane, *Ulster's Men: Protestant Unionist Masculinities and Militarization in the North of Ireland, 1912–1923* (Montreal: McGill University Press, 2012)

McDermott, Jim, *Northern Divisions: The Old IRA and the Belfast Pogroms, 1920–1922* (Belfast: Beyond the Pale Publications, 2009)

McGarry, Fearghal, *Eoin O'Duffy: A Self-Made Hero* (Oxford: Oxford University Press, 2005)

McGreevy, Ronan, *Great Hatred: The Assassination of Field Marshal Sir Henry Wilson MP* (London: Faber, 2022)

Miller, David, *Queen's Rebels* (Dublin: University College Dublin, 2007)

Moore, Cormac, *Birth of the Border: The Impact of Partition in Ireland* (Dublin: Merrion Press, 2019)

Morrissey, Conor, 'Scandal and anti-Semitism in 1916: Thomas Dickson and *The Eye-Opener*', *History Ireland*, 24/4 (2016), 30-34

Ó Coinn Seán, *Defending the Ground: B (Ballymacarrett) Company, 2nd Battalion, 1st Brigade, 3rd Northern Division, Irish Republican Army 1920–1922* (Belfast: Short Strand Community Tourism and Heritage Initiative, 2017)

O'Connell, Sean, 'Violence and Memory in Twentieth-Century Belfast: Stories of Buck Alec Robinson', *Journal of British Studies*, 53/3 (2014), pp. 734–56

O'Connor, Emmet, *Rotten Prod: The Unlikely Career of Dongaree Baird* (Dublin: UCD Press, 2022)

BIBLIOGRAPHY

O'Halpin, Eunan, and O'Corráin, Daithí, *The Dead of the Irish Revolution* (New Haven, CT: Yale University Press, 2020)

Ó Néill, John, *Belfast Battalion: A History of the Belfast IRA, 1922–1969* (Ballygarran: Litterpress, 2018)

Parkinson, Alan, *Belfast's Unholy War* (Dublin: Four Courts Press, 2004)

Parkinson, Alan, *A Difficult Birth: The Early Years of Northern Ireland, 1920–1925* (Dublin: Eastwood, 2020)

Parr, Connal, 'Expelled from yard and tribe: The "Rotten Prods" of 1920 and their political legacies', *Studi Irlandesi*, 11/11 (2021), pp. 299–321

Patterson, Henry, *Class Conflict and Sectarianism: The Protestant Working Class and the Belfast Labour Movement 1869–1920* (Belfast: Blackstaff Press, 1980)

Peden, G.C., *The Treasury and British Public Policy* (Oxford: Oxford University Press, 2000)

Phoenix, Eamon, *Northern Nationalism: Nationalist Politics, Partition and the Catholic Minority in Northern Ireland, 1890–1940* (Belfast: Ulster Historical Foundation, 1994)

Radford, Mark, *The Policing of Belfast, 1870–1914* (London: Bloomsbury, 2015)

Reid, Colin, 'Protestant Challenges to the "Protestant State": Ulster Unionism and Independent Unionism in Northern Ireland, 1921–1935', *Twentieth Century History*, 19/4 (2008), pp. 419–45

Ryder, Chris, *The RUC: A Force Under Fire* (London: Mandarin, 1992)

Scalone, Franceso, Pozzi, Lucia, and Kennedy, Liam, 'Religion and Child Death in Ireland's Industrial Capital', *Social Science History*, 47 (2023), pp. 425–51

Smith, Colin, *Singapore Burning* (London: Penguin, 2006)

Smyth, William, *Toronto, the Belfast of Canada: The Orange Order and the Shaping of Municipal Culture* (Toronto: University of Toronto Press, 2015)

Staniland, Paul, 'Armed Groups and Militarized Elections', *International Studies Quarterly*, 29/4 (2015), pp. 694–705

Taylor, James, *The First Battalion Royal Irish Rifles in the Great War* (Dublin: Four Courts Press, 2002)

Taylor, James, *Guilty but Insane: J. C. Bowen-Colthurst – Villain or Victim?* (Cork: Mercier Press, 2016)

Townshend, Charles, *Political Violence in Ireland: Government and Resistance since 1848* (Oxford: Oxford University Press, 1984)

Townshend, Charles, *The Partition: Ireland Divided, 1885–1925* (London: Allan Lane, 2021)

Walker, Graham, '"Protestantism Before Party": The Ulster Protestant League in the 1930s', *The Historical Journal*, 28/4 (1985), pp. 961–7

Walsh, Brendan, 'Life Expectancy in Ireland since the 1870s', *The Economic and Social Review*, 48/2 (2017), pp. 127–43

Wilson, T.K., *Frontiers of Violence: Conflict and Identity in Ulster and Upper Silesia, 1918–1922* (Oxford: Oxford University Press, 2010)

Wilson, T.K., 'The Most Terrible Assassination That Has Stained the Name of Belfast', *Irish Historical Studies*, 37/145 (2010), pp. 83–106

BIBLIOGRAPHY

Wright, Damien, *Churchill's Secret War with Lenin: British and Commonwealth Military Intervention in the Russian Civil War* (Warwick: Helion and Company, 2017)

Wright, Frank, *Northern Ireland: A Comparative Analysis* (London: Gill and Macmillan, 1988)

UNPUBLISHED RESEARCH

Dunne, Eugene, 'The Experiences of the Aristocracy in County Westmeath during the Period 1879 to 1923' (PhD Thesis, National University of Ireland Maynooth, 2016)

Magill, Christopher, 'East Ulster and the Irish Revolution, 1920–1922' (PhD Thesis, Queen's University Belfast, 2014)

Newman, Seán, 'For God, Ulster and the "B-Men": The Ulsterian Revolution, the Foundation of Northern Ireland and the Creation of the Ulster Special Constabulary' (PhD Thesis, Birbeck, University of London, 2020)

Raume, Geoffrey, '999 Queen Street West: Patient Life at the Toronto Hospital for the Insane' (PhD Thesis, University of Toronto, 1997)

ONLINE RESOURCES

Ancestry, https://www.ancestry.co.uk/

- Ireland, Grand Lodge of Freemasons of Ireland Membership Registers, 1733–1923
- Ireland Civil Registration Deaths Index
- Ireland Civil Registration Births Index

The Auxiliaries, https://www.theauxiliaries.com

Dictionary of Irish Biography, https://www.dib.ie

Dublin Fusiliers, https://www.dublin-fusiliers.com/

Find My Past, https://www.findmypast.co.uk/

- Historical Belfast Directories
- Royal Irish Constabulary HO 184 Series
- TNA WO 363 First World War Soldiers' Documents

Historic Hansard, https://api.parliament.uk/historic-hansard/index.html

Historic-UK-com, https://www.historic-uk.com

History Hub, http://historyhub.ie

History Ireland, https://www.historyireland.com/

Irish Story, https://www.theirishstory.com/

North Irish Horse, http://www.northirishhorse.com.au/

PRONI, Ulster Covenant, https://www.nidirect.gov.uk/services/search-ulster-covenant

Western Front Association, Fold 3, https://www.westernfrontassociation.com/pension-records/

ENDNOTES

INTRODUCTION

1   Public Record Office of Northern Ireland [PRONI], HA/5/193, Shooting of Owen McMahon and Family and barman Edward McKinney (seven in all) at 3 Kinnaird Gardens, Belfast: Witness Statements.

2   For brevity the McMahon and McKinney murders are hereafter referred to as 'the McMahon murders'.

3   David Trimble, 'Glorifying the Gun', *Daily Telegraph*, 15 January 2001.

4   Laurence Marley, 'The McMahon Murders: Class and Killing in Belfast', in Darragh Gannon and Fearghal McGarry (eds), *Ireland 1922: Independence, Partition, Civil War* (Dublin: Royal Irish Academy, 2022), p. 110.

5   BBC Radio Ulster, 'Year 21: The District Inspector', first broadcast 18 June 2021, available at https://www.bbc.co.uk/programmes/p09lw4dh [accessed 5 February 2023].

6   Brian Hanley, 'The RIC Was Never a Normal Police Force; Commemorating It Would Be a Travesty', *Irish Times*, 13 January 2020; Department of Justice of Ireland, 'Press Release: Statement by Minister for Justice and Equality, Charlie Flanagan on the Decade of Centenaries Commemoration of the Dublin Metropolitan Police and Royal Irish Constabulary', 6 January 2020.

7   Bryan Follis, *A State Under Siege: The Establishment of Northern Ireland* (Oxford: Clarendon Press, 1995), p. 95; Arthur Hezlet, *The 'B' Specials* (London: Tom Stacey, 1972), p. 65.

8   Ibid.; Tim Pat Coogan, *Michael Collins: A Biography* (London: Head of Zeus, 2016), pp. 315–16.

9   Royal Norfolk Regiment Museum [NWHRM], 106, Intelligence Reports 1921–22.

10   NWHRM, Officers' Biographies Book: Henry Papworth, Eric Hayes, Harold Watling and Robert Scott; Peter Hart, *The 2nd Norfolk Regiment: From Le Pardis to Kohima* (Barnsley: Pen and Sword: 1998), 79–80; 180–2; The National Archives of the UK [TNA], WO 339/59478, Lt. R.P. Scott.

11   John Ramsden, *The Box in the Attic* (London: Shoot Raw, 2019), pp. 2–15.

12   NWHRM, Officers' Biographies Book: Charles George Wickham.

13   Letters from Lieutenant Colonel Charles Wickham, British Police Mission Athens, to his daughter Anne Ramsden, 1946, reproduced in Ramsden, *The Box in the Attic*, pp. 240, 252.

14   *The Belfast and Province of Ulster Directory, 1921–1922* (Belfast: Belfast Newsletter, 1921), p. 1413.

CHAPTER ONE: KILLING THE MCMAHONS

1   'Belfast Slaughter', *Evening Echo*, 25 March 1922.

2   'The McMahon Murders', *Belfast Newsletter*, 27 March 1922.

3   'Story of Horror', *Evening Echo*, 25 March 1922; 'Irish Terrorism', *Coventry Evening Telegraph*, 25 March 1922; PRONI, HA/5/193, McMahon Inquests, Report by DI William Lynn, 25 March 1922.

ENDNOTES

4   Quoted in Joe Baker, *The McMahon Family Murders and the Belfast Troubles* (Belfast: Glenravel, 1995), pp. 3–4; 'Fiendish Midnight Crime', *Freeman's Journal*, 25 March 1922.

5   'Father and Five Sons Shot', *Northern Whig*, 25 March 1922; 'Second Lieutenant Charles Berwitz', *Northern Whig*, 24 August 1916.

6   House of Commons, *Hansard*, 28 March 1922.

7   NWHRM, 106, Intelligence Reports 1921–22, Report by Capt. H. Papworth, 25 March 1922.

8   'The McMahon Murders', *Belfast Newsletter*, 27 March 1922.

9   'Orangemen Ordered to Clear Out', *Pall Mall Gazette*, 28 March 1922.

10   Military Archives of Ireland [MAI], Military Service Pensions Collection [MSPC], 24SP308, John Cusack; MSP34REF4970, Desmond Crean; National Library of Ireland [NLI], MS 49,554/22/5/23, Accounts of the Provisional Government of Ireland, 1921–1926, Receipt from Patrick O'Driscoll, Provisional Government of Ireland, acknowledging payment of expenses for trip to Belfast, 22 February 1922; J. Anthony Gaughan, *Alfred O'Rahilly: Public Figure* (Dublin: Kingdom Books, 1989), p. 69.

11   National Archives of Ireland [NAI], TSCH/3/S1801 A, Memorandum: The Massacre of the McMahons, undated.

12   'Interview with Badly Wounded Survivor', *Irish News*, 25 March 1922.

13   NLI, MS 44,060/4, Letter from Terence O'Keeffe to Mr McCarthy, 28 January 1974.

14   NLI, 44,061/6, Copy of Statement of Seán Montgomery, relating to the War of Independence in Belfast; 'Buncrana Man Slain in 1922 Belfast Bloodbath', *Derry Journal*, 11 January 2013.

15   'Terrible Belfast Tragedies', *Irish News*, 24 March 1922; TNA, HO 184/33, Constable Michael McKinney.

16   'Who Were the Murderers?', *Evening Echo*, 25 March 1922.

17   NLI, 44,061/6, Copy of Statement of Seán Montgomery, relating to the War of Independence in Belfast.

18   PRONI, HA/5/193, Statements; MIC150/1: Journal of District Inspector W. Lynn, 24-25 March 1922.

19   TNA, WO 372/23/27139, Mabel Rose McMurtry; WO 372/13/55936, James Alexander McMurtry; Registry of Deeds Ireland [RODI], Deeds Grant Index: Mary L. Watson, Grantor, to Mabel R. McMurtry, Grantee, 1921, Memorial Number 208; *Belfast Gazette*, 27 January 1921.

20   'Death of W.J. Purdy', *Belfast Telegraph*, 13 November 1915; Western Front Association, WW1 Pension Records and Ledgers, 12/MP/412: William James Purdy; *Belfast and Ulster Directory*, 1920 and 1921/1922, p. 452; 'The Protection of Animals', *Northern Whig*, 17 January 1918; RODI, Deeds Grant Index: Luis Berwitz, Grantor, to Rosabell Purdy, Grantee, 1920, Memorial Number 207.

21   PRONI, HA/5/193: Shooting of Owen McMahon and Family and barman Edward McKinney (seven in all) at 3 Kinnaird Gardens, Belfast: Witness Statements.

22   Tim Wilson, 'The Most Terrible Assassination that Has Stained the Name of Belfast', *Irish Historical Studies*, 37/145 (2010), p. 84.

23   PRONI, HA/32/1/130, St Mary's Hall, Documents Seized: Found in Attaché Case – St Mary's Hall, 18 March 1922; HA/5/193: Minute by Samuel Watt to Sir Richard Dawson Bates, 30 March 1922.

24   'Allegation Against Policemen', *The Irish Times*, 17 April 1922.

25   PRONI, HA/5/193, McMahon Inquests, Report by DI William Lynn, 23 August 1922.

26   PRONI, BELF/6/5/2/1, Belfast Spirit License Register, 1887–1893.

27   'Belfast Woman Routs Gunmen', *Ballymena Telegraph*, 29 April 1922; 'War on Catholics Goes On', *Irish Independent*, 25 April 1922; 'Belfast Compensation Claims', *Belfast Newsletter*, 15 September 1921.

28   'Lady and Daughter Shot', *Irish News*, 22 May 1922.

29   NWHRM, 106, Report by Capt. H. Papworth, 28 September 1921; 'Popular Belfast Man's Death', *Freeman's Journal*, 23 January 1915.

ENDNOTES

30 PRONI, FIN/15/7/'C1'/537, Vincent Shields, North Derby Street.

31 'Belfast Woman Routs Gunmen', *Ballymena Telegraph*, 29 April 1922; 'War on Catholics Goes On', *Irish Independent*, 25 April 1922.

32 Email correspondence from DI William Lynn's son to the author, 8 October 2023; 'Sinn Féin Scenes', *Irish Weekly and Ulster Examiner*, 23 March 1918; Police Museum of Northern Ireland [PMNI], District Inspectors' Records: William Lynn.

33 PRONI, HA/5/193, McMahon Inquests, Report by DI William Lynn, 23 August 1922.

34 PRONI, PM/8/1/1, Personal and Official Correspondence of Sir Wilfred Spender, Letter from Sir Wilfred Spender to Sir James Craig, 8 March 1922.

35 Diarmaid Ferriter, *A Nation and Not a Rabble: The Irish Revolution, 1913–1923* (London: Profile, 2015), pp. 150–84.

36 MAI, Bureau of Military History [BMH] Witness Statement [WS] 410, Thomas McNally; MSPC, MSP34REF59029, Robert Haskin.

37 MAI, BMH WS 410, Thomas McNally; WS 289, Roger McCorley; MSPSC, 24SP11139: Seamus Woods; TNA, HO 267/253, Arrest of Colonel Woods: Letter from Sir Stephen Tallents to Sir John Anderson, 23 November 1923.

38 Ferriter, *A Nation and Not a Rabble*, pp. 185–99; 236–56.

39 PRONI, D640/11/1, Crawford Papers, Diary 1920–1923.

40 Brian Barton, *The Government of Northern Ireland, 1920–1923* (Belfast: Athol Books 1980), pp. 2–17.

41 A.C. Hepburn, *Catholic Belfast and Nationalist Ireland in the Era of Joe Devlin* (Oxford: Oxford University Press, 2008), pp. 223–4.

42 Charles Townshend, *The Partition: Ireland Divided, 1885–1925* (London: Allan Lane, 2021), pp. 45; 14–51; Robert Lynch, *The Partition of Ireland: 1918–1925* (Cambridge: Cambridge University Press, 2019), pp. 152–4.

43 'The War Against Protestants', *Belfast Newsletter*, 9 May 1922.

44 University College Dublin Archives [UCDA], Richard Mulcahy Papers, Letter from Richard Mulcahy, Minister for Defence, to Arthur Griffith, President of Dáil Éireann, 24 March 1922.

45 MAI, MSPC, DP6925, Joseph O'Sullivan.

46 'Letter from London', *Irish Weekly and Ulster Examiner*, 11 August 1951.

47 'Appeal for Dunn and O'Sullivan', *Bellshill Speaker*, 4 August 1922.

48 The British ultimatum after Wilson's death and the kidnapping of a senior National Army officer, General J.J. O'Connell, by the anti-Treaty IRA were critical to the commencement of the Civil War on 28 June 1922. The latter was a *casus belli* that allowed the provisional government to evade the charge that it had merely given in to British threats. Prime Minister David Lloyd George's government blamed the anti-treaty IRA for Wilson's murder. Minister for Defence Richard Mulcahy denied having anything to do with the attack. However, Ronan McGreevy has argued that the order to kill Wilson in response to the violence in the North of Ireland likely came from Michael Collins in early 1922. The Parliamentary Archives [TPA] LG/F/185/1/5, Draft Conclusions of a Conference of Ministers held at 10 Downing Street on Thursday, 22 June 1922, at 5 p.m. Ronan McGreevy, *Great Hatred: The Assassination of Field Marshal Sir Henry Wilson MP* (London: Faber and Faber, 2022), pp. 378–83.

49 IRA Volunteer Desmond Crean, a former actor and the owner of a wholesale wine and whiskey business in Belfast, may have had some input into the Nixon Memo. He was the IRA point of contact for a number of RIC witnesses cited and in 1924 was working in 'a civil position' in military intelligence in Dublin. UCDA, Ernest Blythe Papers, P24/176, Activities of District Inspector Nixon; MAI, MSPC, MSP34REF4970, Desmond Crean; NAI, 1911 Census, Michael Desmond Crean, https://www.census.nationalarchives.ie/reels/nai001543547/ [accessed 28 January 2024].

ENDNOTES

50 'The Condition of Ireland', *The Spectator*, 5 May 1922.

51 The grievances and realities of sectarian discrimination were outlined by a British judge, Lord Cameron, in his 1969 report – *Disturbances in Northern Ireland: Report of the Commission appointed by the Governor of Northern Ireland* (London: HM Stationary Office, 1969).

52 Cormac Moore, *Birth of the Border: The Impact of Partition in Ireland* (Dublin: Merrion Press, 2019), p. 97; Cormac Moore, 'Partition at 100: Draconian Powers Aimed at Nationalists', *Irish News*, 27 April 2022.

CHAPTER TWO: BELFAST'S DESCENT

1 Robert Lynd, *Home Life in Ireland* (London: Mills and Boon, 1909), p. 185.

2 John Gray, *City in Revolt: Jim Larkin and the Belfast Dock Strike 1907* (Dublin: SIPTU, 2007), p. 25.

3 Emrys Jones, *A Social Geography of Belfast* (London: Quantum Reprints, 1965), pp. 58–60; Paddy Devlin, *Yes We Have No Bananas: Outdoor Relief in Belfast, 1920–1939* (Belfast: Blackstaff Press, 1981), p. 23.

4 Franceso Scalone, Lucia Pozzi and Liam Kennedy, 'Religion and Child Death in Ireland's Industrial Capital', *Social Science History*, 47 (2023), p. 436; Brendan Walsh, 'Life Expectancy in Ireland since the 1870s', *The Economic and Social Review*, 48/2 (2017), p. 131.

5 PRONI, T3580/1, Memoir of Mr Frederick McGinley's Working Life.

6 James Kelly, 'The Pogrom', *Capuchin Annual* (1943), p. 481; NLI, MS 44,060, Seán O'Mahony Papers, 'Volunteer Peter Shevlin', by Peter Quinn.

7 MAI, BMH WS 410, Thomas McNally.

8 Gray, *City in Revolt*, pp. 123–34.

9 Kieran Glennon, *From Pogrom to Civil War; Tom Glennon and the Belfast IRA* (Cork: Mercier Press, 2013), p. 266; Niall Cunningham, 'The Social Geography of Violence During the Belfast Troubles', *CRESC Working Paper Series*, Working Paper No. 122, the University of Manchester, March 2013.

10 'Attacked and Stabbed', *Freeman's Journal*, 26 July 1920.

11 Mark Radford, *The Policing of Belfast, 1870–1914* (London: Bloomsbury, 2015), pp. 9, 111, 169; T.J. Campbell, 'Pogroms: 1857–1935', *Capuchin Annual* (1943), p. 464; 'The Funeral of Curran', *The Witness*, 8 June 1886.

12 Thomas Carnduff, 'I remember', *The Bell* 5/4 (1943), p. 278; Thomas Carnduff, *Life and Writings*, (ed.) Peter Gray (Belfast: Lagan Press, 1994), pp. 69–70.

13 A non-commissioned officer is a member of the armed forces who has been promoted from the ranks – to the position of lance corporal, sergeant, staff sergeant etc – but does not hold an officer's commission and rank (lieutenant, captain, major etc.).

14 P.K. Kemp, *History of the Norfolk Regiment* (Norwich: Soman-Wherry Press, 1953), pp. 3–9.

15 Stathis Kalyvas, 'Fear, Preemption and Retaliation', in S.M. Saideman and Marie-Joelle Zahar (eds), *Intra-State Conflict, Governments and Security: Dilemmas of Deterrence and Assurance* (Abingdon: Routledge, 2008), p. 27.

16 'Ulster's Leader', *Belfast Newsletter*, 13 July 1920.

17 TNA, CO 904/113, County Inspectors' Reports, Belfast, July 1920.

18 Emmet O'Connor, *Rotten Prod: The Unlikely Career of Dongaree Baird* (Dublin: UCD Press, 2022), pp. 46–7.

19 'Black Day in Belfast', *Northern Whig*, 14 February 1929.

20 Moore, *Birth of the Border*, pp. 36–7.

21 Kieran Glennon in his admirably forensic history of the IRA in Belfast noted that the Belfast Brigade rolls of volunteers grew from 367 in June 1921 to 835 by the end of the year. TNA, CO 904/116, Belfast, July 1921. Glennon, *From Pogrom to Civil*, pp. 89–90.

ENDNOTES

22 'Officers and Snipers', *Larne Times*, 21 August 1920.

23 'Belfast Riots Inquest', *Belfast Newsletter*, 11 August 1920; 'The Belfast Riots', *The Light Bob Gazette: The Regimental Paper of the Somerset Light Infantry* 23/3 (1920), p. 8; 'the Battle of Seaforde', https://collections.nationalmuseumsni.org/object-belum-w2011-512 [accessed 12 March 2024].

24 'Ballymacarrett Scenes' *Belfast Newsletter*, 11 August 1920.

25 The recently deceased 15th Duke of Norfolk would have been offended; he was a strident opponent of home rule and a supporter of Ulster's right to self-determination. C.F.N. Macready, *Annals of An Active Life: Volume 2* (London: Hutchinson, 1925), p. 609; 'The Duke of Norfolk on Home Rule', *Londonderry Sentinel*, 13 November 1913; Imperial War Museum [IWM], Field Marshal Sir Henry Wilson Papers [HHW] 2/2G, Letters from General Sir Nevil Macready to Field Marshal Sir Henry Wilson, 2 September 1921, 26 November 1921 and 16 January 1922.

26 In 1935 the Norfolk Regiment was awarded a 'royal' prefix. George V was especially fond of the Holy Boys, as he was of his Sandringham Norfolk estate. The year 1935 was his silver jubilee and the 250th anniversary of the regiment's formation. Here I have used 'Royal Norfolks' when referring to the regiment since 1935. See Neil Storey, *The King's Men: The Sandringham Company and Norfolk Regiment Territorial Battalions, 1914–1918* (Barnsley: Pen and Sword, 2020); Kemp, *History of the Norfolk Regiment*, p. 10.

27 '1st Battalion News', *Cabar Feidh: the Regimental Journal of the Seaforth Highlanders*, 1/1 (1922), p. 46.

28 Macready, *Annals of An Active Life: Volume 2*, p. 609; IWM, HHW, 2/2G, Letters from General Sir Nevil Macready to Field Marshal Sir Henry Wilson, 2 September 1921, 26 November 1921 and 16 January 1922.

29 Kelly, 'The Pogrom', p. 483.

30 MAI, BMH, WS 746, Seán Culhane; 'Dastardly Lisburn Crime', *Belfast Newsletter*, 22 August 1920.

31 Christopher Magill, 'East Ulster and the Irish Revolution, 1920–1922', (PhD Thesis, Queen's University Belfast, 2014), pp. 56–60; 'Dastardly Lisburn Crime', *Belfast Newsletter*, 22 August 1920; *Illustrated London News*, 4 September 1920.

32 *Irish Weekly and Ulster Examiner*, 4 September 1920; NAI, TAOIS/s1451, Belfast Atrocities, 25 August 1920.

33 TNA, CO 904/112 and CO 904/113, County Inspectors' Reports, Belfast, August and September 1920.

34 O'Malley interview with Tom McNally, 3rd Northern Division, republished in Síobhra Aiken et al., *The Men Will Talk to Me: Ernie O'Malley's Interviews with the Northern Divisions* (Dublin: Merrion Press, 2018), p. 110; MAI, BMH, WS 417, David McGuinness; UCDA, Richard Mulcahy Papers, P7/B/77, Memorandum from Seamus Woods, OC 3rd Northern Division, 27 July 1922.

35 NAI, LOU 13, Minute Book AOH 1906–1925, Report from the National Secretary, 7 September 1920; UCDA P7/A/29, Richard Mulcahy Papers, Letter from Seán MacEntee to the President of Sinn Féin, 5 November 1921.

36 MAI, BMH, WS 417, David McGuinness; MSPC, MSP34REF6061, Peter Burns; NAI, LOU 13 Minute Book AOH 1906–1925, Report from the National Secretary, 8 June 1922.

37 MAI, MSPC, MSP34REF7576, Patrick McCarragher; MSP34REF2556, Frank Booth; BMH, WS 289, Roger McCorley; WS 412, Joseph Murray.

38 Follis, *A State Under Siege*, p. 17.

39 Nevil Macready, *Annals of an Interesting Life, Volume 2* (London: Hutchinson, 1924), p. 488. For a nuanced discussion of the foundation of the USC see also Christopher Magill, *Political Conflict in East Ulster, 1920–1922* (Woodbridge: Boydell, 2020), pp. 81–4.

40 PRONI, CAB/5/1, Letter from Lieutenant Colonel Wilfred Spender to Major General Archibald Cameron.

ENDNOTES

41 TNA, CO 906/27, Notes on Police, Estimate of Police Numbers; 'War on the IRA', *Irish News*, 16 March 1922.

42 NLI, 44,061/6, Copy of Statement of Seán Montgomery; 'Policemen Killed', *Freeman's Journal*, 10 July 1921.

43 'Red Weekend in Belfast', *Northern Whig*, 11 July 1921.

44 IRA volunteer from B (Ballymacarett) Company quoted in Seán Ó Coinn, *Defending the Ground: B (Ballymacarrett) Company, 2nd Battalion, 1st Brigade, 3rd Northern Division, Irish Republican Army 1920-1922* (Belfast: Short Strand Community Tourism and Heritage Initiative, 2017), p. 49.

45 W.J. Williams, *Report of the Irish White Cross to 31 August 1922* (Dublin: Martin Lester, 1922), p. 49; 'Sinn Féiners at Armagh', *Northern Whig*, 5 September 1921.

46 MAI, MSPC, MA/MSPC/A/71, Fermanagh Brigade; MSP34REF28880, Patrick Mullarkey; 'Remarkable Outburst', *Fermanagh Herald*, 27 November 1920.

47 Ernie O'Malley interview with Seamus Woods, 3rd Northern Division, republished in Aiken et al., *The Men Will Talk to Me*, p. 94.

48 NAI, TSCH/3/S1801 A, Memorandum by Commission of Belfast Catholics into Police Conduct: 'A Few Facts Concerning Murders Organised and Carried out by Belfast Police, 1920-1921'.

49 James Kelly, *Bonfires on the Hillside: An Eyewitness Account of Political Upheaval in Northern Ireland* (Belfast: Fountain Press, 1995), pp. 137-8.

50 General Registry Office of Northern Ireland [GRONI]. Death Certificate: Ellen Dunbar Nixon, died 22 October 1922, registered 3 November 1922 [in author's possession].

51 'Death of Mrs. Nixon', *Northern Whig*, 12 October 1922.

52 TNA, HO 144/22569, DMP transferred to RIC, Memorial re. Special Consideration on Disbandment, 6 March 1922; MAI, MSPC, MSP34REF943, James Brennan.

53 PMNI, District Inspectors' Records: John W. Nixon.

54 PRONI, D640/6/18, Fred Crawford Papers, Statement about Glenravel Barracks.

55 TNA, CO 904/116, Belfast, July 1921; MAI, BMH, WS 156, DI J.J. McConnell.

56 MAI, BMH, WS 289, Manus O'Boyle.

57 MAI, BMH, WS 156, DI J.J. McConnell.

58 PRONI, HA/32/1254, District Inspector Nixon, Letter from DI Nixon, dated 11 July 1922; NAI, TAOIS/S1011, Northern Advisory Committee Meeting, 11 April 1922; NWHRM, 106, Report by Lt. E.C. Hayes, 10 April 1922.

59 NAI, TAOIS/S1011, Northern Advisory Committee Meeting, 11 April 1922.

60 Although given the name 'Peter' in his Sinn Féin statement, there was no Constable Peter Flanagan recorded as serving in Belfast in 1922. NAI, TSCH/3/s11195, Northern Ireland Outrages 1922, Witness Statement by Constable Flanagan, Brown's Square Barracks, Belfast, 23 March 1922; TNA, HO 184/33: Patrick Flanagan.

61 Aiken et al., *The Men Will Talk to Me*, p. 94.

62 NAI, TAOIS/3/s11195, Witness Statement by Constable Michael Furlong, Leopold Street Barracks, Belfast, 23 March 1922.

63 NAI, TSCH/3/S1195, Northern Ireland Outrages, Statement by Constable Flanagan, Brown's Square Barracks, 23 May 1922.

64 Staffordshire Regiment Museum, SSR/7740/12, Questionnaire re: Ireland answered by Major General John Meredith Benoy.

65 Macready, *Annals of an Interesting Life, Volume 2*, pp. 600-1; IWM, HHW 2/2G, Letter from Major General Sir Archibald Cameron to General Sir Nevil Macready 18 December 1921.

66 PRONI, HA/32/1254, District Inspector Nixon, Letter from Sir Richard Dawson Bates, Minister for Home Affairs, to John M. Andrews, Minister for Labour, 4 August 1922.

67 IWM, HHW 2/2F, Letter from General Sir Nevil Macready to Field Marshal Sir Henry Wilson, 2 September 1921.

253

ENDNOTES

68   Two additional brigades were deployed in Northern Ireland during the spring of 1922 to reinforce the border. From February Colonel Commandant Herbert Potter took command of operations in Belfast; Cameron remained in overall command of 'Ulster District'. Princeton University Library Special Collections [PULSC], Herbert Cecil Potter Letter to his Mother, 19 March 1922.

69   Mark Sturgis, *The Last Days of Dublin Castle: The Dublin Castle Diaries* (Dublin: Irish Academic Press, 1999), p. 219.

70   PRONI, HA/5/962, Robert Simpson, Memorial signed by William H. Byers, 22 April 1922; Kelly, *Bonfires on the Hillsides*, pp. 71–2.

71   IWM, HHW 2/2F, Letter from General Sir Nevil Macready to Field Marshal Sir Henry Wilson, 23 September 1921.

72   IWM, HHW 2/2G, Letter from Major General Sir Archibald Cameron to General Sir Nevil Macready, 18 December 1921.

73   'A Family's Trials', *Freeman's Journal*, 25 November 1921.

74   IWM, HHW 2/2F, Letter from General Sir Nevil Macready to Field Marshal Sir Henry Wilson, 4 November 1921.

75   IWM, HHW 2/2G, Letter from General Sir Nevil Macready to the Secretary of State for War, Sir Laming Worthington-Evans, 20 January 1922.

76   PRONI, HA/32/1254, Letter from DI Nixon, 11 July 1922; HA/32/1/7, Control of the Police, Minute from A.P. Magill, Ministry of Home Affairs, 23 January 1922.

77   PRONI, HA/20/A/1/4, Allegations against the Norfolk Regiment, September to December 1921.

78   PRONI, HA/32/1254, Letter from DI Nixon, 11 July 1922.

79   Wilson, 'The Most Terrible Assassination', p. 102.

80   PRONI, CAB/6/37, Letter from A.W. Hungerford to Prime Minister Sir James Craig, 8 March 1922.

81   NWHRM, 106, Report by Capt. H. Papworth, 20 January 1922.

82   PRONI, D640/11/1, Crawford Papers, Diary 1920–1923.

83   PRONI, D640/12/2, History of the Formation of the Ulster Brotherhood.

84   Keith Haines, *Fred Crawford – Carson's Gunrunner* (Donaghadee: Ballyhay Books, 2019), pp. 287–8.

85   Ibid., p. 292.

86   PRONI, D640/12/2, History of the Formation of the Ulster Brotherhood; Haines, *Fred Crawford*, pp. 278–92.

87   'Coote Attacks Craig', *Anglo-Celt*, 16 June 1921; House of Commons, *Hansard*, 2 November 1920.

88   'Wild Orange Oratory at Belfast Meetings', *Irish News*, 17 November 1921.

89   'Ulster Ex-Servicemen's Association, *Northern Whig*, 16 May 1921.

90   PRONI, D1288/1A, Senator Joseph Cunningham Papers, Memo of Interview with Mrs Cunningham, widow of Senator Joseph Cunningham, 6 January 1966.

91   'Anti-Socialist Campaign', *Belfast Newsletter*, 5 October 1921; 'Ex-Minister of Labour Dies at 87', *Belfast Telegraph*, 24 June 1965.

92   TNA, WO 35/88B/2, Disturbances, Rioting in Belfast, August to September 1921, Letter from Command. 15 Infantry Brigade to [illegible], 12 September 1921.

93   IWM, Field Marshal Sir Henry Wilson Papers, HHW 2/2G, Letter from Major General Archibald Cameron to General Sir Nevil Macready, 9 January 1922.

94   'The Belfast Imps', *Weekly Freeman*, 25 February 1922.

95   Magill, *Political Conflict in East Ulster*, p. 1.

96   The company commanders were Sam McCrea, John Kelly and James Lyle. 'The Ulster Imperial Guard', *Larne Times*, 19 November 1921.

97   TNA, HO 267/48, Imperial Secretary to the Governor of Northern Ireland, Report by Sir Stephen Tallents to Sir John Anderson [March 1924].

ENDNOTES

98 'Ulster Imperial Guards', *Belfast Telegraph*, 14 November 1921.

99 'The Wellington Hall', *Belfast Newsletter*, 17 November 1921.

100 Paul Staniland, 'Armed Groups and Militarized Elections', *International Studies Quarterly*, 29/4 (2015), pp. 694–705.

101 Orange Heritage Museum [OHM], Orange and Black Loyalist Defence Association [OBLDA], Minutes of an Executive Committee Meeting held on 11 November 1921; PRONI, PM/2/4/225/1-5, Memorandum by W.A. Magill, Assistant Secretary, Ministry of Home Affairs, to Secretary of the Cabinet, 24 February 1931.

102 PRONI, PM/2/4/225/1-5, Memorandum by W.A. Magill, Assistant Secretary, Ministry of Home Affairs, to Secretary of the Cabinet, 24 February 1931.

103 'Ulster Specials Honoured', *Northern Whig*, 18 October 1924.

104 Sam Waring was shot in the back in Belfast city centre on 20 June 1922 after a special constable accidentally discharged a rifle. TNA, WO 339/13448, Samuel Waring; 'Special Constable Wounded', *Belfast Newsletter*, 21 June 1922.

105 TNA, HO 267/258, Organisation of the RUC, Letter from Sir Stephen Tallents to Sir John Anderson, 27 February 1923.

106 IWM, HHW 2/2G, Letter from Major General Archibald Cameron to General Sir Nevil Macready, 9 January 1922; Letter from General Sir Nevil Macready to Field Marshal Sir Henry Wilson, 11 January 1922.

107 Chris Ryder, *The RUC: A Force Under Fire* (London: Mandarin, 1992), p. 53.

108 Macready to Worthington-Evans, 8 March 1922, quoted in Paul Canning, *British Policy Towards Ireland, 1921–1941* (Oxford: Clarendon Press, 1985), pp. 57–8.

109 Jim McDermott, *Northern Divisions: The Old IRA and the Belfast Pogroms, 1920–1922* (Belfast: Beyond the Pale Publications, 2009), p. 182.

110 PRONI, D640/11/1, Col. Fred Crawford Diary, 13 June 1922.

111 Kelly, *Bonfires on the Hillside*, pp. 12–18.

112 This episode was related in an interview given by a Belfast republican to the historian Jim McDermott. In this account 'Haw Haw' or 'Ha-ha' is identified by the interviewee as being an officer in the Seaforth Highlanders. McDermott, *Northern Divisions*, p. 175; Hart, *The 2nd Norfolk Regiment*, pp. 79–80.

113 MAI, BMH, WS 492, John McCoy.

114 NLI, MS 8,457/12, Art O'Briain Papers, Report of the Belfast Catholic Protection Committee, 25 April 1922; Hart, *The 2nd Norfolk Regiment*, pp. 181–2.

115 PRONI, HA/32/1/130, St Mary's Hall, Documents Found in St Mary's Hall, Belfast, 18 March 1922.

116 PRONI, HA/32/1/130, Report by City Commissioner to Divisional Commander, 18 March 1922; Patrick Long, 'Eoin O'Duffy', *Dictionary of Irish Biography*, https://www.dib.ie/biography/oduffy-eoin-a6728 [accessed 20 July 2022]; TNA, HO 267/253, Letter from Sir Stephen Tallents to Sir John Anderson, 23 November 1923.

117 There was an especially large intelligence haul in late December 1921/early January 1922. NWHRM, 106, Reports by Capt. H. Papworth, 30 December 1921, 1 and 10 January 1922.

118 PRONI, D1633/2/25, Personal Diary of Lady Lilian Spender, 11 August–December 1921.

119 TNA, CO 904/116, Belfast, September 1921.

120 NLI, 44,061/6, Copy of Statement of Seán Montgomery.

121 Andrew James was the first fatality, shot dead near York Street on 20 November 1921. Three days another two Imps, Bertie Phillips and David Cunningham, were shot dead. The following month Walther Pritchard, a popular Royal Irish Rifles veteran and former Royal Navy sailor Ben Lundy were also killed. Herbert Hassard, another war veteran and Imp, was fatally wounded by Norfolks

ENDNOTES

soldiers on 8 March – he was also a member of the Ulster Protestant Association. 'Killed by Two Bullets', *Northern Whig*, 25 November 1921; 'Vere Street Shooting', *Belfast Telegraph*, 21 February 1922; 'East End Fatalities', *Northern Whig*, 28 November 1921; 'Riot Victim's Funeral', *Northern Whig*, 21 December 1921; 'Funerals of Victims', *Northern Whig*, 17 February 1922; 'Ulster Imperial Guard', *Weekly Telegraph*, 19 November 1921; 'Funerals of Riot Victims', *Belfast Newsletter*, 13 March 1922.

122 TNA, WO 35/160/27, Death of Alexander Turtle, 2 January 1922, Belfast.

123 IRA intelligence indicated that 'an ex-Special' called Stanley Hassan was involved in the killing of Private Barnes. His name does not appear in 1 Norfolks intelligence reports. MAI, IE/MA/HS/A/988/15, Part of captured file titled List of persons employed in RUC Headquarters, Waring Street, Belfast 10 August 1922; NWHRM, 106, Report by Capt. H. Papworth, 6 January 1922; 'Alleged Shooting with Intent to Murder', *Northern Whig*, 6 September 1921; 'Vere Street Shooting', *Belfast Telegraph*, 21 February 1922; 'First Soldier Victim', *Irish News*, 3 January 1922.

124 NAI, NEBB/1/1/1, Statement of Occurrences in Belfast from 1 January to 20 January 1922.

125 'Young Soldier's Death', *Belfast Newsletter*, 12 January 1922.

126 'Mother of Private Barnes' *Belfast Telegraph*, 27 January 1922.

127 IWM, HHW 2/2G, Letter from Field Marshal Henry Wilson to General Macready, 14 February 1922.

128 NAI, TAOIS/3/S11195:, Summary Record of the Occurrences of the latest outbreak in which 'A' and 'B' Class Specials, and Imperial Guards participated, 11 February 1922.

129 NEBB/1/1/6, Belfast Pogroms, Summary of Atrocities in Ulster, 1922, January–April: 1 January 1922; 10 February 1922; 10 March 1922; NAI, TAOIS/3/S11195, Copy of a note sent to a patient, 15 February 1922.

130 IWM, HHW 2/2G, Letter from General Sir Nevil Macready to the Secretary of State for War, 9 February 1922; PRONI, HA/32/1/289A, Arrest and Internment of Gunmen: Report on Robert Craig by DI Spears, 29 October 1922.

131 NWHRM, 106, Report by Capt. H. Papworth, 14 February 1922.

132 Ibid., 16 February 1922.

133 Ibid., 7 February 1922.

134 'Another Day of Tragedy', *Belfast Newsletter*, 15 February 1922.

135 NWHRM, 106, Report by Capt. H. Papworth, 25 February 1922.

136 Ibid., 16 February 1922.

137 'Orangeman's Death', *Belfast Newsletter*, 5 February 1922; 'The Late Mr Waring', *Belfast Telegraph*, 17 February 1922.

138 NWHRM, 106, Report by Capt. H. Papworth, 17 February 1922.

139 Ibid., 26 February 1922.

140 McDermott, *Northern Divisions*, p. 181.

141 'Murder Campaign', *The Irish Weekly and Ulster Examiner*, 14 October 1922; 'Cold-Blooded Murder', *Northern Whig*, 13 March 1922.

142 NWHRM, 106, Report by Capt H. Papworth, 9 March 1922. 'Four Killed; Eight Wounded', *Northern Whig*, 8 March 1922; 'Funerals of Victims', *Northern Whig*, 13 March 1922.

143 'Appeals from Recorder', *Northern Whig*, 14 February 1923; NWHRM, 106, Report by Capt. H. Papworth, 9 March 1922; NAI, NEBB/1/1/6, Belfast Pogroms, Summary of Atrocities in Ulster, 1922: 8 March 1922.

144 'Inquiry into the Death of Lt. E.S. Bruce', https://www.cairogang.com/soldiers-killed/bruce/inquiry/inquiry.html [accessed 26 January 2023]; NLI, MS 49,930, Art O'Briain Papers, Fragment of document on the murder of Lieutenant Edward Stevenson Bruce in Alfred Street, Belfast on 10 March 1922.

ENDNOTES

145 PRONI, HA/5/176, Firing at a Funeral, Rioting and Looting of Mr McKenna's Public House at Whitehouse.

146 Ibid.; 'Man Brutally Murdered', *Irish News*, 13 March 1922; NAI, TAOIS/3/S11195, Witness Statement by Sergeant John Murphy, Springfield Road Barracks, Belfast, 23 March 1922.

147 'The Tunnelled Yards', *Belfast Telegraph*, 30 March 1922.

148 NWHRM, 106, Report by Capt. H. Papworth, 23 March 1922.

149 TNA, WO 35/159B, Courts of Inquiry in lieu of Inquests, Special Constable Charles Vokes, 20 March 1922.

150 'Mad Blood Lust', *Freeman's Journal*, 9 March 1922.

151 PRONI, PM/8/1/1, Personal and Official Correspondence of Sir Wilfred Spender, Letter from Sir Wilfred Spender to Sir James Craig, 8 March 1922.

152 IWM, Field Marshal Sir Henry Wilson Papers, HHW 2/2H, Letter from General Sir Nevil Macready to Sir Henry Wilson MP, 14 March 1922.

153 '1st Battalion News', *Cabar Feidh: the Regimental Journal of the Seaforth Highlanders*, 1/1 (1922), p. 46.

154 IWM, HHW 2/2/G, Letter from General Nevil Macready to the Secretary of State for War, 8 March 1922.

155 IWM, LAWG/3, Lionel Gundry-White Papers, Ledger containing the names of people whom he met between 1921 and 1925, with subjective appraisals of their qualities and failings.

156 NWHRM, 106, Report by Capt. H. Papworth, 12 March 1922.

157 PULSC, Herbert Cecil Potter Letter to his Mother, 19 March 1922.

158 'Outrage on Belfast Children', *Irish News*, 14 February 1922.

159 PULSC, Herbert Cecil Potter Letter to his Mother, 19 March 1922.

160 'Four Deaths', *Freeman's Journal*, 5 June 1922.

161 PRONI, CAB/6/43, Alleged Neglect of S/C to Assist the Military, Letter from Major General A.R. Cameron, Command. Ulster District to Prime Minister Sir James Craig, 6 June 1922.

162 Heggart was nonetheless awarded the King's Police Medal six months later. PRONI, CAB/6/43, Report from District Inspector Richard Heggart to City of Belfast Commissioner, Royal Ulster Constabulary, 6 June 1922; Letter from Major General Arthur Solly-Flood to the Secretary to the Prime Minister, 8 June 1922; 'The King's Police Medal', *Londonderry Sentinel*, 17 February 1923.

163 TNA, HO 184/46, Richard Robert Heggart; PMNI, District Inspectors' Personal Records, Richard Heggart.

164 TNA, WO 106/6156, Report on the intelligence section of the General Staff Branch, Northern Ireland District, 1922–1936; Robert Black, *Honours and Medals Awarded to the Royal Ulster Constabulary GC, 1922–2001* ((Belfast: Royal Ulster Constabulary George Cross Foundation, 2015), p. 21.

165 TNA, CAB/21/254, Draft Conclusion of a Meeting of the Provisional Government of Ireland Committee, 6 June 1922.

166 Suspected accomplices of Arthurs included William Morrow and Archibald Pollock. PRONI, HA/32/1/289A, Arrest and Internment of Gunmen, Report on William Morrow and Archibald Pollock by DI Spears, 29 October 1922; 'Belfast Assizes', *Derry Journal*, 28 July 1922; 'Belfast Crime Outbreak', *Northern Whig*, 6 October 1922.

167 PRONI, HA/5/2194, Joseph Arthurs: Minute by DI R.R. Spears.

168 PRONI, CAB/6/43, Letter from Sir Winston Churchill, Secretary of State for the Colonies to Sir James Craig, Prime Minister of Northern Ireland, 6 June 1922; Letter from Sir James Craig to Sir Winston Churchill, 8 June 1922.

169 Kieran Glennon, 'The Dead of the Belfast Pogrom – Counting the Cost of the Revolutionary Period, 1920–22', *The Irish Story*, 27 October 2020, and 'The Dead of the Belfast Pogrom –

ENDNOTES

Addendum', *The Irish Story*, 20 January 1922; Robert Lynch, 'The People's Protectors? The Irish Republican Army and the Belfast Pogroms, 1920-1922', *Journal of British Studies* 37/2 (2008), p. 375; Brian Hughes, *Defying the IRA? Intimidation, Coercion and Communities during the Irish Revolution* (Liverpool: Liverpool University Press, 2016), p. 165; IWM, HHW 2/2F, Letter from General Sir Nevil Macready to Field Marshal Sir Henry Wilson, 4 November 1921.

CHAPTER THREE: AFTERMATH

1   'The 1920 Riots', *Irish Weekly and Ulster Examiner*, 7 December 1940.
2   PRONI, BELF/6/5/2/8, Spirit License Register, 1901–1910; BELF/6/5/2/2, Spirit License Register, 1893–1900.
3   RODI, Deeds Grant Index, Patrick McMahon, Grantor, to Provident Association of London: Grantee, 1921, Memorial Number 185; *Belfast and Ulster Directory, 1921-1922*, p. 770; '£1,200 Betting Case', *Belfast Telegraph*, 5 November 1927; 'Death of James Dempsey', *Belfast Newsletter*, 11 March 1909.
4   *Belfast and Ulster Directory, 1921/1922*, p. 1413.
5   In 1923 the York Street property passed to John McMahon after Tom's death. PRONI, BELF/6/5/2/8:, Spirit License Register, 1901–1910; PRONI, BELF/6/5/3/1, Spirit License Register, 1911–1923.
6   PRONI, BELF/6/5/2/8, Spirit License Register, 1901–1910.
7   'Belfast Police Intelligence', *Belfast Newsletter*, 8 June 1912.
8   The connection was also sincerely felt – the McMahon family retained a strong connection to Glentoran football club for many decades after the murders. 'The Late Mr Patrick McMahon', *Belfast Telegraph*, 8 December 1936; 'Death Notice', *Belfast Telegraph*, 29 May 1958.
9   'Ulster Prisoner of War Fund', *Northern Whig*, 7 September 1918.
10 'Fiendish Midnight Crime', *Freeman's Journal*, 25 March 1922.
11 'Father and Five Sons Shot', *Northern Whig*, 25 March 1922.
12 PRONI, FIN/18/1/22, Belfast and Ulster Family Grocers and Spirit Dealers Association.
13 'Belfast Compensation Claims', *Northern Whig*, 23 December 1921.
14 'Impudent Street Robbery', *Northern Whig*, 18 October 1921.
15 'Raid on Public House', *Belfast Newsletter*, 26 January 1921.
16 'Other Cases Dealt With', *Northern Whig*, 20 December 1921; 'Putting Down Crime', *Belfast Newsletter*, 26 January 1922.
17 'Raiders Shoot Barman', *Irish News*, 19 November 1921.
18 NAI, TAOIS/s1451, Belfast Atrocities, 25 August 1920.
19 '18000 Compensation', *Belfast Newsletter*, 25 February 1924.
20 PRONI, HA/5/193, Shooting of Owen McMahon and Family and barman Edward McKinney (seven in all) at 3 Kinnaird Gardens, Belfast, Witness Statement by Eliza McMahon.
21 NWHRM, 106, Report by Capt. H. Papworth, 26 March 1922.
22 House of Commons, *Hansard*, 28 March 1922.
23 Ryder, *The RUC*, p. 56.
24 'The Agreement', *Church of Ireland Gazette*, 7 April 1922.
25 NWHRM, 106, Report by Lt. E.C. Hayes, 4 April 1922.
26 Sir Winston Churchill Archives, Cambridge University [CHAR], 22/12 B, Letter from Sir James Craig to Sir Winston Churchill, 7 April 1922.
27 CHAR, 22/13, Letter from Sir Winston Churchill to Sir James Craig, 24 May 1922.
28 PRONI, CAB/6/43, Alleged Neglect of S/C to Assist the Military, Letter from Sir James Craig, Prime Minister of Northern Ireland, to Sir Richard Dawson Bates, Minister for Home Affairs, 10 June 1922.

ENDNOTES

29 NAI, Documents on Irish Foreign Policy, Extract from a Letter from George Gavan Duffy to Ormonde Grattan Esmonde (Madrid), 22 May 1922, https://www.difp.ie/volume-1/1922/northern-ireland/288/#section-documentpage [accessed 28 January 2024].

30 'Belfast Incendiarism', *Belfast Newsletter*, 31 March 1922.

31 NAI, TAOIS/s1011, North East Advisory Committee, Minutes of a Meeting on 11 April 1922.

32 NWHRM, 106, Report by Lt. E.C. Hayes, 2 April 1922; 'Havoc in Labourer's Family', *Northern Whig*, 1 April 1922.

33 'Belfast Murder Series', *Belfast Telegraph*, 11 July 1922.

34 NWHRM, 106, Report by Lt. E.C. Hayes, 2 April 1922.

35 NAI, NEBB 1/1/10, Northern Ireland Minorities, Statutory Declaration by Gerard Tumelty, 16 Arnon Street, 2 April 1922.

36 UCDA, Michael Hayes Papers, P53/66, Statutory Declaration by Daniel McGrath [undated]; 'Further Shocking Crimes in Belfast', *Irish News*, 2 April 1922.

37 His real name was Joseph McCrory.

38 NWHRM, 106, Report by Lt. E.C. Hayes, 2 April 1922.

39 NAI, NEBB 1/1/10, Statutory Declaration by William Kitson, 15 Stanhope Street, 3 April 1922.

40 NWHRM, 106, Report by Lt. E.C. Hayes, 2 April 1922.

41 NAI, NEBB 1/1/10, Statutory Declaration by Catherine Hatton, 9 Stanhope Street, 2 April 1922.

42 'Awful Vengeance Enacted', *Belfast Telegraph*, 3 April 1922.

43 NWHRM, 106, Report by Lt. E.C. Hayes, 2 April 1922.

44 NLI, 44,061/6, Copy of Statement of Seán Montgomery, relating to the War of Independence in Belfast.

45 NWHRM, 106, Report by Lt. E.C. Hayes, 4 April 1922.

46 NAI, NEBB/1/1/1, Belfast Atrocities, Belfast Summary, 3 April 1922.

47 NWHRM, 106, Report by Lt. E.C. Hayes, 4 April 1922.

48 NAI, TSCH/3/S1801 A, Memo random for Michael Collins, Extracts from Statutory Declarations Re Arnon Street and Stanhope Street Massacres.

49 Hereafter, for brevity, I have not repeatedly cited the Nixon Memo whenever it is mentioned. UCDA, Ernest Blythe Papers, P24/176, Activities of District Inspector Nixon.

50 MAI, MSPC, 24SP12908, Henry Russell MacNabb; NAI, TSCH/3/S1801 A, Memo random for Michael Collins, Extracts from Statutory Declarations Re Arnon Street and Stanhope Street Massacres; NWHRM, 106, Report by Lt. E.C. Hayes, 2 April 1922.

51 NAI, TSCH/3/S1801 A, Memo random for Michael Collins, Extracts from Statutory Declarations Re Arnon Street and Stanhope Street Massacres.

52 NWHRM, 106, Report by Capt. H. Papworth, 17 March 1922.

53 NWHRM, 106, Report by Lt. E.C. Hayes, 3 April 1922.

54 'Further Shocking Crimes in Belfast', *Irish News*, 2 April 1922; 'More Shooting Crimes in Belfast', *Irish News*, 3 April 1922; TNA, WO 363, Burnt Records, William Kitson, Royal Irish Rifles.

55 NWHRM, 106, Report by Capt. H. Papworth, 27 November 1921; MAI, MSPC, MSP34REF11033, John Morgan.

56 NWHRM, 106, Report by Lt. H.F. Watling, 6 May 1922; MAI. MSPC, MSP34REF6084, Charles McWhinney.

57 NAI, NEBB 1/1/10, Statutory Declaration by George Murray, 12 Arnon Street, 3 April 1922.

58 NWHRM, 106, Report by Lt. E.C. Hayes, 4 April 1922.

59 PRONI, MIC150/1, Journal of District Inspector W. Lynn, 1-10 April 1922.

60 NAI, TAOIS/s1011, North East Advisory Committee, Minutes of a Meeting on 11 April 1922.

61 NAI, NEBB/1/1/3, Belfast Pogrom, 'Secret Document', 10 April 1922.

ENDNOTES

62 McGrath's name in the 1922 military census appears just below that of Lieutenant Joseph Mack, who was accused of participating in the Countess Bridge massacre near Killarney on 7 March 1923 in which four republican prisoners were murdered. Mark McLoughlin, *Strength of Comradeship: The Milltown Murder* (Kildare: Kildare County Council, 2023), 82; MAI, MSPC, 3P1065, Daniel McGrath; Military Census, Private Daniel McGath, Dublin Guard, Kerry Command, Killarney, 12–13 November 1922.

63 NAI, NEBB/1/1/1, Belfast Summary, 21 May 1922.

CHAPTER FOUR: A TERRIBLE VICTORY

1 Oxford University Bodleian Library Special Collections, MS. Eng. c. 2803, AP Magill Papers, A.P. Magill Unpublished Memoir.

2 NAI, NEBB 1/1/10, Northern Ireland Minorities, Statutory Declaration by Isaac Catney, 14 April 1922.

3 'Joy Street Ambush', *Northern Whig*, 14 June 1922.

4 NWHRM, 106, Report by Lt. E.C. Hayes, 10 April 1922; 'Deaths and Wounds', *Northern Whig*, 19 April 1922.

5 The unionist press gave a different account to that of DI Heggart, who confirmed that 1 Norfolks shot Johnston. Initially it was claimed that Johnston had answered a call for assistance by a sergeant of the Norfolk Regiment and had then been shot accidentally. Later it was suggested that he was 'murdered by unknown persons' and *dum dum* bullets had been used. PRONI, ANT/1/2/C/30/40, Report to the Divisional Commander from DI Richard Heggart, 19 April 1922; NEBB/1/1/6, Belfast Pogroms, Summary of Atrocities in Ulster, 1922, January–April, 18 April 1922.

6 NLI, MS 8,457/12, Report of the Belfast Catholic Protection Committee, 5 May 1922.

7 TNA, BT 377/7/118210, William Madden; 'Funeral Scenes', *Freeman's Journal*, 20 May 1922; 'Renewed Belfast Shootings', *Larne Times*, 20 May 1922.

8 NWHRM, 106, Reports by Lt. H.F. Watling, 13 and 18 May 1922.

9 NAI, NEBB/1/1/8, Belfast Atrocities, 12 April 1922.

10 NWHRM, 106, Report by Lt. E.C. Hayes, 12 April 1922; Report by Lt. H.F. Watling, 25 April 1922; NAI, TAOIS/S1011, Northern Advisory Committee Meeting, 11 April 1922.

11 It was rumoured that Fr Murray, a priest in Ardoyne, was an 'IRA chaplain'. TNA, CO 906/26, Notes of Conversations with opponents and representatives of the Northern Ireland Government and Establishment, Minutes of a Meeting Held at 10 Downing Street, 16 June 1922; NWHRM, 106, Report by Capt. H. Papworth, 30 December 1921.

12 In 1922 20 per cent of Northern Ireland's police was made up of Catholics, predominantly those policemen who transferred directly from the old RIC. This share declined over the subsequent decade. Ryder, *The RUC*, 60; TNA, CO 906/27, Notes on Police Forces; CHAR 22/13, Points for Discussion by the Secretary of State with Sir James Craig, 9 May 1922; Townshend, *The Partition*, p. 234; NAI, TSCH/3/S1801 A, Letter from Prime Minister James Craig to Chairman of the Provisional Government, Michael Collins, 25 April 1922.

13 NWHRM, 106, Report by Lt. H.F. Watling, 24 May 1922.

14 NLI, n.526, p.799, Charlotte Despard, Diary of events in Belfast in May to July 1922.

15 Ibid.

16 NLI, 44,061/6, Copy of Statement of Seán Montgomery, relating to the War of Independence in Belfast.

17 NAI, NEBB/1/1/6, Belfast Pogroms, Summary of Atrocities in Ulster, 1922, January–April, 19 May 1922.

18 NWHRM, 106, Report by Lt. H.F. Watling, 20 May 1922.

ENDNOTES

19 NLI, 44,061/6, Copy of statement of Seán Montgomery, relating to the War of Independence in Belfast.

20 NWHRM, 106, Report by Lt. H.F. Watling, 23 May 1922; 'Other Notable Events', *Ballymena Telegraph*, 2 September 1922.

21 NAI, NEBB/1/1/6, Belfast Pogroms, Summary of Atrocities in Ulster, 1922, January–April, 26 May 1922.

22 NLI, n.526, p.799, Charlotte Despard, Diary of events in Belfast in May to July 1922.

23 NWHRM, 106, Report by Lt. H.F. Watling, 1 June 1922.

24 PRONI, D640/11/1, Crawford Papers, Diary 1920–1923.

25 NAI, NEBB 1/1/10, Northern Ireland Minorities: Statutory Declaration by Susan McCormick, 150 Donegall Pass, 9 June 1922.

26 NAI, TAOIS/3/s1451, Belfast Atrocities, 5 June 1922; 22 June 1922.

27 NWHRM, 106, Report by Lt. H.F. Watling, 3 June 1922.

28 TNA, CO 906/26, Notes of Conversations with opponents and representatives of the Northern Ireland Government and Establishment, Talk at Victoria Barracks, 27 June 1922.

29 NAI, TAOIS/3/s1451, Belfast Atrocities, 27 June 1922.

30 'The Official Report', *Belfast Newsletter*, 17 June 1922.

31 NAI, TAOIS/3/s1451, Belfast Atrocities, 9 June 1922, 5 August 1922; 'With the First Battalion', *Cabar Feidh: The Regimental Journal of the Seaforth Highlanders*, 1/4 (2022), p. 165.

32 NAI, TAOIS/3/s1451, Belfast Atrocities, 9 June 1922, 5 July 1922, 26 August 1922; 'The Official Report', *Belfast Newsletter*, 17 June 1922.

33 Glennon, *From Pogrom to Civil War*, pp. 143–4.

34 MAI, BMH, WS 429, Thomas Flynn.

35 MAI, MSPC, MSP34REF6070, Thomas Flynn; UCDA, Richard Mulcahy Papers, P7/B/77, Six County Memorandum, Report of Meeting, 3 August 1922.

36 UCDA, Richard Mulcahy Papers, P7/B/77, Memorandum from Seamus Woods, OC 3rd Northern Division, to General Headquarters, 27 July 1922; NAI, TAOIS/3/s1451, Belfast Atrocities, 17 May 1922.

37 Tomás Ó Fiaich Library, Armagh, Cardinal Joseph MacRory Papers, Memorandum from Louis J. Walsh to Bishop MacRory, undated [*c*. 1922].

38 NAI, TAOIS/S1011, Northern Advisory Committee Meeting, 11 April 1922.

39 MAI, BMH, WS 412, Joseph Murray.

40 Aiken et al., *The Men Will Talk to Me*, p. 91; MAI, BMH, WS 412, Joseph Murray.

41 TNA, CO 906/26, Notes of Conversations with opponents and representatives of the Northern Ireland Government and Establishment, Talk at Victoria Barracks, 27 June 1922.

42 Nevertheless, Craig's government claimed that the police were not able to push back an IRA assault and occupation of the village of Belleek in County Fermanagh in early June 1922 – a task eventually completed by the British Army. TNA, CO 906/27, Notes on Police, Estimate of Police Numbers; TPA, LG/F/185/1/4, Memorandum, 'British Operations for Clearing the Pettigo-Belleek Triangle', 6 June 1922.

43 CHAR 22/12 B, Letter from Sir Winston Churchill to Sir James Craig, 19 April 1922.

44 Townshend, *The Partition*, p. 234.

45 TNA, HO 267/258, Letter from Sir Stephen Tallents to Sir John Anderson, 27 February 1923.

46 The IRA also had an intelligence network inside the Belfast postal service. The RUC denied that Stapleton had access to its most sensitive intelligence, telling the government that the files he stole were mostly 'harmless'. PRONI, CAB 9B/18, District Inspector Nixon, Report by Minister of Home Affairs Sir Richard Dawson Bates to Prime Minister Sir James Craig, 22 October 1922; Letter from Robert Megaw, Ministry of Home Affairs, to Prime Minister Sir James Craig, 7

ENDNOTES

September 1922; PRONI, HA/32/1/271, Enquiry into the Disappearance of A.T.P. Stapleton; MAI, MSPC, 24SP1108, James Tully; 24SP12059, Rory McNicholl.

47 TNA, HO 267/48, Report by Tallents, 15 October 1922; '"A" Specials Mutiny', *Mid-Ulster Mail*, 19 December 1925; G.C. Peden, *The Treasury and British Public Policy* (Oxford: Oxford University Press, 2000), p. 69.

48 TNA, HO 45/24851, Ireland, Proposed Formation of Ulster Territorial Division from 'C1' Constabulary, Letter from the Secretary of State for War, Stephen Walsh, to the Prime Minister of Northern Ireland, James Craig, 6 March 1924; Memorandum, 'Ulster Special Constabulary', undated.

49 'The Special Constabulary', *Belfast Newsletter*, 20 December 1923.

50 'The Special Constabulary', *Northern Whig*, 20 December 1923.

51 PRONI, D1327/11/2/1/1, North Belfast Ulster Unionist Labour Association Club, York Street, Letter from W. McWilliam to A.W. Hungerford, 10 March 1923.

52 *The Irish Protestant and Orange and Black Magazine*, 2/2 (1924).

53 PRONI, HA/32/1254, District Inspector Nixon, Letter from DI Nixon, 11 July 1922.

54 PRONI, HA/32/1254, Letter from Dawson Bates to Craig, 23 October 1922; CAB 9B/18, District Inspector Nixon, Letter from W. B. Spender to Samuel Cunningham MP, 8 October 1923; Letter from R. Scott, R. Armstrong, J. Rutherford, J.R. Hunter and J. McCurry to RUC Inspector General, 1 August 1923.

55 TNA, HO 267/48, Report by Tallents, 15 October 1922.

56 PRONI, HA/32/1254, Letter from Dawson Bates to Craig, 23 October 1922; Memorandum of the Ulster Unionist Labour Association, Belfast, 7 October 1922.

57 PRONI, HA/32/1254, Resolution of Castleton Temperance LOL, 867, 10 August 1922; Letter from 'the Orange Brotherhood' to Sir Richard Dawson Bates, undated.

58 *The Irish Protestant and Orange and Black Magazine*, 2/5 (1924).

59 PRONI, HA/32/1254, Letter from Dawson Bates to Craig, 23 October 1922.

60 'Recent Belfast Murder', *Belfast Newsletter*, 13 September 1923.

61 PRONI, CAB 9B/18, District Inspector Nixon, Letters from Robert Megaw, Ministry of Home Affairs, to Prime Minister Sir James Craig, 5 September 1923; 6 September 1923.

62 PRONI, HA/32/1254, Letter from Craig to Megaw, 8 September 1923.

63 TNA, HO 144/3915, Letter from Sir Stephen Tallents to Sir John Anderson, 29 February 1924.

64 UCDA, Richard Mulcahy Papers, P7/B/287, Memorandum from Seamus Woods, OC 3rd Northern Division to Commander-in-Chief of the National Army, General Richard Mulcahy, 29 September 1922.

65 'Belfast Orangeism', *Northern Whig*, 5 January 1924.

66 'The Orange Order', *Belfast Newsletter*, 30 January 1924.

67 PMNI, District Inspectors' Records, John W. Nixon, Letter from CI John McNally to DI Henry Lenthall, 5 March 1924; J.W. Nixon Confidential Papers, Memorandum by Samuel Watt, Permanent Secretary of the Ministry of Home Affairs to Inspector General RUC, 21 February 1924; TNA, HO 184/27, Samuel Williamson.

68 TNA, HO 144/3915, Letter from Tallents to Anderson, 28 February 1924.

69 'In and Around Belfast', *Northern Whig*, 29 January 1924.

70 Ibid.; Royal Ulster Constabulary, Certificate of Character, Constable Henry Clougher Gordon, 1 June 1922–17 April 1924, dated 8 June 1925 [copy in author's possession].

71 *The Irish Protestant and Orange and Black Magazine*, 2/5 (1924).

72 Ibid.

73 TNA, HO 267/48, Report by Tallents to Anderson [March 1924].

74 Ibid.

ENDNOTES

75 'Woodvale Contest', *Belfast Telegraph*, 17 November 1933.

76 Colin Reid, 'Protestant Challenges to the "Protestant State": Ulster Unionism and Independent Unionism in Northern Ireland, 1921–1935', *Twentieth Century History*, 19/4 (2008), p. 435.

77 'Appeal to Electors by J.W. Nixon MP', *Belfast Telegraph*, 5 February 1943.

78 PMNI, Diary of District Inspector William Henry Moffatt, Entry for 19 July 1944.

79 Reid, 'Protestant Challenges to the "Protestant State"', p. 435.

80 Loyalists had also not forgiven Londonderry for suggesting in March 1922 that they had been guilty of 'outrages that are as reprehensible as those committed by Sinn Féin'. See Fearghal McGarry, *Eoin O'Duffy: A Self-Made Hero* (Oxford: Oxford University Press, 2005), pp. 270–315; Kelly, *Bonfires on the Hillside*, pp. 137–8; Marquis of Londonderry, *Ourselves and Germany* (London: R. Hale, 1938), p. 1; N.C. Fleming, *The Marquis of Londonderry; Aristocracy, Power and Politics in Britain and Ireland* (London: Tauris, 2005), p. 97.

81 NAI, NEBB/1/1/8, Belfast Atrocities, 3 May 1922; TNA, HO 184/37, Patrick Naughten., 'Mr Cooper's Bigotry', *Derry Journal*, 17 August 1925.

82 'Ex-Inspector Nixon', *Belfast Newsletter*, 19 November 1925.

83 'Alderman Nixon Libel Action', *Northern Whig*, 25 November 1925; 'Alleged Attempt to Pack a Jury', *Manchester Guardian*, 25 November 1925.

84 'Stormy Days in North', *Larne Times*, 23 February 1935.

85 'Nixon Wins Libel Action', *Irish Weekly and Ulster Examiner*, 23 February 1935.

CHAPTER FIVE: THE BROWN'S SQUARE GANG

1 The Cork IRA claimed that an RIC officer called Gordon, born in Leitrim and who had been wounded while serving in the British Army during the war, was responsible for killing Volunteer Thomas Dwyer near the town of Thurles, County Tipperary, on 29 March 1920. MAI, BMH WS 719, Maurice Forde, Peadar McCann, Thomas Daly, Sean Kenny, Michael Keogh, Joseph O' Shea and Timothy O'Sullivan; 'James Gordon', http://www.bloodysunday.co.uk/shot-by-ira-as-spies/gordon-j/j-gordon.html [accessed 5 December 2020]; UCDA, Ernest Blythe Papers, P24/176, Activities of District Inspector Nixon.

2 Eugene Dunne, 'The Experiences of the Aristocracy in County Westmeath during the Period 1879 to 1923' (PhD Thesis, National University of Ireland Maynooth, 2016), pp. 311–12.

3 NAI, 1911 National Census of Ireland entry for Robert Gordon and Henry C. Gordon, Derrycarne Estate, Drumod, County Leitrim; TNA, WO 363/MIS-SORTS112/27, Sergeant Henry Gordon.

4 Dunne, 'The Experiences of the Aristocracy in County Westmeath', pp. 311–12.

5 TNA, HO 184/35, Henry C. Gordon.

6 'Victims of Belfast Outrages', *Belfast Newsletter*, 16 March 1922; 'Inquests on Belfast Victims', *Northern Whig*, 16 March 1922.

7 Henry Gordon was admitted to the W.T. Braithwaite Masonic Lodge which met at the Freemason's Hall on Belfast's Crumlin Road in 1920. TNA, WO 363, Sergeant Henry Gordon, https://search.findmypast.co.uk/record?id=GBM%2FWO363-4%2F007258700%2F02096&parentid=GBM%2FWO363-4%2F7258700%2F168%2F2096 [accessed 14 December 2021]; Grand Lodge of Freemasons of Ireland Membership Registers Collection, *Freemasons of Ireland Membership Registers, Volume V*, Henry Clougher Gordon, H.T. Braithwaite, Belfast 441; 'In and Around Belfast', *Northern Whig*, 29 January 1924.

8 'Capture in North Street', *Belfast Newsletter*, 3 March 1922.

9 TNA, HO 184/32, RIC Service Records, Alexander Sterritt; MAI, IE/MA/HS/A/988/7, Captured Documents, Notes made by MA at District Constabulary HQ Brown's Square, 7 July 1922.

10 TNA, HO 267/48, Report by Tallents to Anderson [March 1924].

263

ENDNOTES

11 MAI, MSPC, MSP34REF32265, Neil Blaney.

12 IWM, HHW 2/2G, Letter from Field Marshal Henry Wilson to General Sir Nevil Macready, 22 December 1921.

13 MAI, MSPC, IRA Medal Application: MD6733, John O'Kane; NWHRM, 106, Report by Lt. E.C. Hayes, 12 April 1922.

14 Not all the Norfolks' intelligence reports were downbeat. Shortly afterwards Lieutenant Harold Watling noted that police-army relations were improving; the former were, for the most part, 'doing their duty' in Ardoyne. NWHRM, 106, Report by Lt. E.C. Hayes, 20 April 1922; Report by Lt. H.F. Watling, 23 April 1922.

15 Sergeant William McCartney (Antrim); Constable James Glover (Antrim); Constable Edwin Caldwell (Londonderry); Constable Berry Preston (Armagh); Constable Thomas Topping (Antrim); Constable Ernest Burton (Antrim). NAI, TSCH/3/S1801 A, Memorandum by Commission of Belfast Catholics into Police Conduct: 'A Few Facts Concerning Murders Organised and Carried out by Belfast Police, 1920–1921', and UCDA, Ernest Blythe Papers, P24/176, Activities of District Inspector Nixon.

16 County Inspector Richard Harrison (Limerick); DI John Nixon (Cavan); Head Constable John Giff (Carlow/Wicklow); Head Constable Robert Pakenham (Mayo); Sergeant Patrick Clancy (Donegal); Sergeant Constable Joseph Carr (Monaghan); Christopher Clarke (King's County); Sergeant George Hicks (Tipperary); Sergeant William Reid (Donegal); Constable Samuel Cooke (Wexford); Constable Alexander Earl (Louth); Constable Joseph Glass (Sligo); Constable James Golden (Sligo); Constable Henry Gordon (Leitrim/Cavan); Constable Thomas Haire (Sligo); Constable Matthew Maher (Mayo); Constable John Norris (Longford); Constable James Russell (Queen's County); Constable Alexander Sterritt (Donegal); Constable William Sherwood (Limerick/Leitrim). There is some confusion over the identity of Constable Glass – one provisional government report suggests he was an 'A' special constable and not RIC Constable Joseph Glass. The Belfast IRA believed that Constable Maher had played a role in the murder of Limerick mayor George Clancy. (Maher had transferred to Belfast in 1920, but had relatives in County Tipperary.) NAI, TSCH/3/S1801 A,: 'A Few Facts Concerning Murders Organised and Carried out by Belfast Police, 1920–1921'; UCDA, Ernest Blythe Papers, P24/176, Activities of District Inspector Nixon; NAI, TAOIS/3/S11195, Witness Statement by Constable Green, Mountpottinger Barracks, Belfast [undated, c. 1922]; MAI, IE/MA/HS/A/988/15, Part of captured file titled List of persons employed in RUC Headquarters, Waring Street, Belfast 10 August 1922; TNA, HO 184/36, Matthew Maher.

17 TNA, HO 184/29, Robert Pakenham.

18 An example is the extreme politics supported by Anatolian Greeks who had been forced to abandon their homes in the new Turkish state and seek refuge in Athens. André Gerolymatos, *An International Civil War: Greece, 1943–1949* (New Haven, CT: Yale University Press, 2016), pp. 8–9; 'Editorial', *Herald and County Down Independent*, 5 December 1925. For a discussion of radicalism among ethnic Germans during this period see also Michael Mann, *The Dark Side of Democracy: Explaining Ethnic Cleansing* (Cambridge: Cambridge University Press, 2006), pp. 196–8.

19 NAI, TSCH/3/s11195, Witness Statement by Constable Andrew McCloskey, Leopold Street Barracks, Belfast, 22 March 1922; TNA, WO 374/69180, Thomas Topping; HO 184/33, William Sherwood.

20 NAI, TAOIS/3/S11195, Witness Statement by Sergeant John Murphy, Springfield Road Barracks, Belfast, 23 March 1922.

21 NAI, TSCH/3/S1801 A, Memorandum by Commission of Belfast Catholics into Police Conduct, 'A Few Facts Concerning Murders Organised and Carried out by Belfast Police, 1920–1921'.

22 UCDA, Ernest Blythe Papers, P24/176, Activities of District Inspector Nixon.

23 There was no Constable Norton serving in Belfast in 1921; this may instead refer to Constable John Norris.

ENDNOTES

24 TNA, WO 35/162, Registry of Cases, John Gaynor, John McFadden and Edward Trodden.

25 PRONI, FIN 18/1/55, Belfast Riots, Inquests on Persons Killed, Report from City Commissioner to RIC Divisional Commander, 28 September 1920; Ernie O'Malley interview with Seamus Woods, 3rd Northern Division, republished in Aiken et al., *The Men Will Talk to Me*, p. 90.

26 'Military Verdict', *Irish Weekly and Ulster Examiner*, 13 November 1920.

27 TNA, HO 184/47, RIC Officers Register, John William Nixon.

28 TNA, HO 184/46, RIC Officers Register, Richard Dale Harrison.

29 MAI, MSPC, DP376, Michael Garvey.

30 TNA, WO 35/150, Military Inquest: Michael Garvey.

31 MAI, MSPC, MSP34REF53374, Hugh McShane.

32 TNA, WO 35/149A, Military Inquest, Daniel and Patrick Duffin, 1921.

33 Alan Parkinson, *Belfast's Unholy War* (Dublin: Four Courts Press, 2004), p. 116; NAI, TSCH/3/S1801 A, 'A Few Facts Concerning Murders Organised and Carried out by Belfast Police, 1920–1921'.

34 'Murder in Crowded Street', *Ballymena Weekly Telegraph*, 30 April 1921; NLI, 44,061/6, Copy of Statement of Seán Montgomery, relating to the War of Independence in Belfast; PMNI, District Inspectors' Records, John Ferriss.

35 TNA, WO 374/65548, Thomas Burrows Stewart; HO 184/52, Auxiliary Division No. 1, Thomas B Stewart.

36 TNA, HO 184/35, Henry C. Gordon.

37 'Death Notice: Alexander McCabe', *Belfast Telegraph*, 16 March 1964; Robert Black, Hugh Forrester and Stephen White, *Marking the Sacrifices and Honouring the Achievements of the Royal Ulster Constabulary GC* (Belfast: Royal Ulster Constabulary George Cross Foundation, 2022), p. 288.

38 'Four Deaths in Belfast', *Freeman's Journal*, 25 April 1921; MAI, BMH, WS 412, Joseph Murray.

39 MAI, BMH WS 1016, Seamus McKenna.

40 NLI, 44,061/6, Copy of Statement of Seán Montgomery, relating to the War of Independence in Belfast.

41 The RIC account contradicts that of the IRA, stating that Constable Caldwell did return fire. MAI, MSPC, MSP34REF7576, Patrick McCarragher; BMH, WS 389, Roger McCorley; 'Another Belfast Murder', *Northern Whig*, 14 March 1922.

42 'Policeman Murdered', *Irish News*, 13 March 1922; 'Walked Smilingly in Death's Shadow', *Ballymena Telegraph*, 18 March 1922.

43 'Springfield Road Shooting', *Northern Whig*, 7 September 1921.

44 'A Cowardly Attack', *Northern Whig*, 11 June 1921; MAI, BMH, WS 389, Roger McCorley.

45 TNA, HO 184/32, RIC General Register, Joseph Carr; Thomas Haire.

46 TNA, WO 35/154, Military Inquest, Alexander McBride, 1921; NAI, TSCH/3/S1801A, 'A Few Facts Concerning Murders Organised and Carried out by Belfast Police', 1920–1921.

47 See, 'Auxiliaries Transfers', https://www.theauxiliaries.com/resignations/RIC-RUC/police-transfers.html [accessed 17 July 2022].

48 'Funerals of Victims', *Irish Weekly and Ulster Examiner*, 25 July 1921.

49 TNA, WO 35/151A, Courts of Inquiry, Malachy Halfpenny.

50 MAI, MSPC, MA/MSPC/RO/404, Ardoyne Company, H. Bradley, Herbert Street.

51 NWHRM, 106, Report by Lt. E.C. Hayes, 8 April 1922.

52 'Belfast's Two Nights of Horror', *Irish News*, 13 June 1921.

53 TNA, WO 35/151A, Courts of Inquiry, Malachy Halfpenny.

54 'Twice Wounded in France', *Ballymena Telegraph*, 18 June 1921.

55 'The Fate of Kerr', *Northern Whig*, 13 June 1921; TNA, WO 35/153A, Military Inquest, William Kerr.

56 Ibid.

ENDNOTES

57   Ibid.; NAI, TSCH/3/S1801A, 'A Few Facts Concerning Murders Organised and Carried out by Belfast Police', 1920–1921.

58   Ibid.; WO 35/153A, Letter from H. Toppin to the Deputy Adjutant General, Ireland Command, 27 July 1921.

59   Hugh McAree has repeatedly been misidentified as a Catholic and a nationalist. He was a member of the Orange Order and signed the Ulster Covenant at Belfast City Hall. 'Further Deadly Conflicts in Belfast', *Irish News*, 15 June 1921; 'Murdered Little Boy', *Belfast Telegraph*, 15 June 1921; 'Funeral of Riots Victims', *Northern Whig*, 20 June 1921; PRONI, Ulster Covenant, Hugh McAree, 1 Sackville Street.

60   TNA, WO 35/153A, Military Inquest, William Kerr; 'Falls Road Terror', *Irish News*, 11 June 1921.

61   Both the 1922 Commission report and the Nixon memo do not mention the abduction of two men on Durham Street at 12.30 a.m., less than an hour before the kidnapping and murder of Halfpenny, Kerr and McBride. A lorry 'full of armed men' in civilian dress pulled up outside a shop and residence on the street. Two male members of the family were dragged out, told they were to be shot and ordered to walk fifteen paces. Residents in other houses on the street opened their windows and looked out – they were shouted at to close them. The armed men were confused about their whereabouts and the identity of the individuals they were supposed to target. The killings may have been called off because of the number of witnesses. 'Ordeal of Brothers', *Belfast Telegraph*, 13 June 1921.

62   PRONI, HA/32/1/130, Index to Documents Found at St Mary's Hall, 18 March 1922.

63   Aiken et al., *The Men Will Talk to Me*, p. 108.

64   NLI, LO 1728, *Weekly Irish Bulletin*, [undated] April 1922.

65   Ibid., 19 June 1922.

66   TNA, HO 184/47, RIC Officers Register, John William Nixon; HO 184/15, John Nixon.

67   NAI, TAOIS/3/s11195, Witness Statement by Constable Michael Furlong, Leopold Street Barracks, Belfast, 23 March 1922; 'Assizes Intelligence', *Northern Whig*, 18 March 1921; 'Ulster Winter Assizes', *Northern Whig*, 19 January 1921; TNA, HO 184/32, Michael Furlong.

68   'Adair' was possibly Special Constable James Adair, who lived on the Oldpark Road, and is included in an IRA list of special constables. NAI, TAOIS/3/s11195, Witness Statement by Constable Michael Furlong, Leopold Street Barracks, Belfast, 23 March 1922; UCDA, Michael Hayes Papers, P53/166, Statement taken from Constable Kehoe, Brown's Square Barracks [c. April 1922]; MAI, IE/MA/HS/A/988/15, Part of captured file titled 'List of persons employed in R.U.C Headquarters, Waring Street, Belfast 10 August 1922'.

69   NAI, TSCH/3/s11195, Witness Statement by Constable William Duffy, Mount Pottinger Barracks, Belfast, 23 March 1922.

70   Aiken et al., *The Men Will Talk to Me*, pp. 90, 94.

CHAPTER SIX: TAKING A DELIGHT IN KILLING

1   PRONI, HA/5/2192, Alexander Robinson, Persons Recommended for Internment; TNA, AIR 5/796, Ulster District HQ, Weekly reports of political and military situation, September 1922.

2   PRONI, HA/32/1/289A, Arrest and Internment of Gunmen, William John Nesbitt; Protestants Who Have Been Interned, May 1923; 'Three Shot Dead in Belfast', *Freeman's Journal*, 18 September 1922.

3   'Firearms Charges in Police Court', *Northern Whig*, 21 March 1922.

4   Ulster Folk and Transport Museum [UFTM], Interview R83 11, Alexander Robinson; 'Belfast Assault Case', *Northern Whig*, 10 August 1921; PRONI, HA/5/962, Robert Simpson, Memorial signed by William Grant MP; NAI, TAOIS/s1451, Belfast Atrocities, 27 August 1922; 17 September 1922; TNA, BT 351/1/116252, James Rafferty.

5   'Riots in Belfast', *Belfast Telegraph*, 23 July 1921; Devlin, *Yes We Have Got No Bananas*, p. 44.

266

ENDNOTES

6   NWHRM, 106, Report by Capt. H. Papworth, 5 October 1921.

7   UFTM, Interview R83 11, Alexander Robinson.

8   PRONI, HA/5/2192, Alexander Robinson, Persons Recommended for Internment; NAI, TAOIS/ s1451, Belfast Atrocities, 27 August 1922; 17 September 1922; 'Peace of Belfast Broken', *Ballymena Telegraph*, 14 October 1922.

9   PRONI, HA/5/2192, Alexander Robinson, Persons Recommended for Internment; HA/32/1/289A, Arrest and Internment of Gunmen, William John Nesbitt; Protestants Who Have Been Interned, 14 May 1923; NAI, TSCH/3/S1195, Northern Ireland Outrages, Statement by Sergeant Martin Bruen, 23 March 1922; 'Death of Sergeant Bruen', *Irish Weekly and Ulster Examiner*, 29 April 1922; UFTM, UNMNI034/190, Danny Robinson.

10   PRONI, HA/5/2192, Alexander Robinson, Letter from Annie Armstrong to Sir Richard Dawson Bates, 26 October 1922.

11   PRONI, HA/5/2192, Handwritten note by DI C. O'Beirne, undated; HA/32/1/289A, Arrest and Internment of Gunmen: Protestants Who Have Been Interned, 14 May 1923; Letter by H. Toppin, Ministry of Home Affairs, to Stephenson, 7 November 1922; Minute by H. Toppin, 18 November 1922; Report by H.C. P.M. Fallon, 13 November 1922; 'A Mysterious Crime', *Belfast Newsletter*, 7 October 1922; 'B Special Internee', *Belfast Telegraph*, 28 November 1922.

12   PRONI, HA/5/2192, Note by DI C. O'Beirne to Commissioner, 20 July 1923; Library and Archives Canada [LAC], Canadian Immigration Service, Passenger List and Border Entries, Alexander Robinson, 8 April 1928; UFTM, Interview R84 135, Fred Heatley, 1983; Sean O'Connell, 'Violence and Memory in Twentieth-Century Belfast: Stories of Buck Alec Robinson', *Journal of British Studies*, 53/3 (2014), p. 743.

13   PRONI, HA/5/2205, George G. Scott, Representations Against Internment Order, interned 10 November 1922; HA/32/1/289A, Arrest and Internment of Gunmen, Protestants Who Have Been Interned, 14 May 1923; HA/5/2210, John Williamson, Report by Head Constable James Wilkin to DI Richard Heggart, 1 October 1922; TNA, ADM 188/734/43940, George Graham Scott.

14   PRONI, HA/32/1/289A, Arrest and Internment of Gunmen, Return of Internees, 14 May 1923.

15   PRONI, HA/5/2210, John Williamson.

16   These were George Gray, Frederick Pollock, Robert Simpson and Robert Waddell. PRONI, HA/5/2223, Robert Craig; HA/32/1/289A, Arrest and Internment of Gunmen, Report on Thomas Pentland by DI Spears, 29 October 1922; Protestants Who Have Been Interned, 14 May 1923.

17   *The Irish Protestant and Orange and Black Magazine*, 2/5 (1924).

18   PRONI, HA/5/2223, Robert Craig.

19   PRONI, HA/5/962, Robert Simpson, Note from DI R.R. Spears to Commissioner, 16 February 1923.

20   Ibid., Letter from Robert Craig to Sir Richard Dawson Bates, 10 July 1922.

21   Ibid., Letter from Sir Richard Dawson Bates to Sam McGuffin MP, 1 November 1922.

22   Ibid., Robert Simpson hearing, 6 June 1923.

23   Ibid., Petition from Robert Simpson, 21 August 1923.

24   Ibid., Conditions of Release form 27 March 1925.

25   MAI, Collins Papers 05-02-23, Report by Intelligence Officer, 3rd Northern Division to Deputy Director of Intelligence, IRA General Headquarters, 24 January 1922.

26   PRONI, BELF/1/1/2/66/11, George Harper, Statement of Catherine Kearney, 25 August 1921.

27   'Vere Street Shooting', *Belfast Telegraph*, 21 February 1922; 'Ulster Imperial Guard', *Irish News*, 21 February 1922.

28   'The Tunnelled Yards', *Belfast Telegraph*, 30 March 1922; NWHRM, 106, Report by Captain H. Papworth, 23 March 1922.

29   'Savage Belfast Crime', *Freeman's Journal*, 26 May 1922; 'Echo of Bombing Charge', *Belfast Telegraph*, 4 May 1922; 'Belfast City Commission', *Northern Whig*, 2 May 1922.

ENDNOTES

30   PRONI, HA/5/2261, Samuel Ditty, Letter from DI John Nixon [undated].
31   Ibid., Resolution of Members of B Constabulary, Craven Street.
32   Ibid., Letter from Lieutenant Colonel P.J. Woods, 4 February 1923.
33   Ibid., Samuel Ditty; HA/5/962A, Andrew Scott.
34   PRONI, HA/32/1/652, James Mulgrew, Letter from Samuel Mulgrew, undated; Letter from Harry Taylor JP, 28 January 1924; Letter from Harry Taylor JP to Lieutenant Colonel Horace Gaussen, 11 January 1924.
35   Ibid., James Mulgrew, Note on James Mulgrew, February 1938.
36   NLI, 44,061/6, Copy of Statement of Seán Montgomery; PRONI, BELF/6/1/2/14, Inquests, Death of Herbert Phillips, 22 November 1921.
37   'Law Reports', *Northern Whig*, 4 May 1922; 'Duncairn Gardens Victim', *Irish News*, 24 November 1921.

CHAPTER SEVEN: THE NOTORIOUS DAVID DUNCAN

1   'Action Against Freeman's Journal', *Northern Whig*, 8 June 1923
2   NAI, DFA/10/3/42, Libel Action by David Duncan, Letter from Seán Lester, Director of Publicity to Gearóid McGann, Office of the President of the Executive, 4 June 1923.
3   'Action Against Freeman's Journal', *Northern Whig*, 8 June 1923; NAI, TAOIS/e3791, David Duncan Libel Proceedings.
4   Archives of Ontario [AOO], RG 10-270, Ontario Hospital Patient File, 20977 – David Duncan, Clinical Report, Dr H. Frank, 15 December 1938.
5   AOO, RG 10-270, Clinical Record, Dr J.G. Dewan, 8 February 1935; 8 June 1923; NAI, TAOIS/3/ S3791, David Duncan Libel Proceedings; 'Belfastman Libelled in Dublin Newspaper', *Belfast Telegraph*, 8 June 1923.
6   David Duncan would continue to misstate his age throughout his life. The wrong year of birth is also etched on his grave – 1890. GROI, Birth Certificate for David John Duncan, born 19 February 1891. Duncan gave a wrong date of birth for his RIC service and that in the French Foreign Legion. He also repeatedly gave conflicting statements about his age during his nearly five years of hospitalisation in Toronto, Canada. TNA, HO 184/42, David Duncan; Museum of the Foreign Legions of France, Aubagne [MFLF], Record of Service for 2nd Class Legionnaire David Duncan, 1925–6; AOO, RG 10-270, Clinical Record, Dr J.G. Dewan, 8 February 1935; 'Imperial Veterans Register Complaints', *Globe and Mail*, 8 June 1939.
7   AOO, RG 10-270, Clinical Record, Dr J.G. Dewan, 8 February 1935; James Taylor, *The First Battalion Royal Irish Rifles in the Great War* (Dublin: Four Courts Press, 2002), pp. 24–8; 'Belfastman Libelled in Dublin Newspaper', *Belfast Telegraph*, 8 June 1923; War Diary of 1st Battalion, Royal Irish Rifles, 1914–15.
8   PRONI, D12581/2/2, Letters from Lieutenant J.H.H. Pollock on active service to his parents, 1915–1917.
9   Charles Bean, *Official History of Australia in the War of 1914-1918: Volume II – The Story of ANZAC from 4 May 1915 to the evacuation of the Gallipoli Peninsula* (Canberra: Government of Australia, 1941), p. 699.
10   'Notes on the Battle of Sari Bair', by Captain F.E. Eastwood, reproduced in *War Diary of 6th (Service) Battalion, Royal Irish Rifles at Gallipoli* (Kindle edition, 2017).
11   Bean, *Official History*, p. 699.
12   PRONI, D1581, Field Message Book of Lieutenant J.H.H. Pollock, Royal Irish Rifles, Entry for 10 August 1915.
13   *War Diary of 6th (Service) Battalion, Royal Irish Rifles at Gallipoli* (Kindle edition, 2017).

ENDNOTES

14 Cyril Falls, *The History of the First Seven Battalions; The Royal Irish Rifles in the Great War Volume II* (Aldershot: Gale and Polden, 1925), pp. 81–2; Royal Dublin Fusiliers, 'The Salonika Campaign', http://www.dublin-fusiliers.com/salonika/salonica.html [accessed 12 August 2023]; Richard Grayson (ed.), *The First World War Diary of Noël Drury, 6th Royal Dublin Fusiliers* (Woodbridge: Boydell, 2022), pp. 112, 160, 189, 227.

15 Army List, 2nd Lieutenants, October 1916, copy made available by the Royal Ulster Rifles Museum.

16 AOO, RG 10-270, 20977 – David Duncan, Conference Report, 1 May 1935.

17 LAC, Militia and Defence personnel files (1870–1948) – 17644: File number 413-4-10, David Duncan, Lt. Royal Irish Fusiliers, Letter from David Duncan, 10 February 1931; AOO, RG 10-270, David Duncan, Clinical Record, Dr J.G. Dewan, 8 February 1935.

18 AOO, RG 10-270, Letter from J.R. Howitt, Superintendent, Ontario Hospital, to the Medical Director, Ex-Services Welfare Society, 15 November 1938.

19 AOO, RG 10-270, Clinical Record, Dr J.G. Dewan, 3 February 1935; TNA, WO 95/4585, War Diaries, 2nd Battalion, Royal Irish Fusiliers, Appendix 1 Vol. 33, August 1917; 2nd Lt. David Duncan, https://www.theauxiliaries.com/men-alphabetical/men-d/duncan-d/duncan.html [accessed 6 May 2024].

20 AOO, RG 10-270, Clinical Record, Dr J.G. Dewan, 8 February 1935; 'Belfastman Libelled in Dublin Newspaper', *Belfast Telegraph*, 8 June 1923; *London Gazette*, 28 June 1918.

21 Damien Wright, *Churchill's Secret War with Lenin: British and Commonwealth Military Intervention in the Russian Civil War* (Warwick: Helion and Company, 2017), p. xviii.

22 Royal Fusiliers Museum [RFM], RFM.ARC.571, Unpublished Memoir of Major E M Alfrey, Russia, May–October 1919, p. 16.

23 National Army Museum, 1966-02-68, Recollections of Acting Sergeant E S Virpsha: North Russian Expeditionary Force 1918–1919.

24 RFM, RFM.ARC.571, Unpublished Memoir of Major E M Alfrey, Russia, May–October 1919, p. 76.

25 'Dyer's Battalion' was commanded by a Canadian soldier, Captain Royce Dyer; its ranks were largely made up of Russian prisoners, including captured Bolshevik soldiers. Wright, *Churchill's Secret War with Lenin*, p. 116.

26 RFM, RFM.ARC.573.1, Typescript memoir of an unnamed Fusilier sent to North Russian Front.

27 RFM, RFM.ARC.571, Unpublished Memoir of Major E M Alfrey, Russia, May–October 1919, pp. 84–5.

28 Wright, *Churchill's Secret War with Lenin*, p. 174.

29 Dennis Gordon, *Quartered in Hell: The Story of the North American Expeditionary Force* (Missoula, MT: Doughboy Historical Society, 1982), p. 68.

30 Gordon, *Quartered in Hell*, p. 291.

31 RFM, RFM.ARC.571, Unpublished Memoir of Major E M Alfrey, Russia, May–October 1919, pp. 150–1.

32 GROI, Copy of a Marriage Certificate – David John Duncan and Sarah Jane Silvester Cockrill, 17 December 1919; TNA, WO 372/6/113056, Medal Card of David Duncan.

33 'Belfast Shopkeeper Shot: Ex-Officer Charged with Murder', *Belfast Newsletter*, 24 February 1922; PRONI, BELF/6/1/2/14, Inquests, Death of James McIvor, 25 November 1921; PRONI, PM/2/4/225/1-5, Letter from Bro. David J. Duncan, 16 Laughton Avenue, Toronto, Canada, to Sir James Craig, Prime Minister of Northern Ireland, 4 February 1931.

34 'Fenians' – originally an Irish rebel movement based on the ancient *Fianna* warriors – can be used as a derogatory way to refer to Catholics in general. PRONI, ANT/1/2/C/30/106, David Duncan and Robert Halliday – Riotous Behaviour; 'Ulster Winter Assizes', *Northern Whig*, 15 January 1921.

35 'The Terror', *Daily News*, 4 March 1922.

ENDNOTES

36 PRONI, PM/2/4/225/1-5, Memorandum by W.A. Magill, Assistant Secretary, Ministry of Home Affairs, to Secretary of the Cabinet, 24 February 1931; TNA, HO 185/52, Auxiliary Division Journal – No. 1: David Duncan.

37 *Belfast and Ulster Directory*, 1920 and 1921/1922, pp. 402, 675.

38 UCDA, Richard Mulcahy Papers, P7/A/29, Memorandum on the Cromwell Clubs, by Alderman John Harkin, forwarded by Seán MacEntee to 'Uachtaráin', 5 November 1921; 'Parade of Belfast Loyalists', *Belfast Telegraph*, 1 November 1921.

39 'Riot Victim's Funeral', *Northern Whig*, 21 December 1921.

40 NLI, MS 8,457/12, Report of the Belfast Catholic Protection Committee, 18 May 1922.

41 The property was owned by the Catholic O'Dempsey family. Before his death in 1909, James Dempsey had been a Nationalist city councillor and president of the Licensed Vintners Association. RODI, Deeds Grant Index, Memorial Number 185, *Patrick McMahon, Grantor, to Provident Association of London: Grantee, 1921*; *The Belfast and Province of Ulster Directory, 1921–1922*, p. 770; '£1,200 Betting Case', *Belfast Telegraph*, 5 November 1927; 'Death of James Dempsey', *Belfast Newsletter*, 11 March 1909.

42 PRONI, BELF/1/1/2/67/8, The King versus David Duncan, 2 February 1922.

43 'Belfast Disturbances', *Northern Whig*, 24 November 1921.

44 MAI, IE/MA/HS/A/988/15, Part of captured file titled List of persons employed in RUC Headquarters, Waring Street, Belfast, 10 August 1922.

45 'Serious Charge Against Ex-Officer', *Belfast Newsletter*, 6 October 1922; 'Deaths', *Belfast Newsletter*, 7 October 1930.

46 PRONI, PM/2/4/225/1-5, Letter from Bro. David J. Duncan, 16 Laughton Avenue, Toronto, Canada, to Sir James Craig, Prime Minister of Northern Ireland, 4 February 1931.

47 'Sequel to Belfast Tragedy', *Belfast Newsletter*, 18 January 1922; PRONI, BELF/1/1/2/67/8, Shooting at Patrick McMahon and Murdering James McIvor.

48 NWHRM, 106, Report by Capt. H. Papworth, 4 December 1922.

49 PRONI, MIC150/1, Journal of District Inspector W. Lynn, 29 December 1921.

50 'Belfast Commission', *Belfast Newsletter*, 27 February 1922; 'Wounded Man's Agony', *Freeman's Journal*, 25 November 1921.

51 PRONI, BELF/1/1/2/67/8, Shooting at Patrick McMahon and Murdering James McIvor.

52 'Another Murder Charge', *Northern Whig*, 24 February 1922.

53 'Belfast Shopkeeper Shot: Ex-Officer Charged with Murder', *Belfast Newsletter*, 24 February 1922.

54 Bernard Monaghan was badly wounded by another National Army soldier who accidentally shot him in the face on 4 February 1923. He returned to north Belfast and received a pension from the Free State for his wound. He served in the British Merchant Navy during the Second World War. MAI, MSPC, 4P467, Bernard Monaghan; TNA, BT 395/1/68418, Bernard Monaghan.

55 *The Belfast and Province of Ulster Directory, 1921–1922* (Belfast: Belfast Newsletter, 1921–22), p. 774; 'Meeting of Mr Duff's Supporters', *Northern Whig*, 23 April 1914.

56 NLI,44,061/6, Copy of Statement of Seán Montgomery, relating to the War of Independence in Belfast.

57 'Heavy Firing in City', *Freeman's Journal*, 18 May 1922; 'The Fate of Robert Dudgeon', *Belfast Telegraph*, 18 May 1922; 'Belfast Bloodshed', *Ballymena Telegraph*, 20 May 1922.

58 PRONI, PM/2/4/225/1-5, Memorandum by W.A. Magill, Assistant Secretary, Ministry of Home Affairs, to Secretary of the Cabinet, 24 February 1931.

59 *The Old Stubborns*, Vol. 1 (1908); TNA, WO 339/13448, Samuel Waring.

60 'Death of Mr S. Waring, JP', *Belfast Newsletter*, 31 May 1926; 'How Ulster Kept the Twelfth', *Ballymena Weekly Telegraph*, 22 July 1922.

61 PRONI, ANT/1/2/C/32/45, Court File, William James Quinn 1922.

ENDNOTES

62 NAI, TSCH/3/s11195, 22 March 1922; TNA, HC 184/31, Andrew McCloskey, Leopold Street Barracks, Belfast, 22 March 1922.

63 A principal British objective – realised by Younghusband – was to force the Dalai Lama to accept a British veto over Tibet's foreign relations. James Taylor, *Guilty but Insane: J.C. Bowen-Colthurst – Villain or Victim?* (Dublin: Mercier Press, 2016), pp. 29–33.

64 Both Dickson and McIntyre were known for their crude tabloid journalism; Dickson also expressed racist, antisemitic views. 'Sheehy-Skeffington, a kind-hearted eccentric with an aversion to violence, was fitted for martyrdom; Dickson and MacIntyre were not.' Conor Morrissey, 'Scandal and anti-Semitism in 1916: Thomas Dickson and *The Eye-Opener*', *History Ireland*, 24/4 (2016), 30-34.

65 Taylor, *Guilty but Insane*, pp. 92–5; MAI, MSPC, MSP3321180, Patrick Nolan.

66 'Belfast Gunmen Again', *Belfast Newsletter*, 31 March 1922; 'Belfast B Specials', *Belfast Newsletter*, 14 May 1927; MAI, MSPC, 24SP11514, Joseph McPeake.

67 NWHRM, 106, Reports by Capt. H. Papworth, 13 and 28 October 1921; 'Belfast Volunteer Defence Corps', *Belfast Newsletter*, 22 October 1915; 'Commander of M2', *Belfast Newsletter*, 26 January 1932; PRONI, AUS/1/28, Special Constabulary, Belfast Volunteer Defence Corps rejoining projected Special Constabulary.

68 Edward Lowry Turner, http://www.northirishhorse.com.au/6UD/Turner%20EJL.html [accessed 19 July 2022]; 'Belfast Civic Affairs', *Northern Whig*, 15 February 1923.

69 PRONI, HA/32/1/296, Ulster Protestant Voters' Association, Report, Head Constable Wilkin, 6 October 1922; 'Belfast', *North Down Herald*, 23 January 1926.

70 PRONI, HA/32/1/296, Ulster Protestant Voters' Association: Report, Head Constable Wilkin, 6 October 1922.

71 'Lowry Turner', *Northern Whig*, 17 August 1927.

72 PRONI, D1327/11/5/10, Ulster Unionist Council: Letter from J.M. Andrews, 3 July 1922; 'Open-Air Meetings', *Northern Whig*, 29 November 1923; 'Death of Sir T. McConnell', *Northern Whig*, 23 May 1938.

73 'Open-Air Meetings', *Northern Whig*, 29 November 1923.

74 NAI, NEBB/1/1/15, Director of Intelligence Office: Protestant Representatives on Conciliation Committee [*c.* 1922].

75 TNA, CO 906/24, Irish Office, Diary, and notes on Northern Ireland Government personalities, 1922.

76 There is some discrepancy in IRA accounts as to the amount of ammunition acquired from UVF sources, principally by Dr Russell McNabb and Belfast IRA intelligence officer Seán Cusack. Dr McNabb's brother, who stored the UVF ammunition at his Belfast shop, claimed that two million rounds passed through his 'hands'. A statement written in support of Seán Cusack's pension application suggested that he was instrumental in sourcing one million rounds of ammunition from the UVF. What is not in doubt from the various testimonials of Defence Forces senior officers and former IRA commanders is that the ammunition was considered to be important by Michael Collins and others in IRA general headquarters. MAI, MSPC, 24SP12908, Henry Russell MacNabb; MSP34REF47899, James McNabb; 24SP308, Seán Cusack; MSP34REF2556, Frank Booth; BMH, WS 389, Roger McCorley.

77 NAI, NEBB 1/1/10, Northern Ireland Minorities, Statutory Declaration by William Barrett, 168 Grosvenor Road, 7 June 1922.

78 NAI, TAOIS/S1011, Advisory Committee Meeting in Belfast, 15 May 1922; 'Belfast Claims Court', *Belfast Newsletter*, 24 February 1922; 'Petition Against Licensing Act', *Northern Whig*, 7 February 1924.

79 NAI, NEBB 1/1/10, Telegram to Michael Collins from James McKenna, Greencastle, Belfast, 20 March 1922; RODI, Land Registry Index, Parish of Belfast or Shankill, 1920–1923; PRONI, BELF/6/5/3/1, Spirit License Register, 1911–1923.

80 PRONI, HA/32/1/390, William Nesbitt: Letter from George Turkington, Grove Street [undated];

ENDNOTES

Letter from Annie Armstrong to Sir Richard Dawson Bates, 7 July 1923.

81 PRONI, BELF/6/5/3/1, Spirit License Register, 1911–1923.

82 RODI, Daniel McMahon, grantor, to Frederick McNair, grantee, 1922.

83 'Belfast Claims Court', *Northern Whig*, 10 October 1922.

84 NAI, NEBB 1/1/10, Statement by Mrs and Mrs McCleeve [*sic*], 8, North Queen Street, 13 April 1922; 'The Ulster Elections', *Belfast Telegraph*, 26 November 1923; PRONI, HA/5/2220, Robert Waddell: Note for Major Shewell from Colonel Toppin, 17 March 1923.

85 NAI, NEBB 1/1/10, Statement by Mrs McCleeve [*sic*], 8, North Queen Street, 13 April 1922.

86 'Christmastide Murder', *Belfast Telegraph*, 28 January 1922; PRONI, BELF/6/5/3/1, Spirit License Register, 1911–1923; 'Foul Belfast Murder', *Belfast Telegraph*, 31 December 1921.

87 Stanley Cohen, *States of Denial: Knowing About Atrocities and Suffering* (Oxford: Blackwell Publishers, 2001), p. 59.

88 GROI, Birth Certificate for Jane Heaslip, Kilnaleck, 7 July 1869; NAI, 1911 National Census, entry for Thomas Heaslip, Ballymackinroe, Cavan Rural, County Cavan.

89 UCDA, P67/69, Seán MacEntee Papers, Handwritten report of an attack by the RUC and Special Constabulary on King Street, May 1922.

90 MAI, MSPC, MSP34REF6048, Patrick McMahon.

91 'The Sting of Conscience', *Witness*, 24 March 1922; 'Eleven Inquests Today', *Belfast Telegraph*, 22 March 1922.

92 See entry for Lieutenant Samuel Waring, Leicestershire Regiment, https://royalleicestershire regiment.org.uk/entity/128723-waring-samuel?q= [accessed 23 March 2023].

93 Stathis Kalyvas, *The Logic of Violence in Civil War* (Cambridge: Cambridge University Press, 2006), p. 339.

94 PRONI, BELF/6/5/3/1, Spirit License Register, 1911–1923; 'License Premises Looted', *Belfast Newsletter*, 16 July 1921; 'Sale of Very Valuable License Premises', *Belfast Telegraph*, 6 October 1924.

95 *Belfast and Ulster Directory*, 1920 and 1921/1922, p. 594; 'Transfer of Licence', *Belfast Newsletter*, 9 April 1920.

96 Pension Ledger Card for Corporal David Duncan, Royal Fusiliers, copy made available by the Royal Ulster Rifles Museum.

97 PRONI, HA/32/1/130, Index to Documents Found at St Mary's Hall, 18 March 1922.

98 Land Registry of Northern Ireland, Memorial between Patrick McMahon and Thomas Corr, 30 November 1923, Book 20, No 80; *Belfast and Ulster Directory*, 1921/1922, p. 594.

99 House of Commons, *Hansard*, 28 March 1922.

100 NWHRM, 106, Report by Capt. H. Papworth, 4 January 1922; MAI, IE/MA/HS/A/988/15, Part of captured file titled List of persons employed in RUC Headquarters, Waring Street, Belfast 10 August 1922.

101 PRONI, BELF/1/1/2/68/9, Barnsley Sloan, Joseph Clarke and Joseph McKee – intimidation of Josephine Moan and forcing her to leave her home.

102 NAI, NEBB/1/1/2, Summary of Outrages in Belfast, 1922: Document marked 'Secret' and accompanying anonymous letter, 10 April 1922.

103 Western Front Association, WW1 Pension Records and Ledgers, 12/MB/No1977, Henry Brett.

104 PRONI, BELF/1/1/2/68/6, Henry Brett and William Wilson - murder of Mary Wilson during sectarian trouble in the Argyle St area of Belfast.

105 Interview with Reverend Brian Black, Belfast, 2 June 2022; PRONI, HOS/28/1/14/1/3, Case book – Males, Alexander Kennedy, Previous History, Dr H.A. Skillen, 169 Duncairn Gardens.

106 Interview with Reverend Brian Black, Belfast, 2 June 2022.

107 PRONI, HOS/28/1/14/1/3, Case book – Males, Alexander Kennedy, Previous History, Dr H.A. Skillen, 169 Duncairn Gardens.

ENDNOTES

108 Ibid., Entry for 4 April 1921.

109 Ibid., Alexander Kennedy, Entry for 7 February 1921.

110 Ibid., BG-7-KA-15, Record of Death, Alexander Kennedy, January 1924; BG-7-G-133, Belfast Workhouse Admission Records, Alexander Kennedy, 1922–4.

111 MAI, MSPC, MSP34REF11751, Seamus Keaveney.

112 MAI, BMH WS 410, Thomas McNally.

113 Interview with Reverend Brian Black, Belfast, 2 June 2022.

114 NWHRM, 106, Report by Capt. H. Papworth, 24 March 1922.

115 Ibid., 14 January 1922.

116 PRONI, HA/32/1/289A, Arrest and Internment of Gunmen, Protestants Who Have Been Interned, 14 May 1923.

117 PRONI, MIC150/1, Journal of District Inspector W. Lynn, 9-10 April 1922.

118 AOO, RG 10-270, David Duncan, Ward Admission Record, 1 April 1935.

119 'Police Sergeant Assaulted', *Belfast Newsletter*, 6 October 1922; 'In the Police Courts', *Irish News*, 6 October 1922.

120 PRONI, PM/2/4/225/1-5, Memorandum by W.A. Magill, Assistant Secretary, Ministry of Home Affairs, to Secretary of the Cabinet, 24 February 1931.

121 'Belfastman Libelled in Dublin Newspaper', *Belfast Telegraph*, 8 June 1923; AOO, RG 10-270, David Duncan, Clinical Record, Dr J.G. Dewan, 8 February 1935.

122 MFLF, Record of Service for 2nd Class Legionnaire David Duncan, 1925–6.

123 GRONI, Marriage Certificate, Emily Clements and David Duncan, Belfast, 2 June 1928.

124 GROI, Death Certificate for Sarah Duncan, 8 Whitworth Terrace, Drumcondra, Dublin, died 20 September 1937.

125 LAC, Canadian Immigration Service, Passenger List and Border Entries, David Duncan, 5 April 1929; PRONI, PM/2/4/225/1-5, Memorandum by W.A. Magill, Assistant Secretary, Ministry of Home Affairs, to Secretary of the Cabinet, 24 February 1931; 'Imperial Veterans Register Complaints', *Globe and Mail*, 8 June 1939.

126 LAC, Canadian Immigration Service, Passenger List and Border Entries, Emily Duncan, 9 March 1930.

127 TNA, WO 363, Matthew Clements, Royal Irish Rifles; LAC, Passenger Lists and Border Entries, Matthew Clements.

128 AOO, RG 10-270, David Duncan, Clinical Record, Dr J.G. Dewan, 8 February 1935; William Smyth, *Toronto, The Belfast of Canada: The Orange Order and the Shaping of Municipal Culture* (Toronto: University of Toronto Press, 2015), pp. 199–213.

129 Ibid.

130 PRONI, PM/2/4/225/1-5, Letter from Bro. David J. Duncan, 16 Laughton Avenue, Toronto, Canada, to Sir James Craig, Prime Minister of Northern Ireland, 4 February 1931; AOO, RG 10-270, Clinical Record, Dr J.G. Dewan, 8 February 1935.

131 Ibid.

132 PRONI, PM/2/4/225/1-5, Letter from Bro. David J. Duncan, 16 Laughton Avenue, Toronto, Canada, to Sir James Craig, Prime Minister of Northern Ireland, 4 February 1931.

133 OHM, OBLDA, Minutes of an Executive Committee Meeting held on 11 November 1921.

134 Kelly, *Bonfires on the Hillside*, p. 18; PRONI, HA/32/1/289A, Arrest and Internment of Gunmen, Protestants Who Have Been Interned, May 1923; HA/5/2192.

135 Hunger was a daily reality. A report by a social worker noted that children in the area were malnourished, and adults frequently suffered from anaemia. Toronto City Archives, Series 1807, File 2 / 530914, Neighbourhood Workers' Association, Riverdale, Minutes, 22 March 1939; AOO, RG 10-270, Clinical Record, Dr J.G. Dewan, 8 February 1935.

ENDNOTES

136 The resolution was proposed by Reverend Morris Zeidman, a Polish-born convert to Presbyterianism from Judaism. Toronto Reference Library Special Collections, L35, Toronto Loyal Orange County Lodge fonds, Series 1, Volume 2d, Executive Committee, Minutes, Meeting, February 1940.

137 Smyth, *Toronto, The Belfast of Canada*, pp. 230–2; AOO, RG 10-270, Ontario Hospital Patient File, 20977 – David Duncan, Clinical Report, 9 November 1936.

CHAPTER EIGHT: THE PATIENT BY THE WINDOW

1 AOO, RG 10-270, Ontario Hospital Patient File, 20977 – David Duncan, Clinical Record, Dr J.G. Dewan, 8 February 1935.

2 'Nixon Wins Libel Action', *Irish Weekly and Ulster Examiner*, 23 February 1935; 'Alderman J.W. Nixon', *Belfast Telegraph*, 19 October 1934; 'Alleged Book Libel', *Daily Telegraph*, 20 October 1934; 'Ulster MP's Libel Trial', *Manchester Guardian*, 19 February 1935; 'Court Echo of the Murder of the McMahon Family', *Irish News*, 19 February 1935.

3 'Nixon Libel Suit', *Belfast Telegraph*, 2 February 1935.

4 'Apology', *Derry Journal*, 4 September 1925; 'Sequel to Nixon Libel Suit', *Northern Whig*, 28 November 1925.

5 AOO, RG 10-270, Physician's Certificate, Dr Charles Homer McCuaig, 21 February 1935.

6 Ibid., Admission Notes, 1 April 1935.

7 Ibid., Physician's Certificate, Dr Charles Homer McCuaig, 21 February 1935.

8 PRONI, PM/11/7, Prime Minister's Tour of Canada, Colonel Baptiste Johnston to Sir Robert Gransden, 4 April 1950.

9 AOO, RG 10-270, Ontario Hospital Patient File, 20977 – David Duncan, Clinical Record, Dr J.G. Dewan, 8 February 1935.

10 Ibid.

11 AOO, RG 10-270, Clinical Record, Dr C.H. Lewis, 30 August 1935.

12 Ibid., Clinical Record, Dr J.G. Dewan, 14 February 1935; Letter from Dr J.R. Howitt to Dr R.C. Montgomery 6 November 1937.

13 Ibid., Clinical Record, Dr E Barton, 18 April 1935.

14 Ibid., Progress Note, Dr J.G. Dewan, 12 March 1935.

15 Ibid., Clinical Record, Dr J.G. Dewan, 8 February 1935.

16 Ibid., Clinical Report, Dr H. Frank, 15 December 1938.

17 Ibid., Record of Magistrate's Hearing, 25 February 1935; Warrant for the detention of David Duncan, 1 April 1935.

18 'Belfast Murders', *Irish News*, 7 January 1922.

19 AOO, RG 10-270, Letter from Lt. Col. Baptist Johnston to John Thompson, 13 February 1936; Memorandum from B.T. McGhie, Deputy Minister, Department of Health to McIntyre Hod, Secretary, Attorney General's Department, 15 December 1938.

20 Ibid., Letter from J R Howitt, Superintendent, Ontario Hospital to Dr R G Montgomery, Director, Hospitals Division, Department of Health, Toronto, Ontario, 28 September 1937.

21 Ibid., David Duncan, Social Record, 25 April 1938; Clinical Record, 3 October 1938, 15 November 1938; Letter from David Duncan to Superintendent, 2 March 1939; 'Imperial Veteran Heard', *Globe and Mail*, 24 June 1939.

22 Ibid., Letter from Dr J. Sommer, Toronto General Hospital, to Dr J.R. Howitt, Ontario Hospital, 5 July 1939, 'Imperial Veterans Register Complaints', *Globe and Mail*, 8 June 1939; 'Imperial Veteran Heard', *Globe and Mail*, 24 June 1939.

23 AOO, RG 10-270, Clinical Report, 9 November 1939; Valerie Hauch, 'Once Upon a City: Toronto's Notorious Police Chief', *Toronto Star*, 10 June 2016.

274

ENDNOTES

24 Ibid., Clinical Record, 31 December 1939.

25 Ibid., David Duncan, Visitors' List.

EPILOGUE

1 Kemp, *History of the Norfolk Regiment*, pp. 10–11.

2 Ernest's sister Nelly continued to run the family shop in Fakenham until her death in the late 1960s. I am grateful to Mr Peter Boggis, Fakenham and District Community Archive, for this information and photographs of Pte. Barnes' grave.

3 Hart, *The 2nd Norfolk Regiment*, pp. 180–2.

4 Colin Smith, *Singapore Burning* (London: Penguin, 2006), p. 342.

5 NWHRM, Officers' Biographies Book, Eric Hayes.

6 'The Murder Campaign', *Irish Press*, 12 November 1973.

7 'Divided Views on New Defence Force', *Fermanagh Herald*, 22 November 1969.

8 See Edward Burke, *An Army of Tribes: British Army Cohesion, Deviancy and Murder in Northern Ireland* (Liverpool: Liverpool University Press, 2018), pp. 78–95.

9 Huw Bennett, *Uncivil War: The British Army and the Troubles, 1966–1975* (Cambridge: Cambridge University Press, 2023), pp. 209–14.

10 Bennett, *Uncivil War*, pp. 260–64. For an insightful discussion of the British state's longstanding dilemma when confronting loyalism see Frank Wright, *Northern Ireland: A Comparative Analysis* (London: Gill and Macmillan, 1988), pp. 11–12.

11 'The McMahon Murders', *Irish Weekly and Ulster Examiner*, 9 October 1937.

12 Email correspondence from DI William Lynn's son to the author, 8 October 2023.

13 'Death Notice', *Belfast Telegraph*, 29 May 1958; 'Obituary: Mr. B. McMahon', *Irish Weekly and Ulster Examiner*, 7 June 1958.

14 'McMahon-Nugent Wedding', *Evening Herald*, 31 December 1935.

15 'Shot Newry IRA Men are Buried', *Belfast Telegraph*, 18 May 1974.

16 Information provided by Norah Glynn (the grandniece of Owen McMahon) and her husband Joe Glynn, Dublin, 9 August 2022.

17 Roy Garland, *Gusty Spence* (Belfast: Blackstaff, 2001), p. 45.

18 Robinson also claimed that his mother raised the illegitimate daughter of the Earl of Shaftesbury at their home in Andrew Street. UFTM, Interview R83 11, Alexander Robinson.

19 PRONI, HA5/693, Alexander Robinson: Grounds for Internment; Ed Moloney, *Voices from the Grave* (London: Faber and Faber, 2010), p. 36.

20 Emily Moulton, 'New painting replaces paramilitary mural', *Belfast Telegraph*, 13 August 2009.

21 GROI, Copy of the Marriage Certificate of John William Nixon and Kathleen Elizabeth Shannon, 11 January 1928.

22 'Obituary', *Belfast Newsletter*, 25 January 1982; Interview with a granddaughter of John William Nixon Senior, England, 4 February 2023.

23 AOO, RG 10-270, Ontario Mental Health Clinic, Social Services Record, David Duncan; Letter from M.R. Gordon, Neighbourhood Workers' Association, Riverdale District, to Dr J.R. Howitt, Ontario Hospital, 5 May 1938.

24 Mary McAleese, *Here's the Story: A Memoir* (London: Penguin, 2020), pp. 7–8, 97–108, 267–79; Niamh Horan, 'Mary McAleese still haunted by early life in "a hell on earth created by Christians"', *Belfast Telegraph*, 14 November 2021.

25 Stephen Dempster, 'Loyalist paramilitary groups in NI "have 12,500 members"', *BBC News*, 2 December 2020; Lisa O'Carroll, 'Loyalist paramilitaries suspected as hoax device disrupts Irish minister's Belfast speech', *The Guardian*, 25 March 2022.

INDEX

1922 Commission Report 131, 132, 134, 138, 144

Abercorn, James Hamilton, 3rd Duke of 119
Adair, Special Constable 149
Agnew, Alex 120
Ancient Order of Hibernians (AOH) 39–40, 140, 143
Anderson, Andrew and Lizzie 52
Anderson, John 116–17
Anderson, Winifred 17, 18
Anglican Church 84
Anglo-Irish Treaty 6–7, 19, 22, 61
Armistice Sunday (1921) 56
Armstrong, Annie 155, 156, 157, 193
Armstrong, James 199
Armstrong, William 194–5, 199
Arnon Street Massacre 88, 90, 91, 92, 94–7, 98, 112, 208
Arthurs, Joseph 74, 156
Ataturk, Mustafa Kemal 170, 171
Auxiliary Division 40, 47, 126, 134, 139, 142, 143, 151, 176–7; Catholics terrorised by 145–6, 147; IRA and 135–7

Babington, Sir Anthony 124
Bales, John 135
Bannon, Sarah 182
Barnes, Private Ernest John 63–4, 160, 227
Barrett, Constable William 30, 192
BBC series xiv
Beattie, Robert 99–100, 178
Belfast 27–8, 30; Alexandra Dock 32; Alton Street 90; Andrew Street 152, 153; Ardoyne 44, 45, 50, 99, 100, 105, 129, 138; Ariel Street 161, 207; Arnon Street Massacre 88, 90, 91, 92, 94–7, 98, 112, 208; Campbell Street 94; Coal Quay 39; Falls Road 27, 29, 36, 38, 59, 108, 109, 131;

Foundry Street 38; Garmoyle Street 62–3; Grosvenor Road 31; Havana Street 128; Joy Street 98; Kashmir Street 36, 131; Malvern Street 161, 207; Marrowbone area 44, 45, 50, 83, 100, 110, 128; North Queen Street 30, 63, 67; Old Lodge Road 46, 86, 107, 143, 199; Oldpark Road 110, 115, 116; Park Street 86–7, 89; St Peter's Place 106; Sandy Row 31; Seaforde Street 38, 72–3; Shankill Road 32, 44–5, 93, 107, 113, 195, 199; Short Strand 36, 86; Springfield Road 45, 136, 137, 144; Stanhope Street 66, 86, 88, 91, 93–5, 99, 105, 107, 109, 127, 161, 162; Sussex Street 63–4; Tiger's Bay 63; Wall Street 67, 70, 108, 161; Weaver Street 72, 105, 154, 202, 203; Woodford Street 86; York Road 105, 113, 164, 167–8, 179, 184, 209; York Street 30, 31, 64, 67, 68, 152–3, 154, 155, 180, 193, 207, 209
Belfast City Council 112, 117, 121, 178
Belfast pogrom xvi, 19, 60, 75, 97, 123–4, 129, 148, 149, 199, 205, 207, 209; see also Arnon Street Massacre
Belfast Volunteer Defence Corps 189
Belfast War Hospital 71, 108
Belleek RIC Station 108, 143
Berwitz, Louis and Charles 5
Bickerstaff, Commander William 57, 80, 118, 120, 190, 198, 199
Black, Revd Brian 204
Black, Henry 180
Black and Tans 126, 144, 180
Blaney, Neal 128
Blaney, Patrick 167–8
Bloody Friday (1972) 232

Boer War xix, 23, 33, 103, 123, 167, 189, 204–5
Bolam, Ernest 135
bomb attacks 65, 67, 70, 72, 86, 161, 168, 203
Boundary Commission 118
Bowen-Colthurst, Captain John 188, 197
Boyd, Constable David 138
Boyd, Robert 54, 55, 58
Bradley, Annie 141–2
Bradley, Daniel 163
Bradley, Hugh 140–1
Brierty, Patrick 81–2
British Army 50–1, 228–9; 10th (Irish) Division 20, 169; 15th Infantry Brigade 47, 72; 16th Divisions 20; 36th (Ulster) Division 169; Black Watch 204–5; Essex Regiment, 1st Battalion 69, 70; Guards Machine Gun Regiment 9–10; intelligence 17, 61, 73–4, 182; IRA and 53, 61–2, 72; Irish Guards 8, 122, 126, 130, 134; lower ranks of xx–xxi; loyalists and 51, 59, 72–3, 74, 99; Norfolk Regiment, 2nd Battalion 61, 228; North Russia Relief Force 173–5; Operation Banner 229; police and 110; Protestant mob and 150; Royal Field Artillery 94, 139–40; Royal Inniskilling Fusiliers 57; Royal Irish Fusiliers xxi, 10, 99–100, 172, 173–4, 175, 189; Royal Irish Rifles 56, 57, 67, 94, 99, 157, 162, 163, 169–71, 185, 189, 213; Seaforth Highlanders, 1st Battalion 37, 68, 70–1, 107–8; Sherwood Foresters 186; Somerset Light Infantry 73, 107, 145, 189; South Staffordshire Regiment, 2nd Battalion 47; Special Constabulary and 59, 65, 68, 69, 70, 71–2, 73, 102–3,

276

INDEX

105–6; veterans 30, 95, 99–100, 122, 126, 157, 162, 185, 188, 189, 204–5; Worcestershire Regiment, 4th Battalion 69; *see also* Norfolk Regiment, 1st Battalion
British Colonial Office 84
British Empire Union 55
Britten, Frederick, County Inspector 119
Brown, James 137
Brown, Private James 69
Brown, T.W., Justice 183–4
Browne, Robert 81–2
Brown's Square Barracks 45, 86, 89, 93, 96, 106, 107, 124, 125–51, 163, 198; Norfolk Regiment's reports on 128, 129
Bruce, Daniel 72
Bruce, Lieutenant Edward 68
Bruce demesne 5, 9, 13, 18, 188, 197, 207
Bruen, Sergeant Martin 155, 197, 208
Burn, Harry, MP 55, 118
Byers, William 48, 49

Cahoon, Samuel 80
Caldwell, Constable Edwin 130, 133, 136–7
Cameron, General 48, 49–50, 55, 58, 73
Campbell, Thomas, *Hohenlinden* 31–2
Campbell, T.J. 79
Campbell, William 137
Carnduff, Thomas 32–3
Carson, Sir Edward 23, 34, 54, 163
Carter-Campbell, Colonel Commandant George 47, 48, 55, 145, 146
Catholic publicans, attacks on 15–18, 192, 199
Catholics 23, 28, 29, 30, 31, 39; anti-Catholic sentiment 55, 64–5, 100; attacks on 32–3, 38–9, 66–7, 68–9, 104, 106, 116, 152–3, 193; Auxiliaries and 145–6; civil rights demonstrations 228–9; Cronje Clan 33; ex-servicemen, threats to 64–5; exodus from Belfast 105; gangs 33; IRA offensive, opposition to 39; killings 49, 67, 75, 104, 106, 107, 115, 126, 133, 134, 138–45, 152, 181–2, 184–5, 202–3, 204; loyalist attacks 167–8, 176, 178, 179–80, 182, 192; loyalist perception of 23–4, 84–5; police raids 83; pubs owned by 81; RIC attacks 46–7, 128–9, 130,

133, 134, 138–45, 150; Special Constabulary attacks 152–5, 163, 179–82, 192; *see also* Arnon Street Massacre
Catney, Patrick 176
Chermside, Special Constable William 196
Churchill, Randolph 31–2
Churchill, Winston 5–6, 57, 74–5, 84, 85, 110, 173
Civil Contingencies (Special Powers) Act (1922) 51, 101, 102
civil rights demonstrations 228–9
Clancy, Sergeant Patrick 129, 130, 131
Clarke, Alice 136
Clarke, Constable Christy 133, 134, 136–7
Clarke, Joseph 202
Clements, Mathew 212, 225
Coates, Sir William 159
Cochrane, Revd Samuel 69, 183
Cole, Private 108
Collins, Michael 7, 19, 23, 40, 44, 86, 101–2, 108, 191
Collins-Craig Pact 84, 85, 230
Conlon, Constable Thomas 42
Connolly, Patrick 164
Coote, William, MP 53, 55, 56, 62, 84–5, 114, 120, 190
Cosgrove, Joe 180
Court Street Barracks 155, 197, 208
Coveney, Simon 236
Craig, Sir James 14, 19, 22, 23, 26, 37, 41, 49; British Army and 50–1; British government's ultimatum 72; 'C1' Special Constabulary 58; Collins and 101–2; Collins-Craig Pact 84, 85, 230; criticism of 120; Duncan's letter to 213–14; internment request 48; IRA and 64; loyalist pressure on 163; Nixon and 116, 119; perception of 37, 38, 50, 56, 84; Sinn Féin and 62; Special Constabulary and 74, 84, 85, 111–12
Craig, Robert 65, 158–9
Crawford, Colonel Fred 22, 45, 51, 52–3, 59, 106, 153
Crawford's Tigers 53, 153
Crean, Desmond 7
Cromwell Clubs 177–8
Cronjé Clan 33
Crossey, John 204
Crummey, Frank 101, 109, 160
Culhane, Seán 38
Cunningham, Joseph 54
Cunningham, Special Constable Thomas 196
Curran, James 32

Cusack, Seán 7, 206

Dames-Longworth, Travers 126
Davey, James 142
Davison, Sir Joseph 112, 113, 120, 153, 186, 213
Dawson Bates, Sir Richard 37, 47, 50, 51, 103–4, 114, 119, 155; 'B' Specials, letter from 162–3; Nixon, views on 115; Norfolk Regiment, views on 69–70; perception of 48–9, 70, 110; prisoner release ordered by 158; resignation 122
Day, Lieutenant Colonel Francis 64, 71, 103
de Valera, Éamon 18, 22, 54, 177
Deane, Private George 108
Despard, Charlotte 103–4, 105
Devany, James 82
Devlin, Joe, MP 6, 9, 18, 39, 83, 132, 201
Dewan, John 220
Dickinson, Private Arthur 65
Dinsmore, Head Constable Robert 142
Ditty, Special Constable Samuel 162, 163, 208
Dixon, Herbert 194
Dodds, William 193
Donaghy, Joe 42
Donald, Thompson, MP 53
Donaldson, Mary 104
Donnelly, Francis 86
Donnelly, Francis, Jnr 86, 157
Donnelly, Joseph 86, 157
Donnelly, Lizzie 106
Donnelly, Mary Ann 86
Doran, Jane 106
Downey, Mary 10, 11, 15, 148, 199, 209
Drennan, William F. 194
Dudgeon, Robert 185
Duffin, John 133
Duffin, Patrick and Daniel 133, 134, 136
Duffy, Constable William 150
Duncan, David: acquittal on murder charges 184; Auxiliary Division and 176–7, 185; background 168, 198; British Army and 168–9, 171–2, 173, 175–6; 'C1' Constabulary 185, 210–11, 213, 214; Catholics attacked by 176; Cromwell Clubs 177, 178; death 225; emigration to Canada 212–14; French Foreign Legion 167, 201, 211, 218, 221; grave 234; Imperial Guards and 167, 177, 178, 179, 200, 202, 213; IRA

277

INDEX

intelligence on 200; letter to Craig 213–14; libel trial 167, 173; McMahon murders and 200, 206, 209–10; McMahon, Patrick, attempted murder of 179–80, 183, 185, 200, 222, 223; marriages 176, 211, 212, 226; mental state 172, 173, 186, 200, 201, 206, 210, 213, 216, 217–25; military pension, termination of 200, 206; murder accusation 181, 182–4; psychiatric hospital, commital to 219, 220–5, 235
Duncan, Emily (*née* Clements) 213, 216, 218, 220, 222, 223–4, 225, 234–5
Duncan, Joseph 177, 202
Duncan, Sarah (*née* Cockrill) 176, 211, 213
Dunne, Reginald 24

Earl, Constable Alexander 130
Earle, Constable Thomas 134
Easter Rising (1916) 20, 21, 73, 103, 162, 188, 196
Eastwood, Captain Francis 170
Elliott, George 164
Ewart, Major Gerald 56
Expelled Workers' Relief Committee 35

Fallon, Head Constable Peter 156
Fannon, William 164
Fee, Commandant David 51, 187, 188
Ferriss, DI John 133, 134
First World War xvii, xviii, xix, 8, 20, 169; Gallipoli campaign 20, 71, 169–71; home rule, postponement of 19; veterans 30, 94, 95, 99–100, 122, 126, 157, 162, 186
Flanagan, Constable Patrick 46–7
Fletcher, DI Thomas 119
Fraser, Becky 146
Fraser, William 146
Freeland, General Ian 228
Freeston, Lieutenant Colonel William 145, 146
French, Field Marshal Sir John 33, 102
French Foreign Legion xxi, 167, 175, 210, 211, 218, 221
Furlong, Constable Michael 46, 125, 149–50

Galbraith, James, Imperial Guard 160–1, 200, 202
Garvey, Michael 132, 197
Gault, Joseph 164, 200

Gaussen, Lieutenant Colonel Horace 163
Gavan Duffy, Charles 85
Gaynor, John 131, 132
Gelston, John, City Commissioner 43, 58, 96, 113, 114, 116, 117, 132, 209
General Election (1918) 21
George V, King 23, 71, 106–7
Giff, Head Constable John 118, 122, 124, 129, 131, 138, 140, 143, 150
Gilfillan, DI Ewing 73, 74, 217
Gillan, Constable Thomas 132
Gillespie, Sergeant James 122, 123, 218
Girvin, James 86–7
Glass, Constable 137–8
Glenravel Barracks 3–4, 91, 97
Glover, Constable James 131, 132, 134, 137, 142
Glover, Samuel 142
Golden, Constable 134
Good Friday Agreement (1998) 230
Goodwin, Colonel William 57, 58, 185, 213
Gordon, Constable Henry 118, 125–6, 130, 134, 138, 140, 151; Arnon Street Massacre 89, 90, 92, 93, 95, 96; McMahon murders and 92, 125, 149, 196; Nixon's defence of 127; resignation 120
Gordon, John 54–5
Gormanston Camp 126, 134, 142, 143, 146–7
Grant, Private James 99
Grant, William, MP 55, 57, 118, 153, 155, 156
Gundry-White, Lieutenant Lionel 71, 99

Haire, Constable Thomas 130, 134
Haldane, Lieutenant Colonel Maldwyn 158, 214
Halfpenny, Malachy 134, 139–43, 147
Halfpenny, Winifred 141, 147
Hall, Special Constable Thomas 86
Halliday, Robert 176
Hamill, Arthur 3–4
Harkin, John 177–8
Harper, Jordy, Imperial Guard 63–4, 160, 161, 164, 198, 200, 202
Harrison, Richard, County Inspector 131
Hassard, Herbert 67–8, 178
Hatton, Catherine 90, 161
Hayes, Lieutenant Eric xvii, 86, 90, 91, 92, 94, 101, 128, 129, 228
Heggart, DI Richard 73–4, 162, 163
Henry, Sir Denis 123

Hermon, John 65
Hiatt, Lieutenant Cuthbert 146, 161–2
Hicks, Constable George 133, 134
Horgan, Constable Edward 42
Howitt, John 223
Huey, George 118, 190
Hughes, Brendan (the Dark) 232–3
Hughes, Owen 233

Irish Free State 22, 23, 64, 120; Provisional Government 7, 24, 84, 85, 91, 192
Irish Protestant Benevolent Society 219
Irish Republican Army (IRA) xvi, 5, 6, 7, 65, 95, 98, 231; 3rd Northern Division 92, 108; anti-Treaty IRA 22, 25, 97, 108, 128; Ardoyne Company 128, 141; arms 40, 191, 206; arrests 127; arson attacks 40, 43, 85, 86, 104; assassinations 21–2, 24, 34, 38, 104; Auxiliaries and 135–7; Belfast IRA 7, 21, 29, 35, 61, 90–1, 108, 147; bombings 232–3; British Army and 53, 59, 61–2, 72; Catholic constables and 45, 46; Catholic opposition to 39; collection book seized by RIC 9; Craig's government and 64; ex-British soldiers and 94, 95; intelligence network 8, 111, 125, 168, 180, 187, 200–1, 202; internees, release of 22; loyalist reprisals 104; murder gangs, Imperial Guards and 160; northern offensive 23, 104, 109; RIC, attacks on 32, 42, 43, 46, 86, 104; RIC, republicans killed by 131–3; Special Constabulary, attacks on 59

James, Cadet Eric 143, 145
Jennings, John 106
Johnston, Colonel Baptist 219–20
Johnston, James 202, 203
Johnston, Special Constable Thomas 161–2, 198
Jones, David 64, 193

Kalyvas, Stathis 33–4, 198
Kane, John 106
Kearney, Catherine 160
Keaveney, Seamus 206
Kehoe, Constable Myles 150
Kelly, James 182, 222
Kelly, James (journalist) 28, 29, 48–9, 60, 122, 214
Kelly, John 58
Kelly, Sergeant 116

278

INDEX

Kennedy, Alexander (Alick) 167, 204–6
Kennedy, Barney 72
Kennedy, Dinah 205
Kennedy, Kathleen 72
Kerr, Alice 144–5, 147
Kerr, William 134, 143–4, 145, 147
Kitson, William 88–9, 94, 95
Knocker, Margaret 181–2
Knox, Major General Sir Alfred xix

Lambe, Patrick 154
Laverty, Revd Bernard 46, 191
Lavery, Hugh 82
Leathem, Edward and George 153–4
Leathes, Major Carteret 52, 189
Lee, Officer Cadet 143
Leneghan, Paddy 235
Leopold Street Barracks 8, 44, 46, 83, 133, 187
Lloyd George, David 19, 25, 26, 40, 48, 57, 74, 227; Craig and 102; de Valera and 22; North Russian Relief Force 173, 175
Loughran, Daniel 181
Loughridge, Lieutenant James, RAMC 139, 140, 145
Love, Head Constable William 183
loyalist paramilitaries xviii, 14, 19, 40, 54, 99; Catholics attacked by 154, 164, 167–8, 176, 178, 179–80, 182, 192; killings 65, 67, 162, 164; the Pass Gang 32–3; recruitment as policemen 26; reprisals 104, 201; RIC and 52; Shankill butchers 230
loyalists 31, 35, 84; British Army and 51, 59, 72–3, 74, 99; Catholics, perception of 23–4, 84–5; sectarian attacks 32–3, 36, 38, 106
Lucas, Sergeant William 43
Lundy, Ben 65
Lusted, Alfred 52
Lyle, James, Imperial Guard 188–9, 197–8
Lynd, Robert 27
Lynn, Alex 126–7
Lynn, Robert, MP 54, 56, 118, 163, 217
Lynn, DI William 9, 10, 15, 18–19, 151, 182, 183; Arnon Street massacre investigation 96; background 19; Duncan and 210, 222–3, 230–1; McMahon murders investigation 15, 19, 209
Lynwood, Lieutenant Colonel Ian 99, 228
Lyons, William 57

MacBride, Maud Gonne 103
McAleese, Martin 236
McAleese, Mary (née Leneghan) 235–6
McAlinden, Martin 231–2
McAnaney, Hugh 68–9, 178, 185
McAnaney, Mary 68–9
McAree, Hugh 146
McArt's Fort 29
McBride, Alexander 80, 134, 137, 138–9, 147
McBride, Elizabeth 138–9, 193
McCabe, Alexander 134–5
McCall, Michael 203–4
McCarragher, Patrick 137
McCartney, Sergeant William 177
McCloskey, Constable Andrew 187–8
McCloskey, James 143
McClune, James 30
McClune, William 36
McConnell, DI J.J. 45, 46
McConnell, Olive 235
McConnell, Tom, MP 55, 190–1
McCoo, Special Constable Nathaniel 98
McCorkey, Revd William 57
McCorley, Roger 21, 40, 59, 61, 135, 137
McCormick, Susan 106
McCoy, John 60–1
McCreeve, Elizabeth 193–4
McCrory, Joseph 88–9, 90, 94
McCuaig, Charles 219
Mac Curtain, Tomás 38
McDonald, Constable James 138
MacDonald, Ramsay 111
McDougall, Esther 161, 162
McDrury, Mary, Norah and Sarah Jane 235
McElroy, Mary and Rose 106
MacEntee, Seán 177–8, 195
Mac Eoin, Seán 6
McFadden, John 131
McGinley, Frederick 28
McGrath, Daniel 88, 97
McGregor, Nellie 36
McGuffin, Sam, MP 159
McGuinness, Charles, Nomad 123–4
McGuinness, David 39
McGurnaghan, Patrick 160, 182, 202
McIvor, James 181, 182, 183–4, 200, 213, 222, 231
McKay, Alex 54
McKee, Joseph 164, 202
McKelvey, Joe 21, 61
McKenna, Bernard 89, 90
McKenna, Seamus 135–6

McKinney, Edward xiii, xiv, xvii, 4, 6, 8, 9, 11, 13, 15, 195
McKinney, Constable Michael 8
McMahon, Bernard 6, 79, 80, 81
McMahon, Bernard (son of Owen) xiii, 13
McMahon, Daniel 6, 79–80, 81, 82, 193
McMahon, Daniel (son of Owen) 83
McMahon, Eliza (née Downey) xiii, 3, 4, 6, 10, 79, 199, 230; children 82–3; evidence given by 10–11, 13, 15
McMahon, Frank (son of Owen) xiii, 4, 13, 83
McMahon, Gerald (son of Owen) xiii, 4, 12, 13
McMahon, John 6, 81
McMahon, John (son of Owen) xiii, 4, 6, 11, 12, 14, 82–3, 231; description of the killers 7–8, 10; evidence given by 12–14, 15, 148, 201, 208, 209
McMahon, Leo (son of Owen) xiii, 231
McMahon, Lily (daughter of Owen) xiii, 6, 10, 11, 12, 14, 199, 231
McMahon, Michael (son of Owen) xiii, 4, 6, 10, 11, 12, 13, 15
McMahon, Owen xiii, xx, 4, 6, 11; background 8–9, 79; brothers 6, 185; business interests 79, 80–1; estate, value of 82; family 82–3; Sinn Féin and 9, 14
McMahon, Patrick (son of Owen) xiii, 4, 83
McMahon, Patrick xx, xxi, 6, 79–80, 81, 179, 194; complaint to police 206; damages awarded to 82; departure from York Road 184, 201; Duncan's attempt to murder 179–81, 183, 185, 200, 222, 223, 231; raids on premises 81, 179–80, 198
McMahon, Rose 193, 194
McMahon, Thomas 6, 80
McMahon family: burials 6; neighbours 9–10; rumours about 25–6
McMahon murders 12, 13–14, 97, 123; acquittal of accused 184; aftermath of murders 4–5, 83, 86, 235; commission of inquiry not established 101; description of murderers 198, 208, 209; door broken down with sledgehammer 9, 92, 125, 149; inquests 15; investigations into 9; motive for xv, 10, 26, 195–8, 201, 203, 204, 206–7, 231;

279

INDEX

murderers' disappearance 207; reactions to their murder 5–6, 24; Sinn Féin investigation 148; suspects 164, 203, 204, 205–6, 208; witness affidavits 14; *see also* Duncan, David; Nixon, DI John William

McMichael, James, Imperial Guard 161

McMullan, Nellie 184–5

McMurtry, Charles 104

McMurtry, James 9–10

McMurtry, Mabel 3, 9–10

McNabb, Russell 7, 92, 109, 191, 192–3

McNally, John, County Inspector 119

McNally, Thomas 21, 29–30, 147

Macready, General Nevil 36, 37–8, 41, 49–50, 55, 70–1, 74, 75

MacRory, Joseph, Bishop 6, 40, 96, 100–1, 109

McWhinney, Charles 95, 127

Madden, Patrick 62, 193

Madden, William 100, 178

Magee, Sergeant John 162

Magill, Andrew 98, 185, 214

Markievicz, Constance, Countess 21

Martelli, Captain Esmond 174

Martin, Robert 164

Mater Hospital, attack on 106–7

Mayes, Captain Thomas 57, 112

Megaw, Robert 113, 116

Millar, Margaret 49

Millar, Samuel 72

Ministry of Home Affairs 10, 14, 57, 98, 119, 155, 185, 190

Mitchell, Thomas 114

Moan, Josephine 202

Moffatt, DI William 121

Monaghan, Bernard 181, 183, 184

Montgomery, Seán 8, 9, 42, 62, 90, 136, 164, 184–5

Moody, Special Constable Andrew 86

Moore, Sir William 124

Morgan, John (Armoured Car) 94–5

Morgan, Margaret 132–3

Morgan, Brother Michael 36

Mountpottinger Barracks 150

Mulcahy, Richard 24, 25

Mulgrew, Special Constable James 163, 164, 208

Mullan, Peter 154

Mullaney, Thomas 107

Murdoch, Charlie 207

Murphy, Sergeant John 68

Murray, Charles 104

Murray, George 95

Murray, Revd Hugh 101

Murray, James 192–3

Murray, Joseph 109, 135

Musgrave Street Barracks 142, 143, 145, 147, 177

National Army 7, 22, 24, 25, 61, 97, 117, 128, 184

Naughten, Constable Patrick 122

Neeson, Katherine 67

Nesbitt, Special Constable William 152–3, 154, 155, 193

Nixon, John 233–4

Nixon, DI John William, xiv, xv, 43–7, 50, 86, 101, 142, 208; 'B' Specials and 51–2, 80, 91; behaviour, concerns about 112–13, 115–17, 118–19; Belfast City Council, seat on 121; bigotry 131; 'C' District and 51, 52, 112, 113, 132; Catholic constables, views on 46; Catholics, attitude towards 47; descendants 233; dismissal 119–20; family 233; identification parade, refusal to arrange 96; investigations blocked by 151; libel trial 122–4, 217, 218; looters arrested by 107; McMahon murders and 25, 92, 93, 122–3, 195–6, 217–18; marriage 233; MBE awarded to 112; 'murder gang' and 132, 137–8; NI House of Commons, election to 121–2; Norfolk Regiment, views on 51, 52; obstruction of investigations 147; Orange Order and 112, 117–18, 119, 120; perception of 101, 115, 121; proposed dismissal of 114–15, 119–20; radicalism 130; reprisal gang run by 187; reprisal murders, absence from 150; Sinn Féin intelligence reports 130–1; Stanhope Street, IRA and 93–4; supporters 112, 118, 120, 164, 190; threats issued to superiors 117; *see also* Nixon Memo

Nixon, Kathleen (Kay) (*née* Shannon) 233

Nixon, Nellie (*née* Moore) 44

Nixon, Detective Sergeant Sam (DMP) 44

Nixon Memo 25, 92, 93, 125; constables named in 133–4, 149; evidence ignored by 147–8, 188; RIC murder gang victims 131–4, 138–40, 144–6

Nolan, Patrick 188

Norfolk Regiment, 1st Battalion xv–xvi, xvii, 33, 35–7, 46, 51,

59–60, 104, 207; Arnon Street massacre report 86–91, 92, 93, 95, 96; arrests made by 161–2; 'C' Company 62–3; departure from Belfast 227; ex-British soldiers, IRA and 94; Holy Boys (nickname) 37, 63; Imperial Guards, street battles with 62–4; intelligence reports 61–2, 65, 84, 86–91, 92, 93, 95, 96, 182; IRA and 86; loyalist attacks 99, 100, 108; loyalist perception of 69–70; motto 'Firm' 37; police atrocities, prevention of 71–2; police, concerns about 65; police districts (C and D), command of 70; prevention of attacks 71–2, 91, 99, 100; Protestants shot by 67–8; reports on killings by Special Constabulary 87, 88–9, 90, 91; RIC members identified by 128; Special Constablulary and 59, 65, 69, 70, 71–2, 86–91, 92, 93, 100; street battles with Imperial Guards 62, 161; violence in Belfast 62–3

North East Belfast Unionist Club 64

Nugent, John Dillon, MP 39–40

O'Beirne, DI Cornelius 155

O'Daly, Commandant Patrick 97

O'Donnell, Alexander 82

O'Donnell, Constable 91–2

O'Driscoll, Patrick 7, 168

O'Duffy, Eoin 42–3, 61, 100, 112, 122

O'Kane, John 128

O'Keeffe, Terence 8

O'Keeney, Hugh 200–1, 208

O'Keeney, John 15–16, 18

O'Keeney, Rose 16, 18

O'Malley, Ernie 150

O'Neill, James 199

O'Neill, Sam 81, 82, 198

Orange and Black Loyalist Defence Association 57

Orange Order 31, 39, 48, 57; espionage network 52; Nixon and 112, 117, 118–19, 120, 186; Rising Sons of India LOL 169; Robert Peel Loyal Orange Lodge 116, 117, 118, 119; Royal Arch Purple 213; in Toronto 212, 215; tributes to Special Constabulary 112; Twelfth of July demonstrations 29, 34; York Road Loyal Orange Lodge 153

Orangemen 6, 36, 37, 50, 51, 99, 113, 114

O'Sullivan, Joe 24–5

INDEX

Pakenham, Head Constable Robert 124, 129–30, 155, 197
Papworth, Captain Harry xvii, 6, 51, 61–2, 65, 66, 99, 182, 207
Park, Minnie 160–1
Parkinson, Lieutenant Fred 69
Pearse, Patrick 21
Pentland, Thomas 158
Phillips, Bernie, Imperial Guard 161, 164
Pinder, Captain William 154, 189
Pollock, Frederick 155, 156
Pollock, Lieutenant James 171
Potter, Colonel Commandant Herbert 72, 107
Presbyterian Church, Townsend Street 57
Preston, Constable Berry 130, 131, 132
Pritchard family 79
Pritchard, Walther 178
Protestants 20, 23, 28, 33; killings 75, 86, 104, 106, 107, 146; publicans 193, 194–5, 199; rioting and 150; Southern 24, 53
Purdy, Beatrice 3–4
Purdy family 5, 10, 198–9
Purdy, Rosabell 3, 10, 198–9
Purdy, William 10, 199
Purdysburn Mental Hospital 205, 233–4

Quinn, William 186–7

Rafferty, Jane 152, 155–6, 233
Reid, Sergeant William 131, 138
riots 29–32, 36, 39, 43, 69, 82, 99, 105, 110, 129, 143, 146, 149, 150, 156
Robb, William, Sergeant 183, 184
Robinson, Special Constable Alec 152, 154–7, 160, 164, 198, 212, 214, 230, 232–3
Roche, James (magistrate) 210
Rogan, Constable John 138
Royal Air Force (RAF) 110, 186
Royal Irish Constabulary (RIC) xiv, 30, 119; 'B' District 37, 45, 131; British Army and 71–2; 'C' District 44, 45, 47, 51, 52, 73, 126, 127, 132, 143, 162; Catholics attacked by 46–7, 128–9, 130, 150; Catholics in 45, 46, 91–2, 134, 136, 192; Crimes Special Branch 73; criticism of 74, 126–7; Crossley tenders and 142; 'D' District 3, 9, 19, 143, 155, 210; fatalities 34, 43, 86; IRA attacks 32, 42, 43, 46, 86, 104; IRA collection book seized by 9; killings 131–3; McMahon

murder file 14, 15; Nixon Memo and 131–2; perception of 37–8; Special Constabulary 7, 8, 9, 14, 24, 41; Transport Division 141, 143; Ulster Division 31; *see also* Auxiliary Division; Ulster Special Constabulary (USC)
Royal Ulster Constabulary (RUC) xviii, xix, 25, 26, 31, 42, 45, 110, 111, 154, 155; arrests of UPA members 158; Catholics and 101, 156; informants 152; Orange Order and 118; Special Branch 121
Russell, Constable James 138
Russian Civil War (1918–20) xix, xxi, 173, 174, 175
Ryan, Edward 66

St Mary's Hall 43, 95, 108, 195, 200
St Matthew's Catholic Church 36, 38
St Patrick's Church 105, 191
Saunders, Thomas 182
Scott, Andrew 163
Scott, Special Constable George 155, 157, 164, 208
Scott, Constable Herbert 192
Scott, Lieutenant Colonel Robert xvii–xviii, 60–1, 66, 228
Second World War xix, 61, 228
sectarian attacks 7, 23–4, 32–3, 36, 38–9, 42, 43, 49, 66–7, 235; RIC and 46–7; *see also* Arnon Street Massacre
sectarianism, employment and 34–5
Shankill Unionist Association 186
Sharkey, Constable Hugh 137
Sheehy Skeffington, Francis 188
Sherlock, Mary 74
Sherwood, Constable 130
Shevlin, James 115
Shevlin, John 115, 116, 117, 196
Shields, Kathleen 17, 18
Shields, Vincent 17, 208
Shields, William 17
Simpson, Robert 159, 164
Sinn Féin 5, 7, 9, 14, 25, 39, 48; Arnon Street massacre, report on 90, 91, 92, 93; boycott organised by 35; Craig and 62; General Election (1918) 21; intelligence reports 130–1; investigators 125, 130; loyalist attack, report on 99; McMahon murders, investigation into 148; police and 45, 108–9; Treaty negotiations 42
Sloan, Barnsley, Imperial Guard 161, 202

Smith, Margaret 202–3
Smyth, Colonel Gerald 34
Solly-Flood, Major-General Sir Arthur 101, 110, 111, 113, 114–15
Spallen, William 87, 90
Spears, DI Reginald 74, 159
Spence, Gusty 229–30, 232
Spender, Lady Lilian 62
Spender, Colonel Wilfred 19, 41, 62, 70
Spratt, Harry (Harry Brett) 202, 203–4
Springfield Road Barracks 68, 131
Staniland, Paul 57
Stapleton, Pat 111
Steele, William 57
Sterritt, Sergeant Alex 118, 130, 132, 138, 140, 158; evidence at Halfpenny inquest 143; McMahon murders and 125, 149, 196; perception of 127, 131
Sterritt, Constable William 127
Stewart, Hector 66
Stewart, James 36
Stewart, Special Constable Thomas 134
Sturdy, Special Constable Thomas 146
Sullivan, Sergeant James 137
Swanton, Mary 79
Swanzy, DI Oswald 38, 39, 56
Swindles, John 93

Tallents, Sir Stephen 102, 110, 111, 116–17, 127
Taylor, David 163
Taylor, Commander Harry 56, 84, 112, 118, 120, 162–4, 187, 188, 189
Telford, James 104–5
Tennyson, William 126, 127
Thaxton, Kate xvi, xvii
Thompson, Joseph 67
Toppin, Colonel Henry 155
Topping, Constable Thomas 130
Toronto Lunatic Asylum xxi, 216
Traynor, Daniel 163
Tregenna, Richard 55, 56, 118
Trenchard, Sir Hugh 110
Trimble, David xiv
Trodden, Edward 131
Troubles, the 110, 229–30, 232, 234, 236
Tully, James 111
Tumelty, Ellen (*née* Spallen) 87–8
Tumelty, Gerard 87
Turkington, James 190
Turner, Captain Edward 189–91
Turner, Constable George 86–7, 91, 92

281

INDEX

Turner, Lance Corporal Reggie 62, 202, 228
Turtle, Alex, Imperial Guard 63, 202, 228
Twaddell, William, MP 18, 55, 56, 104

Ulster Brotherhood 53, 153
Ulster Club 48, 49
Ulster Covenant 130
Ulster Defence Association (UDA) 229, 230, 232, 236
Ulster Defence Regiment (UDR) 229, 230
Ulster Ex-Servicemen's Association 54, 186, 189
Ulster Imperial Guards (Imps) 54, 55, 56–8, 62, 184, 196, 202; attacks on Catholics 68–9; British Army, street battles with 62–4, 65–6; 'C1' Specials, incorporation into 57–8, 161, 214; Duncan and 167, 177, 178; IRA report on 200–1, 202; murder gangs 160, 187–8; Norfolks and 65, 161; North Belfast Regiment 68; perception of 58
Ulster Prisoner of War Fund 81
Ulster Protestant Association (UPA) 65, 157, 158–9, 160
Ulster Protestant Voters' Defence Association 190
Ulster Special Constabulary (USC) 24, 25, 26, 57, 150, 151; 'A' Class 41, 42, 47, 64, 111, 146, 196; attacks by 98; attempted rapes 98; 'B' Class 41, 42, 47–8, 49, 50, 51–2, 55, 56, 62, 65, 80, 189, 190, 208; 'B' Class, cuts to 116; Belfast, control of 109–10; British Army and 102–3; British Army reports on 105–6; 'C' Class 41, 89, 95; 'C1' Class 41–2, 58, 65, 93, 110, 111, 152–3, 157,

185, 189, 198, 208; Catholics attacked by 152–5, 163, 179–82, 192; Catholics, recruitment of 100; Churchill's views on 74–5, 84; Craig and 74, 84, 85, 111–12; Devlin's criticism of 83; establishment of 40–1; estimated costs 111; fatalities 64, 66, 69, 196, 207; Imperial Guard, incorporation of 57–8, 62, 161, 213, 214; intelligence network 189; IRA attacks on 59; letter to Dawson Bates 162–3; McMahon murders and 208; manpower shortages 58; murder suspects 162, 163, 187; Norfolk Regiment and 59, 65, 69, 70, 71–2, 86–91, 92, 93, 100; Norfolk Regiment's reports on killings 87, 88–9, 90; Orange Order tributes 112; perception of 41, 72, 103; UDR, incorporation into 229; witness assaulted by 96; see also Arnon Street Massacre
Ulster Unionist Labour Association (UULA) 54, 55, 57, 64, 114, 118, 178, 190–1, 193
Ulster Unionist Party (UUP) 53, 121, 177
Ulster unionists 22–3
Ulster Volunteer Force (UVF) 34, 41, 130, 232, 236; arms importation 22, 37; arms, theft of 206; home rule, opposition to 20; mural 233; North Belfast Regiment 99, 205; perception of 54–5; weapons handed to NI government 50, 65; weapons, sale of 191, 206
Ulster Workers' Council 230
United Irishmen 28

Vance, Elizabeth 193
Victoria Barracks 111
Vokes, Special Constable Charles 69

Walsh, Joseph 88, 90, 93, 94, 96, 97, 148
Walsh, Louis J. 109
Walsh, Margaret 96
Walsh, Michael 88, 90
Walsh, Robert 90
Walsh, Stephen, MP 111–12
Waring, Samuel 186
Waring, Captain Samuel 56, 58, 66, 114, 185–7, 188, 197, 198
Waring, William 66, 196, 204, 205, 206
Watling, Lieutenant Harold xvii, 106
Watt, Samuel 119–20
Weston, Ann 36
Wickham, Lieutenant Colonel Charles xviii–xix, 38, 48, 49, 58, 73, 101, 111, 112; Nixon and 112–13, 117, 118–19, 120
William III, King 29
Williams, DI George 15, 92
Williamson, James, KC 183
Williamson, Special Constable John 157–8, 214
Williamson, Samuel 119
Wilson, Field Marshal Sir Henry 37, 49, 50, 69–70, 72, 107, 128; assassination 24, 25, 26
Wilson, John 179
Wilson, Mary 204
Wilson, William 203–4
Wolfe Tone, Theobald 28
Woods, Colonel Philip 163
Woods, Seamus: Auxiliaries and 135; IRA and 21, 39, 43, 61, 104, 108, 109, 117, 132, 136; Nixon, views on 150; RIC Constable killed by 137
Woodthorpe, Lieutenant John 36
Worthington-Evans, Laming 59

York Street Barracks 17
Young Citizen Volunteers 10, 199
Younghusband, Colonel Francis 188

282